Compromise and the American Founding

Why is today's political life so polarized? This book analyzes the ways in which the divergent apprehensions of both "compromise" and the "people" in seventeenth-century England and France became intertwined once again during the American founding, sometimes with bloody results. Looking at key moments of the founding, from the first Puritan colonies to the beginning of the Civil War, this book offers answers of contemporary relevance. It argues that Americans unknowingly combined two understandings of the people: the early modern idea of a collection of individuals ruled by a majority of wills and the classic understanding of a corporation hierarchically structured and ruled by reason for the common good. Americans were then able to implement the paradigm of the "people's two bodies." Whenever the dialectic between the two has been broken, the results had a major impact on American politics. Born by accident, this American peculiarity has proven to be a long-lasting one.

ALIN FUMURESCU is Assistant Professor of Political Science at the University of Houston. In 2013, he won the American Political Science Association's Leo Strauss Award for the best doctoral dissertation in the field of political philosophy. He is the author of *Compromise: A Political and Philosophical History* (2013), which has been translated into Chinese and Romanian. He has written several book chapters on compromise in edited volumes, and he is regularly an invited guest speaker to international conferences on compromise.

Compromise and the American Founding

The Quest for the People's Two Bodies

ALIN FUMURESCU
University of Houston

CAMBRIDGE
UNIVERSITY PRESS

CAMBRIDGE
UNIVERSITY PRESS

University Printing House, Cambridge CB2 8BS, United Kingdom

One Liberty Plaza, 20th Floor, New York, NY 10006, USA

477 Williamstown Road, Port Melbourne, VIC 3207, Australia

314–321, 3rd Floor, Plot 3, Splendor Forum, Jasola District Centre, New Delhi – 110025, India

79 Anson Road, #06-04/06, Singapore 079906

Cambridge University Press is part of the University of Cambridge.

It furthers the University's mission by disseminating knowledge in the pursuit of education, learning, and research at the highest international levels of excellence.

www.cambridge.org
Information on this title: www.cambridge.org/9781108415873
DOI: 10.1017/9781108235358

© Alin Fumurescu 2019

First published 2019

Printer in the United Kingdom by TJ International Ltd. Padstow Cornwall

A catalogue record for this publication is available from the British Library.

ISBN 978-1-108-41587-3 Hardback

Contents

Acknowledgments

As I grow older, I fancy there might be some truth in the saying that wisdom comes with age. Eventually, you come to realize that even such a solitary act as the writing of a book is made possible only thanks to the existence of those who are there for you whenever they are needed most, often when you don't even realize it.

The friendly atmosphere in the Department of Political Science at the University of Houston put my mind at ease and made it possible to concentrate on topics that otherwise can be regarded as eccentric by people interested in a more quantitative and nonphilosophical approach to politics. Wholehearted thanks are naturally due to my fellow theorists, faculty and graduate students alike, who in our workshops gave helpful feedback when I was presenting various parts of the manuscript.

Particular thanks to Jeremy Bailey and to Jeffrey Church who made me feel welcome at the University of Houston from the very beginning, and who are as great as friends as they are as scholars. From all of our intelligent and promising graduate students who kept my hopes up for the future, special thanks are due to Anna Marisa Schön and Scott Hofer who provided much-needed help in various stages of the preparation of the manuscript. And when it came to editing, even more thanks are due to Ana, who, probably because she is not my PhD student (yet she is my daughter), proved to be an extremely helpful – and demanding – copyeditor.

The support of the Jack Miller Center for the Tocqueville Forum cofounded with Jeremy Bailey made it possible to bring to campus a brilliant collection of guest speakers, and – as everyone who went through this process knows very well – the life of the mind is nourished by such regular encounters. A small grant from the Division of Research at the University of Houston proved very useful when finishing the last phases of publishing this book, proving once again that political philosophy does not necessarily have to be the Cinderella of the Social Sciences.

The professionalism of the team from Cambridge University Press never ceases to impress me. My special gratitude goes to my editor, Robert Dreesen, who, throughout all these years – and apparently in the years to come – proved that it is possible to go above and beyond the strict requirements of his position, becoming, as Al Farabi put it, "the spur" that everyone needs every now and then.

Last but not least, I am grateful, as usual, for all the love and resilience of my wife, Anca, and of my children, Ana, Andrei, and Alec, who, through all the challenges of their teenage and young adult Romanian-American days, made me proud. Unknowingly, they served as a constant reminder that our future depends on a proper understanding of the past. Therefore, this time, to them I dedicate this book, with all my love, so they won't forget.

I

Introduction

"One political being called a people ..."

Thus when in the Constitution of the Commonwealth of Massachusetts, it is said that the body politic is formed by a social compact in which the whole people covenants with each citizen and each citizen with the whole people, the words whole people in the first part of the sentence, have not the same meaning as they have in the second. In the first part they mean the portion of the people capable of contracting for the whole and with the whole—in the second, they mean the sum of total human beings bound by and included in the compact.

– *John Quincy Adams*

Like most American stories, the one of the American people is, by most standards, a success story. Even more impressive, it is the story of a self-made people – an eminently *political* people. After all, the ambition of a handful of Puritans spread in the wilderness to "be set as lights upon a Hill more obvious than the highest mountain in the World" was to be fulfilled to an extent never dreamt of by their contemporaries, albeit through means never imagined by the original protagonists.[1] Also like most American stories, it is one that generally tends to be depicted in broad strokes, with heroes and villains, winners and losers, divided in rather well-circumscribed and easily identifiable camps. Thus, in the winning camp one finds – besides the Puritans – Patriots, Federalists, and Northerners, while the losers' camp is occupied by Loyalists, Antifederalists, and Southerners. One of the primary aims of this book is to use the intellectual history of compromise as a tool for revealing some of the shades and hues that have been erased from this overly simplified picture, thus clarifying key moments in the making of the American people.

[1] Edward Johnson, quoted in Francis J. Bremer (1976), *The Puritan Experiment – New England Society from Bradford to Edwards* (New York: St. Martin's Press), 37.

Surprising considering its purported centrality to America's founding, the subject of compromise has thus far failed to seriously engage the interest of any one scholar, and the extant literature focuses almost exclusively on the role compromise played during the Constitutional debates and in the rhetorical and legal battles over the issue of slavery in the early republic.[2] It is a gap that is important to address, especially under the conditions of extreme polarization and unwillingness to compromise that characterizes today's American politics. For, as I have discussed in greater detail elsewhere, the history of compromise resembles the tip of an iceberg, in that it reveals its own concealment. It is a history that signals overlooked differences in some fundamental assumptions one makes about "the people" and their relationship to the political sphere.[3] This is a history that still has plenty to teach us.

On the one hand, the refusal to compromise with perceived "others," which came to characterize Puritans, Patriots, Antifederalists, and Southerners alike, reveals largely ignored similarities between protagonists that otherwise are considered to have belonged to opposite camps in the story of America's founding. On the other hand, the willingness of Puritans to compromise, if only among themselves, and the calls for compromise made to their opponents not only by Loyalists but also by Federalists, and even by most Northerners until civil war became a reality, signals – other practical and historical consider- ations aside – that these actors might have had a shared understanding of what "the people" stood for, and why they thought a compromising attitude *ought* to be praised.

As such, the story of the American people, precisely because of the ambiva- lence of the term "people" for the protagonists, offers researchers a unique opportunity by combining in a peculiar way the British willingness to com- promise with the French unwillingness to do so, as detailed in my previous work.[4] According to one view, the people is as a collection of equal individuals, ruled by a majority of wills. According to the other, the people is a corporation, hierarchically structured, ruled by reason for the sake of the common good. Philosophically speaking, the former understanding of the people is sympa- thetic to the social compact theory, while the latter supports the political or governmental compact between a people and its leaders. I shall argue that it was precisely this foundational double helix that is largely responsible for the

---

[2] See Chapter 5 for the bibliography on the role played by compromise in the framing and ratification of the Constitution. Peter B. Knupfer (1991), *The Union as It Is: Constitutional Unionism and Sectional Compromises, 1787–1861* (Chapel Hill, London: The University of North Carolina Press) comes the closest to the overall purpose of this book. Yet Knupfer starts his investigation of compromise from the Philadelphia Convention, and his approach, despite some areas of agreement, is significantly different from the one proposed here. See especially Chapters 5 and 6 in this volume.

[3] Alin Fumurescu (2013), *Compromise: An Intellectual and Philosophical History* (Cambridge: Cambridge University Press), 10–11.

[4] Fumurescu, *Compromise*. See further.

versatility of American politics, and its eventual successes, but also for the persistent confusions both between the two understandings of the people and between the social and the political compact, respectively.

Considering all the contemporary implications, it is therefore from this foundational double helix that we ought to begin.

1.1 ONE PEOPLE, TWO BODIES[5]

In their recent book, *Democracy for Realists*, Christopher Achen and Larry Bartels argue that the credibility of "folk theory" of democracy, according to which people rule either directly or indirectly, through their representatives, "has been severely undercut by a growing body of scientific evidence."[6] Backed by a wealth of recent studies, the authors make a claim worrisome to many: None of the two main theories of democratic governance, namely the populist and the elitist, can sustain empirical inspection. Voters do not control public policy, neither directly, through referenda and popular consultations, nor indirectly, by prospectively choosing or retrospectively rewarding leaders that attend to their wishes. Bluntly put, "conventional thinking about democracy has collapsed in the face of *modern* social-scientific research," yet "scholars ... persist uneasily in their *schizophrenia*, recognizing the power of the critical arguments but hoping without hope that those arguments can somehow be discredited or evaded."[7]

Even more recently, Daniele Caramani launched, from a different perspective, an equally concerning warning: According to her analysis, the representation model of party democracy is under attack from two sides – the populist and the elitist/technocratic. Politicians are accused (by the populists) of being either too detached from the people or (by the technocrats) too willing to please them regardless of the consequences. As the argument unfolds, populism and technocracy share the *"homogenous and organic vision of the people,"* "a non-pluralistic view of society and politics." As a result, "both forms believe in an 'external' interest [of the people], detached from the specific group interests and their aggregation. [...] For populism, the general interest can be identified through *the will* of the people. For technocracy, the general interest can be identified through *rational speculation* and scientific procedures."[8] It is, in

---

[5] This section is partially informed by Alin Fumurescu (2013), *Compromise*, and by Alin Fumurescu (2018), "The People's Two Bodies: An Alternative Perspective on Populism and Elitism," *Political Research Quarterly*, 7:4, 842–853.

[6] Christopher H. Achen and Larry M. Bartels (2016), *Democracy for Realists: Why Elections do not Produce Responsive Government* (Princeton: Princeton University Press), 11.

[7] Ibid., 12 (emphases added).

[8] Daniele Caramani (2017), "Will vs. Reason: The Populist and Technocratic Forms of Political Representation and Their Critique to Party Government." *American Political Science Review*, 111:1, 62 (emphases added).

Caramani's own words, a political confrontation framed in terms of "will" versus "reason."

The undertones of Achen and Bartels's book and Caramani's article might be different, but both – and these are only two recent examples from a growing pool of scholarly literature concerned with this topic – point in the same direction: the crisis that democracies must face is related to conflicting understandings of "the people."[9] Absent this clarification, the concept of popular sovereignty, central to any democratic system, remains an empty one, explaining everything and nothing. In Achen and Bartels's view, "the ideal of popular sovereignty plays much the same role in contemporary democratic ideology that the divine right of kings played in the monarchical era." "The doctrine of 'The King's Two Bodies' [...] provided useful leeway for understanding and accommodating the fact that mortal rulers were often less than divine in bearing and behavior." A similar rationale applies to the contemporary understanding of the people. "We ... have our 'two bodies' doctrine: when majorities go seriously astray, it is not the people that 'advised themselves,' but rather the people misadvised by others and misled by misordered counsel."[10]

I shall argue that there is more validity in the paradigm of the people's two bodies than Achen and Bartels seem willing to grant. The paradigm might be nothing more than a fiction, but it is a useful one – like all other fictions on which any government rests. They are the bread and butter of politics. Edmund Morgan's observation is not to be ignored:

> Governments require make-believe. [...] Make believe that the people *have* a voice or make believe that the representatives of the people *are* the people. Make believe that governors are the servants of the people. Make believe that all men are equal or make believe that they are not. [...] Because fictions are necessary, because we cannot live without them, we often take pains to prevent their collapse by moving the facts to fit the fiction.[11]

Far from being "modern" or signaling some "schizoid" thinking, the idea of the people being conceived *at once* as a multitude prone to errors *and* as a sovereign corporate entity that cannot err enjoys a long pedigree. Even if the label of the people's two bodies is recent, the idea behind it is not.[12] It predates

---

[9] See, for example, Christopher Bickerton and Carlo Invernizzi Accetti (2015), "Populism and Technocracy: Opposites or Complements?" *Critical Review of International Social and Political Philosophy*, 20:2, 186–206; Nadia Urbinati (2014), *Democracy Disfigured* (Cambridge, MA: Harvard University Press).

[10] Achen and Bartels, *Democracy for Realists*, 19–20.

[11] Edmund S. Morgan (1988), *Inventing the People: The Rise of Popular Sovereignty in England and America* (New York, London: W.W. Norton & Co.), 13–14 (emphasis in the original).

[12] One could argue that the "people's two bodies" label is inaccurate, since, as a multitude, the people have no *one* distinct body, like they do in the corporate understanding. However, the expression "the body of the people" is currently used mostly in reference to a multitude of voices, which makes the distinction implied by the label even more useful. One should also remember

the transfer of sovereignty from kings to people, and hence the transfer of the idea of the King's Two Bodies to the people's two bodies that came to characterize the revolutionary eighteenth century.[13]

Despite what common misconceptions would have us believe, the doctrine of the King's Two Bodies was far from widespread, and equally far from characterizing the entire medieval period. Even if the doctrine was probably known across Europe, "it was nevertheless in England alone that there had been developed a consistent political, or legal theory of the 'King's Two Bodies.'" The theory, "in all its complexity and sometimes scurrilous consistency, was practically absent from the Continent."[14] According to Queen Elizabeth's lawyers, "the King has in him two Bodies, viz., a Body natural and a Body politic. [...] [H]is Body politic is a Body that cannot be seen or handled, consisting of Policy and Government, and constituted for the Direction of the People, and the Management of the public weal, and this Body is utterly void of Infancy, and old Age."[15] Far from being typically medieval, this "notion had . . . its important heuristic function in the period of transition from mediaeval to modern political thought."[16]

This is not to say that European medieval political thought was deprived of this dual way of thinking when it came to understanding the people. Throughout the Middle Ages, at least from the Roman lawyer Azo onward, "the people" were conceived simultaneously as a whole and as a multitude, as One and as Many. The same rationale informed both the Church and the political bodies.[17] That the body politic was to be distinguished – as later on the political body of the King would be as well – from the physicality of its members was a certitude for the famous Commentator Baldus de Ubaldis, who

---

the frontispiece of the 1651 edition of Hobbes's *Leviathan*, by Abraham Bosse, "with creative inputs" from Thomas Hobbes, in which the body of the sovereign is made up of tiny little persons.

[13] Although the formula of "the people's two bodies" has been previously used, the interpretation offered here differs drastically from the ones proposed by Sheldon S. Wolin (1981), "People's Two Bodies." *Democracy: A Journal of Political Renewal and Radical Change*, 1:1, 9–24, and by Eric L. Santner (2011), *The Royal Remains: The People's Two Bodies and the Endgames of Sovereignty* (Chicago: University of Chicago Press). On the one hand, Wolin identifies in the American tradition a politically active, democratic body and an essentially passive, economic, and antidemocratic one. On the other hand, Santner focuses on the modern transference of sovereignty from the King's Two Bodies to the people's two bodies, mainly from a psychoanalytical perspective centered on the idea of "corporeality." Edmund S. Morgan (1988), *Inventing the People*, whose chapter four is entitled "The People's Two Bodies," comes closer, distinguishing between people as subjects and people as rulers, and between the power to govern and the power to determine the form of government. See further.

[14] Ernst H. Kantorowicz (1957), *The King's Two Bodies: A Study in Mediaeval Political Theology* (Princeton: Princeton University Press), 446, 441.

[15] Quoted in ibid., 7.   [16] Ibid., 447.

[17] David Ciepley (2017), "Is the U.S. Government a Corporation? The Corporate Genesis of Modern Constitutionalism," *American Political Science Review*, 111:2, 418–435. See also Fumurescu, *Compromise*, especially chapter 3.

wrote in the fourteenth century: "Therefore separate individuals do not make up the people, and thus properly speaking the people is not men, but a collection of men into a body which is mystical and taken as abstract, and the significance of which has been discovered by the intellect."[18] Like the General Will that Rousseau would later describe, this "mystical body of the commonwealth" (*corpus mysticum republicae*) could not err.[19]

As modern as it might seem today, the idea that governments are the creation of the corporate people and that rulers are responsible and subordinate to the people was a common trope throughout the entire medieval period.[20] For example, Jacques Almain and John Mair, two lecturers at the University of Paris, "were ... explicit ... about the power of the secular community over the ruler. The community retained a constituent power. It could change both the ruler and the form of the constitution for reasonable cause."[21] The first monarchomachian theories of justified resistance were based, not on some proto-social contractarianism, but on the medieval political contract between the people and their rulers. Thus, in Beza's words, "those have the power to depose a King who have the power to create him."[22]

There is no doubt, however, that in the medieval and even the early modern French understanding, the people entitled to remove an unworthy king were not the multitude but the *optimates*, i.e., the most reasonable part of it (*maior et sanior pars.*) However, who exactly could fulfill this role was open to debate. For François Hotman they were the supreme magistrates in the Estates, while for Beza, in the case of corruption of the Estates, the role could devolve to inferior magistrates. Yet, despite these differences, all authors from the period, Protestants and Catholics alike, carefully distinguished between the people as a conceptual whole and the majorities, i.e., between the people as One and the people as Many. They would all have agreed with Bodin who had previously argued that "in popular assemblies votes are counted, not weighed, and the number of fools, sinners, and dolts is a thousand times that of honest men."[23]

---

[18] Quoted in Joseph Canning (1987), *The Political Thought of Baldus de Ubaldis* (Cambridge: Cambridge University Press), 187.

[19] It would be undoubtedly interesting to analyze how Rousseau's distinction between the General Will and the will of all (as simple majority of individual wills) relates to the paradigm of the people's two bodies. It would constitute, however, an entire project in itself.

[20] This understanding was common in both Western Europe and the Byzantine Empire. See Anthony Kaldellis (2015), *The Byzantine Republic: People and Power in New Rome* (Cambridge, MA: Harvard University Press) for a similar argument and a wealth of examples.

[21] John H. M. Salmon (2007), "France," in Howell A. Lloyd, Glenn Burgess, and Simon Hodson, eds. *European Political Thought: 1450–1700* (New Haven and London: Yale University Press), 462.

[22] Theodore de Bèze (1970), *Du Droit de Magistrates*, introduction, édition et notes par Robert M. Kingdon. Geneva: Librairie Doz, 45. For more details and examples, see Fumurescu, *Compromise*, chapter 3.

[23] Jean Bodin [1955], *Six Books of the Commonwealth*, abr. and tr. M.J. Tooley (Oxford: Basil Blackwell), VI.4, 193.

In this context, corporations (or offices) could have been represented and/or made compromises, but unique individuals could not. The general understanding was that no one could represent someone else in full, for no one could represent someone else's uniqueness. Since the internal self was impossible to represent, it was beyond the realm of political compromises, which are inherently public. Consequently, regardless of the circumstances, for the medieval individual, compromise could only involve the external, public self (*forum externum*), *qua* member of a corporation, but never the inner, private self (*forum internum*). Thus, compromise, both as a method of arbitration (*arbitratio*) and as a method of election (*electio*) was a neutral term, neither to be praised nor to be feared, since there was no fear of "*being* compromised."

Early modernity put an end to this understanding. Challenged by the various pressures of change, the dialectic of the individual between the two fora split across the Channel between a centrifugal individualism – focused almost exclusively on *forum externum* as the visible, trusted self – and a centripetal individualism, for which *forum internum* represented the only true self while *forum externum* was relegated to the status of a mere costume. As a result, by the beginning of the seventeenth century, Great Britain pioneered the understanding of the people as a collection of individuals, united via mutual compact or compromise, with every single Englishman virtually represented in Parliament. As Gilbert Burnet put it, "The true and Original Notion of Civil society and Government, is, that is a Compromise."[24] Naturally, compromise became a foundational virtue as the only way to avoid open conflict. Meanwhile, France continued, for more than a century after, to preserve the medieval understanding of the people as an organic corporation, hierarchically structured. Since the French emphasized centripetal individualism, unlike the medieval *compromissum*, the French *compromis* lost its neutral meaning, being perceived as a threat to one's identity, *qua* individual or *qua* community. The first English and French dictionaries of the seventeenth century reflect well these different understandings.[25]

The American case is different from both the British and the French in that in the New World the modern understanding of "the people" took a peculiar twist – and so did the usage of compromise. As I shall show in detail in the next chapter, thanks to the Puritan bidimensional covenant, the idea of equal individuals consenting to form a new political body and to subject themselves to a new form of government was far from a mere philosophical idea. It was a living reality, hence the later attractiveness of the social contract theory for American political thinking. At the same time, once this new body of people was formed, the details of setting up a specific form of government and its daily function was entrusted in the hands of an elected aristocracy of merit, driving

---

[24] Gilbert Burnet (1688), "An Inquiry Into the Measures of Submission to the Supream Authority ...," in *A Collection of papers relating to the present juncture of affairs in England*, 2.

[25] For a full exposition of this history, see Fumurescu, *Compromise*.

many scholars to claim that the Puritans were in effect more medieval than modern.[26] In reality, they simply assumed that people enjoyed equal constituent power but different political skills.[27] This dual understanding of the people, both horizontal and vertical, proved to be, politically speaking, a long-lasting legacy.

What sets the American case apart is that they had the opportunity to actually implement both understandings of "the people" without really favoring one at the expense of the other. Some scholars have noticed that "democratic tides" come and go throughout American history.[28] The approach that I propose here overcomes this binary thinking, divided between "republicans" and "radical democrats,"[29] "traditional or radical Whigs" and "Federalists,"[30] "democrats" and "anti-democrats,"[31] or simply "republicans" and "liberals."[32] In effect, I claim that, as in the story of the blind men and the elephant, all interpretations are partially right, and the main problem remains the inability to seize the paradigm of the people's two bodies underlying these labels. By contrast, the interpretation suggested here represents more than the acknowledgment of "multiple traditions,"[33] a "synthesis,"[34] or an "amalgam."[35] It invites the reader to see the whole elephant.

---

[26] Stephen Foster (1991), *The Long Argument – English Puritanism and the Shaping of New England Culture, 1570–1700* (Chapel Hill: The University of North Carolina Press); Donald S. Lutz (1988), *The Origins of American Constitutionalism* (Baton Rouge: Louisiana State University Press).

[27] Richard A. Ryerson (2016), *John Adams's Republic: The One, the Few, and the Many* (Baltimore: John Hopkins University Press), 12.

[28] See, for example, Anthony S. King (2012), *The Founding Fathers v. The People* (Cambridge, MA: Harvard University Press), 100.

[29] Ibid., 130–150.

[30] Donald S. Lutz (1980), *Popular Consent and Popular Control: Whig Political Theory in the Early State Constitutions* (Baton Rouge: Louisiana State University Press).

[31] Merrill Jensen (1970), *The Articles of Confederation: An Interpretation of the Social-Constitutional History of the American Revolution, 1774–1781* (Madison: University Wisconsin Press).

[32] When it comes to interpreting the founding through "republican" vs. "liberal" lenses, the literature is by now too voluminous to review. Suffice is to say, with the risk of simplifying, that among the promoters of the republican readers one finds scholars such as Barnard Baylin, Gordon Wood, and J. G. A. Pocock, while in the liberal camp one finds names such as Joyce Appleby, Isaack Kramnick, Thomas Pangle, Michael Zuckert, or Mark Hulliung. Most of them and some of their disciples will be mentioned and quoted throughout this book.

[33] Alan Gibson (2007), *Understanding the Founding: The Crucial Questions* (Lawrence: University Press of Kansas).

[34] Mark A. Noll (2002), *America's God – From Jonathan Edwards to Abraham Lincoln* (Oxford: Oxford University Press).

[35] Michael P. Zuckert (2005), "Natural Rights and Imperial Constitutionalism: The American Revolution and the Development of the American Amalgam," *Natural Rights Liberalism from Locke to Nozick*, Ellen Frankel Paul, Fred D. Miller Jr., and Jeffrey Paul, eds. (Cambridge: Cambridge University Press), 27–55.

The paradigm of the people's two bodies does not merely recognize the existence of these different understandings. Instead it reveals why they were accepted by most of this book's protagonists, *at the same time*, in a display of dialectic thinking that is hard to conceive today when talking about "the people." Much as Denis de Rougemont argued, in *Man's Western Quest*, that, all religious considerations aside, Christianity shaped a particular understanding of the world, I claim that Puritanism helped mold a certain *forma mentis* that contributed to a unique political *Weltanschauung*, by training the American mind to "assume incompatibles."[36] As hard as it is to accept today, the idea of an "aristocracy of merit" dominated the American psyche and rhetoric for more than a century before it was replaced by competing concepts, such as "republicanism" or "democracy," but at the same time, equally indisputable was the right of ordinary citizens to approve the general form of government and to elect or remove this "aristocracy" from office.

Thus, what for us today may appear as "schizophrenia" was, for a long period of time during the American founding, a suitable way for dealing with a political reality that could not (and still cannot) be confined in the peculiarly contemporaneous "either-or" model of the people: either ruled by wills or by reason, either artificial creation or organic whole, either One or Many. As a result, the question of popular sovereignty was addressed in a more creative way than democratic theory does today. In this respect at least, Achen and Bartels may rest assured: The founders were more realist than many contemporaries when it came to (not) trusting the people *qua* multitude to make complex political judgments, yet also less cynical than some technocrats that the same multitude was able to make mostly sound decisions about basic principles of government.

From the perspective proposed here, Caramani's worries also appear misplaced. Historically speaking, populism, understood as direct or indirect rule *of* the people by a majority of votes, and technocracy, understood as rule *for* the people's general interest, have neither been inherently incompatible nor have necessarily shared "a homogenous and organic vision of the people," but rather the opposite, if only because the organic vision is inherently inimical to homogeneity. The general interest is not incompatible with the aggregate interests of the groups composing it, if "the people" is understood – as it used to be – as a corporation of corporations. Hence, populism or elitism per se are less of a problem; all politicians are and will be, to various degrees, both populist and elitist, while popular leaders and technocrats are forced sooner or later to

---

[36] According to de Rougemont, accepting that Christ is simultaneously "true God" and "true man" paved the way for modern physicists to finally accept that a photon is, at the same time, a wave and a particle. Overcoming the binary logic, in which "*tertium non datur*," marked the beginning of modern physics; Denis de Rougemont (1956), *Man's Western Quest – The Principles of Civilization*, trans. from French by Montgomery Belgion (New York: Harper & Brothers Publishers), 115–118.

become politicians, as Caramani also acknowledges. The main problem, I suggest, might be a misconception of "the people" that creates unrealistic expectations both *for* and *from* the electorate, and *for* and *from* the elites that are supposed to act on its behalf. Thus, far from being a mere linguistic artifice, the people's two bodies proves a useful paradigm for dealing simultaneously with the pitfalls of elitism and populism while taking advantage of both.

After all, words do matter precisely because their meanings are not settled.

1.2 COMPROMISE AND THE CHALLENGE OF REALISM

There is no denying that such a sweeping overview of the entire founding era raises an entire set of challenges, both theoretical and practical. To begin with, the jury is still out on when the American founding begun and when it ended. For some, it started in 1611, with *Virginia Articles, Laws, and Orders*; for others, in 1730s, with Benjamin Colman's sermon, *Government the Pillar of Earth*; or as late as in the 1760s, with Abraham Williams's *An Election Sermon* (1762). It also may have ended (or even begun) in 1787, in 1805, or in 1860.[37] However, since this is a book not about the American founding per se but about the founding of the American *people* – a distinction that is easily yet undeservedly overlooked – it seems appropriate to start from the very beginning, with the arrival on the shores of the New World of the first group of American Pilgrims and Puritans. This is not to deny the existence of the Native Americans, or the fact that the colony of Virginia was by 1620 already well established. But, as I will elaborate further in the next chapter, it would be hard to deny that for the making of the American *people*, unlike the Puritans, these groups (and many others) have provided less important contributions, insofar as the *idea* of a people implies a certain set of contrived beliefs.

A similar rationale applies to establishing the ending of the research period. Here, the distinction between the founding of America and the founding of the American people becomes even more relevant. While the existence of a distinctive American *identity* was generally accepted decades before the Revolutionary War, and the reality of an independent *country* became a matter of fact after the Declaration of Independence, things were much muddier when it came to agreement on the existence of an American *people*. As shown in Chapter 6, John Taylor's 1820 book, *Construction Construed*, stated: "Common consent is necessary to constitute a people, and no such consent, expressly or implied, can be shewn, by which all the inhabitants of the United States have ever

---

[37] See, for example, Bruce Frohnen, ed. (2002), The American Republic – Primary *Sources* (Indianapolis: Liberty Fund); Charles S. Hyneman and Donald S. Lutz (1983) *American Political Writing during the Founding Era, 1760–1805* (Indianapolis: Liberty Press); Ellis Sandoz, ed. (1998), *Political Sermons of the American Founding Era, 1730–1805* (Indianapolis: Liberty Press); Knupfer, *The Union as It Is*.

constituted themselves into *one* people. *This could not have been effected without destroying every people constituted within each state, as one political being called a people* cannot exist within another."[38] Disturbed as one might feel today about such statements, one has to acknowledge that for Thomas Jefferson, drafter of the Declaration of Independence and by then former president of the United States, Taylor's book was "sent by heaven to our aid."[39] It took a Civil War and more than 600,000 deaths to replace the formula "the United States *are*" with the one currently employed, "the United States *is*." Only then was the question of the existence of one American people finally put to rest, and it is where our story ends as well.

However, establishing the time frame is only the first of many methodological challenges. The next is to address the distinction between "people" and "nation." Why focus on the birth of the former and not of the latter? It is an important question that ought to be seriously considered, and a proper answer would probably require writing another book. Suffice is to say that the American people is primarily a *political* people, and was in this respect, from the very beginning, an outlier case. With the risk of oversimplifying the argument, in most cases, a "people" is identified primarily as a community of traditions, language, religion, culture, etc. In the modern understanding, a "people" becomes a "nation" once it acquires (or at least demands) political autonomy over a territory, via the emergence of the nation-state.[40] Lincoln, for example, used this distinction between "people" and "nation," during the famous Lincoln–Douglas debates, while attacking Douglas for not being coherent when making appeals to people's sovereignty.[41]

What is popular sovereignty? We recollect that at an early period in the history of this struggle, there was another name for this same thing – *Squatter Sovereignty*. It was not exactly Popular Sovereignty but Squatter Sovereignty. What do those terms mean? What do those terms mean when used now? [. . .] What was Squatter Sovereignty? I suppose if it had any significance at all it was *the right of the people to govern themselves*, to be sovereign of their own affairs while they were squatted down in a country not their own, while they had squatted *on a territory that did not belong to them, in the sense that a State belongs to the people who inhabit it – when it belonged to the nation* – such right to govern themselves was called "Squatter Sovereignty."[42]

---

[38] John Taylor (1820), *Construction Construed and Constitutions Vindicated* (Richmond: Shepherd and Pollard), 47 (emphasis added).

[39] Thomas Jefferson to Archibald Thweatt, January 19, 1821, in Paul Leicester Ford, ed., (1899), *The Writings of Thomas Jefferson* (New York: G.P. Putnam), vol. 10, 184.

[40] Throughout the Middle Ages, a "nation" was strictly culturally defined. As such, the distinction between "*ethne*" (Greek) and "*natio*" (Latin) was blurred. Only by the beginning of modernity, with the emergence of the nation-state, did this cultural identity begin to be politicized.

[41] See further Chapter 6.

[42] Quoted in Roy P. Basler, ed., (1953), *The Collected Works of Abraham Lincoln*, vol. 2, 487 (emphasis added).

Nevertheless, pervasive as it turned out to be, the concept of the nation-state also proved to be practically a very dangerous one. Rhetoric does matter. "Political beliefs, actions, and practices are partly constituted by the concepts which political actors hold about those beliefs, actions, and practices."[43] Whenever one talks about a "nation" as a political community, passions tend to flare up between different nationalities that unavoidably must coexist within the same state. Various proposals have been made to address the problem, from "civic nationalism" to "multiculturalism," in the attempt to accommodate national minorities' rights and to defuse the potentially explosive danger of nationalism.[44] Significant progress has been made in this direction, by constitutionally accommodating various cultural groups within the framework of the state, yet the results are still failing to meet the expectations.[45] That, at least at a subconscious level, the nation (culturally defined) remains assimilated with the state (politically defined) is demonstrated by the persistence in both everyday language and formal communications of expressions such as "National Gross Domestic Product," "National Gross Income," "national holidays," "National Bank," and the like, instead of the accurate "State Gross Product," "State Gross Income," "state holidays," "State Bank," etc.[46]

In the United States, however, "people" and "nation" tend to be conflated – and for cause. Like the modern nation, the American people was first and foremost politically, not culturally, defined. Even if, as we shall see, American history is marked by the development of its own brand of identity politics, including anti-immigration politics, overall the idea that a people is politically

---

[43] James Farr (1989), "Understanding Conceptual Change Politically," in Terrence Ball, James Farr, and Russel L. Hanson, eds., *Political Innovation and Conceptual Change* (Cambridge: Cambridge University Press), 27.

[44] The following is but a small sample of the literature addressing the topic: Benedict Anderson (2006), *Imagined Communities: Reflections on the Origins and Spread of Nationalism*, 2nd ed. (London: Vero); Brian Barry (2001), *Culture and Equality: An Egalitarian Critique of Multiculturalism* (Cambridge, MA: Harvard University Press); Peter J. Burke and Jan E. Stets (2009), *Identity Theory* (Oxford: Oxford University Press); Joseph H. Carens (2000), *Culture, Citizenship, and Community: A Contextual Exploration of Justice as Evenhandedness* (Oxford: Oxford University Press); Chaim Gans (2003), *The Limits of Nationalism* (Cambridge: Cambridge University Press). Jurgen Habermas (2001) *The Postnational Constellation: Political Essays* (M. Pensky, Trans.) (Cambridge, MA: MIT Press); Will Kymlicka (1995), *Multicultural Citizenship: A Liberal Theory of Minority Rights* (New York: Oxford University Press); Anthony D. Smith (2001), *Nationalism: Theory, Ideology, History* (Cambridge: Polity Press).

[45] Article 3 of the German *Grundgesetz*, for example, states that "no person shall be favored or disfavored because of sex, parentage, race, language, homeland and origin, faith, or religious or political opinions" (official translation). Similarly, the first article of the latest French constitution (1958) assures "the equality of all citizens before the law without distinction based on origin, race, or religion."

[46] I am grateful to Anna Marisa Schön for bringing some of these observations to my attention.

defined proved very resilient.[47] During the same speech quoted above, Lincoln elaborates on this point as well – and deserves a lengthier quotation:

We are now a mighty nation ... We run our memory back over the pages of history for about eighty-two years [...] and we fix upon something that happened away back, as in some way or other being connected with this rise of prosperity. We find a race of men living in that day whom we claim as our fathers and grandfathers; they were iron men, they fought for the principle that they were contending for; [...] We have besides these men – descended *by blood* from our ancestors – among us perhaps half our people who are *not* descendants at all of these men, they are men who have come from Europe – German, Irish, French and Scandinavian – men that have come from Europe themselves, or whose ancestors have come hither and settled here, *finding themselves our equals in all things. If they look back through this history to trace their connection with those days by blood, they find they have none*, they cannot carry themselves back into that glorious epoch and make themselves feel that they are part of us, but when they look through that old Declaration of Independence they find that those old men say that "We hold these truths to be self-evident, that all men are created equal," and then they feel that ... *they have a right to claim it as though they were blood of the blood, and flesh of the flesh of the men who wrote that Declaration,* and so they are. That is the electric cord in that Declaration that links the hearts of patriotic and liberty-loving men together, that will link those patriotic hearts as long as the love of freedom exists in the minds of men throughout the world.[48]

Because of this American overlapping between "nation" and "people," the contemporary focus on nation and nationalism risks to obscure what I believe is a more important concept, namely "the people." After all, the American nation is no longer a questionable concept. The role of the people in American democracy, however, remains heavily disputed, hence it was on "the people" that I have chosen to focus.

It was not the only choice that I had to make. Other choices, some of them quite painful, had to be made as well, if only to keep the length of the book manageable. Although the chapters unfold chronologically, some historical aspects are emphasized at the expense of others. One could question, for example, the space allocated to the religious subtleties that characterized Puritanism and the Great Awakening, in contrast to, say, the events of the Revolutionary War. Yet I did so for a couple of reasons. First, because, for the past two decades or so, these religious movements that left an undeniable mark on the founding era have become increasingly overlooked – and whenever they are invoked it is usually in the wrong context and for the wrong reasons.

---

[47] Here is a small sample of the literature considering the peculiarity of American nationalism: Ali Behdad (2005), *A Forgetful Nation: On Immigration and Identity in the United States* (Durham: Duke University Press); Richard T. Hughes (2003), *Myths America Lives By* (Urbana: University of Illinois Press); Roger M. Smith (1988), "The 'American Creed' and American Identity: The Limits of Liberal Citizenship in the United States," *Western Political Quarterly* 41:2, 225–251.

[48] Quoted in Roy P. Basler, ed., (1953), *The Collected Works of Abraham Lincoln*, vol. 2, 499–500 (emphasis added).

Second, as Alexis de Tocqueville observed in the *Democracy in America*'s chapter suggestively entitled "*On the Point of Departure and Its Importance for the Future of the Anglo-Americans*," in America, "liberty looks upon religion as its comrade in battle and victory, as the cradle of its infancy and divine source of its rights."[49] Even more important, one has to take into consideration that the first "peoples" voluntary created by the American Puritans were, unlike any of their European counterparts, theologico-political communities. The Christic appeal to "Render unto Caesar the things that are Caesar's, and unto God the things that are God's" (Matthew 22:21) had no traction in New England, except for Roger Williams and the colony of Rhode Island. Thus, the ways in which religion modified their apprehension of the self modified their understanding of political representation as well. As we shall see, it proved to be, in theological parlance, both a blessing and a curse.

To some extent, the very topic of the book imposed other choices. Since this is not a book concerned with recreating the details of the American founding, but rather one that aims to combine conceptual history with the history of political thought, I will not delve into the historical details more than is necessary for establishing the background against which this enterprise takes place.[50] As I looked at compromise throughout the founding era both as a concept and as a practice, I selected those texts and contexts that I found more useful for understanding the extent to which the rhetoric of compromise – both in everyday language and as a conscious political appeal – matched the practice of it. Part of the reason was rather pragmatic: establishing the relationship between the rhetoric and the practice of compromise has contemporary implications that go beyond mere historical and theoretical interest. The same motivation drove the highlighting of some particular concepts in the writings of the era at the expense of others, perhaps equally important, such as "liberty," "natural rights," "state," and so forth.[51] Thus, throughout the book, the focus will remain primarily on how the willingness to compromise (or the lack thereof) was associated with different understandings of "the people," with the hope that illuminating this connection then might help us better understand many of our contemporary plights.

After all, regardless of the historical context, a political compromise has inherently two sides: an affective and a contractual one. One can look at a

[49] Alexis de Tocqueville [2004] *Democracy in America*, translated by Arthur Godhammer (New York: The Library of America), 13, 49.

[50] For a more detailed discussion of the similarities and differences between conceptual history, history of ideologies, philosophical history of ideas, philosophical history of the political, *Begriffgeshichte*, and of the authors associated with each of them, see Fumurescu, *Compromise*, 6–9.

[51] See, for example, Terrence Ball, James Farr, and Russel L. Hanson, eds. (1988), *Political Innovation and Conceptual Change* (Cambridge: Cambridge University Press); Daniel T. Rodgers (1987), *Contested Truths: Keywords in American Politics since Independence* (New York: Basic Books, Inc.).

compromise as involving mutuality and sacrifice for the sake of a greater good, but one can also look at it through a pseudo-commercial lens, as a bargain between competing interests. Hence, "its meaning can change as the emphasis on one or another element is changed."[52] The former is largely characteristic of the republican emphasis on a common good and the rejection of factionalism, and thus of the political compact between the people as a whole and its ruler(s); meanwhile the latter is closer to the classic liberal *Weltanschauung*, and thus to the social contract theory, ruled by a majority of wills. In the former case, political representation presupposes a representation of groups, corporations, or communities; in the latter, a representation of individuals.

Hence, by its very nature, the study of the concept of compromise requires a dual methodological approach, at the intersection of the so-called "realist" and "moralist" or "normative" approaches in political theory. Although – as in the case of all methodological labelling – I suspect a bit of scholarly vanity at work, it is important to clarify where my approach fits inside this literature. The past decade has witnessed an explosion of this controversy among political theorists. Sparked by the publication in 2005 of Bernard Williams's collection of essays, the debate took off after 2010, with calls for "an approach which gives greater autonomy to distinctively political thought," as opposed to the moralistic and normatively driven contemporary political philosophy, for which John Rawls and his successors of various flavors are held responsible.[53] Despite the differences among the supporter of "realism," they all share the idea that political thought ought to re-emphasize the political, i.e., what realistically can be done considering historical circumstances. And although none of them deny that politics implies normative commitments, they refuse to confuse political philosophy with moral philosophy or psychology, rejecting anything close to an "ideal, normative theory," disconnected from reality (the realist constraint). Notwithstanding, the risk of "realism," as skeptics are quick to point out, would be to give up any attempt to improve the world, accepting it "as it is."

Considering all of the above, it would be tempting to subsume the approach proposed here under the label of "realist" political theory, but it would also be

---

[52] Knupfer, *The Union as It Is*, 13.

[53] Bernard Williams (2005), *In the Beginning Was the Deed: Realism and Moralism in Political Argument*, ed. Geoffrey Hawthorn (Princeton: Princeton University Press), 3. As a sample of the participants on both sides of this debate, see Michael Freeden (2012), "Interpretive Realism and Prescriptive Realism," *Journal of Political Ideologies*, 17:1, 1–11; Katrina Forrester (2012), "Judith Shklar, Bernard Williams and Political Realism," *European Journal of Political Theory*, 11:3, 247–272; William Galston (2010), "Realism in Political Theory," *European Journal of Political Theory*, 9:4, 385–411; Edward Hall (2017), "How to Do Realistic Political Theory," *European Journal of Political Theory*, 16:3, 283–303; William E. Scheuerman (2013), "The Realist Revival in Political Philosophy, Or: Why New is Not Always Improved," *International Politics*, 50:6, 798–814; Matt Sleat, ed. (2018) *Politics Recovered: Essays on Realist Political Thought* (New York: Columbia University Press); Enzo Rossi (2016), "Facts, Principles, and (Real) Politics," *Ethical Theory and Moral Practice*, 19, 505–520.

reducing it to one side of the coin. While it remains historically and politically sensitive, and it avoids jumping to value judgments about the actors discussed or about their decisions, it does not shy away from normative considerations. After all, even the supporters of the realist approach end up calling for "a return to political philosophy's traditional blend of normative and descriptive descriptions."[54]

To give, for now, just one example from a contemporary perspective, it would be easy to condemn the Northerners and even Lincoln himself for their willingness to compromise with the Southerners on the institution of slavery for the sake of preserving the Union. Nevertheless, once one sheds contemporary glasses and refrains from post hoc judgments, one must concede that realistic abolitionists could not peek into the future, and thus were forced to compromise on one principle (slavery) in order to preserve the other (the Union). One must also admit that, in and of itself, this tough choice presupposes a normative commitment. It is completely *realistic* to assume that *moral* considerations matter, even if only because sometimes they ought to be compromised. There are no straightforward, objective rules on when to compromise or how much. Max Weber's observation about this political plight still stands:

In truth, politics is an activity of the head but by no means only of the head. In this respect the adherents of an ethics of conviction are in the right. But whether we should act in accordance with an ethics of conviction or an ethics of responsibility, and when we *should* choose one rather than the other, is not a matter on which we can lay down the law to anyone else. [...] I find it immeasurably moving when a mature human being – whether young or old in actual years is immaterial – who feels the responsibility he bears for the consequences of his own actions with his entire soul and who acts in harmony with an ethics of responsibility reaches the point where he says, "Here I stand, I can do no other." That is authentically human and cannot fail to move us. For this is a situation that *may* befall *any* of us at some point, if we are not inwardly dead.[55]

This is even truer in the case of political compromise, in which not only principles, ideologies, and interests come into play but also affections. Thus, it involves both objective and subjective considerations. It is often difficult, if not altogether impossible, to find even a minimum consensus on so many respects. And even if the paradigm of the people's two bodies does not automatically presuppose a *theoretical* compromise between the two competing understandings of the people, in *practice*, such compromises were often necessary for maintaining the Union.

It is important to note that neither the corporate conception of the people nor the understanding of the people as a collection of individuals is inherently

---

[54] Rossi, "Facts," 505.
[55] Max Weber (2005), "Politics as a Vocation," in Michael L. Morgan, ed., *Classics of Moral and Political Theory*, Fourth edition (Indianapolis and Cambridge: Hackett Publishing Company), 1248 (emphasis in the original).

friendly *or* hostile to compromise. Rather, the two approaches resemble Machiavelli's famous comparison between the state of Turkey, ruled authoritarian by the Sultan, and the state of France, ruled by the king with the help of an envious nobility: "Comparing the two states, anyone can see that, though conquering the Turkish state might be hard, once conquered, it would be easy to hold. On the other hand, to take the state of France would be relatively easy in some ways, but to hold onto it would be very hard."[56] In a similar way, the American founding teaches us that, as a general rule, under republican premises, compromises are difficult to arrive to, yet once the agreement takes place, chances are they will be long-lasting. In contrast, under liberal assumptions, political compromises are easier to reach yet hard to keep.

As long as the idea of a corporate people is accepted by the parties involved, all efforts are directed toward creating a concurrent majority that takes into consideration the demands of the minority. The process tends to drag on, for the stakes are high, but once the solution is agreed on, it will be long praised by everyone as a gesture of goodwill from all parties. In counterdistinction, once the people is understood as a multitude of equal individuals, compromise becomes the only way of creating a people by setting up, through voluntary consent, an impartial arbitrator or a *compromissarius*.[57] Yet once this new people is created, the inherent *inequality* between a majority and a minority – the basic principle of the social contract theory – makes any political compromise ephemeral, by switching the emphasis from its affective component to its contractual one. A good example would be President Trump's comment to his fellow Republicans in February 2018. According to CNN, "While Trump initially suggested Republicans may need to compromise to reach a deal with Democrats on immigration, he then turned his sights to the 2018 election as an alternative. 'To get it done we'll have to make some compromises,' Trump said, 'unless we elect more Republicans.'"[58] According to the founders' criteria, such compromises would qualify as compromises "without a heart," mere bargains between the competing interests of a majority and a minority. Naturally then, once the majority changes, the old compromise becomes void.

As we shall see, the story of founding of the American people is filled with both types of compromises.

1.3 E PLURIBUS UNUM

If the American people was over two centuries in the making, it is because its creation began not with three groups defined by different cultures – moralistic

---

[56] Niccolo Machiavelli [1977], *The Prince*, Translated and edited by Robert M. Adams (New York: W.W. Norton & Company), 13.

[57] Fumurescu, *Compromise*.

[58] www.cnn.com/2018/02/01/politics/president-donald-trump-gop-retreat/index.html, last accessed June 13, 2018.

in New England, individualistic in the Middle Atlantic, and traditionalistic in the South – and not even with thirteen groups, but with many more.[59] Practically, as I will show in Chapter 2, each group of Puritans and Pilgrims arriving on the shores of the New World *actually* created new, theologico-political "peoples" through the express consent of individuals to found both a church and a political community. "One could also speak of their creating a society, but this term is not quite strong enough."[60]

They were covenanted people, and covenantal theory permeated their entire *Weltanschauung* despite, or precisely because of, its sophistication. The Puritans distinguished between the covenant of works, the covenant of grace, and the covenant of justification, but also between the inner covenant of each individual with God, the church covenant, and the covenant of each church with God. More will be said about the distinction between covenant, compact, and contract. For now, suffice it to say that out of these multiple covenants only two proved to be long-lasting: the horizontal church covenant, among the members to form a church and a political community; and the vertical covenant between each church and God, that was politically reflected in the covenant of the newly created people with their elected leaders. It is easy to understand why this bidimensional covenant can be mistaken as either a proto-social contract theory or as a medieval political contract. However, the similarities in form cannot obscure the major differences in their fundamental assumptions about human nature and political membership.

The American Puritans, unlike their English counterparts, distrusted *forum externum*, for, like the French, they suspected it of being tainted with hypocrisy. Nor did they trust *forum internum*, as the French did, for, as the English, they believed it was deceitful, easy prey to devil's tricks. As a result, they rejected both the British centrifugal individualism and the French centripetal form of individualism, embracing one of their own, which I labeled, for lack of a better word, "purged individualism." Essentially, it presupposed to purge one's *forum internum* by effectively turning it inside out, thus replacing *forum externum* for everyone to see. Through detailed public confessions (admission tests) the internal self became the visible, external one, and the authenticity of its conversion or "purity" had to be vetted by the "visible saints." It was the necessary precondition for being admitted as a full member, with voting powers, in both the church and the political community. Put in modern parlance, no "conversion narrative," no "citizenship." To be admitted in the community, the invisible ought to be made visible.

By requiring the external approval of the hierarchy of saints, this purged individualism began a collision course with the horizontal understanding of the

---

[59] For the famous tri-partition, see Daniel J. Elazar (1972), *American Federalism: A View from the States* (New York: Thomas Y. Crowell) and Chapter 4 in this volume.
[60] Donald S. Lutz (1988), *The Origins of American Constitutionalism* (Baton Rouge: Louisiana State University Press), xxiv.

people *qua* free and equal individuals. As communities expanded, older and more educated religious authorities began to be contested, and the pendulum swung from "objectivity" to "subjectivity," from reason to will, and from the community to the individual. As shown in Chapter 3, by the beginning of the eighteenth century, the American colonists became more British than their brethren across the Atlantic. Yet, by the same token, they also began developing their own particular identities.[61] Because the Great Awakening ended up permanently destroying the old theologico-political communities, new ways of identifying were needed. Since the British assumption was that a people was held together primarily by its own elected legislative body, the colonial assemblies came to be seen as the equivalent of the British Parliament.

As the tensions between the metropole and the colonies intensified, the idea of different peoples inside the empire of Great Britain, held together only by political contracts between the king and each colony, became increasingly attractive. As the "arbitrator" or *"compromissarius"* between different parts of the empire, the role of the king for the colonists was emphasized to the extent that, to the surprise of many, including Lord North, they became more Tories than Whigs.[62] In order to defend their corporate rights, the colonists had no choice but to renounce any pretention of being represented by or in the Parliament, either virtually or actually, as the social compact theory demanded, and make appeal to the political one, for all extra-colonial relationships. Thanks to the paradigm of the people's two bodies, throughout the Imperial Debate, the colonists proved more versatile, at least as far as theoretical justifications were needed on both sides of this confrontation.

This cherished corporate identity at the colonial level made the Patriots increasingly unwilling to compromise, and when the time came, King George metamorphosed almost overnight in the colonial psyche and pamphlets from a benevolent Father into "the perfect scapegoat."[63] Although largely ignored in the first years after its adoption, the Declaration of Independence managed to depict the king as the main culprit of all colonial infringements of corporatist rights, all the while reaffirming that "consanguinity" and the "Ties of our common Kindred" do not matter when "it becomes necessary for one People to dissolve the Political Bands which have connected them with another."[64]

[61] Bernard McConville (2006), *The King's Three Faces: The Rise and Fall of Royal America, 1688–1776* (Chapel Hill: University of North Carolina Press); Nancy L. Rhoden (2013), "The American Revolution (I) – The Paradox of Atlantic Integration" in Stephen Foster, ed., *British North America in the Seventeenth and Eighteenth Centuries* (Oxford: Oxford University Press).

[62] Eric Nelson (2011), "Patriot Royalism: The Stuart Monarchy in American Political Thought, 1769-75" in *The William and Mary Quarterly*, 68:4.

[63] Gerald Stourzh (2010) [1970], *From Vienna to Chicago and Back: Essays on Intellectual History and Political Thought in Europe and America* (Chicago: University of Chicago Press), 25.

[64] Barry Alan Shain, ed. (2014), The Declaration of Independence in Historical Context: American State Papers, Petitions, Proclamations & Letters of the Delegates in the First National Congress (New Haven and London: Yale University Press).

As I will discuss in Chapter 4, the fear of a tyrannical executive left an undeniable mark on the state constitutions – and not only the first ones. These foundational documents shared a common feature: the emphasis switched one more time from the corporatist and hierarchical vision of the people to the horizontal and egalitarian one, and granted extended powers to the state legislatures. This commonly held egalitarian approach makes it easy to discuss the state constitutions of the late eighteenth century together with the ones from the first half of the nineteenth ones, despite some undeniable differences between the former and the latter.

Three of these differences are worth emphasizing. The first one is the transfer of the constitutional power from the legislatures, in which it initially resided, to the state ratifying convention, thus increasing popular control. The second is the relatively rapid abandonment of the secrecy of the debates in these conventions – a decision that, as we shall see in greater detail later, impaired the chances to compromise and opened the door for a populist rhetoric. Finally, the third one is the increasingly rapid move away from providing representation for corporations – towns, counties, and the like – to providing representation for individuals.

Yet the corporatist vision of the colonial peoples was not to be abandoned when it came to establishing the Articles of Confederation. As in the case of the now largely forgotten Articles of the Confederation of the United Colonies instituted by the Puritans more than a century before, the theoretical equality of corporations, regardless of their actual size, made a compromise possible, despite the marked differences among the newly created thirteen states. It was no small feat, considering that just a few years before these differences – economic, religious, cultural, etc. – were considered by most actors and outsiders impossible to overcome. According to an anonymous British observer, the association of so many different peoples amounted to nothing more than "a rope of sand."[65] He was proven wrong. Even if the Articles of Confederation turned out to be short lived and deficient in many respects, it was a constitution that formalized the idea of dual citizenship and made possible the compromises of the Philadelphia Convention – the topic of Chapter 5.[66]

To claim to have something new to say about the compromises that took place during the Philadelphia Convention and the successive ratifying conventions might appear pretentious, considering the amount of scholarship already dedicated to this topic. Nevertheless, without challenging (most of) these interpretations, I suggest that the main reason why the Constitution was, for generations to come, reverentially referred to as "the greatest of all

---

[65] "Some Thoughts on the Settlements and Government on our Colonies in North America," 10 March 1763, Add. Mss (Liverpool Papers), British Library – quoted in Jack P. Greene (1982), "The Background of the Articles of Confederation," *Publius*, 12:4, 19.

[66] Donald S. Lutz (1990), "The Articles of Confederation as the Background to the Federal Republic," *Publius*, 20:1, 55–70, 66.

compromises" was not primarily because it set up an example of how meaningful compromises can be reached by combining appeals to interests and to affections, but because it formalized with a surprising degree of success the paradigm of the people's two bodies. The fact that the famous three words that open the Constitution, "We the People," were never elaborated upon in the text that followed, far from being a weakness, allowed a lot of room for maneuver in defining "the people." The delegates present in Philadelphia in the summer of 1776 were faced, in this respect alone, with a double challenge: first, to decide if the United States was made up of one or of several peoples (or nations); second, to decide which of the two understandings of the people ought to be given priority.

Both of these challenges were solved through compromise. Elbridge Gerry's observation made in the convention, on July 5, proved convincing enough for most delegates: "We were neither the same Nation not different Nations. We ought not therefore to pursue the one or the other of these ideas too closely."[67] The second compromise about the people was the hardest. Since in the Articles of Confederation the principle was clearly in favor of representing the people in their "corporate capacity," and the Articles proved defective, for politicians like Hamilton it meant that it was "the great and radical vice in the construction of the existing Confederation," and ought to be replaced with its counterpart – representation of individuals.[68] Fortunately, the end result represented a compromise between the two, and not just by ensuring the representation of individuals in the House of Representatives and of the corporate peoples in the Senate, but by creating a mechanism of checks and balances that would prevent, so to speak, one body of the people from taking over the other.

As Tocqueville noticed, "In America, the struggle between these two camps," one "wishing to restrain the power of the people, the other to extend it without limit," "never took the violent form that has often distinguished it in other countries. Both parties agreed about the most essential points," and, as he went on to explain, many of one camp's principles "ultimately became part of their adversaries' creed." Therefore, the Federalists success was, in his view, "one of the most fortunate events attending the birth of the great American Union," and he believed that "the federal Constitution ... is a lasting monument to their patriotism and wisdom."[69]

However, not all the compromises of the new Constitution were to be applauded and, unsurprisingly, not all of them proved long-lasting. The (in)

---

[67] In James Madison (1985), *Notes of Debates in the Federal Convention of 1797* (Athens: Ohio University Press), 243.

[68] *The Federalist* (2001), 71.

[69] Alexis de Tocqueville [2004] *Democracy in America*, translated by Arthur Goldhammer (New York: The Library of America), 200–201.

famous Three-Fifths Compromise might have been necessary at that time both for finalizing the draft and for increasing the likelihood of its ratification, but it also turned out to be the least defendable. Nevertheless, as I will show in Chapter 6, for the first decades of the new republic, the institution of slavery was neither in the forefront of political debates nor a direct threat to the Union. To the despair of the most committed abolitionists, such as William Lloyd Garrison, slavery was mainly discussed as an economic and constitutional problem, not as a moral one.

As a matter of fact, the first serious threat to the Union came not from the South but from the New Englanders. What they perceived as a growing wave of populism, exploited by the Southern aristocrats, was seen as a direct threat to the republican principles upheld throughout the Revolutionary War and beyond by the American people.[70] This rather forgotten episode in American history has two valuable lessons to teach us. On the one hand, it shows that when a minority feels constantly abused, rightfully or not, by a majority, compromises become more difficult if not altogether impossible, being refused by both parties as either unnecessary (by the majority) or as "too little, too late" (by the minority). On the other hand, it also suggests that populism and the existence of an aristocracy of wealth, far from being incompatible, may very well coexist.[71]

As discussed in the same chapter, a similar ambiguity manifested in the development of mass politics during the first half of the eighteenth century. While enfranchising and mobilizing more and more strata of the white male population, it also meant a setback in terms of political rights for many white women and free blacks.[72] Such developments were part of a larger one, marked by the emergence of a political rhetoric increasingly attacking an "otherness" defined in terms of not just gender or race but also of religion, ethnicity, place of birth, etc. As we shall see, some strange alliances took place during that period, showing how dangerous it can be to make sweeping correlations between increased political activism and tolerance. Fortunately, by the same token, the problem of slavery finally came to be posed as a moral one, and thus one that could no longer be subjected to political compromises. In the end, in one of the last ironies of the American founding, it was the South, not the North, that refused to compromise on what it perceived as a direct threat to the Southern peoples' identity, thus initiating a devastating civil war.

---

[70] Davis S. Brown (2016), *Moderates: The Vital Center of American Politics, from the Founding to Today* (Chapel Hill: University of North Carolina Press).

[71] I will elaborate on the issue of populism in Chapter 6.

[72] See, for example, Andrew W. Robertson (2015), "Jefferson Parties, Politics, and Participation: The Tortuous Trajectory of American Democracy," in Daniel Peart and Adam I. P. Smith, eds., *Practicing Democracy*.

By now, it should come as no surprise that the Civil War was, in Lincoln's interpretation, "essentially a people's contest." As such, "no compromise by public servants could in this case be a cure."[73]

1.4 THE PEOPLE'S TWO BODIES – THEN AND NOW

More about the contemporary implications will be said in the concluding chapter. For now, let us notice that even if never labeled as such, the paradigm of the people's two bodies proved a powerful tool in crafting a distinct American people. It might not be an accident that the English language allows one to say both "the American people *is* a hard-working people" and "the American people *are* hard-working people."[74] For both the British and for American colonists, the people were primarily conceived as a *political* people, hence assimilated with the "nation." As Sir Roger L'Estrange put it as a widely accepted truth, "The people are the nation; and the nation is the people."[75] Therefore, unlike in continental Europe, in Great Britain and in the United States, there are no references to "national minorities," but instead to "ethnic minorities."[76]

There was, however, from the very beginning, a crucial difference between the two: while for the British the idea of a political people was just that – an idea – for the American colonists it was a living reality. Furthermore, in seventeenth-century Great Britain, the understanding of the people was sharply divided between that of the Tories, for which the multitude was but an unruly mob, and that of the Whigs, for which the legal equality of the individuals was a fundamental assumption. For people like L'Estrange, this latter approach was opening the gates of anarchy. After positing what he saw as a self-evident truth, "the people are the nation; and the nation is the people," he continued with what, for him, was the crux of the matter: "*But do we speak of the multitude or of the community?*" For the fervent royalist the answer was clear: "If of the community, why do ye not rather call it the government? If of the multitude; they have no right of acting, judging, or interposing."[77] By contrast, the

---

[73] Abraham Lincoln (1861), *Message to Congress in Special Session, in The Collected Works of Abraham Lincoln* (1953), Vol. 4, 439.

[74] In contrast, for example, in French (*le peuple*), Italian (*il popolo*), German (*das Volk*), or Romanian (*poporul*), the only possible usage of "the people" is in singular, like a corporate entity.

[75] Roger L'Estrange (February 10, 1683), *Observator in Dialogue*, quoted in Steven C.A. Pincus (2006), *England's Glorious Revolution, 1688-1689: A Brief History with Documents* (New York: Palgrave Macmillan), 143.

[76] The Romans also understood "the people" (*populus*) to be the assembly of citizens, while the multitude was referred to as *plebe*. The ways in which "nation" and "people" changed their meanings across time and space is a fascinating topic, but one that does not constitute the object of this book.

[77] L'Estrange, *Observator*, 143 (emphasis added).

American strength was to being able to accommodate both visions of the people, without creating an unsurpassable gap between the two.

Recently, David Ciepley has argued efficaciously that the US Constitution "is neither a contract among individuals to form a people," as many scholars still argue, "nor a contract between a people and a ruler." In other words, it is neither a social nor a political contract. Instead, it "should be seen as a popularly issued corporate charter."[78] As persuasive as it may be, Ciepley's argument remains one-sided. As we shall see, the simultaneous appeal to chartering *and* to the ruler/political compact was a common trope throughout the founding era. As for the Constitution, the drafters themselves saw it as a combination between a social and a political compact. Madison wrote in a letter dated February 15, 1830, that "[t]he original compact is the one implied or presumed, but nowhere reduced to writing, by which a people agree to form one society. The next is a compact, here for the first time reduced to writing, by which the people in their social state agree to Government over them. These two compacts may be considered as blended in the Constitution of the United States."[79]

Thus, it appears that, for this book's protagonists, the distinction between charter, social, and political contract was not as clear-cut as Ciepley suggests. He claims that "a sovereign (the People) promulgates a charter (a written constitution) that establishes a government with juridical personhood. [...] Substitute 'king' or 'Parliament' for 'People,' and this description ... is indistinguishable from a description of the formation and operation of an 18th century corporation."[80] If, as Ciepley rightfully claims, "the federalists could thus appeal to both populist and antipopulist sentiments by turn," it was not simply because "the institutional matrix of our modernity turned out to be quite 'medieval.'"[81] The corporatist sovereign people is only half of the story. The paradigm of the people's two bodies allows space for both the people as corporation and for the people as multitude, without reducing the first to simply chartering a constitution and then fading into the background, like a crowd of "investors." Thus, Donald Lutz's interpretation appears both more complex and more accurate:

Take a charter ... and replace the king as the highest civil authority with "the people." The people as grantor give a monopoly of political power to government officials, who collectively become the grantee, or government. [...] Establish institutions whereby the grantee can make all collective decisions ... as long as the decisions are agreeable to the grantor and not contrary to the provisions in this "charter" that serves as a kind of higher law. In outline form, you have described how a charter lends himself to

---

[78] David Ciepley (2017), "Is the U.S. Government a Corporation? The Corporate Genesis of Modern Constitutionalism," *American Political Science Review*, 111:2, 419.

[79] Quoted in Garry Rosen (1999), *American Compact: James Madison and the Problem of Founding* (Lawrence: University Press of Kansas), 20.

[80] Ciepley, "Is the U.S. Government a Corporation?", 419.   [81] Ibid., 432, 434.

structuring a constitution with a legally enforceable content and the overtones of a contract. (Lutz 1988, 38–39)

Distinguishing between two types of contracts and two different understandings of the people, while applying to both the label of "social compact," appears to be an American staple, as shown also in John Quincy Adams's lecture delivered at the Franklin Lyceum in November 25, 1842. Adams made clear that he considered "the Constitution of the Commonwealth of Massachusetts," the Constitution of the United States ("this great confederated Union"), and "the North American Declaration of Independence" all founded on the principles of the social compact – "the principles of Sidney and Locke ... together with the subsequent writings of Montesquieu and Rousseau" (Adams 1842, 29). If we ignore the name-dropping, what he understood by "social compact" was an altogether different matter. Very much in line with Hamilton or Madison, he carefully separated the two understandings of the people:

Thus when in the Constitution of the Commonwealth of Massachusetts, it is said that the body politic is formed by a social compact in which the *whole people* covenants with each citizen and each citizen with the *whole people*, the words *whole people* in the first part of the sentence, have not the same meaning as they have in the second. In the first part they mean the portion of the people *capable* of contracting for the whole and with the whole—in the second, they mean the sum of total human beings bound by and included in the compact. (Adams 1842, 8 – emphasis in the original)

All the misogynist remarks and inadvertencies aside,[82] Adams deserves credit for pointing out the ambiguity of all founding documents on this subject – unfortunately a feat rarely matched by contemporary scholars. Hence, going beyond the founders' misuse of the social compact label, while recuperating both the distinction they made between the two types of compacts and their respective understandings of the people, is a long-overdue enterprise. As I will discuss in more details in the last chapter, these distinctions are important not just in political theory but in political practice and rhetoric as well, if we want to avoid the Scylla of false elitism and the Charybdis of populist appeals.

By resting their political theory solely on the governmental compact and the corporatist understanding of the people, the medieval authors justified, created, and reinforced false hierarchies that in the long run proved damaging for society and self-defeating for the ruling class. A different type of danger may arise from the opposite direction. By exclusively and indiscriminately using the rhetoric of the social compact, with its implied mechanical equality between individuals, contemporary liberal democracies run the risk of making the cultivation and promotion of the chords of affection and of statesmanship more difficult. When "elitism" as a concept is ostracized in politics, both rhetorically

---

[82] Adams assumes that families are the building blocks of the social compact to argue against women's electoral franchise, considers Hobbes a theoretician of the divine rights of kings, same as Filmer, etc.

and institutionally, the gates of populism become wide open. And, as the history of the Founding teaches us, excesses on either side can be extremely pernicious for building meaningful political compromises.

The first example of how difficult is to maintain the balance between the two comes from the Puritan experiment.

2

The Uncompromising Puritans

"If the whole conclave of Hell can so compromise ..."

> Satan labours to compromise the business, and bring it to a composition between him and Christ.
>
> – William Gurnall[1]

That the first Puritans to set foot on the shores of North America were no friends of compromise goes almost without saying. After all, the very label that they came to embrace is in itself quite suggestive. That they were to be a major influence on what was to become "the American spirit" is also widely accepted, albeit sometimes qualified.[2] Despite the many claims to the contrary, it follows that the American people was founded not just on compromise but also on a deeply rooted uncompromising attitude.[3] Given these misconceptions, it is

---

[1] Ironically, Gurnall's "Puritanism" has been contested because of his compromising position after the Restauration and the passing of the Act of Uniformity.

[2] As many recent scholars have pointed, it would be exaggerate to credit Puritanism with an overwhelming influence on the founding, ignoring other influences from mainstream Anglicans, Quakers, Catholics, Jews, Native Americans, and so forth. Yet it would be equally exaggerate to reduce the role played by Puritanism to a mere influence among others. See further.

[3] For quotes supporting the argument that "America (or the American people) was founded on compromise," from Alexander Hamilton to President Obama, see Fumurescu, *Compromise*, 1–2. Since then, the number of similar claims has increased, both in the academia and in the public sphere. For the academia, see, for example, Michael J. Faber (2015), "The Federal Union Paradigm of 1788: Three Anti-Federalists Who Changed Their Minds," *American Political Thought: A Journal of Ideas, Institutions, and Culture*, 4, 527–556; David Brian Robertson (2013), The Original Compromise: What the Constitution's Framers Were Really Thinking (New York: Oxford University Press). For the public sphere, see President Obama's seventh and last State of the Union address: "Democracy grinds to a halt without a willingness to compromise." www.cbsnews.com/news/obama-state-of-the-union-2016/

worth deciphering where this refusal to compromise came from and what its underlying assumptions were, in order to better understand its political consequences.

"Puritanism" is undoubtedly a rather fluid term, "a movement whose essence was ambiguity,"[4] to the extent that some came even to question the relevancy of the label.[5] Yet the frustrating difficulties in defining it are actually revealing of a built-in ambivalence operating at various levels, which makes the movement appear not only paradoxical but at the same time appealing even today to a wide – and oftentimes contradictory – variety of positions. "American Puritanism managed to combine the traditional and the radical, the voluntary and the authoritarian, as well as a host of other diametrically opposed impulses, into one organic whole that apparently thrived on its own internal conflicts".[6]

It is an observation shared, in different wordings, by many scholars – and for cause. The Puritans were both focused on the afterlife *and* deeply concerned with this world, both individualistic *and* communitarian, firm believers in the doctrine of predestination *while* praising the strength of will. They also fled religious persecution *yet* were deaf to any calls for toleration, were enemies of imposed hierarchies *while* reinforcing their very own, etc. – and all of the above while refusing to compromise on any side of these bipolarities.[7] I argue that the best way to decipher these paradoxes is by taking a closer look at the Puritans' uncompromising attitude. Far from being typically British, it resembles more the French suspicion of compromise, without, however, becoming identical to it. But in order to make sense out of these ambivalences, one has to take into consideration the other side of the coin as well. The same Puritans *were* willing to compromise plenty of differences, but only *among themselves*, as long as they perceived such differences as not threatening to the purity of their much cherished theologico-political communities. For, as I shall try to demonstrate, the uncompromising attitude manifested itself only toward the perceived

---

[4] Stephen Foster (1971), *Their Solitary Way: The Puritan Social Ethic in the First Century of Settlement in New England* (New Haven and London: Yale University Press), xvi.

[5] For a discussion on the challenges of defining Puritanism and the contemporary relevancy of the label, see, for example, Michael P. Winship (2001), "Where There Any Puritans in New England?", *The New England Quarterly*, 74:1, 118–138.

[6] Foster, *Their Solitary Way*, xvi.

[7] See, for example, Wilson Carey McWilliams (1973), *The Idea of Fraternity in America* (Berkeley, Los Angeles, London: University of California Press); Francis J. Bremer (1976), *The Puritan Experiment – New England Society from Bradford to Edwards* (New York: St. Martin's Press); Christopher Hill (1964), *Society and Puritanism in Pre-revolutionary England* (London: Secker & Warburg); Perry Miller (1939), *The New England Mind – The Seventeenth Century* (New York: The Macmillan Company); Michael P. Zuckert (1996), *The Natural Rights Republic – Studies in the Foundation of the American Political Tradition* (South Bend: University of Notre Dame Press); Perry Miller and Thomas H. Johnson, eds. (2001), The Puritans – A Sourcebook of Their Writings (Mineola: Dover Publications, Inc.); David A. Weir (2005), *Early New England – A Covenanted Society* (Cambridge: William B. Eerdmans Publishing Company).

"outsiders," whether they were Catholics, Anglicans, Quakers, Baptists, or other so-called Enthusiasts. In other words, the willingness to compromise or its lack thereof was intimately related to group and self-identification. This ambivalence was made possible by the fact that they were able to actually implement a bidimensional covenant: the first one horizontal, between equal individuals to create a new theologico-political people; the second one vertical, between this new formed people and its elected aristocracy of merit.

Therefore, the first part of the chapter shows how the American Puritans were different from their English brethren. Generally speaking, the Puritans viewed the Church of England as a compromise between Catholicism and Protestantism, and hence in need of purification.[8] Yet the first colonists enjoyed more freedom – religious, political, and geographical – than did the Puritans at home.[9] Far from religious persecution and political overseeing, they were largely free to organize their churches and towns as they saw fit. In case of discord, the dissatisfied ones could move elsewhere, creating new churches and eventually new colonies – options not available to the Puritans that chose to remain in England and were forced to compromise. But this was not the only difference between the two versions of Puritanism across the Atlantic. The American Puritans felt that they had something more to prove, not just to England but to the entire world – namely, that they were able to become "a shining city on a hill," a beacon of light for the rest of the world.[10] All these reasons concurred in highlighting the importance of preserving their identity unaltered and uncorrupted, making them suspicious of any form of compromise with "otherness."

As shown in the second part, this "strange brew of ideas, mixing communitarian, theocratic, and even totalitarian elements with a forward-reaching commitment to individual rights,"[11] this "witches' brew that went under the name of Puritan social thought,"[12] was facilitated by a peculiar form of individualism that set them apart and shaped their apparently paradoxical character. Puritans did not embrace a centripetal individualism, focused almost exclusively on the inner self, as did the French during the same period of time, for "the very names of Self and Own should sound in the watchful Christian's

[8] John Adair (1982), Founding Fathers – The Puritans in England and America (London, Melbourne, Toronto: J.M. Dent & Sons Ltd), 89–90; Bremer, *The Puritan Experiment*, 28.
[9] See Adair, *Founding Fathers*; Sacvan Bercovitch (1975), *The Puritan Origins of the American Self* (New Haven and London: Yale University Press); Stephen Foster (1981), "New England and the Challenge of Heresy, 1630 to 1660: The Puritan Crisis in Transatlantic Perspective," *The William and Mary Quarterly*, 38:4, 624–660; Weir, *Early New England*.
[10] John Winthrop (1630), *A Model of Christian Charity*, in Miller and Johnson, *The Puritans*, 199.
[11] Benjamin T. Lynerd (2014), Republican Theology: The Civil Religion of American Evangelicals (New York: Oxford University Press).
[12] Foster, *Their Solitary Way*, 171.

ears a very terrible, wakening words, that are next to the names of sin and satan."[13] Yet neither did they adopt the British centrifugal version, for to be concerned with the outer self was to be a hypocrite, caring more about the "dead bark" than about the living soul.[14] Pure (pardon the pun) and simple, they demanded from themselves and from their followers that the selves be turned inside out, bringing one's *forum internum* into the light, effectively replacing *forum externum,* so it could be purified under the scrutiny of peers.[15] In sum, they did not maintain the medieval dialectical relationship of the two fora, but neither did they emphasize one at the expense of the other, as happened throughout the seventeenth century across the Channel. Instead, they chose to "purge" one by transforming it into the other.

Given this, one can understand why, despite being outwardly as uncompromising as the French, the Puritans were not afraid of compromising themselves, their consciences, and everything that for the French understanding represented one's unique *forum internum.* This hidden, "inward" self was the friend of Satan, and the only way to clean it was by stripping it of all possible deceiving veils of privacy – something utterly inconceivable to the French, whose fear of compromise originated precisely in the possibility of outsiders arbitrating over one's *forum internum.* For lack of a better term, I label this Puritan form of individualism "purged individualism."[16] Any other form of individualism was, for Thomas Hooker and his contemporaries, "the Devils first Handsale, his Masterpiece, that Grand Fundamentall Designe on which he has built his Kingdom ever since."[17] This strategy of turning the inside out, of making the invisible visible and the private public, by bringing the hidden into the light, was considered the only way of not only creating *"visible* saints"[18] but also collapsing the distance between the *visible* church and the invisible one.[19]

This peculiar form of individualism helped forge a peculiar understanding of the community as well. In Miller's words, "to understand the Puritan mind we must endeavor to comprehend how the two kingdoms, the inward and the

---

[13] Richard Baxter (1830), "Christian Directory" in *Practical Works,* ed. William Orme, 23 vols. (London), 422.

[14] Uriam Oakes (1673), *New England Pleaded with* ..., quoted in Miller and Johnson, *The Puritans,* 71.

[15] For more details on the French centripetal individualism and the British centrifugal one, and their relationship with compromise, see Fumurescu, *Compromise.*

[16] I thank my colleague, Naomi Choi, for suggesting it.

[17] Quoted in Foster, *The Solitary Way,* 43.

[18] Edmund S. Morgan (1963), *Visible Saints: The History of a Puritan Idea* (New York: New York University Press). In the preface, Morgan acknowledges as the inspiration for his title Geoffrey Nuttall's (1957), *Visible Saints: The Congregational Way, 1640–1660* (Oxford: Basil Blackwell), arguing that "what Mr. Nuttall says about the term 'visible saints' is as true of the New England Congregationalists as of the English." Or even more so, one might add. See further.

[19] Michael P. Winship (2012), Godly Republicanism: Puritans, Pilgrims, and a City on a Hill (Cambridge, MA: Harvard University Press), 225.

social, were for that mind forever inseparable."[20] In the long run, this legacy created a "critical ambiguity" in understanding the people.[21] If the Puritans are still viewed by many as "medieval," it is because, like the French, they clung tightly to the hierarchical and corporatist vision of the people as *universitas*, ruled by a "voluntary aristocracy" for the good of the whole.[22] If, however, they are also seen as friends or even forerunners of the social contract and liberalism, it is because the reality of political and religious communities created by the free consent of their members made actual what for their English brethren remained just a virtual representation of each and every individual. They mutually promised, i.e., *com-promised*, to obey the rules and the laws of the community accepted by the majority. The former, corporatist understanding of the people was suspicious of compromises of any sorts, fearing a threat to both the uniqueness and virtues of its members and the identity of the community. The latter was conducive to compromise, for the equality of the parties was implied.

Not surprisingly, this ambiguity fully manifested itself in the Puritans' covenantal theory, often mistaken for proto-contractarianism, while in effect it shared with different versions of contract theory just the form yet neither the substance nor the basic assumptions.[23] Besides the distinctions they made between the covenant of works, the covenant of grace, and the covenant of justification, the Puritans managed – for a while – to juggle at the same time three others, loosely related to the first ones: the covenant of each individual with God (the inward covenant "betwixt God and the soul only," as Hooker had it), the church covenant (the visible one, among the saints), and the covenant of each church with God.[24] While the church covenant resembled in its horizontality the social contract theory, by creating a religious community with an accepted government from the free accord of its individual members, the vertical covenant of each church with God was modeled after the classic, medieval governmental contract between the people as a hierarchical *universitas* and its ruler. However, if the latter could be broken by the ruler, the former could not be broken but by the community, for God always keeps His promises.[25] Yet since the same logic applied not just to the heavenly governance but to worldly governments as well, it opened the door for the right of a

---

[20] Perry Miller (1939), *The New England Mind – The Seventeenth Century* (New York: The Macmillan Company), 407–408, 433.

[21] Mark A. Noll (2002), *America's God: From Jonathan Edwards to Abraham Lincoln* (Oxford, New York: Oxford University Press), 91.

[22] Foster, *The Solitary Way*, xii.

[23] Robin W. Lovin (1984), "Equality and Covenant Theology," *Journal of Law and Theology*, 2:2, 241–262. For a review of the literature considering the connection between natural rights and protestant politics, see Zuckert, *The Natural Rights Republic*, especially ch. 6. Zuckert advances his own explanation.

[24] Miller, *The New England Mind*, 375–381; 413–417; 445–448.   [25] Ibid., 413.

community – political or religious – to justly rebel against its rulers.[26] This vertical version of covenant was suspicious of compromises of any sorts with outsiders, for they threatened both the identity of individuals and the identity of the community. The horizontal one was conducive to compromise, for the equality of the parties was implied. Thus, unknowingly for its protagonists, the paradigm of the people's two bodies became a living reality hand in hand with an ambivalent attitude toward compromise.

As a result of this ambiguity, the American Congregationalists became fervent supporters of the Parliament and of Oliver Cromwell during the Civil War perceived as God's sign that they were on the right path, and they reaped the benefits of its victory. At the same time, though, they exposed themselves to the same accusations of abuses of power from the inside. The result, as shown in the last part of the chapter, was that this uncompromising attitude came with a price, namely the rapid fragmentation of the movement, despite repeated pleas for unity. In order to survive, the Puritans were forced to appeal to what they hated most, namely to compromises, of which noticeable examples are the Half-Way Covenant and the Saybrook Platform.[27] Politically speaking, the change was associated with a switch of their focus from the governmental contract to the social one, based on the equality of individual wills and, implicitly, on rule by majority. Ironically, it was precisely this willingness to compromise that ensured the survival of the movement for a few more decades. And although Puritanism was officially dead by the time of the first Great Awakening in the 1740s, it also made possible its long-lasting influence. As the following chapters will try to demonstrate, the legacy of the people's two bodies was revived and adapted, playing a crucial role throughout the entire American founding, whenever the question of political compromises came to the forefront. It is a forgotten legacy, but one we are still living with.

2.1 "PURITANISM WAS IN THE EYE OF THE BEHOLDER"

Patrick Collinson's cleverly coined phrase[28] captures well the conflicting meanings that Puritanism shares conceptually with compromise. Both terms can, were, and still are used with both negative and positive connotations, and both prove hard to define because of their built-in ambiguity. As I will try to prove in the following pages, this is no accident, for the two share more history than one is usually aware of. After all, timewise, the origins of the term "Puritan" overlaps with the split in the usage of "compromise" across the Channel,

---

[26] Bremer, *The Puritan Experiment*, 91–92; Miller and Johnson, *The Puritans*, 187–188; Samuel Willard (1694), *The Character of a Good Ruler* (Boston, an election sermon preached on May 30), quoted in Miller and Johnson, *The Puritans*. See further.

[27] Bremer, *The Puritan Experiment*; Hill, *Society and Puritanism*.

[28] Patrick Collinson (1980), "A Comment: Concerning the Name Puritan," *Journal of Ecclesiastical History*, 31, 483.

namely the end of the sixteenth and the beginning of the seventeenth centuries. One feature appears, however, to be almost constant from the beginning of the movement – the unwillingness of its members to compromise in matters of faith. For, as Robert Browne (1550?–1633) fervently believed, "real ministers would not compromise with Antichrist."[29]

The jury is still out on who first used the label "Puritans" to designate – Initially with undoubtedly negative connotations – the nonconformist Anglicans broadly defined. The formerly accepted evidence that the Frenchman Pierre de Ronsard used it for the first time in 1562 is highly questionable.[30] What is certain, however, is that, at least by 1587, the impassioned Catholic Ronsard was able to see the major problem of Reformation in general, one that would end up destroying Puritanism in particular, namely its inner centrifugal tendency. Once it was agreed that everyone was equally entitled to interpret the Bible as she or he saw fit, the djinn of fragmentation was out of the bottle. In Ronsard verses,[31]

> *Les Apostres jadis preschoient tous d'un accord,*
> *Entre vous aujourdhuy ne regne que discord;*
> *Les uns sont Zvingliens, les autres Lutherists,*
> *Les autres Puritains, Quintins, Anabaptistes,*
> *Les autres de Calvin vont adorant les pas,*
> *L'un est predestine, & l'autre ne l'est pas …*

Most likely, the originator of the label was the Archbishop Parker who grumbled as early as 1566 about the queen's lack of support for his struggle to restrain "precisians and puritans."[32] The blamed ones, realizing that they were, in modern parlance, victims of a PR attack, started off by rejecting the label, as shown in a petition to the Privy Council about 1580: "The adversary … very cunningly hath new-christened us with an odious name … of Puritanism; we detest both the name and the heresy."[33] "I know no Puritan," wrote Udall in 1588, "but Satan taught the papists so to name the ministry of the gospel."[34]

Yet the victims were no shrinking violets either, and they were convinced they occupied the moral high ground. In a world in flux, they offered stability.

---

[29] Winship, *Godly Republicanism*, 47.

[30] Malcolm Smith (1972), "Ronsard and the Word Puritan," *Bibliotheque d'Humanisme et Renaissance*, T. 34, No. 3, 483–487.

[31] Quoted in ibid., 485 – "Formerly, the Apostles preached all the same/Today, among yourselves is nothing but discord./ Some are Zvingliens, other Lutherists/Other Puritans, Quintins, Anabaptists,/Yet others adore in Calvin's footsteps/One is predestined, the other is not …" (my translation).

[32] Quoted in Adair, *Founding Fathers*, 86.   [33] Quoted in Hill, *Society and Puritanism*, 14.

[34] J. Udall (1588) [1879], *Diotrephes* (ed. A. Arber), 9, quoted in Hill, *Society and Puritanism*, 14. For a more detailed history of the evolution of the term, and bountiful examples, see Hill, *Society and Puritanism*, 14–20.

"Anglicanism seemed to many to be a faith without a character, a compromise church based on the principle that the shape of most ecclesiastical matters was a matter of indifference. Puritanism, in contrast, generated in its members a sense of conviction."[35] Eventually, some of the so labeled decided that the best way to win this PR war was to embrace the term and change the negative connotations to positive ones. As a result, they fought back. "For labeling was a two-way process. When they were dubbed 'puritans,' godly Protestants responded with the antipuritan, a caricature of their critiques."[36] They wrote pamphlets, sermons, tracts, depicting their adversaries as ignorant, dim-witted despisers of religions. Only from the mouth of an atheist (Atheos) could one find accusations such as this: "You that are precise puritans do find fault where there is none, you condemn men for every trifle."[37] Indeed, "Puritans, more than most people, tended to see things in bipolar terms. He who is not with the Lord is against him, after all, and men do not receive grace by degree."[38] Religiously speaking, it was an "all or nothing" approach.

The problem, however, was – then, as now – circumscribing Puritanism, since there were so many gradations of it, and the changes between mainstream Anglicans and Puritans were mostly incremental. Defining its boundaries proved an impossible task.[39] As this was not sufficient, the label of Puritanism did not apply just to religious matters. There were:

First a Puritan in politicks, or the Politicall Puritan, in matters of State, liberties of people, prerogatives of sovereigns, etc. Secondly An Ecclesiasticall Puritan, for the Church Hierarchie and ceremonies, who was at first the onely Puritan. Thirdly A Puritan in Ethicks or moral Puritan says to consist in singularity of living, and hypocrisie both civill and religious which may be called the vulgar Puritan, and was the second in birth and had maede too many ashamed to be honest.[40]

Thus, from its inception, the Puritan movement was forced to confront head-on the challenge of identification and self-identification, which could only enhance their anti-compromising attitude. Eventually, the confusion grew to the point where neither the supporters nor the detractors of the movement appeared to know what they were talking about, and people started begging

---

[35] Bremer, The Puritan Experiment, 28.

[36] Christopher Haigh (2004), "The Character of an Antipuritan," The Sixteenth Century Journal, 35:3, 672.

[37] George Gifford (1582), A Briefe discourse of certain points of the religion which is among the common sort of Christians, which may be termed the Countrie Divinitie (London), fols. 3r, 76r, quoted in Haigh, "The Character," 672.

[38] Foster, The Solitary Way, 33.

[39] Adair, Founding Fathers; Miller and Johnson, The Puritans; Winship, "Where There Any Puritans in New England?"

[40] Joseph Mead to Sir Martin Stuteville of Dalham, Suffolk, April 14, 1623, British Museum, Harleian MSS, 389, quoted in Kenneth Shipps (1976), "The Political Puritan," Church History, 45:2, 196. I shall return to the issue of hypocrisy shortly.

that either the king or the Parliament or both come up with a precise definition of a Puritan "so that those who deserve the name may be punished, and others not calumniated."[41] However, Sir Robert Harley's premonition – "I think the Parliament will not proceed to define a Puritan"[42] – proved accurate. The answer never came, yet neither history nor William Laud waited for it. The rise of the High Church to power marked the beginning of the Puritans' persecution, as vaguely defined as they were, and many believed that the Anglican Church was on its way to a return to Catholicism. Ironically, thanks to this persecution, the question of identity was partially solved, if only in the negative.

It is not the aim of this chapter to disentangle the multitude of reasons that converged in what came to be known as the Great Migration of the 1630s, when some 21,000 Englishmen moved across the Atlantic. There are several studies with this declared purpose, working out all the minutiae of economic, social, and political reasons, but all agree that among the main reasons was the Puritans' sense of their divine mission. In Tocqueville's blunter and perhaps less nuanced words, "they tore themselves away from the pleasures of home in obedience to a purely intellectual need. They braved the inevitable miseries of exile because they wished to ensure the victory of *an idea*."[43] This idea was first and foremost a religious one, but its implications were secular as well, for it infused a powerful sense of divine mission in *this* world. As William Bradford from Plymouth had it, "England was the first nation to which Lord gave the light of the gospel after the darkness of poppery,"[44] but because of their lack of perspectives at home and the decline of the Protestant movement across Europe, many came to believe that the New England settlements would be able to offer a model of Puritanism that would (re)convert first England and eventually the rest of the world.

The well-known quote from Winthrop at the board of Arbella – "wee shall be as a City upon a Hill. The eies of all people are upon Us" – was not an accident, but the norm among a people with a widespread sense of a higher mission.[45] While at the time this was not an uncommon Puritan trope even in England, only in the colonies did it take a central place – and for good reason. Edward Johnson, too, wrote that the purpose of the Massachusetts Bay colony was to "be set as lights upon a Hill more obvious than the highest mountain in the World," while clergyman John Norton spoke of New England as "holding forth a pregnant demonstration of the consistency of Civil-Government with a

[41] Ruttland MSS, aprox 1620, quoted in Hill, *Society and Puritanism*, 19.

[42] Portland MSS. (H.M.C.), III, p. 13, quoted in Hill, *Society and Puritanism*, 19.

[43] Alexis de Tocqueville (2004), *Democracy in America*, translated by Arthur Goldhammer (New York: The Library of America), 37 (emphasis in the original).

[44] Quoted in Bremer, *The Puritan Experiment*, 34.

[45] John Winthrop (1630), *A Model of Christian Charity*, in Miller and Johnson, *The Puritans*, 199.

Congregational-Way." They were not fleeing "from duty in time of danger"[46] –
explained John Norton – but Providence Divine shutting up the door of service
in England, and on the other hand opening one in New England."[47] Their belief
in a "manifest destiny" made them feel the weight of being "the climax of world
history, the ultimate revelation through events of the objective toward which
the whole of human activity had been tending from the beginning of time."[48]
The "errand into the wilderness" made the parallel with the tribulations of
Israel, and hence with the Old Testament,[49] much more powerful. If
Anglicanism encouraged a sense of nationalism, Puritanism, regardless of sheer
numbers, aimed higher, to internationalism,[50] despite the particularism inherent in the Old Testament and the universalism of the New one. From the very
beginning, this vetero-testamentary parallel gave to the Puritan settlers in New
England a particular understanding not only of their distinctive identity but
also of the entire covenantal theory. "In Europe ... the covenant was utilized as
an instrument of reformation. In the New World, the covenant was an instrument of formation; the foundational covenants of the civil realm and the church
laid the basis for the community."[51]

No matter how strong the ties with their English brethren and how great
their indebtedness to England, the fact that the New Englanders could actually
implement their vision created almost from the very beginning a particular form
of Puritanism. "They were thoroughly reactionary, highly original, and, by
consequence, uniquely American."[52] They belonged to England, indeed, but
to the New, not the Old one. "The immigrants were agreeing by the mid-1630s
that, in the words of John Cotton, the time had come to 'enjoy the libertye, not
of some ordinances of god, but of all and all in Puritye.' Compromises were a
thing of the past."[53] It was therefore a precious identity, to be cherished and
jealously protected. "The more fervent their commitment to the task of leading
godly lives, the more reluctant they were to compromise" – an attitude shared
by clergy and lay Puritans as well.[54] "Those who journeyed to America had the

---

[46] See also John Cotton: "It is a serious misrepresentation, unworthy of the spirit of Christian truth,
to say that our brethren ... fled from England like mice from a crumbling house ..." – quoted in
Francis J. Bremer (1994), *Shaping New England – Puritan Clergymen in Seventeenth Century
England and New England.* (New York: Twayne Publishers), 77.

[47] Quoted in Bremer, *The Puritan Experiment*, 37–38.

[48] Miller and Johnson, *The Puritans*, 86.

[49] See, for example, Jim Sleeper (2009), "American Brethren: Hebrews and Puritans," *World
Affairs*, 172:2, 46–60.

[50] Bremer, *The Puritan Experiment*, 34.

[51] Weir, *Early New England*, 221. I shall return in the third part to the particularities of American
coventalism and its relationship with the Puritan uncompromising general attitude.

[52] Foster, *The Solitary Way*, 45.

[53] David D. Hall (2011), *A Reforming People: Puritanism and the Transformation of Public Life in
New England* (Chapel Hill: The University of North Carolina Press), 18.

[54] Francis J. Bremer (2015), *Lay Empowerment and the Development of Puritanism* (New York:
Palgrave Macmillan), 49.

opportunity to shed compromise with prescribed nonessentials and to implement what they felt was the best form of church government and worship." This uncompromising attitude did not go unnoticed back home. "The New England experiment provoked fears among those left behind. [...] The claims for the purity of colonial practices seemed to imply criticisms of those in England who continued to make compromises as the price for comprehension within the established church."[55] Despite their common ancestry and even common religious tenets with their brethren across the Atlantic, they thought about themselves as different, voluntary created theologico-political communities: as Donald Lutz put it, not just different societies, but different peoples.[56]

So persuaded were they of their own mission that many came to believe that responsible for Cromwell's success during the Civil War was less his army (although some shipped back to England in order to help the war effort) than the Puritans' prayers from across the Atlantic. As William Hooke put it, it was the duty of the American Puritans to "lye in wait in the wilderness, to come upon the backs of God's enemies with the deadly Fasting and Prayer, murtherers that will kill point blanke from one end of the world to the other."[57] The strategy appeared to be working, for not only did Cromwell come out victorious and the king beheaded, but his Protectorate proved extremely beneficial for the American Puritans. His closest religious advisers were Thomas Godwin and John Owen, both Congregationalist disciples of John Cotton, which helped Congregationalism win the battle for influence with their Presbyterian brethren in England – for a while, that is.

With the death of Cromwell and the Restauration, the American Puritans' hopes to redeem England came to a screeching halt, and their belief in their divine purposefulness was seriously shaken. So important was this self-understanding that, to a large extent, this single event can be said to have marked the beginning of the end for the Puritans. It forced them not only to reconsider their mission and identity but also, as we shall see in a more detailed fashion later, to do the unthinkable in order to ensure their preservation – to compromise among themselves and with others. Even if, on a rhetorical level, "the need to stand against adversity without surrender or compromise ... became a standard theme of late seventeenth century Puritan writing," in practice they became both more democratic and more liberal.[58] The new strategy proved at least in part successful, since it ensured the movement's survival for another half century or so.[59]

---

[55] Bremer, *Shaping New England*, 60, 61. See also Hall, *A Reforming People*, 19.

[56] Donald S. Lutz (1988), *The Origins of American Constitutionalism* (Baton Rouge: Louisiana State University Press), xxiv.

[57] Quoted in Bremer, *The Puritan Experiment*, 109.   [58] Bremer, *Shaping New England*, 93.

[59] The fact that the end of Puritanism is as hard to define as its beginnings also speaks volumes about their challenging identity.

Although they disagree on the degrees, most scholars agree on the important impact the Puritans had on the American Founding – and among the first to acknowledge this was, rather unsurprisingly, Tocqueville. As "[i]n a manner of speaking, the whole man already lies in swaddled in his cradle," so "[e]very people bears the marks of its origins"[60] – and, according to him, the American people's origins were to be found in Puritan New England. These origins are to be found in Puritan New England, not because it was the only "ingredient," but because it proved to be the most important one. "The civilization of New England was like a bonfire on a hilltop, which, having spread its warmth to its immediate vicinity, tinges even the distant horizon with its glow."[61] Some features typically associated with Puritanism were able to inform the American *Weltanschauung* beyond New England to an extent that the Anglicans, the Quakers, and so forth were never able to attain in America's formative years. "In their obsessive self-chronicling, which grew in intensity with their sense of dissolution as a community, they guaranteed for themselves a unique afterlife in American culture. 'Whether *New England* may live anywhere else or no,' Cotton Mather proclaimed, 'it must *Live* in our *History*'."[62]

The majority of contemporary scholars agree wholeheartedly.[63] For Perry Miller, Puritanism "has become one of the continuous factors in American life and American thought," and "its role in American thought has been almost the dominant one," shaping "the American mind."[64] For John Adair, "we are all, in varying degrees, heirs to the Puritan tradition,"[65] while for Bercovitch (1975) the title of his book speaks for itself: *The Puritan Origins of the American Self*. The examples could go on and on, but what is important to notice is that almost without exception the emphasis is less on the Puritans' religious ideas as on how these shaped a particular sense of the self. Even if, in the past decades, the picture of the founding became more nuanced and the accuracy of talking about a single Puritan mind became questionable,[66] Foster's recommendation remains valuable: one should not get so entangled in taxonomical debates to deny "a real and continuing historical entity out there," nor should we play

---

[60] de Tocqueville, *Democracy in America*, 31.   [61] Ibid., 36.
[62] Andrew Delbanco (1989), *The Puritan Ordeal* (Cambridge, MA: Harvard University Press), 248. It is worth remembering that Cotton Mather was the one to coin the word 'American'.
[63] Some scholars have argued that the role of Puritanism during the founding has been exaggerated, since Virginia was created some thirteen years before the Massachusetts Bay Colony (yet the Puritans had a definite contribution in its founding and financing as well), or that Scottish Enlightenment was, overall, more influential. No one denies, however, the Puritan influence on the American mores.
[64] Miller and Johnson, *The Puritans*, 1.   [65] Adair, *Founding Fathers*, xii.
[66] See, for example, Bremer, *Shaping New England*.

"blind men to the elephant" to the extent we deny the fact that Puritanism shaped a way of thinking and a particular sense of the self.[67]

Yet, an even better proof for the endurance of this legacy is less the scholarly appraisal than politicians' appeal to it. From right to left, from Ronald Reagan's repeated references to the Pilgrims to Bill Clinton's New Covenant, they speak volumes about the popular attraction of the Puritan mind. All ideological considerations aside, Sleeper's observation deserves a somewhat lengthier quotation:

> The political idioms of George W. Bush and his neoconservative allies, on the one hand, and Barack Obama and custodians of the civil rights movement, on the other, are both staked in Hebraic and Puritan sub-soils that have nourished distinctively American dimensions in civil-republican life: think of early-nineteenth-century Whig and Methodist linkages of public works to civil society's "internal," spiritual, and moral improvements. Recall Abraham Lincoln's prosecution of the Civil War in what he came to see as Calvinist terms. Then there are the social gospel crusaders for economic justice in that century and, in the twentieth, the latter-day puritan Woodrow Wilson's "War to End all Wars." And there are also, on the one hand, the McCarthyite witch hunts of "un-American" activists and, on the other hand, the almost religious enthusiasm in many liberals (and many others') responses to Barack Obama's biblically resonant speeches during the 2008 campaign.[68]

It is worth pondering where this popular fascination with Puritanism comes from, beyond just being an undeniable part of the American founding. If it would have been only for that, the attraction of this movement would not have survived outside the academic circles,[69] a bloody civil war, two world wars, among many other smaller ones, but also the emergence of mass consumerism, the explosion of hedonism, or the digital revolution, regardless of the still enduring reputation of Puritans as joy-killers.[70] Apparently, nothing could be more distant from Puritanism, than, say, the Facebook phenomenon. Yet, as we shall see, appearances may be deceiving.

I suspect that, as a matter of fact, it is this built-in ambivalence of Puritanism that resonated across centuries with the American longing for "having cake and eating it too," made possible by their paradigm of the people's two bodies. Regardless of what time period they occupied or what their interests were, Americans were able to find in Puritanism what they were looking for:

---

[67] Stephen Foster (1991), *The Long Argument – English Puritanism and the Shaping of New England Culture, 1570-1700* (Chapell Hill and London: The University of North Carolina Press), 5.

[68] Sleeper, "American Brethren: Hebrews and Puritans," 46–47.

[69] The only period when Puritanism in America had a rather bad scholarly reputation was in the decades that bridged the end of the nineteenth and the beginning of the twentieth centuries. The reasons for this peculiarity are beyond the scope of this chapter.

[70] No matter how exaggerated we know this reputation to be today, at its core, the argument still stands, if one is to consider just the interdiction of Christmas celebrations, the forbidding of wedding bands, etc.

individualism *and* corporatism, particularism *and* universalism, privacy *and* publicity, meritocracy *and* egalitarianism, social *and* governmental compact, brotherhood *and* exclusion, etc. After all, Collinson was right – Puritanism *is* in the eye of the beholder – but only because the movement had, from its very inception, all of these features. This apparently paradoxical character gave it a distinct intellectual and moral flavor; it allowed it to flourish but also contributed to its dismissal.[71] In order to better understand why, one has to return once again to the uncompromising origins of the Puritan self that distanced it from its European counterparts, both English and French, and not just by an ocean. To use Tocqueville's imagery, if one can know the man from the cradle, one can also know the baby from the womb.

2.2 "... AS THE ENTRAILS OF A CREATURE CUT DOWN THE BACK"

Considering their jealously protected identity, it comes as no surprise that the American Puritans' usage of compromise differed significantly from that of the British. A survey of the Colonial Papers reveals plenty of instances in which "compromise" was used with the British neutral or even positive meaning of avoiding open conflict by settling or arbitrating differences. In all these instances, however, the authors are not Puritans. It is either the king himself writing, for example, to Sir Thomas Lynch, Governor of Jamaica – "... it is his Majesty's pleasure that in case Samuel Gerrard cannot compromise and end the accounts, and that he stand in need of the Governor's help that he require said John Head and John Mohun to render to said Samuel Gerrard all goods belonging to said merchants"[72] – or officers of the Crown, like in the case of the letter to the King of the Representation of the Council for Plantations concerning New England: "Moreover there are many differences between the colonists concerning boundaries, which if not compromised cannot be determined without civil war, except by the King's sovereign power."[73] In the *Journal of the Assembly of Virginia*, a non-Puritan colony dominated by Anglicans, "compromise" is used with the same meaning: "The dispute, over the joint committees [...] was resumed, the Lieutenant Governor again charging the burgesses to get to business. [...] A compromise was arranged. Robert Beverley was permitted to stay in the town until he had furnished the burgesses with the information desired."[74] In New Hampshire it was Richard

---

[71] Adair, *Founding Fathers*, xi.
[72] Date: February 21, 1672; TNA Catalogue Reference: SP 44/31, p. 84 d; Calendar Reference: Vol 7 (1669–1674), pp. 332–333.
[73] Date: August 12, 1671; TNA Catalogue Reference: CO 1/27, Nos. 15, 16, 17|CO 389/5, pt. 2, p. 5; Calendar Reference: Vol 7 (1669–1674), p. 244.
[74] Date: November 27, 1682; TNA Catalogue Reference: CO 5/1407, pp. 26–35; Calendar Reference: Vol 11 (1681–1685), p. 554.

Chamberlain, the educated lawyer and royal appointee as secretary of the province, who spent only a few years in the colonies, using "compromise" as pacifying method:

I hope that what I am about to write may not be disagreeable. For several times at the meeting of the Assembly the Council pressed and threatened me if I refused the oath of secrecy. I told them that I intended to be guided alike by my duty to the Council here and to the ancient laws of England. As a compromise I suggested that the matter might stand over till I received instructions from England.[75]

There is also no doubt that the American Puritans were familiar with the procedure of compromise as arbitration and actually used it extensively to solve disputes *among themselves*. After all, as David Hall put it, no matter how uncompromising was their attitude toward others, "even in New England, politics was a matter of negotiation and compromise."[76] As in the classic Roman *compromissum* as *arbitratio*, it was a method to avoid appearing in the court of law, only in this case the rationale was different – far from being a way to avoid the embarrassment associated with appearing in the public sphere for airing the dirty laundry, it was yet another exercise of love between fellow saints. The fact that "a preference for compromise [was] more conducive to social peace" did not hurt either.[77] "As a matter of deliberate policy incorporated into the town covenant, the townspeople agreed to refer their controversies to two or three impartial 'arbitrators' chosen by the town or by the parties involved, and for a full half-century the rule of love did take substantial business away from the rule of the law courts."[78] The householders from Lancaster, for example, vowed that they would never "goe to Lawe one with an other in actions of Debt or Damages ... but to end all such Controversies among ourselves by arbitration or otherwise."[79] Yet despite all evidence of fact, they refused to use the word "compromise" to describe these arbitrations.

Not only that, but the American Puritans consistently refused to use the word – as did their English brethren – as equivalent for "contract" or "compact," even when the situation appeared to demand it. In England, Gilbert Burnet, for example, used "compromise" to explain his *theoretical* version of the social contract:

The true and Original Notion of Civil Society and Government, is, that is a compromise made by such a Body of Men, by which they resign up the Right of demanding Reparations, either in the way of Justice against one another, or in the way of War,

---

[75] Date: May 14, 1681; TNA Catalogue Reference: CO 1/46, No. 138, ICO 5/940, pp. 5–9; Calendar Reference: Vol 11 (1681–1685), pp. 48–49.
[76] Hall, *A Reforming People*, 20. [77] Ibid., 139. [78] Foster, *The Solitary Way*, 48.
[79] Quoted in Hall, *A Reforming People*, 139.

against their Neighbours; to such a single Person, or to such a Body of Men as they think fit to trust with this.[80]

The Puritans, while having created actual societies and actual governments by compacts, never used the word "compromise" as an equivalent for "compact," although they came really close – they "mutually promised," i.e., co-promised to subject themselves to the laws of their own making. So did the settlers from the Piscataqua River, when, unable to form a church, they wanted to form at least a civil government, in 1642: "And this wee have *mutually promised* and engaged to doe." A few more examples should suffice. The famous Mayflower Compact, signed on November 11, 1620, states that, "We do solemnly and mutually . . . covenant and combine ourselves into a civil body politic . . . We, whose names are under-written [. . .] *promise* all due Submission and Obedience [to the Body Politick]." Also, one of the first church covenants, that of Charlestown-Boston Church, on July 30, 1630, begins with the words: "We whose names are hereunder written . . . do hereby solemnly and religiously, as in His most holy Presence, *Promise* & bind ourselves," while the Providence Agreement of August 20, 1637, stipulates: "We whose name are hereunder [. . .] do *promise* to subject ourselves in active and passive obedience to all such orders and agreements as shall be made *for the public good* of the body in an orderly way, *by the major consent* of present inhabitants."[81]

However, while the Puritans did not embrace the French negative usage of compromise – after all, they were still (more or less) loyal subjects of His Majesty, the King – they did borrow the French suspicions of it, which is reflected in their usage of the term. There were two main areas of concern. First, that, on the outside, compromising with other non-Puritanical beliefs, i.e., tolerating them, meant acknowledging the fallibility of religion and the lack of a foundational truth. John Cotton, for example, was vehemently against those who claimed that, under the ill-defined label of Christianity,

. . . all may be reconciled, the bloud of a dead man, and God, life, and death, heaven and hell, and all, shall be reconciled. *It shewes what great reason we have everlastingly to stand out against all compromising with them*, and all subjection to any thing that pertaines to that Religion, for they have farced truthes, [. . .] they are such, as in very truth, have not the blood of the Lord *Iesus* in them, but are as the blood of a dead man, as they have them, and corrupt and pollute them.[82]

The other main area of concern was on the inside, the very soul of the Puritan, over which Satan and Christ waged war. According to William

---

[80] Gilbert Burnet (1688), "An Inquiry Into the Measures of Submission to the Supream Authority . . .," in *A collection of papers related to the present state of affairs in England*, 2. For a lengthier analysis of Burnet's works, see Fumurescu, *Compromise*, 262–265.

[81] Quoted in Donald S. Lutz (1988), *The Origins of American Constitutionalism* (Baton Rouge: Louisiana State University Press), 25–30 (emphases added).

[82] John Cotton (1642), *The Pouring Out of the Seven Vials* (London), 45 (emphasis added).

Gurnall, the sinner's conscience might be deceived and appeased by a more-than-willing to compromise devil:

The command saith, Now repent. The imperative hath no future tense. God saith "To-day, while it is to-day:" The devil saith, To-morrow. Which wilt thou obey, God or him? [...] *Satan labours to compromise the business, and bring it to a composition between him and Christ*: when conscience will not be pacified, then Satan, for quiet's sake, will yield to something, as Pharaoh with Moses. [...] If God hath the matins, he looks for the vigils, and thus he is contented the day should be divided.[83]

Since conscience was suspected of corruption, a close watch was imposed to prevent its further contamination, both from the inside and, first and foremost, from the outside. As Nathaniel Ward put it, "[H]e that is willing to tolerate any Religion, or discrepant way of religion, besides his owne, unless it be in matters merely indifferent, either doubts of his owne, or is not sincere in it." Such a tolerant attitude, went the argument, would destroy not just religion but all moral life. "If the devil might have his free option, I believe he would ask nothing else, but liberty to enfranchise all other Religions." Hence, "that State that will give Liberty of Conscience in matters of religion, must give Liberty of Conscience and Conversation in their Morall Laws, or else the Fiddle will be out of tune, and some of strings cracke." "Truth is the Parent of all Liberty *whether politicall and personall*," and therefore the supporters of "Tolerating all Religions" proved more daring than "the Deville himselfe ... for feare it would break his winde and wits to attend such a Province." "If *the whole conclave of Hell can so compromise*, exadverse, and diametricall contradictions, as to cosmopolitize such a multimonstruous mafery of heteroclyts and quickdiblets quietly; I trust I may say with humble reverence, they can doe more than the Senate of heaven." Ward's conclusion is straightforward:

I dare take upon me, to be the Herauld of New-England so farre, as to I proclame to the world, in the name of our Colony, that all Familists, Antinomians, Anabatists, and other Enthusiasts, shall have free Liberty to keep away from us, and such as will come to be gone as fast as they can, the sooner the better.[84]

The issue of toleration became intimately connected with the one of hypocrisy, i.e., of the discrepancy between the outward and the inward self – an issue that, it is worth remembering, also divided Frenchmen and Englishmen during the entire seventeenth century.[85] In medieval parlance, the proper relationship between *forum externum* and *forum internum* was seen differently across the Atlantic. Who created the hypocrite – the tolerant person or the

---

[83] William Gurnall [1845], *The Christian in Complete Armour; or A Treatise on the Saints' War with the Devil* ... carefully revised and corrected by the Rev. John Campbell, D.D., London, Printed for Thomas Tegg, 73, Cheapside, MDCCCXLV, 11–12 (emphasis added).

[84] Nathaniel Ward (1645 [1647]) *The Simple Cobbler of Aggawam in America* ... (London) – quoted in Miller and Johnson, *The Puritans*, 227, 230–232.

[85] Fumurescu, *Compromise*, 99, 124, 134.

uncompromising one? As Richard Baxter confesses, for many Anglicans, "Puritans" came to be equated with "Hypocrites."[86] By the mid-seventeenth century, while England was making the first steps toward religious toleration, the American Puritans stuck, disturbingly for many, to their uncompromising position. This difference in vision is nicely captured in a correspondence between John Cotton and Sir Richard Saltonstall, initially First Assistant to John Winthrop, but who returned to England in 1631 and was appointed ambassador in Holland. After his return from Holland, Saltonstall was worried that his former New Englishmen insisted so much on outward submission that they practically invited hypocritical behavior, and complained that former appeals to common sense fell onto deaf ears:

Truly, friends, this your practice of compelling any in matters of worship to do that whereof they are not fully persuaded is to make them sin, for so the Apostle (Rom. 14 and 23) tells us, and *many are made hypocrites thereby, conforming in their outward man for fear of punishment.*[87]

Cotton's reply was as polite and harsh as the accusation. After explaining that all the cases presented by Saltonstall were "just sufferings" and not even too harsh, he concluded:

As for compelling men to worship, that did not make them sinners if the worship was lawful. [...] Better to make men hypocrites than allow them to continue as profane persons. '*Hypocrites give God part of his due, the outward man, but the profane person gives God neither outward nor inward man*'.[88]

Based on this rationale, nonmembers of the church were required to attend religious services side by side with the members in most Puritan communities,[89] and also to pay taxes despite not having a right to vote.[90] The well-known outcry "no taxation without representation" would have to wait some hundred years more. Winthrop's rationale made perfect sense: "If we here be a corporation established by free consent ... then no man hath right to come into us &c. without our consent."[91]

However, Cotton's attitude toward hypocrites changed drastically when it switched from the "outsiders" to the "insiders." What for the people outside the church was acceptable and even recommended as better than nothing, for the members of the church was unpardonable. About the same time he replied to Saltonstall (ca. 1654) he also published in his *The New Covenant* a couple of sections, one entitled "Swine and Goats," the other "Hypocrites and Saints." In both, he made the distinction between the "notoriously wicked" and the

---

[86] Adair, *Founding Fathers*, 104.
[87] Richard Saltonstall, ca. 1650, quoted in Adair, *Founding Fathers*, 241 (emphasis added).
[88] Quoted in Adair, *Founding Fathers*, 242, emphasis added.
[89] Bremer, *The Puritan Experiment*, 102.   [90] Miller and Johnson, *The Puritans*, 192.
[91] John Winthrop (1637), quoted in Miller and Johnson, *The Puritans*, 200.

Hypocrites. "Of Hypocrites two sorts (and you shall find them in the Church of God) some are washed Swine, others are Goats." The washed Swine, after hearing the word of God "have been stomach sick of their sins, and have rejected their wicked courses, but yet their swines heart remaineth in them." Therefore, once they see a puddle, they cannot refrain but "readily lye down in it: But they are a grosser kind of Hypocrites." The subtler ones, thus the more dangerous, are the capricious Goats. They may climb "upon the tops of the mountains," looking like saints, yet they may descend as fast as they climbed.

[The washed swine] will crop grasse a while in a fair Pasture, but if you keepe them long there, they will not delight in such manner of feeding, but will rather choose to go into mire; but as for goats they will delight in the Commandments of the Lord, Isa. 58.2. It is not very hard thing unto them, nor grievous for them to keep solemne fasting dayes together, they come willingly, they delight to come, therefore *the difference will be hardly discovered, and unles you be a Christian of a very cleere discerning, you will not finde the difference.*[92]

Or, in Shepard's words, "it is clearer than the day that many who are *inwardly* ... the children of the devil are *outwardly* ... the children of God,"[93] and only "the godly could recognize that distinction."[94] Both Cotton's suspicions about the gap between the inward and outward man, and its solution – a careful scrutiny by peers – informed many, if not most, of the Puritans' practices. Even as late as 1689, in his ordination sermon, "the newly chosen minister of Salem Village, Samuel Parris, referred to himself as charged with 'making a difference between the clean, & unclean; so as to labour to cleanse & purge the one, & confirm & strengthen the other'."[95]

The position that set them apart from both Frenchmen and Anglicans can be summarized as follows: On the one hand, *forum internum* (one's inner self), was corrupted by the Fall and by itself could not resist the shrewd attacks mounted against it by the devil. Not surprising then, the self was "the great snare," "the false Christ," a spider's "webbe [spun] out of our bowels," hence the necessity to root out "the Devils poison and venome or infection of Self."[96] "You must be empty, if ever Christ fills you," warned William Crashaw of one of the first waves of colonists before their departure.[97] The damned were

---

[92] John Cotton (1654), "Swine and Goats," "Hypocrites and Saints," *The New Covenant, or a Treatise ...*," 44–47, 6469 (emphasis added), quoted in Miller and Johnson, 314–318.

[93] Michael McGiffert, ed. [1972] (1994), *God's Plot – Puritan Spirituality in Thomas Shepard's Cambridge* (Amherst: University of Massachusetts Press), 17 (emphasis added).

[94] Francis J. Bremer (2014), "To Tell What God Hath Done for Thy Soul: Puritan Spiritual Testimonies as Admission Tests and Means of Edification," *The New England Quarterly*, vol. 87:4, 637.

[95] Anne S. Brown and David D. Hall (1997), "Family Strategies and Religious Practice: Baptism and the Lord's Supper in Early New England" in *Lived Religion in America – Toward a History of Practice*, David D. Hall, ed. (Princeton: Princeton University Press), 45.

[96] Quoted in Bercovitch, *The Puritan Origins*, 18.

[97] William Crashaw (1618), quoted in Delbanco, *The Puritan Ordeal*, 82.

defined by self-affection, self-fullness, self-honor, etc., while the redeemed ones were characterized by self-emptiness and self-denial.[98] On the other hand, *forum externum* (the outer self) could be deceiving as well, if not even more so. The Englishmen that relied only on it, said Urian Oakes in *New England Pleaded with*, were "like the Cinnamon Tree, nothing good but the bark."[99] Therefore, adopting a centripetal individualism was not an option, but neither was the centrifugal individualism, embraced by most Englishmen.

The solution was to replace one's *forum externum* with one's *forum internum*, by externalizing the latter, making it public for everyone to see. This was the *Auto-Machia*, the Self-Killing, as George Goodwin entitled a poem extremely popular throughout the entire seventeenth century.[100] In Edward Taylor's vivid description, one had to descent into "A varnisht pot of putrid excrements," hoping that once they were brought out, "Then Lord, my tumberill/Unload of all its Dung, and make it cleane."[101] This turning inside-out, this stripping oneself of any "covers" that might hide corruption, is graphically captured by Henry Hammond in a sermon from his early Puritan years. In Michael McGiffert's words,[102]

Sins are to be ferreted out … Hammond brings to the first task "the seat, the lungs, the bowels" Anglicans scorned as emotional overkill. He summons the Paul's Cross crowd [...] to "shrift and winnow and even set our hearts upon the rack." It is the "solemnest work of our soul" to "prevent God's inquest with our own" by "cut[ting] ourselves up (becoming as "naked and discernible," in Hammond's graphic image, "as the entrails of a creature cut down the back"). "Every cranny of our souls" must be diligently searched and cleansed.[103]

This "purged individualism" puts in a new light scholarly claims that "Puritan theology was an effort to externalize and systematize this subjective mood,"[104] or that "the Puritans' urge for self-denial stems from the very subjectivism of their outlook" and "their humility is coextensive with personal assertion." It illuminates what Bercovitch calls "the dilemma of Puritan identity,"[105] together with an entire series of Puritan features that have puzzled scholars for many years. It helps explain, for example, why their piety did not

---

[98] Bercovitch, *The Puritan Origins*, 17.

[99] Urian Oakes (1648), *New England Pleaded with*, 34, quoted in Miller and Johnson, *The Puritans*, 71.

[100] George Goodwin (1607), *Auto-Machia*, trans. Joshua Silvester (London), no pagination.

[101] Quoted in Bercovitch, *The Puritan Origins*, 16.

[102] It is worth noticing the graphic corporeality of the imagery used by the Puritans: blood gushing, entrails, purgation, excrements, poison were all common tropes. One could speculate how the austerity of their meetinghouses, stripped of icons and incense, with any of the visual incentives of the ceremonial liturgy, was thus compensated in sermons and writings by such graphic descriptions.

[103] Michael McGiffert (2005), "Henry Hammond and Covenant Theology," *Church History*, 74:2, 270.

[104] Miller, *The New England Mind*, 5.   [105] Bercovitch, *The Puritan Origins*, 18.

translate into a flight from this world and a solitary life, for what was the peculiar emphasis on the "calling" of each individual but a desire to externalize the inner self? "God is the Generall, appointing to very man his particular calling ... And as in campe, no souldier can depart his standing, without the leave of the Generall."[106] Purging one's inside by exposing it to others' scrutiny was also part of the emphasis put on public confession, not punishment, during the relatively few trials of the era, for "confession opened the way to reconciliation and restoration."[107]

From here comes the "obsession" with keeping diaries in which to record all the minutiae of one's thoughts. According to Richard Rogers's written confession, this daily outpouring of the inner thoughts and feelings on paper helped him "know mine own heart better ... and to be better acquainted with the divers corners of it and what sin I am most in danger of and what diligence and means I use against any sin and how I go under any affliction."[108] However, the diaries were not enough for externalizing the inner self, for ultimately they were still relying solely on individual judgment. What was needed was more radical. It involved public confession and voluntary submission to the judgment of the elect, more fitted to evaluate the soul's purity and to pilot it through the "reefs and shoals" involved in this "psychological dissection"[109] – something that would have been anathema for the French, worried about compromising themselves, i.e., allowing an unworthy third party to judge one's *forum internum*. Quite the opposite, for the self-denying Puritans.

The Massachusetts churches no longer made the conventional assumption that persons knowledgeable in Christianity who conducted themselves as sincere Christians and "visible saints" for purposes of church admission. Now they wanted some glimpse of the process by which God had worked saving faith in their souls. [...] [Aspirants] would have to offer a public description of that process. The conversion narratives were the most ambitious expression to date of the old puritan ambition to collapse the distance between the visible church, consisting of the saved and the damned alike, and the invisible church of the saved, whose members were known with certainty to God alone.[110]

In order to be accepted into the Church, faith had to be demonstrated, and a simple confession was not deemed sufficient. Aspirants had also to explain "what work of grace the Lord has wrought in them." "For ministers like Thomas Shepard, evidence of faith should include a description of one's pre-conversion preparation for grace," a practice criticized vehemently by English Presbyterians such as Richard Baxter.[111] Nevertheless, for the American

---

[106] William Perkins (1626–1631) *The Workes of that Famous and Worthy Minister of Christ in the University of Cambridge, Mr. William Perkins* (London: I. Legatt, 3 vols), quoted in Morgan, *Visible Saints*, 35.

[107] Hall, *A Reforming People*, 86.   [108] Quoted in Adair, *Founding Fathers*, 93.

[109] Miller, *The Puritan Mind*, 53, 56.   [110] Winship, *Godly Republicanism*, 225.

[111] Bremer, *The Puritan Experiment*, 98–99.

Puritans, public scrutiny was the only right way for founding a congregation. Absent a superior authority to serve as judge, the selection of the "pillars of the church" had to rely on reciprocal scrutiny. Big Brother was replaced by many smaller ones.

Candidates volunteered themselves for this distinction, believing themselves worthy by virtue of their belief, election, and uprights lives. The candidates then questioned each other in order to satisfy themselves that all were of the necessary caliber; those who failed to satisfy their peers were eliminated from further consideration (without jeopardy to their chances for church membership). Those who emerged from these private conferences then volunteered for similar scrutiny from the other members of the community. Those eliminated were replaced by other candidates, and the process was repeated. It usually took a few months for the "pillars" to be selected.[112]

Although experimentally rooted in English Puritanism, the practice of these "conversion narratives," "tests of saving faith," "admission tests," or "relations," as their contemporaries used to label them, soon became the staple of American Puritanism and was institutionalized.[113] The jury is still out on whether John Cotton was the one imposing these admission tests in the beginning of the 1630s, and how generalized was the practice that excluded up to half of the adult population from the sacraments in the late 1630s outside of New Haven.[114] Nevertheless, the general consensus is that even when the "relations" were not a requirement, such confessions were a widely common practice, strongly recommended and encouraged.[115] For example, the Cambridge Platform, while asking for a "profession of faith and repentance," did not mandate "a personal and public confession." And yet it deemed such confessions "lawful, expedient, and useful." "Even in those churches in which personal accounts were not required for membership, puritan clergy recognized that moving stories of the working of God's grace could energize and empower their congregation."[116]

These "relations" were performances in which *how well* one disclosed the depths of one's feelings was as important as *what* was actually said – and the reason can be formulated as follows: the turning of the inside self out meant that both the characteristics of *forum externum*, i.e., sameness and conformity, and the ones of *forum internum*, i.e., uniqueness and authenticity, had to be revealed in the process. Not surprising then, the relatively few confessions whose documentation has survived reveal that these narratives have to meet a double standard.[117] On the one hand, they had to respect a certain structure, touch on certain points, and were oftentimes rehearsed before being actually

[112] Ibid., 100.   [113] Foster, *The Long Argument*, 163.
[114] Winship, *Godly Republicanism*, 225–226.
[115] Bremer, "To Tell What God Hath Done," 658.   [116] Ibid., 653.
[117] Thomas Shepard's *Confessions* contain fifty-one testimonies given between 1637 and 1645, Michael Wigglesworth's *Diary* another six, from around 1653–1657, and reverend John Fiske's *Notebook* yet another twenty-three transcribed between 1644 and 1666.

delivered, "coached by the ministers and vetted by senior saints."[118] On the other hand, they had to come through as "unique" and "authentic," and the best way to do so was by being emotionally persuasive. For "there was a difference between a profession of faith offered by someone whose understanding and emotions had been enlightened by the spirit and someone who was not of the elect, and the godly could recognize that distinctions."[119]

Nevertheless, once the door between private personal experience and public scrutiny had been cracked open, "the laity gave the clergy's directions an unusual twist when they exposed their introspective soul-searchings to each other in the course of their private exercises."[120] Increasingly, women as well as men of all classes gathered in "conferences" to share their spiritual experiences and to make sure they did not misinterpret their "inspirations." Initially at least, such lay conferences were encouraged by ministers as a means of avoiding anarchy and maintaining the unity of the faith.[121] In the long run, however, this transfer of competency to pass judgment from the hands of the "veteran saints" into the hands of laity proved damaging to the "popular aristocracy" or the "elective dictatorship of the wise and virtuous" that represented the religious and political backbone of Puritanism.[122]

The practice of exposing one's *forum internum* to the outside, for either clergy or laity to judge, started to be abandoned. After the Presbyterian William Brattle was called to be the pastor of the Cambridge Congregation, the members of the fourth Puritan house of worship in Boston published the "Brattle Street Manifesto." They declared that public examination of candidates for membership was to be eliminated, all children were to be baptized, communion was to be open to everyone, and all members – men and women alike – were to share in the choice of the pastor and the governance of the church.[123] It signaled the beginning of the end for "purged individualism" – and delivered a serious blow to the hierarchy of saints.

2.3 "… THEY LOOK BACKWARD AS WELL AS FORWARD"

There is a reason why, after so many years, Perry Miller remains the inescapable reference for any Puritan study. Indeed, he can be "both utterly persuasive and profoundly disturbing," but while subsequent literature has refuted many of the details from *The Puritan Mind*, Miller's "basic strategy of explicating the behavior of the Bay Puritans in terms of their theological beliefs and carefully formulated doctrines has been more than vindicated."[124] Considering all of the above, Miller was right when claiming that the Puritans "look backward as

---

[118] McGiffert, *God's Plot*, 137.   [119] Bremer, "To Tell What God Hath Done," 637.
[120] Foster, *The Long Argument*, 163.   [121] Bremer, *Lay Empowerment*, 8–9.
[122] Foster, *The Long Argument*, 75, 168.   [123] Bremer, *The Puritan Experiment*, 215.
[124] Darren Staloff (1998), *The Making of and American Thinking Class – Intellectuals and Intelligentsia in Puritan Massachusetts* (Oxford: Oxford University Press), xiii.

well as forward. They reflect the revolution in society, but not the direction of
the revolt."[125] They hung onto the past while they unwillingly prepared the
future. In a sense, they resembled Klee's Angelus Novus as described by Walter
Benjamin:

His eyes are staring, his mouth is open, his wings are spread. This is how one pictures the
angel of history. His face is turned toward the past. Where we perceive a chain of events,
he sees one single catastrophe which keeps piling wreckage upon wreckage and hurls it
in front of his feet. The angel would like to stay, awaken the dead, and make whole what
has been smashed. But a storm is blowing from Paradise; it has got caught in his wings
with such violence that the angel can no longer close them. The storm irresistibly propels
him into the future to which his back is turned, while the pile of debris before him grows
skyward. This storm is what we call progress.[126]

Regardless of how one chooses to interpret it, the Puritan peculiar form of
individualism went hand in hand with the covenantal theory that came to define
both their religious and their political lives. And once again, their understanding of covenant differed drastically from both the French and the English
versions of contractarianism, while trying almost desperately to maintain a
delicate balance between the two. If the French centripetal individualism,
whether Catholic or Protestant, embraced, politically speaking, the medieval
version of a political or governmental contract between the people as a whole
and their rulers,[127] so did the American Puritans. This corporatist vision of "the
people" was embraced regardless of its legal origination – by royal charter or
by compact or covenant.[128] In both cases, this presupposed (a) an organic,
corporatist vision of the people as *universitas* and, as a result, (b) a belief in a
"natural inequality" among the members of the community. Both assumptions
are well captured by John Winthrop. In a *Modell of Christian Charity*, written
while still on board the *Arrbella*, in the middle of the Atlantic, he reminded his
fellow Puritans that they were united into a single body long before they came
aboard, for "though wee were absent from each other many miles, and had our
imploymentes as farre distant, yet wee ought to account our seules knit together
by this bond of loue, and lieu in the exercise of it, if wee would haue comforte of
our being in Christ."[129] The medieval organic vision permeates and informs
the entire *Modell*. The Puritan idea of calling fitted nicely into this

[125] Miller, *The New England Mind*, 339.
[126] Walter Benjamin (1968) [1940], "On the Concept of History" in *Illuminations*, translated by
Harry Zohn (New York: Harcourt, Brace & World), 294.
[127] Fumurescu, *Compromise*, esp. ch. 7.
[128] For the constitutional legacy of the charter's corporatist understanding of "the people," see
further Chapter 4. See also in Donald S. Lutz (ed.). (2008). *Colonial Origins of the American
Constitution – A Documentary History* (Indianapolis: Liberty Fund).
[129] John Winthrop (1630), *A Model of Christian Charity*, in Miller and Johnson, *The
Puritans*, 197.

Weltanschauung, reinforcing it. In William Perkins's words, the good of the whole was the telos of each and every single calling:

The finall cause or end of every calling, I note in the last words of the description; For the common good: that is, for the benefite and good estate of mankind. In mans body there be sundry parts and members, and every one hath his severall use and office, which it performeth not for it selfe, but for the good of the whole bodie; as the office of the eye, is to see, of the eare to heare, and the foote to goe. Now all societies of men, are bodies, a family is a bodie, and so is every particular Church a bodie, and the common-wealth also: and in these bodies there be severall members which are men walking in severall callings and offices.[130]

In such a community, inequalities among its members are not only unavoidable but actually ordered by God "for the preservacion and good of the whole, [...] soe that the riche and mighty not eate vpp the poore, nor the poore, and dispised rised vpp against their superiors, and shake off their yoake." As a result, it is precisely this hierarchy that binds the people together, for "every man might haue need of other, and from hence they might be all knit together in the Bond of brotherly affeccion."[131]

In a sense, the Puritan corporation was tighter and more demanding of the individual than the medieval *universitas* ever was – and now we are better equipped to understand why. The latter preserved a space for individual autonomy in *forum internum*, reserving the belonging to *forum externum*, while the former, as we have seen, simply replaced the outer self with the inner one. Not surprisingly, as in the French case, this assumed inner hierarchy of membership was suspicious of any form of compromise, for compromise presupposed precisely the equality of the parties.

Yet, only apparently paradoxical, what was impossible between unequal men – namely, compromise – became possible between men and God, thanks to the covenant of grace. As John Preston acknowledged, "He is in heauen, and wee are on earth; hee the glorious God, we dust and ashes; hee the Creator, and wee but creatures; and yet he is willing to enter into Couenant, which inplies a kinde of equality betweene vs."[132] Hence Thomas Manton urged: "Let us compromise all Difference between us and God." "[B]y the blood of the everlasting covenant ... Heaven and Earth are at an accord, and the great quarrel between us and God is compromised and taken up."[133] "God voluntarily condescended to treat with man as with an equal and to draw up a covenant or contract with His creature."[134] And, since in seventeenth-century England compromise and contract or covenant came to be used

---

[130] Perkins, *The Workes*, 750. [131] Winthrop, *A Model*, 195.
[132] Quoted in Miller, *The New England Mind*, 381.
[133] Thomas Manton (1693), *A fourth volume containing one hundred and fifty sermons on several texts of Scripture* ... (J.D. and are to be sold by J. Robinson), 147, 690.
[134] Miller and Johnson, *The Puritans*, 58. I will discuss later the distinction between "covenant" and "contract" and the mistake of conflating the two.

interchangeably,[135] it comes as little surprise if God the Father and God the Son also made a Covenant of Redemption that preceded the one of Grace, which "made God not merely bound by His pledge to the creature, but till more firmly tied by a compact with Himself."[136] "God covenanted with Christ that if he would pay the full price for the redemption of beleevers, they should be discharged. Christ hath paid the price, God must be unjust, or else hee must set thee free from all iniquitie."[137] This covenantal theory might have very well been, in Miller's words, "a possibly over-subtle device" and "a shamelessly pragmatic injunction,"[138] for by a single stroke it held God responsible and gave a central place to individual will in the midst of the doctrine of predestination. "If a man can believe, he has done his part; God then must needs redeem him and glorify him."[139]

It went almost without saying that this inner covenant "betweext God and the soul only," in Thomas Hooker's words, had to be mirrored in the outward, Church-Covenant. "When God by His providence removes all *outward* obstacles, the *inward reception of grace and the outward act become one* ... 'The Covenant of grace is ever included and presupposed in the Covenant of Church'."[140] Richard Mather does an excellent job summarizing the New England logic:

Church-Covenant differs not in substance of the things promised from that which is between the Lord and every particular soule, but onely in some other respects; [...] The one is usually done in private, as in a mans Closet between the Lord and his soule, and the other in some publick assembly.[141]

But, as Hooker is eager to point out, even the covenant that is "usually done in private, as in man's Closet," i.e., in his *forum internum*, externalizing it becomes a must in settled Christian communities, for "there God demands that the covenanted saints become churchmen."[142] What in theory gives preeminence to the "internal covenant" in practice emphasizes the outward one. Absent an over-watching Big Brother, the burden of surveillance fell onto the little brothers, because "a congregational church is by the institution of Christ a part of the militant visible church, consisting of a company of saint by calling, united into one body by an holy covenant, for the publique worship of God, and the mutual edification of one another."[143] "The Covenant of Grace is cloathed with Chuch Covenant in a Politicall visible Church way."[144] Once *forum internum* replaced *forum externum*, there was no other way. By necessity

---

[135] Fumurescu, *Compromise*, chapter 6.   [136] Miller, *The New England Mind*, 405.
[137] Quoted in ibid., *The New England Mind*, 406.   [138] Ibid., 394–395.   [139] Ibid., 377.
[140] Quoted in ibid., 447 (emphasis added).   [141] Ibid., 447.   [142] Ibid., 446–447.
[143] John Cotton, Richard Mather, and Ralph Partridge (1649) *A Platform of Church Discipline*, quoted in Bruce Frohnen, ed. (2002), *The American Republic – Primary Sources* (Indianapolis: Liberty Fund), 49.
[144] Quoted in Miller, *The New England Mind*, 447.

then, since the private became public, the religious community ought to have become a political one as well, "for the worke wee haue in hand, it is by mutuall consent through a special overruleing providence, and a more then an ordinary approbation of the Churches of Christ to seeke out a place of Cohabitation and Consortenship vnder a due forme of Government both ciuill and ecclesiasticall."[145]

"*Both* civil and ecclesiastical" is a key formula for understanding the Puritans' politics. If the creation of a new people and of a church required the consent of free and equal individuals, and the election of the aristocracy of merit trusted in the hands of the majority, the operation of the government and of the church was based on the medieval political contract between the people as a whole and its rulers. Hence, John Cotton's demand: "Look what a King requires of the People, or the people of a King, the very same doth God require of his people, and the people of God ... that is, a Governor, a Provider for, and a protector of his people." Or, in Thomas Hooker's once again more bluntly words, "[t]he Covenant which passeth betwixt God and us, is like that which passeth between a King and his people."[146]

Such a governmental contract did not presuppose, prima facie, any democratic assumption, as it is generally assumed – quite the opposite. "While they believed in popular participation in the electoral process, they denied the legitimacy of popular rule. [...] God, the Puritans believed, had chosen a few to lead the many."[147] For example, in the Agreement of the Settlers at Exeter in New Hampshire (July 5, 1639), the Rulers' Oath asked them to "rule and govern his people according to the righteous will of God," while the people had to swear "to be ruled and governed according to the will and word of God, and such wholesome laws and ordinances as shall be derived therefrom by our honored Rulers and the lawful assistants, *with the consent of the people*."[148] Such inequality was a must, for, in John Cotton words, "If the people be governors, who shall be governed?"[149] This bidimensional covenant was a two-way road. Perry Miller is once again right: "When ... Puritans turned to the theory of contract, it was only in part to protect their rights against absolutism; it was also to justify them in subordinating individuals to the state, once the ideals of the state had been rightly conceived."[150]

As we have seen, the paradigm of the people's two bodies allowed the American Puritans to conceive the people in two dimensions: in the horizontal one, they were equally entitled to agree on forming a new people and establish a government on a general form; in the vertical one, they ought to elect an aristocracy of merit, in which hands to entrust the details of the government

---

[145] Winthrop, *A Model*, 197.   [146] Quoted in Miller, *The New England Mind*, 413.
[147] Bremer, *The Puritan Experiment*, 95.
[148] Quoted in Donald S. Lutz (ed.). (2008), Colonial Origins of the American Constitution – A Documentary History (Indianapolis: Liberty Fund), 4 (emphasis added).
[149] Quoted in Bremer, *The Puritan Experiment*, 91.   [150] Miller, *The New England Mind*, 418.

and the running of its daily operations. On the one hand, the people had the right to depose and replace the rulers, for "if the church have power to chuse their officers and ministers [...] then, in case of manifest unworthiness and delinquency, they have power also to depose them: for to open and shut, to chuse and refuse, to constitute in office, and to remove from office, are acts belonging to the same power."[151] On the other hand, though, the rulers could not compromise with the whims of the majority if they considered such whims detrimental to the community as a whole. Like the French, the Puritans knew that a superior should never compromise with an inferior. When John Winthrop found himself caught in the midst of a battle that challenged his authority, he managed to emerge victorious and cleared of all charges, yet this was not enough. He had to clarify the proper relationship between the people and their magistrates in order to prevent further incidents:

The great questions that have troubled the country, are about the authority of the magistrates and the liberty of the people. It is yourselves who have called us to his office, and *being called by you, we have our authority from God* ... We account him a good servant, who breaks not his covenant. The *covenant between you and us* is the oath you have taken of us, which is to this purpose, that we shall govern and judge your causes by the rules of God's laws and our own, according to our best skill.[152]

It might be tempting to equate the Puritan covenantal theory with contractarianism, but the truth is that the two share only the appearances but nothing of the basic assumptions. Thinking about the first as some primitive, rough form of the latter implies a "liberal contractarian evolutionism," which is historically inaccurate. Rather, covenant theology and contract theories were competitors.[153]

First, as Donald Lutz observed, there were subtle yet significant differences between contracts, compacts, and covenants. The contract was understood as a legally enforced agreement between two or more people; the compact was meant to create a tight knit community; the covenant did the same, only in the presence of a higher witness/authority. "Put another way, a document which is covenant can, by simply removing the reference to higher authority, be changed into a compact."[154] Second, the assumptions about "human nature" differed radically between the Puritan covenant and the social contract theorists. After the Fall, the Puritan man was far worse than any Lockean or even Hobbesian equivalent.

---

[151] John Cotton & all (1649), *A Platform*, quoted in Frohnen, *The American Republic*, 53.

[152] Winthrop, *Little Speech on Liberty*, quoted in Frohnen, *The American Republic*, 34 (emphasis added).

[153] Lovin, "Equality and Covenant Theology." Yet see Zuckert, *The Natural Rights Republic*, for a more nuanced distinction of this "amalgam."

[154] Donald S. Lutz (1994), "The Evolution of Covenant Form and Content as the Basis for Early American Political Culture," in Daniel J. Elazar, ed. *The Covenant in the Nineteenth Century: The Decline of an American Tradition* (Lanham, MD: Rowman and Littlefield Publishers), 39.

What the theologians could not accept was the contractarian view of the human persons who made these agreements. The self-interested, rational individual who calculates the value of proposed social arrangements in terms of his or her own purposes and makes commitments accordingly could not have been the covenant-partner they had in mind. Covenant theology rejected the anthropology of empiricism, and it did so not because we are better than the security-seeking, desire-driven creatures Hobbes described, but because it thought we are worse.[155]

Even the more democratic-minded Roger Williams could agree that without Magistrates, people, like fish, would devour one another.[156] Absent God, and left to our own devices, we would destroy ourselves.

Last but not least, the difference between the two *Weltanschauungs* was that, unlike contractarianism, through the Covenant of Grace and the Church Covenant, one replaced selfishness with a care for the common good. It was precisely this "eudaimonistic ethics" that separated the essentially private contracts from the public covenants.[157] Natural liberty was exchanged for moral liberty, as Winthrop emphasized.

For the other point concerning liberty, I observe a great mistake in the country about that. There is a twofold liberty, natural (I mean as our nature is now corrupt) and civil or federal. The first is common to man with beasts and other creatures ... This liberty is incompatible and inconsistent with authority, and cannot endure the least restraint of the most just authority. [...] The other kind of liberty I call civill or federal; it may also be termed moral, in reference to the covenant between God and Man, in the moral law, and the political covenants and constitutions among men themselves. This liberty is the proper end and object of authority, and cannot subsist without it. [...] If you stand for your natural corrupt liberties and will do what is good in your own eyes, you will not endure the least weight of authority, but will murmur, and oppose, and be always striving to shake off that yoke.[158]

Winthrop was rightfully concerned. What in theory worked marvelously, in practice became problematic. Ideas are stubborn – and the horizontal and egalitarian aspect of covenantal theory challenged the vertical and hierarchical one almost from the very beginning.[159] The fact that, despite theological differences, both Puritans and their own dissenters shared the same uncompromising attitude did not help either. As a matter of fact, Puritanism was a movement doomed to fail from the very beginning because of its own success in what today would be labeled as identity politics.

---

[155] Lovin, "Equality and Covenant Theology," 245.
[156] Roger Williams (1644), *The Bloody Tenent, of Persecution, for Cause of Conscience*, quoted in Frohnen, *The American Republic*, 42–47.
[157] Lovin, "Equality and Covenant Theology," 252.   [158] Winthrop, *Little Speech*, 34.
[159] For a detailed discussion of the differences between "covenants" and "contracts," see also Weir, *Early New England*, 226–227.

2.4 "THEY DON'T WEIGH THE INTELLECTUAL FURNITURE"

The Puritan dissenters were, properly speaking, no dissenters. They were just more Puritan than the Puritans, in the same way in which the Puritans were claiming to be the true Anglicans, and the American Puritans considered themselves more Puritan than their English brethren. Each of them just pushed a little bit further the logical implications of their professed faith. Dissenters such as Anne Hutchinson or Roger Williams were expelled, as later were the Quakers and the Baptists, not only because of their (questionable) antinomianism (expecting God to do everything necessary for salvation) or arminianism (putting too much emphasis on personal efforts) but also because of their reliance, in both cases, exclusively on the inner self, thus downplaying not just the purged individualism but also the role of the hierarchy of saints. Yet Hutchinson and Williams, Quakers and Baptists, did nothing but to push Puritanism to its logical extremes.[160] If both parties proved as unwilling to compromise (with the dissenters usually being even less willing to compromise), the reason is to be found in their focus on a "pure" identity. If disdain for the lukewarm Anglicanism that was stuck, rather comfortably, between Catholicism and Protestantism leads one to cross the Atlantic and leave everything solely for the sake of an idea, as Tocqueville put it, one had better believe that one's ideas were the right ones. As has been proven too many times by history, people have often been willing to even die for their perceived rightful identity – and sometimes they actually did and still do. Then and now, identity politics comes with a price.

On a deeper level, this uncompromising clinging to one's identity reveals a troubling insecurity. "For psychological reasons [the Puritans] needed an official opposition in order to experience their identity."[161] And since in New England, unlike in the Old, there was practically none, they had to invent it. As Bremer astutely observes, "the Puritans' intolerance was in part at least a symptom of their own insecurity."[162] It is a lesson to be remembered, for this need of creating scapegoats was largely responsible for the Puritan movement's fragmentation, let alone the (in)famous Salem's trials. Unlike the case of England, where forced cohabitation required at least some level of compromise, in the colonies this was not the case. Regardless of whether one was excluded from the church and the community or if one voluntarily decided to leave, one was always sure that one could find a community to join or even to create a brand new one, as Roger Williams did.

Roger Williams and Anne Hutchinson are the best-known examples of dissenters, although most likely they were not the first ones, and oftentimes they are "bundled" together, despite their differences, as promoters of secularism – which was never their intention. What they had in common,

---

[160] Adair, *Founding Fathers*, 172; Bremer, *The Puritan Experiment*, 65. See further.
[161] Adair, *Founding Fathers*, 174.   [162] Bremer, *The Puritan Experiment*, 138.

however, was the inner and unshakeable conviction that they were right and the Puritan orthodoxy wrong. Because of this, they were the least tempted to compromise. In the long run, their principled stubbornness paved the road toward the "democratization" and, in the end, the dismissal of the Puritan movement. A bit of history would hopefully clarify this point.

Roger Williams had strong separatist views and could not accept any congregation that refused to repudiate their ties with the Church of England. As a result, he declined the position of teacher offered by the Boston congregation; the Salem congregation withdrew its offer for the same reasons, and he found Plymouth's Pilgrims insufficiently separatist, so he returned to Salem and started preaching as an unofficial assistant to Pastor Skelton. After Skelton's death, Williams was offered the position of formal pastor of the congregation, and began openly preaching the separation of civil affairs from spiritual ones. What is often absent from this well-known picture, however, is that Williams's concerns with the separation of church and state, in modern parlance, was not meant to protect the state from religious interferences – quite the opposite. The aim was to protect the church from state interference, as was the practice in Massachusetts. "Roger Williams's assertion of toleration came not from a political and constitutional scruple but from a conception of the spiritual life so exalted that he could not see it contaminated by earthly compulsion."[163] "His hope was that in a climate of religious freedom, Turkes (Muslims), Jews, Anti-Christians (Catholics), and Pagans (American Indians) could be truly converted instead of just mimicking it."[164]

Obviously, in the eyes of Puritan orthodoxy, such radical teachings were not conducive to maintaining the unity of a theologico-political people, and was a direct threat to the hierarchy of saints, so, after a failed effort at reconciliation from the governor, Williams ended up in front of the General Court in July 1635. In Bremer's suggestive account,

Despite his later reputation as a conciliator, Williams's reaction to the court's decisions was far from conciliatory. He informed the Salem church that he could not in conscience communicate with the other churches of the Bay and that he could not maintain communion with the Salem congregation unless it joined him in renouncing ties with the other churches. Faced with the threats of the General Court and William's own intransigence, the Salem congregation began to back away from its fiery member and ultimate repudiated his views.[165]

After yet another failed attempt from Thomas Hooker presiding over the General Court, Williams was sentenced to depart from the Bay in six weeks. Since he could not, for health reasons, the assistants ordered his deportation to England in January 1636. Winthrop, who disagreed with Williams but did not

[163] Miller, *The New England Mind*, 454.
[164] Teresa M. Bejan (2015), "Evangelical Toleration," *The Journal of Politics*, 77:4.
[165] Bremer, *The Puritan Experiment*, 67.

want him to fall into the hands of Laud, warned him, and he was able to escape to Providence territory, were he eventually ended up founding Rhode Island.

The Hutchinson family arrived in Boston in 1634, just at the beginning of Williams's troubles. Anne Hutchinson's story is also well known, so there is no reason to delve into the details. What is important to notice, however, is that her attack on the Puritan establishment started from a different direction than Williams's. She chose to emphasize what, after all, was another idea at the core of Puritan theology, i.e., the mystical experience of grace, downplaying human actions as means of preparation for grace and/or as signs of sanctification. However harsh, Adair's observation has some truth in it: "[B]y pushing the Puritan gospel to the extremes, Anne had exposed its ultimate illogicality. Despite the intellectual commitment to justification by faith alone, expressed in such doctrines as predestinations, almost all Puritan preachers in practice assumed some form of effort – valuable effort too – on the part of their listeners."[166] For Hutchinson and her followers, the practice of evaluating publicly the most intimate testimonies of grace – the bringing of the inside self out – was, after all, nothing but part of what they called "the Covenant of Works." It was yet another threat to the hierarchical understanding of the people.

Politics and Governor Henry Vane got involved in her tribulations, yet once again the repeated attempts that were made to appease the entire situation were to no effect. Neither Anne Hutchinson nor her followers were willing to compromise. In 1637, Winthrop was reelected governor, while Vane was not even elected among the assistants. In 1638, Anne was formally excommunicated and banished. She and her family settled initially in what would become Rhode Island. By that time, Williams had purchased land from the Native Americans and had founded Providence. The government of the town gave a vote to all men, and they all pledged to abide by the decisions of the majority, "the maior part," but only "in ciuill things."[167]

Assisted by Williams, a wealthy and respected merchant from Anne Hutchinon's group of exiles from the Bay, William Coddington, purchased from the Native Americans the large island of Aquidneck and founded Portsmouth, with him as chief magistrate. However, by then the spirit of "brotherly love" was broken and, in 1639, taking advantage of Coddington's absence from the town, Anne and her followers replaced him with her husband, William Hutchinson. Coddington and his supporters seceded and founded Newport. In 1640, Hutchinson fell out of grace with the inhabitants of Portsmouth, and Coddington managed to unite Newport and Portsmouth as a new colony with himself as governor. The colony proclaimed itself a democracy with religious freedom for all. Eventually, Anne Hutchinson left for Long Island after her husband's death in 1643, only to be killed by Native Americans. Her legacy, however, endured

---

[166] Adair, *Founding Fathers*, 172.   [167] Quoted in Weir, *Early New England*, 102.

through the Quakers and all the other branches labeled as "Enthusiasts" by the orthodox Puritans, and would be revived once again by the Evangelical movement that marked the end of Puritanism.

Neither of the two movements that went hand in hand – namely, democratization and religious fragmentation – could be stopped, despite the intentions of their initiators. Such twists of fate and faith, literally speaking, can be easily understood once one considers "the flexibility of covenant theory and practice," which can "explain, therefore, the various highways and byways that the covenant concept and the various forms of Puritanism took."[168] The emphasis on the vertical or on the horizontal dimension of the covenant made all the difference when it came to compromise, as Williams and Hutchinson came to experience firsthand. "Providence had a reputation for being one of the most argumentative plantations in New England, and within a period of ten years it signed at least five more civil covenants in an attempt to draw its various factions together."[169]

Although Rhode Island would remain for a long period of time an outlier, throughout all the New England colonies the civil franchise expanded almost from the beginning, by the mere force of numbers, and more and more "inhabitants" became "citizens" with voting rights. The "democratic revolution" started in New England almost from the very beginning of colonization, and, as Tocqueville put it, "[e]veryone played a part: those who strove to ensure democracy's success as well as those who never dreamt of serving it; those who fought for it as well as those who declared themselves its enemies."[170] As the electoral franchise expanded and the political power became more centralized, something else happened: direct democracy came to be replaced by representative democracy, yet in both cases the final decision remained in the hands of the majority. If in the Fundamental Orders of Connecticut (1638–1639), for example, the choice of the Governor, the Magistrates, "and other publicke Officers" was to "be made by all that are admitted freemen and haue taken the Oath of Fidelity, and doe cohabitte within this Jurisdiction, hauing beene admitted Inhabitants by the mayor parte," as the locus of power moved upward, at provincial and colonial level, the decision moved into the hands of the legislative.[171]

John Wise's *Vindication* (1717) is the perfect exemplification of this development. As his predecessors, Wise starts off by paying lip service to God's wisdom, yet moves swiftly from Divine Laws to Natural and Human Laws. "It is certain Civil Government in General, is a very Admirable Result of Providence, and an Incomparable Benefit to Man-kind, yet must needs be acknowledged to be the Effect Human Free-Compacts and not of Divine Institution."

---

[168] Weir, *Early New England*, 223.   [169] Ibid., 103.

[170] de Tocqueville, *Democracy in America*, 6.

[171] Compare, for example, the Cambridge Agreement of July 5, 1632 with the Massachusetts Agreement of May 14, 1634, in Lutz, *Colonial Origins*, 45–50.

As Locke later, he agreed that, "The Internal Native Liberty of Mans Nature ...
does not consist in a loose and ungovernable Freedom, or in unbounded
Licence of Acting." Every man "must be acknowledged equal to very Man."
Even if Aristotle suggested that "nothing is more suitable to Nature, than that
those who Excel in Understanding and Prudence, should Rule and Controul
those who are less happy in those Advantages ... there is room for an Answer.
That it would be the greatest absurdity to believe, that Nature actually Invests
the Wise with a Sovereignty over the weak ... for that no Sovereignty can be
Established, unless some Humane Deed, or Covenant Precede." Thus, both the
social compact and the following political compacts were needed for making
legitimate the "rule and control of those who exceed in understanding and
prudence to rule over those who are less happy in those advantages":

> Let us conceive in our Mind a multitude of Men, all Naturally Free & Equal; going
> about voluntarily, to Erect themselves into a new Common-Wealth. Now their Condi-
> tion being such, to bring themselves into a Politick Body, they must needs Enter into
> divers Covenants. They must Interchangeably each Man Covenant to joyn in one lasting
> Society, that they may be capable to concert the measures of their safety, by a Publick
> Vote. A Vote or Decree must then nextly pass to set up some Particular species of
> Government over them ... Then all are bound by the Majority to acquiesce in that
> particular Form thereby settled, though their own private Opinion, incline them to some
> other Model. After a Decree has specified the particular form of Government, then there
> will be need of a New Covenant, whereby those on whom Sovereignty is conferred ...

In some democratic governments, continues Wise, "the representative body can
make but one house," but in others "they make different houses in their grand
sessions, and so one house or state can negative another."

> But in every distinct house of these states, the members are equal in their vote; the most
> ayes makes the affirmative vote, and most no's the negative: *They don't weigh the
> intellectual furniture, or other distinguished qualifications of the several voters* in the
> scale of the golden rule of fellowship; they only add up the ayes and the no's, and so
> determine the suffrage of the house.[172]

It was nothing less than a confirmation of a process of "democratization"
well under way in the colonies. Weir cannot resist the temptation of placing the
colonies on a right–left spectrum, according to their religious tolerance, taken
as a measure of democratization, although he is the first to acknowledge the
inapplicability of this terminology in that historical context. In this picture, the
New Haven Colony would be the strictest, religiously speaking, occupying
therefore the far-right position, followed by the Massachusetts Bay Colony
and then the Connecticut Colony (which from its inception allowed franchise
to nonmembers of the local church.) More toward the "left" would be the New

---

[172] John Wise (1717), *Vindication of the Government of New England Churches*, quoted in Miller
and Johnson, *The Puritans*, 259–269 (emphasis added).

Plymouth Colony, which allowed the imposition of religious uniformity at the town level but not at the colonial one. Finally, the most "leftist" would be Rhode Island, which, as we have seen, was, strictly religiously speaking, the most tolerant one.[173]

After the Restoration, this uncompromising common front against the king broke down according to the "right–left" spectrum proposed by Weir – and now we can understand why. Rhode Island, the colony that in its internal governance got the closest to an embodiment of a social contract theory, was also the first to compromise and to acknowledge the finality of the Restoration in October 1660. It was followed by Connecticut in March 1661 and Plymouth three months later. The two most "rightist" colonies, namely Massachusetts Bay and New Haven, also proved to be less willing to compromise. Massachusetts went through a prolonged political confrontation between royalists, commonwealthmen, and moderates, until finally, in August 1661, the moderates won, and the General Court proclaimed the king in the fashion desired by Whitehall. New Havenites' first response to the Restoration was to reopen negotiations with Peter Stuyvesant in order to resettle in what would become New Jersey, despite their long-lasting history of feud with the Dutch. Furthermore, they organized a network of colonists to hide Edward Whalley and William Goffe, wanted under the charge of regicide. Eventually, they caved in, and New Haven became the last New England colony to proclaim the king, in August 1661.

A key factor in acknowledging the Stuarts was the need for an official royal charter to protect the colonies under the new circumstances. While the role of majorities to control government inside the colonies kept growing, the existence of these charters maintained alive the corporatist understanding of "the people" of each colony, but only insofar as external relations were involved. This second understanding of the people would later prove essential in theoretically justifying the Revolutionary War, but earlier it was also responsible for the first successful attempt at uniting the colonies. In the midst of the Civil War at home, the New Englanders faced two major threats, namely the Native Americans, who were being helped by the French, and the Dutch. To better face these dangers, the colonies decided to combine their forces, so in 1643, Connecticut, New Haven, Massachusetts, and New Plymouth signed "The Articles of Confederation of the United Colonies of New England." (Rhode Island was once again the exception.) More details will be discussed in Chapter 4. For now, suffice is to notice that the Articles, largely forgotten today, bear an almost eerie resemblance to the most famous Articles of the Confederation of 1777. The Articles of Confederation of the United Colonies stipulated that,

The said United Colonies for themselves and their posterities do jointly and severally hereby enter into a firm and perpetual league of friendship and amity for offence and

---

[173] Weir, *Early New England*, 134–135.

defence, mutual advice and succor upon all just occasions both for preserving and propagating the truth and liberties of the Gospel and for their own mutual safety and welfare. (1643)

More than one hundred years later, The Articles of Confederation also stipulated that,

The said states hereby severally enter into a firm league of friendship with each other, for their common defence, the security of their Liberties, and their mutual and general welfare, binding themselves to assist each other, against all force offered to, or attacks made upon them, or any of them, on account of religion, sovereignty, trade, or any other pretence whatsoever. (1777)

Religious appeals aside, there were no major differences between the two documents. Both considered the parties as corporate peoples, thus equal, hence both provided for equal representations (and vote) despite the actual numbers of the populace (two representatives or "commissioners" in the case of the former, no less than two but no more than seven in the case of the latter, yet each colony/state's vote was to be counted as one). Both documents set up a mechanism for solving internal disagreements that resembled "compromise as arbitration," although the sanctions in case of such event remained rather vague. Weir is missing the mark when he asserts that, "the Confederation of New England ... presents an important backdrop to the Articles of Confederation (1777) *and* the Constitution of the United States (1787)."[174] While the first two documents share the basic assumptions about representing corporate peoples, the third one, as we shall see in Chapter 5, puts forward a major change in this understanding. Representing the people as a corporation or as a collection of individuals was not a trifling detail, as history would bear witness, repeatedly, quite soon.

2.5 "...UNTIL A BETTER LIGHT WILL BE AVAILABLE TO GUIDE THEM"

If external threats helped emphasize, on the political level, the corporatist dimension of "the people," on the religious level the dynamics played differently. Here, the "enemy" to be concerned with came mainly from the inside, not from the outside, yet in both cases what was at stake was the identity of the community as a whole. But if the enemies from the outside helped create a centripetal movement of coagulation, the perceived enemies from the inside had the opposite, centrifugal effect, breaking down the unity of the churches. No one likes to share the bed with the enemy, yet in New England, religiously speaking, there were plenty of bedrooms from which to choose. Religious fragmentation went hand in hand with political centralization. As a result,

---

[174] Ibid., 107.

the number of civil covenants started decreasing after the Restoration, while the number of church covenants increased, and, at the same time, the former became more uniform and the latter more and more diversified.[175]

By the second half of the seventeenth century it became increasingly apparent that the Congregationalists' victory was more of a Pyrrhic one. First, after Cromwell's success, England experienced in the 1650s what the Bay colonists had experienced in the 1630s with Anne Hutchinson – "not one form of Antinomianism but a thousand."[176] And although Cromwell tried his best to protect his beloved clergy, after his death, Presbyterianism emerged as the only one able to restrain these "enthusiastic excesses of inner lights," being perceived as a well-balanced compromise between a too hierarchized and Catholicized Episcopialism on the one hand and a too loose Congregationalism on the other. Not surprisingly, Englishmen tended to favor the party they perceived as a compromise between extremes, in the same way in which the Anglicans were initially perceived as "a compromise of sorts between the Catholic and Protestant positions,"[177] and Congregationalists presented themselves as a middle way between Presbyterians and Independents.[178] History has its own ironies.

However, the differences between Old and New England came to play a crucial role. If in the former the aristocratic character of the society was easier to maintain, in the latter the democratic tendencies had plenty of space in which to flourish – the frontier. As soon as 1677, Increase Mather warned that "People are ready to run wild into the woods again and to be as Heathenish as ever, if you do not prevent it."[179] In 1705, Joseph Easterbrooks depicted frontiersmen as people running from the benefits of learning, instruction, and civilization "for worldly conveniences." "By that means [they] have seemed to bid defiance, not only to Religion, but to Civility it self; and such places thereby have become Nurseries of Ignorance, Prophaneness and Atheism."[180] The American Puritans tried their best to withstand these assaults on lessening the prestige of well-educated clergy, yet slowly but surely they were forced to adapt in what came closer to an open market of ideas and increasingly fervent appeals to feelings. In the way in which they conceived their sermons, their contrived simplicity of style – not "more sauce than meat" – became more poetic, and logical or scriptural arguments were gradually replaced by appeals to feelings, getting closer to the Evangelical preaching style.[181]

This change in the preaching style proved not to be enough to reverse the dwindling church membership, so the idea of a Half-Way Covenant became increasingly attractive. According to it, children of baptized individuals could

---

[175] Ibid., 4.   [176] Miller and Johnson, *The Puritans*, 15.   [177] Adair, *Founding Fathers*, 89.

[178] Bremer, *The Puritan Experiment*, 104.

[179] Increase Mather [1677] (1679, 2nd ed., 1685), *A Discourse Concerning the Danger of Apostacy* (Boston), 104.

[180] Joseph Easterbrooks (1705), *Abraham the Passenger* (Boston), 3.

[181] Miller and Johnson, *The Puritans*, 55–79.

themselves be baptized, regardless if the parent(s) had or had not be admitted to full membership in the church.[182] The initiative divided not just leading figures of the Puritan movement but even families: Richard Mather, for example, was in favor, while his two sons, Eleazar and Increase, opposed it. The result was a further fragmentation of the Puritan front, but in relatively short time it proved "a reform preferable to the greatest danger posed by presbyterialists," who sought a parish type of church membership going further than the Half-Way Covenant. "With the clergy still divided into at least two major groups, the General Assembly in 1669 announced that until "better light" was available to guide them, the magistrates would tolerate any polity practiced by congregations adhering to the fundamentals of orthodox theology."[183] It was, in Christopher Hill's words, "New England's attempt to find a compromise between the old and the new conception."[184] Not surprisingly, as many scholars have noticed, Puritanism had no choice but to become "more English as the century passed," taking "its political and many of its ecclesiastical cues from Old England after the Restoration of 1662 and the Glorious Revolution of 1688–1689.[185]

However, if the Half-Way Covenant was for a while able to stop the decline in church membership, it did little to maintain the unity of faith. It was a one-way road. "New England grew by the cellular division of congregations, and the wider the Puritans spread on the ground, the thinner it tended to become."[186] As the individualist side of Puritanism grew, covenants came to be replaced with voluntary contracts of association. "Free will in a society safely dominated by an established Church is one thing; free will in a free contract society is something very different."[187] In Connecticut, a last-ditch effort to stop this centrifugal movement was attempted when in 1708 the General Assembly adopted the Saybrook Platform that included three sections: the first adopted the 1658 Savoy Confession of the English Congregationalists, the second called for the establishment of ecclesiastical consociations in each county, while the third endorsed the 1691 "Heads of Agreement."

With the liberalization of membership requirements, the beginning of the eighteenth century saw the rapid growth of preachers' appeals to the heart, while also questioning the sainthood of saints and denouncing their "aristocratic intellectualism."[188] Puritan sermons tried their best to reverse this trend, claiming that these "intellectual aristocrats" were necessary for the good of the corporate people. For example, in 1711, Ebenzer Pemberton argued in a funeral sermon delivered at Harvard in favor of promoting "good literature":

---

[182] The term "Half-Way Covenant" was in effect an invention of the eighteenth century but has been applied retroactively by historians. See Bremer, *The Puritan Experiment*, 145.

[183] Bremer, *The Puritan Experiment*, 146.   [184] Hill, *Society and Puritanism*, 492.

[185] Weir, *Early New England*, 225.   [186] Adair, *Founding Fathers*, 239.

[187] Hill, *Society and Puritanism*, 495.

[188] Miller and Johnson, *The Puritans*, 16–19; Bremer, *The Puritan Experiment*, 226–228.

This is necessary for the true prosperity and happiness of a people ... This has for ever been in highest esteem among civilized nations ... The more good literature civil rulers are furnished with, he more able they are to discharge their trust to the honour and safety of their people. And learning is no less necessary, as an ordinary medium to secure the glory of Christ's visible kingdom ... When ignorance and barbarity invade a generation, their glory is laid in the dust; and the ruin of all that is great and good among them will soon follow.

Pemberton continues, showing that the restoration of the admiration for intellectual prowess presupposes respecting (and preserving) a fixed hierarchy of callings. The following passage could very well have been written in the fifteenth century: "Thus every man is to serve his generation by moving in his own orb; and discharging those offices that belong to that order that the government of heaven has assigned him to."[189]

The call fell mostly on deaf ears. Increasingly, people "demanded fervent rather than learned ministers and asserted the equality of all men."[190] By all practical measures, as a religious movement, Puritanism was dead before 1740. Nevertheless, its political legacy of voluntarily creating a people with two "bodies" thanks to the bidimensional covenant proved to be long-lasting.

The versatility of this foundational double helix was soon to be put to the test during the Imperial Debate and the Revolutionary War.

[189] Ebenezer Pemberton (1727), *Sermons and Discourses on Several Occasions* (London), 212–213, 220–221.
[190] Miller and Johnson, *The Puritans*, 19.

3

The Uncompromising Patriots

"Friends, brethren, enemies will prove . . ."

... they fell into black-and-white habits of mind in which the patriots could do
no wrong and Britain no right.

– Mark A. Noll

It is said that in a Rorschach test everyone finds what s/he is looking for – which is
why the Puritan legacy has proven so enduring. The previous chapter identified
multiple, seemingly contradictory layers of the Puritans' *Weltanschauung*, suggesting that it is precisely this complexity that helps explain its attractiveness
during the American founding and beyond. This is no accident. Despite their
meager numbers, the first English settlers in New England accomplished
more than the brethren they left behind – they could implement their politico-
theological ideas to an extent otherwise inconceivable in the Old World. By the
unanimous and voluntary consent of the individuals involved they created not
just churches or settlements, not just new societies, but, as Donald Lutz has
pointed out, new *peoples*, despite, not because, of their common ancestry.[1]
Simply put, the American Puritans developed a dual conception of the "people."
One, akin to its seventeenth-century English counterpart, understood "the
people" as a collection of equal individuals who would select, through
an electoral majority, representatives to protect their individual rights. The other,
alike to the medieval and the seventeenth-century French conception, regarded
the people as an organic and hierarchically structured community, contracting
with their rulers for the common good and for the protection of corporate rights.[2]

---

[1] Lutz, *Colonial Origins of the American Constitution*, xxiv. See also Anne S. Brown and David D.
Hall (1997) "Family Strategies and Religious Practice: Baptism and the Lord's Supper in Early
New England" in David D. Hall, ed., *Lived Religion in America: Toward a History of Practice*
(Princeton: Princeton University Press), 45–46.
[2] Fumurescu, *Compromise*.

As a result, the Puritans considered people equally equipped and entitled to give their consent to the initial covenant and the formation of the new religious and political body. They also agreed that everyone was equally equipped and entitled to agree, through a majority vote, to the general form of government, the selections of the rulers, and their eventual removal from office. Unsurprisingly, solving disputes among these equal members through compromise was an accepted and widespread practice. Yet in the covenantal theory this horizontal understanding was always complemented by a vertical one, which explains why the backbone of Puritanism was the natural aristocracy of the wise and virtuous. From this perspective, people were not equally equipped and entitled to rule. After all, according to the doctrine of predestination, few were elected, and the challenge was how to identify them. Only this "elected aristocracy" was entrusted to work out the specific details of the government and to ensure its proper function.[3] This corporatist understanding of the people was suspicious of any attempts to compromise with outsiders, especially on matters of doctrine, such as religious identity. The two "camps" were to be kept apart like Light from Darkness. No compromise between the two was ever acceptable, for the Puritan identity was far too precious to be worth endangering. As we have seen, "Puritans, more than most people, tended to see the world in bipolar terms."[4] The result of this uncompromising attitude was, unsurprisingly, the rapid fragmentation of the movement.

Thus, as I will show in the first part of this chapter, it would be a mistake to hold the First Great Awakening, which started "officially" in 1740, responsible for the disappearance of the Puritan movement.[5] "It must be understood ... that the victim was subsequently a long time dying."[6] As a matter of fact, in some important respects, the Great Awakening – like many Enthusiasts and dissenters before it – was only pushing some major tenets of Puritanism to their logical extremes. It would be equally mistaken to blame the initial promoters of the new movement for completely destroying the Puritans' expectations for educated ministers and well-articulated sermons. Famous preachers like Jonathan Edwards or Gilbert Tennent were equally intellectually equipped and dogmatically articulated.[7] But by switching the emphasis from rationality to feelings, the New Lights contributed, unknowingly and unwillingly, to the

---

[3] See, for example, Foster, *The Long Argument*, 75; Hall, *A Reforming People*, 37–38.

[4] Foster, *Their Solitary Way*, 33.

[5] I use "officially" in quotation marks, because the 1739 arrival of George Whitefield in the colonies is considered by many the beginning of the Great Awakening. However, from 1730s, Jonathan Edwards, for example, had already started to preach a theology based on the "transformative emanations" of the Holy Spirit. As we will see further, the temporal borders of the First Great Awakening are as fluid as the ones of the Puritan movement.

[6] Foster, *The Long Argument*, 290.

[7] Edwin Scott Gaustad (1957), *The Great Awakening in New England* (New York: Harper & Brothers), 47.

damage of an essential feature of Puritanism, namely the fragile balance between the horizontal and the vertical understanding of the people. Thus, they ended shaking the paradigm of the people's two bodies. From then on, matters of doctrine could have been easily compromised, but no compromise was possible between the New and the Old Lights preachers.

The authority of the Old Lights and their ministerial abilities came to be questioned under the claim that their preaching substance and form revealed a suspicious stiffness. When touched by the Holy Spirit – so went the argument – the true believer's thirst for God could no longer be satisfied with a mere "philosophical and moral religion." In other words, the accusation was that purged individualism ends up suffocating the inner self. The Inner Light did not need any other authority from the outside to be authenticated. It was enough for it to be strongly felt. As a result, the church covenant was dropped in favor of the pure covenant of grace. Ironically, as we shall see, this *inner* experience of grace had still to become manifest on the *outside*. *What* was said began to be less important than *how* it was said, which indicated the privileging of form over substance or of the exterior over the interior. Realizing this, Alexander Garden challenged Whitefield in 1741, "only to put the *same* words, which from his mouth produced the boasted effects, into the mouth of an *ordinary* speaker, and see whether the same *effects* would be the consequence."[8] Probably even more revealing for the same movement inside out was the fact that the personal experience of conversion was to be proven by extremely expressive, sometimes even violent signs like groaning, shaking, crying, or fainting.

In the end, like Puritanism before it, the new movement was crushed under its own weight, when ministers began accusing each other of being "unconverted." The uncompromising attitude resulted in hundreds of schisms in New England alone;[9] meanwhile, the enthusiasm of the newly converted started to grow old. The New Lights began to compromise with the Old Lights, and during this process something had irrevocably changed. Salvation was available for all, not just for the elected few; at the same time, populism became a force to be reckoned with, thanks to the emotionalism and egalitarianism espoused during the Awakening. It was also the first sign that egalitarian populism could be as uncompromising, if not more so, than the hierarchically corporatist understanding of "the people." Parochial allegiances were forever lost, and religious pluralism became a fact of life. Without an integration of the grace covenant into a church covenant, the former "peoples" that established New England disappeared and new definitions were required.

---

[8] Quoted in Alan Heimert (1966), Religion and the American Mind: From the Great Awakening to the Revolution (Cambridge, MA: Harvard University Press), 20 (emphases in the original).
[9] Jeremy Gregory (2013), "'Establishment' and 'Dissent' in British North America: Organizing Religion in the New World" in Stephen Foster, ed., *British North America in the Seventeenth and Eighteenth Centuries* (New York: Oxford University Press), 158.

Some scholars argue that these social developments in the colonies prepared the way for the movement for independence even before the Stamp Act Crisis. By encouraging common people to reshape Christianity in their own image[10] and forging an American sense of nationalism, some historians consider the threshold for a First American Revolution completed by 1760.[11] I shall argue in the second part of this chapter that such claims are exaggerated, to say the least. The same rhetoric of liberty was used on both sides of the Atlantic, but the understanding of the people was slightly different. And yet, this apparently insignificant difference ended up fueling an increasingly uncompromising attitude among the Patriots toward the metropole they had grown up admiring and imitating. For the colonists, local corporate rights began to supersede individual rights to the extent that even the freedom of the press was sacrificed in the name of the greater good (i.e., the protection of local interests). While both sides agreed with the idea that people were politically maintained in existence by their legislatures, the practice of instructing their representatives increasingly pushed the colonists to transfer their allegiance from the British Parliament to their local colonial assemblies. Thus, before becoming a full-blown war for independence, the conflict between the two legislatures facilitated confusion between the two types of contract – political and social – and their respective different understandings of "the people."

The third section of the chapter explores in more detail the legacy of the bidimensional Puritan covenant and the subsequent paradigm of the people's two bodies, in an attempt to disentangle the underlying theoretical assumptions of the revolutionary era. Like many contemporary politicians and even scholars, the Patriots made repeated references to social contract theory and to Locke, even when their specific arguments did not warrant parallels, as they shared few – if any – of the basic assumptions of social contract theory. Like Locke, they all agreed that individuals were *equally free* to enter social and political compacts. Yet unlike Locke, they assumed that the general interest of the corporate community so formed was better represented by the prudent, the skillful, and the virtuous from their ranks. Furthermore, the Patriots believed that the rights of the individuals could be sacrificed for the common good if necessary. Because of this peculiar understanding of the people's two bodies, the emphasis during the Imperial Debate was on the political rather than the social compact, a compact between the king and the colonies, embodied in the royal charter.

---

[10] Nathan O. Hatch (1989), *The Democratization of American Christianity* (New Haven: Yale University Press), 9.

[11] From the defenders of the thesis that the First Great Awakening was the foundation of the American Revolution, none was probably more enthusiastic than Heimert's *Religion and the American Mind*. For an excellent interpretation of "the First American Revolution," see Nancy L. Rhoden (2013), "The American Revolution (I) – The Paradox of Atlantic Integration," in Foster, *British North America*, 255.

The last part of the chapter shows that by circumventing the Parliament and by making the king the arbitrator (i.e., *compromissarius*) of all disputes among the various parts of the empire, the Patriots became, to the surprise of many, Tories rather than Whigs, willing to grant the king more authority over the colonies than he had ever before possessed. The uncompromising anti-monarchical stance adopted by Thomas Paine from the moment he set foot ashore in the New World in 1774 was only widely adopted by the Patriots in 1776, by which time King George had become "the perfect scapegoat."[12] The British hoped for a compromise even after the Declaration of Independence, but with the symbolic killing of the father-arbitrator (i.e., the king), compromises with Great Britain were no longer possible. From then on, the Americans would be forced to find new ways of compromising among themselves.

A caveat is in order here. It is not the aim of this chapter to review and analyze all events culminating with the Declaration of Independence. Since this is not a survey work, I will not spend time on the details, nor will I take sides in the debate between various ways of looking at the founding era, although I hope that my interpretation can provide some clarifications.[13] Instead, I will focus almost exclusively on those historical aspects and those texts that show how the increased unwillingness to compromise, manifested more forcefully so in the case of the Patriots after 1776, remained for the entire period closely associated with different representations of "the people." Throughout the course of the Imperial Debate, thanks to the people's two bodies' paradigm, the Americans proved more versatile in adjusting their theoretical arguments according to changing circumstances. As we shall see, Mark Noll was right when claiming that the "Christian republicanism of the early United States was possible only because of considerable ideological flexibility," and this flexibility was related with the understanding of "the people."[14]

3.1 "WE ARE BREAKING TO PIECES IN OUR CHURCHES"

Ironically, the Great Awakening was formally ignited by a Great Compromiser – George Whitefield. While still a member of the Church of England, in which he helped create the Methodist movement, Whitefield had no problem adapting his flamboyant sermons across a wide variety of denominations. As Reverend Roger Price, Commissary for New England, observed of Whitefield with disdain, "to the Quaker he becomes a Quaker; to the Anabaptist an

---

[12] Gerald Stourzh (2010) [1970], *From Vienna to Chicago and Back: Essays on Intellectual History and Political Thought in Europe and America* (Chicago: University of Chicago Press).

[13] For a relatively recent summary of these historiographical debates, see Stephen Foster's "Introduction" in *British North America*.

[14] Mark A. Noll (2002), *America's God: From Jonathan Edwards to Abraham Lincoln* (Oxford: Oxford University Press), 92–93.

Anabaptist; to the Presbyterian and Independent, a Presbyterian and Independent."[15] Yet, as accommodating as he was with his audience, as intransigent he proved to be, from the very beginning, with their ministers. "The twenty-five-years old Whitefield, cocksure and anything but knowledgeable, set the actual terms of the debate over the New England Way, [saying]: 'Many, nay most that preach, I fear, do not experimentally know Christ'."[16] And so began the uncompromising crusade of the New Lights against the Old Lights and of the New Lights among themselves, an enthusiastic crusade that would end up forever altering the Puritan legacy. But in his first and most successful big tour of the colonies, from New England to Georgia, young and unlearned Whitefield was not alone. Most of the times he preached along well-educated and more level-headed American ministers: in New England under Jonathan Edwards, in Pennsylvania and New Jersey under William and Gilbert Tennent, and in Virginia under Samuel Davies.

If the Great Awakening is to be interpreted "not [as] theological," but from the perspective "of opposing theories of the human psychology,"[17] then the educated revivalists are to be found, unlike Whitefield, somewhere in the middle of the spectrum. They placed themselves between the classical supporters of the idea that reason should control passions and the most extreme Enthusiasts for whom the passions stirred by the Holy Spirit were everything that mattered. They believed "that true sainthood consisted of more than unbridled and insubstantial enthusiasm."[18] Jonathan Edwards, for example, acknowledged that, "the increase in the learning, in itself is a thing to be rejoiced in, because it is a good," yet he was also eager to explain why: "if duly applied, [is] an excellent handmaid to divinity." A few lines later, he felt the need to reinforce the handmaid image: "But yet, when God has sufficiently shown men the insufficiency of human wisdom [...] then may we hope that God will make use of the great increase of learning as a handmaid to religion."[19] And even when Gilbert Tennent was nearing the zenith of bitterness against the Old Lights, after the schism of the Presbyterian Church in 1741, he found a place for reason and understanding amid his defense of passions:

---

[15] Quoted in Edwin Scott Gaustad (1957), *The Great Awakening in New England* (New York: Harper & Brothers), 119.

[16] Stephen Foster (1991), *The Long Argument: English Puritanism and the Shaping of New England Culture, 1570–1700* (Chapel Hill and London: The University of North Carolina Press), 295.

[17] Alan Heimert and Perry Miller, eds. (1967), *The Great Awakening: Documents Illustrating the Crisis and Its Consequences* (Indianapolis and New York: The Bobbs-Merrill Company, Inc.), Introduction, xxxix.

[18] Heimert and Miller, *The Great Awakening*, li.

[19] Jonathan Edwards (1777), "A History of the Work of Redemption" in Heimert and Miller, *The Great Awakening*, 23–24.

We know not that we use any Dialect in inculcating the Terrors of the Law, but what accords with Scripture *and* Reason; or that we endeavor to excite the lower Passions, but *after* the Information of the Understanding, and that by scriptural Incentives: Which is so far from being seditious, that is the Duty of every Gospel Minister.[20]

None of them denied the importance of study. After Edwards's death, Tennent wrote in 1758, "As his genius was extraordinary, so it was greatly improved by long and hard study, by which he treasured up much useful knowledge, both divine and human."[21] Their reasonableness also manifested in the fact that they did not equate spiritual liberation with freedom from any law whatsoever.[22]

Notwithstanding, their language resembled the frightening imagery of the first Puritans, and was fully embraced by the revivalists who followed. According to the New Lights' vivid descriptions, men were, in their natural state, nothing but "poor, filthy worms ... brought from wallowing, like filthy swine, in the mire of our sins," while the unconverted ministers were presented as "these Caterpillars [that] labour to devour every green Thing."[23] From this perspective, it is true that "New Englanders took to Whitefield's message because it was already their message, the message they had been born and bred to hear, newly condensed in content."[24] At first sight, the substance of the sermons between the Old and the New Lights did not differ much.[25] But what, theologically speaking, had happened unknowingly to Whitefield decades before his arrival was already starting to forever alter life in the colonies. This theological change helps explain why the Old Lights' reasonableness was to fall prey to radical Enthusiasts such as the young Whitefield.

Classical covenantal theory started to break down around 1700 with an attack on the church covenant. This is not to say that covenantal theory was on the verge of disappearing, but it would never carry the same weight as when it had been able to create politico-theological communities.[26] The first one to signal a major breach with the former understanding was Jonathan Edwards's grandfather, Solomon Stoddard (1643–1729). Unhappy with the compromise

---

[20] Gilbert Tennent (1741), "Remarks upon a Protestation" in Heimert and Miller, *The Great Awakening*, 171 (emphasis added).

[21] Alan Heimert uses this quote to celebrate the memory of his mentor, Perry Miller, in the dedication of his book, *Religion and the American Mind*. See further.

[22] For a discussion on this point, see Robert N. Bellah (1975), *The Broken Covenant: American Civil Religion in Time of Trial* (New York: The Seabury Press), 19–22.

[23] Edwards, "A History," 13; Gilbert Tennent (1741), "The Danger of an Unconverted Minister" in Heimer and Miller, *The Great Awakening*, 72.

[24] Foster, *The Long Argument*, 296.   [25] Ibid., 306.

[26] The following paragraphs are partially informed by C. C. Goen, ed. (1972), *Jonathan Edwards – The Great Awakening* (New Haven and London: Yale University Press), especially 12–32; by Mark A. Noll (2002), *America's God: From Jonathan Edwards to Abraham Lincoln* (Oxford: Oxford University Press), especially 41–49; and by Glenn A. Moots (2010), *Politics Reformed: The Anglo-American Legacy of Covenant Theology* (Columbia and London: University of Missouri Press), especially 98–112.

of the Half-Way Covenant, and what he perceived as a degradation of the way of life in New England, Stoddard arrived at the conclusion that the only solution for restoring piety was to replace the church covenant with a national covenant (where the "Christian nation" was New England, "the Commonwealth of Israel"). Furthermore, instead of preventing people from partaking of the Lord's Supper, as was the common practice, he recommended that they be forced to do so. Considering what he saw as an increased debauchery in the lives of New Englanders, a rising spirit of commercialism, and a growing separation of politics from the church, it seemed clear to him that the Half-Way approach was not enough. Instead of keeping people out of the church, one should force them in.

Stoddard's solution resembled John Cotton's justification from some seventy years earlier, mentioned in the previous chapter. When discussing with Sir Saltonstall the problem of the unconverted being forced to participate in the religious services and paying taxes, without having a right to vote, Cotton argued:

As for compelling men to worship, that did not make them sinners if the worship was lawful. [...] Better to make men hypocrites than allow them to continue as profane persons. '*Hypocrites give God part of his due, the outward man, but the profane person gives God neither outward nor inward man*'.[27]

However, there was one major difference between the two moments in time. In Cotton's case, the unconverted were supposedly tormented for being unable to be accepted among the saints. By Stoddard's time, it became quite clear that for many, being kept apart from the church, far from being a punishment, became an excuse for getting involved in a wide range of ungodly activities. Tellingly, Stoddard's most famous polemic was *The Inexcusableness of Neglecting the Worship of God, Under a Pretence of Being in an Unconverted Condition* (Boston, 1708). Since the purged individualism, requiring the honest turning of the inside out for purification, proved inefficient even in the softened form of the Half-Way Covenant, Stoddard's solution was to practice a reverse strategy: purging the inner self by forcing the outer self to change. In so doing, one at least gives the inner self a chance for purification. After all – went the argument – the Lord's Supper was a seal of God's covenant with all Christian nations, not only with the truly converted ones.

Mere decades later, his nephew, Jonathan Edwards, took an entirely different approach. By then, Edwards had given up all hopes that the *internal* covenant of grace could be cloaked in any *external* covenant, whether a church or a national covenant. The theologico-political communion of the saints, dreamt up by his forefathers, had proven to be just that – a dream.

---

[27] Quoted John Adair (1982), *Founding Fathers – The Puritans in England and America* (London, Melbourne, Toronto: J.M. Dent & Sons Ltd), 242 (emphasis added). Not surprisingly, the issue of hypocrisy would be hotly debated throughout the Great Awakening. See further.

The "political" or external covenants might have been a solution for the Old Testament, but they became futile in the New one: "The New Testament informs us but of one covenant God enters into with mankind through Christ, and this is the covenant of grace ... [It] affords no more foundations for supposing two real and properly distinct covenants of grace, than it does suppose two sorts of real Christians."[28] In some respects, his approach is reminiscent of that of Roger Williams, from a century before: protect the purity of the church by keeping it free of political interference, even if political interference in this case meant a church or a national covenant. The church was to be composed of saints only, but in this case the covenant of grace did not need to be "reinforced" by a church covenant among the elected ones, although it did require "authentication."

As a result, Edwards ended up reviving the Puritanical purged individualism, according to which the inner self was to be exteriorized for everyone to see and judge. "None ought to be admitted as members of the *visible* church of Christ, but *visible* and professing saints."[29] Hence, it was necessary that one's qualifications "be made so *visible* or *audible* to others, that others may *rationally* judge they are there."[30] In 1742, he even managed the impressive performance of having the people from the town of Northampton form a covenant – yet not a church covenant – in which they promised to behave exemplarily in all relationships with each other, including commercial dealings, avoiding "unchristian bitterness," ill-will, holding secret grudges, occasions "to stir up or gratify a lust of lasciviousness," and so on. But the boldest step came at the end of the document: "And being sensible of our weaknesses, and the deceitfulness of our own hearts, and our proneness to forget our most solemn vows, and lose our resolutions, we promise to be *often strictly examining ourselves* by these promises, especially before the sacrament of the Lord's supper."[31]

Despite his overall conciliatory tone, Edwards became as uncompromising as the first Puritans when it came to tolerating the unconverted: "There are two competitors for the kingdom of this world, *Christ and Satan*; the design of a public profession of religion is, to declare on which side men are."[32] But in 1750, when he insisted that no person would be admitted to the Lord's Supper absent a detailed conversion narrative of saving faith, the community of Northampton, which his grandfather Stoddard had opened communion to

---

[28] Jonathan Edwards (1749), *An Humble Inquiry into the Rules of the Word of God* ... quoted in Noll, *America's God*, 46.

[29] Ibid., 45 (emphases added).   [30] Quoted in Heimert, *Religion*, 131 (emphases added).

[31] Jonathan Edwards (1742), "A Town Repents" in Richard L. Bushman, ed. (1970), *The Great Awakening: Documents on the Revival of Religion, 1740-1745* (New York: Atheneum), 166–169(emphases added).

[32] Jonathan Edwards (1752), *Misrepresentations Corrected and Truth Vindicated, in a Reply to the Rev. Mr. Solomon Williams's Book*, quoted in Noll, *America's God*, 45.

all, decided they had enough. They dismissed Edwards with an overwhelming majority of votes (out of 253, only 23 voted for him to stay).

From a practical perspective – though practicality was never in his mind – Jonathan Edwards should have probably listened to his cousin, Solomon Williams (1700–1776), with whom he had had a heated theological exchange. In his *True State of the Question concerning the Qualifications Necessary to Lawful Communion in the Christian Sacraments*, Williams argued against his cousin and alongside Stoddard that there *were* two covenants, one *external* and one *internal*, and that the first was not conditional on the second. It would be a mistake, he claimed rather shrewdly, to confuse entering "into Covenant, with keeping Covenant."[33] Besides, he asked, how can one truly distinguish the unregenerate from the regenerate, based solely on their own confessions and actions? "If human nature was truly sinful, then was it not capable of manufacturing phony conversion narratives?"[34]

Across these theological subtleties, two interrelated trends remained constant: first, the permanent dismissal of the church covenant; and second, the constant appeal to pushing one's inner self out, thus making the invisible visible, for anyone to be able to see and judge. On the one hand, the dismissal of the church covenant marked the disappearance of the theologico-political community. From then on, one's religious identity would never perfectly overlap with one's political identity. At the same time, it marked "a transition from clerical to lay religion, from the minister as an inherited authority figure to self-empower mobilizer, from the definition of Christianity by doctrine to the definition by piety."[35] The hierarchical understanding of the people as well-ordered society was about to be seriously challenged. On the other hand, as we shall see, the constant pressure to voluntarily disclose one's inner self would eventually end up dismissing it altogether. Slowly but surely, most of the colonists would exchange the purged individualism of their forefathers for the classical, centrifugal one, as part of the process of "Anglicization."[36]

Thus, by the time George Whitefield began his first transcolonial tour of Awakening, the ground was already prepared for the "awakening." It was not difficult for him and for the itinerant ministers that mimicked his strategy to take over from their moderate and learned predecessors. All they had to do was to get rid of the increasingly sophisticated dogmatic issues and to rely almost exclusively on the "experience of grace." Tens of thousands gathered to listen to his sermons. According to Whitefield's *Journals*, on October 1740, while preaching for a few days at Edwards's meetinghouse, even "[g]ood

---

[33] Solomon Williams (1751), *The True State of the Question* ... (Boston). Quoted in Noll, *America's God*, 46.
[34] Moots, *Politics Reformed*, 110.   [35] Noll, *America's God*, 44.
[36] Nancy L. Rhoden (2013), "The American Revolution (I) – The Paradox of Atlantic Integration" in Stephen Foster, ed., *British North America in the Seventeenth and Eighteenth Centuries* (Oxford: Oxford University Press), 255–287.

Mr. Edwards wept during the whole time of exercise" and "the people were equally affected."[37] Just a few years later, Jonathan Edwards would weep for an entirely different set of reasons, but for the time being, the Great Awakening was able to impress even the most cultivated minds of New England.

People would convert by the hundreds after just one moving sermon. It was, by all accounts, an intoxicating experience and an instantaneous gratification. As an exponent of the Old Lights, Charles Chauncy was horrified by this view: "[H]ow precarious that Religion must be, which has its Rise from the Passions, and not any thorow Change in the Understanding and Will." The terror this sermon instilled in the audience produced "strange Effects upon the Body such as a swooning away . . . Shriekings and Screamings; convulsion-like Tremblings and Agitations, Strugglings and Tumblings, which in some Instances have been attended with Indecencies I shan't not mention."[38] These new converts "needed to do something appropriate to the kind of conversion they had experienced. They found it in many places by questioning the credentials of old church members."[39]

Once again, compromise was no longer an option. But if before people were unwilling to compromise for dogmatic reasons, now they were unwilling to compromise over a minister's style of preaching, and hence over his claimed sainthood. "Old Lights were not allowed the modest distinction John Winthrop had courteously awarded Roger Williams, the status of *misguided saints* whose works bore evil fruits without prejudicing their own acknowledged election."[40] As a result, over two hundred schisms took place in New England alone during the Great Awakening, and in parts of Connecticut and Western Massachusetts these religious divisions turned into political factions as well.[41]

By 1750 the split over the Awakening was the dominant circumstance of New England, and each side denied the fundamental legitimacy of the position held by the other. Nor was this merely a split at the top. About one in five of the churches in Massachusetts and one in three in Connecticut suffered outright schisms over the Awakening, mostly in form of enthusiasts for the revival either seceding to form Strict Congregational churches, evangelical in piety and Morelian in polity, or going over to the new Separate Baptists.[42]

Many of the Old Lights preachers lost their income and were forced to move out, including, as we have seen, Jonathan Edwards. As a Saybrook minister sorrowfully observed, "we are breaking to pieces in our Churches, very fast in Connecticut."[43] The tables had turned. Almost overnight, the ministers had lost their position of authority inside the churches, and the believers took over.

---

[37] George Whitefield (1960), *Journals* (London), 477 – quoted in Goen, *Jonathan Edwards*, 49.
[38] Quoted in Gaustad, *The Great Awakening*, 94.   [39] Foster, *The Long Argument*, 300.
[40] Ibid., 299 (emphasis added).
[41] Jeremy Gregory (2013), "'Establishment' and 'Dissent' in British North America: Organizing Religion in the New World" in Foster, *British North America*; Foster, *The Long Argument*, 310.
[42] Foster, *The Long Argument*, 291.   [43] Quoted in Gaustad, *The Great Awakening*, 110.

According to some scholars, what was awakened in 1740 was nothing less than "the spirit of American democracy."[44] Christianity became democratic, reshaped "by common people who molded it in their own image."[45] It was the discovery of religious populism.[46]

Not everyone embraced this development. For many of the Old Lights, the idea that the people are a mere collection of equal individuals to be guided by a majority of votes was deeply disturbing. Some were worried that "[t]he elective dictatorship of the wise and virtuous could give way to the still more formidable dictatorship of the many."[47] Jonathan Mayhew was one of them: "[Since] the truth and right have a real existence in nature, independent of the sentiments and practices of men, they do not necessarily follow the multitude or the major part." The idea that truth was just a social convention determined by a majority vote was abhorrent, for "the multitude may do evil, and the many judge falsly."[48] Unsurprisingly, Mayhew conceived of "the people" not horizontally, but vertically, as a well-structured whole. In his famous *Discourse Concerning Unlimited Submission and Non-Resistance to the Higher Powers*, upon the occasion of the centennial of the execution of Charles I, he alluded to a political compact between the rulers and the ruled. He argued not just for the right of "the whole body politic" to rebel but for their duty to do so whenever the ruler became a tyrant. Otherwise, "'tis treason against common sense; 'tis treason against God."[49]

Yet, the fact that Mayhew was a Patriot who vehemently opposed the Stamp Act, coined the phrase "no taxation without representation,"[50] and urged common action among the colonies in the famous sermon *The Snare Broken* (1766) cannot be directly related to his anti-populist views, as tempting as it might be to draw such a connection.[51] Thomas Darling, too, was disgusted by

---

[44] Heimert and Miller, *The Great Awakening*, lxi.

[45] Nathan O. Hatch (1989), *The Democratization of American Christianity* (New Haven: Yale University Press), 9.

[46] I borrow this expression from Ronald P. Formisano (2008), *For the People: American Populist Movements from the revolution to 1850s* (Chapel Hill: University of North Carolina Press), 45.

[47] Stephen Foster (1971), *Their Solitary Way: The Puritan Social Ethic in the First Settlement in New England* (New Haven and London: Yale University Press), 168.

[48] Quoted in Heimert and Miller, *The Great Awakening*, 576.

[49] Jonathan Mayhew (1750), "A Discourse Concerning Unlimited Submission and Non-resistance to the Higher Powers ..." in Bernard Bailyn, ed. (1965) *Pamphlets of the American Revolution, 1750-1776* (Cambridge, MA: The Belknap Press of Harvard University Press), 238–239.

[50] The New England Baptist leader, Isaac Backus, ended up accusing the Congregationalists of hypocrisy. They were claiming "no taxation without representation" while themselves taxing Baptists and other non-Congregationalists. See Gregory, "'Establishment' and 'Dissent.'"

[51] Despite the overwhelming evidence to the contrary, some scholars still consider Mayhew a partisan of the idea that people are nothing but a collection of individuals equally entitled to the right to rebel. See, for example, William T. Reddinger (2016), "The American Revolution, Roman 13, and the Anglo Tradition of Reformed Protestant Resistance Theory," *American Political Thought: A Journal of Ideas, Institutions and Culture*, 5, 359–390.

the idea of bowing to the preferences of the multitude and of a people conceived as a collection of self-interested individuals. Although some ministers were suggesting just that, Darling, while starting from the same premises as Mayhew, ended up in the Loyalist camp: "Who are they that affirm, that the only Criterion of Duty to God is Self-Interest? Who are the Men who say, that the natural Tendency which Thing have to promote our own Interests, is the sole Criterion of moral Good and Evil, Truth and Falsehood, Duty and Sin?"[52] For the time being, the clash within the Great Awakening was not between Patriots-to-be and Loyalists-to-be. It was between two competing visions of "the people," like two branches sprung from the same Puritan tree.

The tensions flaring up between the horizontal, egalitarian, and populist apprehension of the people on the one hand and the vertical, hierarchical, and aristocratic one on the other concluded in a compromise. The Awakening died down as suddenly as it had begun, and the reasons for it were rather mundane. First, it was a matter of sheer numbers; the itinerant ministers ran out of people to convert. The entire movement had been based on the spectacle of dramatic conversions, and now the pool of potential candidates to Awaken had shrunk drastically. The already converted could no longer fuel it, for they could not muster the necessary attention.[53] The second reason was institutional; after ignoring "the cultural and ecclesiastical institutions that had made their miracle possible," the New Lights came to the realization that they were cannibalizing themselves.[54] Scarred by the excesses of the Awakening, people left the Congregationalists in troves, finding refuge either in a more rationalistic religion, heavily influenced by the Scottish Enlightenment, or in the ordered liturgy of the Church of England.[55] "From the 1690s to the 1740s, the Church of England was the fastest growing denomination in British America. By the time of the Revolution it had achieved an unprecedented degree of predominance in the colonies."[56] Moderates like Tennent worked hard to institutionally reconcile the Old and the New Lights and to secure a place for Congregationalists in an increasingly diverse religious landscape. It was too little, too late.

3.2 IN THE WAKE OF THE AWAKENING

By the second half of the 1750s, religious unity was a thing of the past. Although the colonies of New England and Virginia still maintained a certain degree of religious uniformity – the former Evangelical and Congregational, the

---

[52] Heimert and Miller, *The Great Awakening*, 576–577.   [53] Foster, *The Long Argument*, 297.

[54] Ibid., 297. It is no accident that the Quakers, who knew firsthand the dangers of extreme "enthusiasm," were the only denomination that remained largely unscathed throughout the Awakening.

[55] Gregory, "'Establishment' and 'Dissent'," 158. See also Gaustad, *The Great Awakening*, 117.

[56] Evan Haefeli (2013), "Toleration and Empire: The Origins of American Religious Pluralism" in Foster, *British North America*, 128.

latter Anglican – no one would ever again claim that "a people" is defined both religiously and politically. From then on, individuals could and would shop for preachers and denominations in almost consumer-like fashion. For Great Britain this was a welcome development, benefiting imperial interests. This might appear counterintuitive, yet the rulers of the empire knew from historical precedent that while the Church of England was beneficial to England, religious diversity in the colonies better served the interests of London. "England's rulers, in different ways and at different times, felt that a religiously diverse population, deprived of the unity of an established church, could be a reliable instrument of the empire."[57] They were proven right some decades later, during the Revolutionary War, when "pluralism produced more Loyalism than religious unity did. [...] The colonies with the most pluralism were least likely to separate from Britain,"[58] while the colonies of New England and Virginia were in the forefront of the independence movement.[59] Unsurprisingly, the more homogenous the colonial identity, the less the colonists were willing to compromise with the metropole.

As I mentioned earlier, many scholars argue that, by destroying local allegiances, infusing a new sense of equality, and recreating a sense of American exceptionalism, the Great Awakening helped forge American nationalism that would eventually end up in the Declaration of Independence.[60] However, the story is more complicated. In the first half of the eighteenth century, the unmistakable trend in the colonies was toward imperial integration (Anglicization and metropolization). Colonists became increasingly British-like, mimicking British architecture, religion, and – most importantly – British politics.[61] Once the purged individualism was lost, it came to be replaced with the classic British centrifugal individualism, in which *forum externum*, the outer self, was the only significant one. Sin was no longer visualized as internal, but rather as external. It became vice, while salvation became virtue.[62]

Under the influence of the Scottish Enlightenment, promoted by people such as Witherspoon or Hutchinson, even private virtue acquired a public dimension. For Benjamin Rush, educated in Scotland, "private virtue requires a collective effort to cultivate."[63] As a result of this process of "externalization," compromise – a word largely ignored by the ministers of the Great Awakening – returned to use with its typically positive British connotation, as a beneficial

---

[57] Haefeli, "Toleration and Empire," 134.   [58] Ibid., 134.

[59] Barry Alan Shain, ed. (2014), *The Declaration of Independence in Historical Context: American State Papers, Petitions, Proclamations & Letters of the Delegates in the First National Congress* (New Haven and London: Yale University Press), 10.

[60] See, among others, Heimert and Miller, *The Great Awakening*; Noll, *America's God*; Moots, *Politics Reformed*.

[61] Rhoden, "The American Revolution," 258.

[62] Benjamin T. Lynerd (2014), *Republican Theology: The Civil Religion of American Evangelicals* (Oxford: Oxford University Press), 46.

[63] Ibid., 90.

method for solving disagreements.[64] Thus, in 1745, for example, Sempronius
T. Gracchus mentioned with satisfaction that "[t]he Scotch generously con-
sented to a compromise, that they might secure the Liberty of that Nation."[65]

Politically speaking, in the decades following the Glorious Revolution
of 1688, "the oligarchic orders that dominated the colonies [...] faced a
straightforward problem. What would the new imperial order mean to those
living on the empire's far fringes?" The solution was to revive the political
contract theory that was used in 1688, but with a twist. Faithful to the
Congregationalist tradition, John Wise argued for allowing different institutional settings for different parts of the empire. "New England, he believed,
could be in the empire without being of the empire. [...] [T]he imperial fringe's
enthusiasm for protestant monarchy contrasted sharply with the metropolitan
center's apathy toward the monarch."[66] Conversely, England's support for
parliamentary supremacy became increasingly unpopular in the colonies, and
for good reason.

"The more intra-colonial politics looked like its British domestic equivalent,
the more members of the colonial legislatures might begin to conceive themselves as British parliaments in miniature ... and consequently deeply resent an
intervention in their affairs from either Whitehall or Westminster."[67] Across
the Atlantic, they used the same language of freedom and rights, while referring
to the same constitution of Great Britain. "Colonial Whigs did not fight for
American rights. They fought for English rights."[68] In a post-Lockean era, it is
tempting to equate these rights with natural individual rights. This would be
historically inaccurate, because "the crisis that led to the War of Independence
was concerned primarily with British corporate, not individual rights, and was
viewed by the majority of the colonists through the lens of British
constitutional, not abstract natural rights."[69] The same applies to the concept
of liberty. As we saw even in the case of the more moderates New Lights, liberty
was understood as encompassing both rights for the individual and duties
for society. The rhetoric of liberty, which increased in intensity after the Stamp
Act crisis of 1765, built on the same arguments made previously in England

---

[64] After surveying hundreds of pages with sermons and pamphlets from the Great Awakening time
period, I was unable to find a single instance in which "compromise" is used. This surprising
absence is telling in itself.
[65] Sempronius T. Gracchus (1745), *The American Magazine and Historical Chronicle*
(1743–1746), (Boston, July 2, 1745), 277.
[66] Brendan McConville (2006), *The King's Three Faces: The Rise and Fall of Royal America, 1688-
1776* (Chapel Hill: University of North Carolina Press), 40, 43.
[67] Rhoden, "The American Revolution," 263.
[68] John Phillip Reid (1989), *The Concept of Representation in the Age of the American Revolution*
(Chicago and London: The University of Chicago Press), 4.
[69] Shain, *The Declaration of Independence*, 4–5. See also John Phillip Reid (1988), *The Concept of
Liberty in the Age of the American Revolution* (Chicago: The University of Chicago Press), 2.

during the excise crisis of 1733 and the cider and perry excise of 1763.[70] The call was for "ordered resistance," not for rebellion, and "through all their proceedings, the Sons of Liberty insisted that they intended to uphold, not overturn, the established government."[71]

Although the parties "disagreed about what coercive measures constituted a threat to liberty and what defensive measures were justified to protect liberty [...] what they agree on was the rhetoric of liberty."

That fact becomes apparent when we compare the appeals to liberty by Lord North with the appeals of the pro-American opposition in the House of Commons, or the writings of the champion of liberty, Richard Price, with the commentaries of the conservative jurist, Sir William Blackstone. They used the same slogans because they thought similar constitutional thoughts and shared common political values.[72]

Paradoxically, such ideological similarities did not make compromises between the parties easier. On the contrary, they made them impossible, for the arguments were framed by both sides as a matter of principle, much on the patterns of the confrontations between the Puritans and the Dissidents, or between the New and the Old Lights. "Colonial patriots drew their arguments from the same wellspring of ideas as apologists for British policy, each side basing their claims on principles of British liberty so fundamental as to forbid any significant compromise. This shared commitment to the unalterable led to intransigence and paranoia on both sides."[73] Each side pretended to speak in the name of "the people," which, in their eyes, gave them the right to coerce their opponents; after all, the rights of the people had preeminence over the rights of a few individuals. As George Mason put it, "every member of society is in duty bound to contribute to the safety and good of the whole."

And when the subject is of such importance as liberty and happiness of a country, every inferior consideration, as well as the inconvenience of a few individuals, must give place to it; nor is it any hardship upon them as themselves and their posterity are to partake of the benefits resulting from it. Objections of the same kind might be made to the most useful institutions.[74]

Among the "inconveniences" brought forward by this increased unwillingness to compromise was the freedom of the press – one of the first to be sacrificed, not by the Loyalists, but mainly by the Patriots. The first colonial newspaper, *The Public Occurrences*, appeared in September 25, 1690, only to be suppressed twenty-four hours later. The second was published in 1704, but by 1774 the colonists had access to some forty-eight newspapers. Between 1760 and 1775, the newspaper press was expanding nearly twice as fast as

[70] Reid, *The Concept of Liberty*, 4.
[71] Pauline Maier (1972), *From Resistance to Revolution: Colonial Radicals and the Development of American Opposition to Britain, 1765–1776* (New York: Alfred A. Knopf), 96.
[72] Reid, *The Concept of Liberty*, 9.   [73] Rhoden, "The American Revolution," 277.
[74] Quoted in Maier, *From Resistance to Revolution*, 138.

the population.[75] "News, like much else in Atlantic culture, was Janus-faced, creating Imperial loyalties and a consciousness of a distinctive American identity at one and the same time."[76] While reading about the recent political developments across the ocean, the colonists started to think more and more about how these could possibly affect their local interests. It was these concerns that would begin to forge an American identity. Still, as the tensions grew between the colonies and the metropole, most of the publishers tried to maintain a neutral voice and to allow a variety of opinions to be expressed. Even the political *Independent Adviser* published by Samuel Adams began by claiming neutrality:

Our present political state affords matter for a variety of thoughts to insert whatever of general interest might appear proper to publish. We are of no party, nor would we promote any narrow designs. We are ourselves free, and our paper shall be free – free as the constitution we enjoy – free to Truth – Good manners and Good sense, and at the same time free from all licentious reflections, Insolence and Abuse. (January 14, 1748)[77]

Such claims, however, grew increasingly empty after 1765 and the Stamp Act Crisis, when the colonists began dividing themselves into two camps. "Despite their libertarian rhetoric, American resistance leaders proved unwilling to tolerate opposition from the press. Since press freedom existed for the purpose of protecting liberty, they reasoned, there should be no freedom for a press that opposed liberty."[78] Under the protection of anonymity, a handful of activists could assume the role of "public," speaking in the name of the people.[79] Quite soon, it became impossible to satisfy both the Patriots and the Loyalists, so the policy of neutrality was no longer an option. Publishers were forced to take sides, becoming increasingly biased in order to avoid "being ostracized from their communities and harassed by mobs and local authorities."[80] A compromising attitude became a thing of the past. It was no longer possible "to hear and weigh everything that is fairly adduced on either side of the question with equal attention and care," as a Loyalist paper, *Boston Post-Bay Advertise*, claimed as late as February 20, 1775.[81] The expression "fake news" was yet to be coined, but the propaganda machines on both sides already knew how to employ it.[82]

---

[75] Jeffrey L. Pasley (2001), *"The Tyranny of Printers": Newspapers Politics in the Early American Republic* (Charlottesville and London: University of Virginia Press), 33.

[76] Rhoden, "The American Revolution," 266.

[77] Sidney Kobre (1960), *The Development of the Colonial Newspaper* (Gloucester, MA: Peter Smith), 50.

[78] Pasley, *"The Tyranny of Printers,"* 34. See also Bernard Bailyn and John B. Hench, eds. (1980), *The Press & The American Revolution* (Worchester: American Antiquarian Society).

[79] Ibid., 35.   [80] Ibid., 37.

[81] Quoted in Bailyn and Hench, *The Press & The American Revolution*, 239.

[82] For troves of examples of how both sides consciously and deliberately manipulated and distorted the truth, see Philip Davidson (1941), *Propaganda and the American Revolution, 1763–1783* (Chapel Hill: The University of North Carolina Press).

Still, the question remains: If Patriots and Loyalists were so similar in their justifications, both across the Atlantic and within the colonies, how can one explain the development, in a matter of years, of a peculiar political culture in the colonies? "What differences were there between the political processes in 18th century America and 18th century England that could explain the significantly different receptions of the same political ideas?"[83] What made possible "the convergence of the Puritan covenant pattern and the Montequieuan republican pattern,"[84] their "republican theology,"[85] the "theistic rationalism,"[86] "the American synthesis" between Protestantism, republican ideology, and commonsense moral reasoning of Scottish Enlightenment pedigree,[87] or "the American Amalgam"[88] – to name just a few well-known academic descriptions of this peculiarity?

The clear majority of scholars agree on one key factor: "the one clear exception [to all these similarities] was representation [that] departed from British perceptions."[89] Before the Stamp Act Crisis of 1765, the colonists accepted practically without question the authority of the British Parliament. When a year before the crisis, in 1764, the Connecticut Assembly asserted that "[b]y the Common Law of England, every commoner hath a right not to be subjected to Laws made without his consent," this did not *yet* mean that the colonists thought they were not properly represented in the British Parliament.[90] The concept of "consent" was still largely virtual, as the case of Francis Plowden, a conservative common lawyer, demonstrates. As a Roman Catholic, he was not eligible to vote, but this did not prevent him from boasting that "the British constitution is founded upon a democratic basis, the free-will and consent of a free people."[91] Colonists' faith in the Parliament was also not easily shaken. During the crisis of 1765, even the most radical Sons of Liberty kept "blaming the King's servants for the American grievances while acquitting the parliament and, with even greater rhetorical emphasis, the King,"[92] Only after the new Parliament of 1768 not only endorsed the king's condemnation of Massachusetts but asked for punitive measures did the colonists start losing faith in the Parliament's ability to represent their interests.

"Representing their interests" is a key phrase in this context, for it signals how the split in the understanding of representation across the Atlantic began.

[83] Bernard Bailyn (1968), *The Origins of American Politics* (New York: Alfred A. Knopf), x.
[84] Bellah, *The Broken Covenant*, 27.   [85] Lynerd, *Republican Theology*.
[86] Gregg L. Frazer (2012), *The Religious Beliefs of America's Founders: Reason, Revelation, and Revolution* (Lawrence: University Press of Kansas).
[87] Noll, *America's God*.
[88] Michael Zuckert (2005), "Natural Rights and Imperial Constitutionalism: The American Revolution and the Development of the American Amalgam" in Ellen Frankel Paul, Fred D. Miller Jr., and Jeffrey Paul, eds., *Natural Rights Liberalism from Locke to Nozick* (Cambridge: Cambridge University Press), 27–55.
[89] Reid, *The Concept of Liberty*, 4.   [90] Quoted in Reed, *The Concept of Representation*, 12.
[91] Ibid., 13.   [92] Maier, *From Resistance to Revolution*, 106.

In Britain, it was generally accepted that virtually every Englishman was represented in the Parliament. "The maxim that 'the consent of the Parliament is taken to be every man's consent' was certainly strengthened by the notion that a member of the House of Commons represented every citizen and not a single constituency."[93] Thus, there was no real difference between those living in England and those living in the colonies – they were all equally represented.[94] As Thomas Whately put it in 1765, "none are actually, all are virtually represented in Parliament."[95] Even for Jonathan Mayhew, the Parliament did not *rebel* against Charles I, for a people cannot rebel against itself, "[a]nd who so proper to make this resistance as the lords and commons – the whole representative body of the people – guardians of the public welfare?"[96] It followed, logically, that no MP was tied to the wishes of his electors, borough or county, since, in the words of Baron Rovers, "[e]very Englishman of every rank, has a claim to his services."[97] As a matter of fact, in order to be elected an MP, there was no requirement to be resident of the boroughs or counties in which the elections took place. Judge Spencer Cowper confessed to Watkins Williams Wynn that "he had never been in the borough he represented in parliament, nor had he ever seen or spoke with any of his electors."[98]

The American colonists, however, were no longer satisfied with this virtual representation of "every Englishman." They did not want to be represented qua individuals; they wanted their group interest to be represented.[99] As a result, they "drifted backward, as it were, towards the medieval forms of attorneyship in representation."[100] They did not invent a new theory of representation, but instead chose to adopt an older one.[101] The colonists believed that "if the elected representative was in theory accountable to all the people of Great Britain, he was in practice accountable to no one."[102] The long-standing practice of instructions strengthened their theory of representation by attorney as well. In order to check the power of the governors appointed by the crown, throughout the entire period leading to the Revolutionary War, local leaders sought to increase the weight of the colonial assemblies, first by expanding the electoral franchise and, second, by holding the representatives directly

---

[93] Reid, *The Concept of Representation*, 80.

[94] For an excellent discussion of this topic and a trove of significant quotes, see Eric Nelson (2014), *The Royalist Revolution: Monarchy and the American Founding* (Cambridge, MA: The Belknap Press of Harvard University), 80–97.

[95] Quoted in Bailyn, *The Ideological Origins*, 166.

[96] Mayhew, "A Discourse Concerning Unlimited Submission," 239.

[97] Quoted in Reid, *The Concept of Representation*, 81.   [98] Ibid., 82.

[99] The theory of shared interests being represented was present in England as well, only, unlike the case of the colonies, very few interests were actually identified. For a lengthy discussion on this topic and a wealth of quoted from that time period, see Reed, *The Concept of Representation*, especially chapter 4.

[100] Bailyn, *The Ideological Origins*, 164.   [101] Reid, *The Concept of Representation*, 9.

[102] Ibid., 81.

accountable to their constituencies. The voters of Portsmouth, New Hampshire, told their representative that "the giving Instructions ... in affairs of Public Concern ... is a Privilege which must be highly valued by every true Patriot, as giving each Representative an Opportunity of knowing the Mind of their Constituents, to which he ought to pay great Regard." In a private letter, Samuel Adams made a similar argument: "It is a very common practice for this town [of Boston] to instruct their representatives, which among other good purposes serves to communicate their sentiments and spirit to the other towns."[103]

Important as it is, the difference between the "virtual" representation of "every Englishman" and the "actual" representation of local corporate interests does not, in itself, help explain the development of a peculiar American "republican theology," the "American synthesis," or the "American amalgam."[104] In order to understand this peculiarity, one has to clarify the crucial yet oftentimes overlooked distinction between the social and the political compact. Thanks to the Puritans' legacy of the bidimensional covenant, both were present simultaneously in the colonists' political thinking, each – as we have seen in the previous chapter – with a different understanding of "the people." After all, "the hundred years after 1760 were indisputably a period of brilliant innovation and of the extension of New England influence outside of its home territory."[105]

3.3 "HOW THEN DO WE NEW ENGLANDERMEN DERIVE OUR LAWS?"

"American revolutionists, to be sure, hardly qualified as expert contract theorists," for "nearly all failed ... to distinguish between the separate contracts of society and government," even though their "sole actual concern was the contract of government."[106]

Many Whigs, however, believed that their notion of such a contract had come from John Locke. This may well not be true, for Locke's "contract" has been primarily concerned with an original agreement between all members of society to form a political entity; he left implicit the original and subsequent agreement between rulers and ruled.[107]

---

[103] Quoted in Reid, *The Concept of Representation*, 99–100.

[104] I use quotes for "virtual" and "actual" representation in order to signal that these are mostly theoretical labels. In reality, any representation, no matter how "actual" and descriptive, remains largely "virtual."

[105] Foster, *The Long Argument*, 311.

[106] Thad W. Tate (1965), "The Social Contract in America, 1774-1787: Revolutionary Theory as a Conservative Instrument," *The William and Mary Quarterly*, 22:3, 376.

[107] Jerrilyn Greene Marston (1987), *King and Congress: The Transfer of Political Legitimacy, 1774-1776* (Princeton: Princeton University Press), 17.

Bailyn, too, observes that during that era, "[t]he citations [of the classics] are plentiful, but the knowledge they reflect is at times superficial. Locke is cited often with precision on points of political theory, but at other times he is referred to in most offhand way, as he could be relied on the support anything the writers happened to be arguing."[108] This is not to say that there are no exceptions. Reid, for example, makes clear that one legal source used by the Patriots to defend their collective rights was "the original compact." "The original compact, not the social compact, was meant, the contract of government between rulers and the ruled, not the contract by which people agreed to enter into a society."[109]

Nevertheless, one should not judge the Patriots too harshly. After all, even today, many politicians and American scholars alike fail to distinguish between the two theories or dismiss the distinctions as merely "technical."[110] When William Clinton launched his *New Covenant*, meant to be "a solemn agreement between the people and their government," he also made reference to the fact that "the Founders outlined our first *social* compact *between government and their people*."[111] He most likely inspired Obama to claim in his Farewell Address that "we need to forge a new social compact," in the same way in which Newt Gingrich's *Contract with America* was said to inspire Donald Trump's *Contract with the American Voter*. In all cases, the description is of a governmental or political contract, while the label used is that of a social compact.

For their part, contemporary scholars know very well that while the political contract understands the people as a hierarchically structured corporation (*ut universis*), contracting with the rulers for the benefit of the whole, the social compact conceptualizes "the people" as a collection of equal individuals (*ut singulis*), ruled by a government of their choice, by majority of wills, and meant to protect individual rights. This awareness does not prevent many scholars from conflating the two under the generic label of "contract/compact theory," or from directly subsuming the former to the latter, thus remaining heavily indebted to the language of social contract and individual natural rights.[112] When speaking about the First Continental Congress, Brendan

---

[108] Bailyn, *The Ideological Origins*, 28–29. Notably, Bailyn himself tends to conflate the social and governmental compacts, usually mentioning them together in the same context.

[109] Reed, *The Concept of Liberty*, 24.

[110] Robin W. Lowin (1984) "Equality and Covenant Theology," *Journal of Law and Religion*, 2:2., 242.

[111] Speech given at Georgetown University, on October 23, 1991 (emphasis added). The *Contract with America* was also meant "to restore the bonds of trust between the people and their elected officials."

[112] E.g., Edwin G. Barrows and Michael Wallace (1972), "The American Revolution: The Ideology and Psychology of National Liberation," *Perspectives in America History*, 6:193, 250–251; Michael P. Zuckert (2003), "Social Compact, Common Law, and the American Amalgam" in Ronald J. Pestritto and Thomas G. West, eds., *The American Founding and the Social Compact*

McConville, for example, states that "the committee members increasingly maintained that the social contract was dissolved," while it is clear from the context that he is actually referring to the political contract between the colonies and the king.[113]

In order to understand this anomaly, one has to remember that the Puritans' covenantal theory developed simultaneously in two directions. In the horizontal one, a group of individuals had to unanimously consent to form a theologico-political community. It was not just a new society, but a new "people."[114] But once created, this people was understood as an organic, hierarchically structured whole, much like the medieval *universitates* had been understood. From a collection of individuals (*ut singulis*), the people became a corporation (*ut universis*). The refining of details in the new constitution as well as the running of the government was voluntarily entrusted to the hands of a natural aristocracy of the wise and the virtuous.[115] As *universitas*, the people made a vertical covenant with their rulers, in which they retained the right to change the rulers whenever they thought the rulers failed to fulfill their mission to care for the whole.

The legacy of this dual understanding of both the contract theory and of the people allowed future generations to embrace both with almost equal fervor, while also adapting them when necessary. Therefore, the Americans saw no major contradiction between the British constitutional tradition, the Lockean social contract theory, the Montesquieuan republicanism, the Scottish Enlightenment, and the corporate responsibility of a people in the eyes of a God who would reward public virtue and would punish public sin. If it was an "amalgam" or a "synthesis" it was not an artificial one, as the words might suggest, but one with a long pedigree, in which – scholarly claims, such as Bailyn's, to the contrary – one can discern, even if the contours are blurred, "a coherent intellectual pattern."[116]

While scholars usually contrast the *active* liberty in civic humanism or in the classical republican paradigm (to participate in the political decision-making process) with the *passive* liberty in the natural rights tradition (a liberty that

---

(Lanham and Oxford: Lexington Books); Brendan McConville (2006), *The King's Three Faces: The Rise & Fall of Royal America, 1688–1776* (Chapel Hill: University of North Carolina Press); Mark Hulliung (2007), *The Social Contract in America: From the revolution to the Present Age* (Lawrence: University Press of Kansas); Glenn A. Moots (2010), *Politics Reformed – The Anglo-American Legacy of Covenant Theology* (Columbia and London: University of Missouri Press); Eric Nelson (2014), *The Royalist Revolution – Monarchy and the American Founding* (Cambridge, MA: The Belknap Press of Harvard University Press); Thomas G. West (2017), *The Political Theory of the American Founding: Natural Rights, Public Policy, and the Moral Condition of Freedom* (Cambridge: Cambridge University Press).

[113] McConville, *The King's Three Faces*, 291.
[114] Donald S. Lutz (1988), *The Origins of American Constitutionalism* (Baton Rouge: Louisiana State University Press).
[115] Foster, *The Long Argument*.   [116] Bailyn, *The Ideological Origins*, 33.

may be possessed without political activity),[117] the two people's bodies approach, of Puritan descent, offers a solution to this apparent conundrum. Using this approach, one can understand why the Patriots drew on both populist and anti-populist arguments.[118] In the horizontal dimension of the covenant – the one that resembles social contract theory – the people's role, *qua* multitude, is reduced to consent to the formation of the political body and to vote to choose their representatives. However, in the vertical dimension of the covenant, the one that sees people as a corporate entity contracting with the rulers, the degree of participation is determined, as in the medieval *universitates*, by one's place and role in this hierarchical whole. Thus, the entire period of the founding is marked by two different kind of fears: on the one hand, the fear of the licentious mob, the people *qua* headless multitude whose strength relies on numbers; and on the other, the fear of unchecked power and the corruption of hypocritical leaders pretending to rule for the common good.[119] Once conceived of as distinct, each of the people's two bodies became threatening.

Read from this perspective, the writings from the era appear in a new light. In order to confer coherence to their arguments, authors had to modify and adapt parts of the claims of one school of thought so they would not contradict the claims of another. For this reason, the Lockean social contract theory and its corollary, individual natural rights, although popular, were never presented in their "pure" forms. First, as we have seen, the claim was not for individual, but rather for corporate rights, in accordance with the political contract understanding of the people *qua* corporation. Second, the idea that the sole or even main purpose of government was the defense of private interest, instead of the common good, was strongly rejected, for it ran against the basic tenets of both republican and covenantal virtue. In his *Two Discourses on Liberty*, Nathaniel Niles, follower of Jonathan Edwards, argued that such "is the maxim on which pirates and gangs of robbers live in a kind of units."

If we go on this maxim, if we suppose that is a well founded government which has its foundation in private interest, we can by no means blame the tyrant for holding absolute dominion, without condemning ourselves; nor can the tyrant blame his subjects for their rebellion, whenever they apprehend rebellion will be their greatest emolument.[120]

---

[117] See, for example, in no particular order, Joyce Appleby, J. H. Hexter, J. G. A. Pocock, Bernard Bailyn, Phillip Reid, Jack P. Greene, Michael Zuckert, Thomas Pangle, and Benjamin T. Lynerd, to name just a few.

[118] Ronald P. Formisano (2008), *For the People: American Populist Movements from the revolution to the 1850s* (Chapel Hill: The University of North Carolina Press), 20.

[119] See, for example, Reid, *The Concept of Liberty*, 35.

[120] Nathaniel Niles (1774), *Two Discourses on Liberty*, in Charles S. Hyneman and Donald S. Lutz, eds. (1983), *American Political Writing during the Founding Era, 1760–1805* (Indianapolis: Liberty Press), 262.

In a similar vein, Samuel Adams, who envisioned America as a "Christian Sparta," claimed that virtue is the best weapon: "We may look up to Armies for our Defence, but Virtue is our best Security. It is not possible that any State shd (sic) long remain free, where Virtue is not supremely honord (sic)."[121] Gordon Woods's "commercial republic" would have to wait a few more decades before coming into existence.[122]

Furthermore, since virtue, by definition, is not distributed equally, and cannot be delegated to someone else to represent it, it is notably absent from both Hobbes's and Locke's theories; nevertheless, it is central to the Whigs' political theory.[123] According to the Patriots, men are "equally free," not "free *and* equal" as the later formulations would have it. John Tucker pleaded in 1771 in favor of a government "consistent with that natural freedom, to which all have an equal claim,"[124] and the delegates of the *Essex Result* called for in 1778, "Let us be equally free." Article I of the constitution of New Hampshire also read: "All men are born *equally free and independent*; therefore, all government of right originates from the people, is founded in consent and instituted for the general good."[125] John Cartwright, a famous British supporter of the American cause to the extent that he refused a promotion in order to avoid fighting in the Revolutionary War, also claimed that "Equal Liberty [is] God's eternal law."[126]

Since equality in freedom could only encourage public virtue, the connection with covenantal theory – albeit one severely modified in the wake of the Great Awakening – was almost natural. "Americans were as likely to argue for independence from England on grounds of preserving American virtue as they were on grounds of freedom from tyranny."[127] "Of the twenty-nine sermons published by Massachusetts clergy from 1777 to 1783, twenty-two reminded the listeners of their covenant and called them to virtue and piety. Clergy in the Middle Colonies were also conversant in the use of covenantal political theology."[128] They decried corruption, claimed corporate responsibility in the eyes of God, and adopted a providential look on history, as Samuel Langdon,

---

[121] Ibid., 31.

[122] See Gordon Wood (1998) [1969], *The Creation of the American Republic, 1776–1787* (Chapel Hill and London: University of North Carolina Press).

[123] See Gary Rosen (1996), "James Madison and the Problem of Founding," *The Review of Politics*, 58:3, 561–595.

[124] John Tucker (1771), *An Election Sermon*, in Hyneman and Lutz, *American Political Writing*, 162.

[125] *A Collection of the Constitutions of the Thirteen United States* (1786) (New Hampshire: Published by order of Congress), 3 (emphasis added).

[126] Quoted in Reid, *The Concept of Liberty*, 113.

[127] Donald S. Lutz (1980), *Popular Consent and Poplar Control – Whig Political Theory in the Early State Constitutions* (Baton Rouge: Louisiana State University Press), 8.

[128] Moots, *Politics Reformed*, 110.

president at Harvard, did in his Election Sermon, *Government Corrupted by Vice*, delivered in 1775, a month after the beginning of the hostilities:

We must keep our eyes fixed on the supreme government of the ETERNAL KING, as directing all events, setting up or pulling down the kings of the earth at His pleasure, suffering the best forms of human government to degenerate and go to ruin by corruption; or restoring the decayed constitutions of kingdoms and states, by reviving public virtue and religion, and granting the favorable interpositions of His providence.[129]

Few denied that "the general idea of a Civil Society or Government is a Number of Persons [equally free] united by Agreement," very much in line with the claims of the social contract theory. But, as Abraham Williams went on to explain, once the society was formed, it acquired an organic, hierarchical structure, for "a society without different Orders and Offices, like a Body without Eyes, Hands, and other Members, would be uncapable of acting."[130] These "collective Bodies, or Societies" resembled "the natural Body," in that they "[we]re composed of various individuals connected together, related and subservient to each other."[131] Williams was not the first nor the last to embrace this organic vision of the people. Daniel Shute took things further, arguing that piety and virtue cannot make up for the lack of wisdom:

Men may be pious and virtuous and yet not capable of penetrating very far into the nature and connection of things, and therefore unequal in transactions which require more than common abilities. [...] On this in no small degree the welfare of society depends. [...] In this fluctuating state, the community will ... need wise men for pilots, to save the threatened bark from surrounding gaging ruin.

But Shute was the exception. Most writers, like John Tucker, were convinced that the rulers should be not only "men of superior knowledge and wisdom,- well acquainted with the civil constitution," and "able critically to examine the complection of the state," but also, "of great importance ... that rulers be *men of distinguished piety and virtue, who will be likely to rule by example as well as law*."[132] As Hynemand and Lutz observe about many of these pamphlets, "of special interest is the emphasis on communitarian rather than individual-istic principles, and the articulation of the 'politics of deference' commonly held during the colonial era, according to which 'the better sort' should be deferred to in political matters, although all freemen are considered political equal."[133]

---

[129] Frank Moore, ed. (1860), *The Patriot Preachers of the American Revolution, with Biographical Sketches, 1766-1783* (New York: n. p.), 55.

[130] Abraham Williams (1762) *An Election Sermon*, in Hyneman and Lutz, *American Political Writing*, 9.

[131] Ibid., 3–4.

[132] John Tucker (1771), *An Election Sermon*, in Hyneman and Lutz, *American Political Writing*, 166–167 (emphasis added).

[133] Hyneman and Lutz, *American Political Writing*, 175.

The qualifications of the rulers were extremely important because "[a]ll government consistent with ... natural freedom ... is founded in compact, or agreement between the parties – between Rulers and their Subjects, and can be no otherwise." Hence, the responsibility for the common good rested on the shoulders of this aristocracy of merit, while the judge of their performance remained the whole people. Unlike the people *qua* multitude, the people *qua universitas* remained sovereign, unless they willingly transferred this power to their rulers (King, Parliament, or, more often, the King in Parliament): "A supreme legislative and a supreme executive power must be placed somewhere in every commonwealth. Where there is no other positive provision or compact to the contrary, those powers remain in the whole body of the people."[134] In 1776, the Massachusetts General Court took this idea a step further, claiming that, as a matter of fact, this power could never be delegated: "It is a Maxim that, in every Government, there must exist somewhere, a Supreme, Sovereign, absolute, and uncontroulable Power; but this power resides, always in the body of the People, and it never was, or can be delegated to one Man, or a few."[135] Still, the question remained: Who were "the people?" "The million inhabitants of the mainland colonies did not make up a majority of English citizens. Since the colonists cold not deny this fact, they had to muddle the issue."[136]

It was precisely on this understanding of "the people" that the British and the colonists began to drift apart. In England, in accordance with the social contract theory, the legislative came to be understood not just as the supreme power, and "the soul of the people," as Locke had it, but as the people themselves, only of a "better sort." If "power" was associated with the executive or the king, "liberty" was associated with the people, namely the Parliament.[137] Thus, the responsibility of the Commons *qua* people was to the institution of the Parliament itself. Not to the people *qua* electing multitude, nor to the king. As Charles James Fox told the House of Commons, "It was the duty of the electors to chuse us. It is ours to act constitutionally and to maintain the independency of Parliament. Whether that independence be attacked by the people or by the crown, is a matter of little importance."[138] As we have seen already in Jonathan Mayhew's *Discourse Concerning Unlimited Submission* ..., the colonists were still embracing the idea that the Parliament is the whole British people. Hence, the idea that the Parliament could rebel was absurd, for a people could not rebel against itself. The Loyalists too found the

---

[134] James Otis (1764), *The Rights of the British Colonies Asserted and Proved*, in Bailyn, *Pamphlets*, 426.

[135] Quoted in Reed, *The Concept of Representation*, 19.

[136] Willi Paul Adams (1980), *The First American Constitutions: Republican Ideology and the Making of the State Constitutions in the Revolutionary Era* (Chapel Hill: The University of North Carolina Press), 134.

[137] Marston, *King and Congress*, 17.   [138] Quoted in Reed, *The Concept of Representation*, 70.

idea of rebelling against the Parliament blatantly absurd. In the words of Daniel Leonard (writing under the *nom de plume* Massachusettensis), "civil society . . . is nothing more than the union of a multitude of people who agree to live in subjection to a sovereign (i.e., *any power having legislative authority.*)"[139]

Yet as the tensions over taxation mounted, the colonists began to question the authority of the Parliament and the whole idea of virtual representation of "every Englishmen." The famous slogan "no taxation without representation" was little more than a slogan, for the colonists did not actually want to be represented in Parliament by one of their own. As an article in the *Newport Mercury* put it on July 11, 1766, an American sent to parliament would lose "that fellow-feeling which forms the firmest barrier of liberty." Absence from home would "weaken his connections, and lessen his interest [and] having little interest of being re-chosen at a future election, he might be remiss in the duty he owed his constituents."[140] Besides, the American representatives in Parliament would always have amounted to an insignificant minority. In the words of John Taylor, it would have been "a mere mockery of representation." The social contract theory at the scale of the British empire simply did not do for the American colonists.

[England] offered them representation. But they declined it upon the ground that the same species of ignorance . . . would still prevail over a majority of the members. [. . .] But there was another reason for *rejecting a compromise with England*, upon the condition of representation in parliament. [. . .] Now, the people of the colonies would have had no power to remove a member of the parliament elected in Great Britain; nor would the laws passed by a majority in that country, but operating exclusively in this, affect any individual of that majority.[141]

Daniel Dulany understood very well what was at stake: "Whether, therefore, upon the whole matter the imposition of the stamp duties is a proper exercise of constitutional authority or not depends upon the single question, whether the Commons of Great Britain are virtually the representatives of the commons of America or not."[142] Obviously he concluded in the negative, as did Richard Bland's own analysis: "I flatter myself, by what has been said, your Position of a virtual representation is sufficiently refuted; and that there is really no such Representation known in the British Constitution, and consequently that the

---

[139] Daniel Leonard (1773), *To All Nations of Men*, in Hyneman and Lutz, *American Political Writing*, 210 (emphasis added).

[140] Quoted in Edmund S. Morgan (1988), *Inventing the People: The Rise of Popular Sovereignty in England and America* (New York and London: W. W. Norton & Co.), 42.

[141] John Taylor (1820), *Construction Construed and Constitution Vindicated* (Richmond: Shepherd & Pollard), 302 (emphasis added).

[142] Daniel Dulany (1765), Considerations on the Propriety of Imposing Taxes on the British Colonies, in Bernard Bailyn, ed. (1965) *Pamphlets of the American Revolution, Vol. 1, 1750-1765* (Cambridge, MA: The Belknapp Press of Harvard University Press), 610.

colonies are not subject to an internal taxation by Authority of Parliament."[143] The idea of virtual representation "was stretching the fiction of representation beyond its elastic limit, and it pushed the colonists into a strenuous affirmation of the local, subject character of representation."[144]

The colonists did not deny the idea of the supremacy of the legislative and its ability to speak in the name of the people, but they began applying it exclusively *inside* the colonies, not as far as the *external* relationships of each colony was concerned. After all, as Dulany argued, "the colonies have a complete and adequate legislative authority, and are not only represented in their Assemblies *but in no other manner*."[145] If the theory of social contract was widely accepted inside the colonies, it was the political contract theory that offered the colonists a theoretical justification for resistance. As James Otis put it, "the relation of modern colonies to their mother state is founded on political compact."[146]

The idea of the political contract informed the entire thinking of the American Whigs, regardless of whether they discussed the British constitution or their own constitutive charters. As early as 1756, an anonymous essayist wrote in *Boston Gazette and Country Journal* that Magna Carta "is in short the constitution of English government – the basis of English law – the compact – the standing perpetual rule over which *no man not any body of men distinct from the whole may claim any just superiority*."[147] "[The British] constitutional laws are comprised in Magna-Charta, or the great charter of the nation. This contains, in general, the liberties and privileges of the people, and is, virtually, *a compact between the King and them*," wrote Tucker in the same Sermon mentioned above.[148] The same idea was defended by Stephen Hopkins in *The Rights of Colonies Examined*: "This glorious constitution, the best that ever existed among men, will be confessed by all to be founded by compact and established by consent of the people."[149]

The transfer of the political compact from the British constitution to the colonial charters was not just natural; it also reinforced the colonists' sense of distinctive colonial identities. "Nor were the benefits of these famous compacts 'between the sovereign and the first patentees' valued only in the particular province in which they had survived. Everywhere in the colonies the existing charters were prized as 'evidential of the rights and immunities belonging to all the King's subjects in America.'"

---

[143] Richard Bland (1766), *An Inquiry into the Rights of the British Colonies*, in Hyneman and Lutz, *American Political Writing*, 86.

[144] Edmund S. Morgan (1988), *Inventing the People: The Rise of Popular Sovereignty in England and America* (New York and London: W.W. Norton & Co.), 240.

[145] Dulany, *Considerations*, 618.

[146] James Ottis (1765), *A Vindication of the British Colonies*, in Bailyn, *Pamphlets*, 557.

[147] Quoted in Bailyn, *The Ideological Origins*, 69 (emphasis added).

[148] John Tucker (1771), *An Election Sermon*, in Hyneman and Lutz, *American Political Writing*, 163 (emphasis added).

[149] Stephen Hopkins (1765), *The Rights of Colonies Examined*, in Bailyn, *Pamphlets*, 507.

Those who viewed the world in the light of covenant theology could see the colonial charters as valid not merely in the eyes of law but in the eyes of God as well: 'our charter ... was a solemn covenant between [the King] and our fathers' – a 'sacred' covenant by which the crown has contracted with a morally regenerate people ...'' – yet another example how covenant theology, republicanism, and political contract theory got easily blended in early American political thought.[150]

The special covenant between the Puritans and God was not put aside, as Brendan McConville argues, but the "imperial contract" did call "for the realization of spiritual identity in a temporal Protestant political culture."[151] The corporatist understanding of the people allowed colonists a double move. On the one hand, they could claim independence from the British Parliament:

Should the analogy between the colonies and corporation be admitted [...] it would amount to this: the colonies are vested with a complete authority to all intents and purposes to tax themselves as any English corporation is to make a bylaw in any imaginable instance for any local purpose whatever, and the Parliament doth not make laws for corporations upon subjects in every respect proper for bylaws.[152]

On the other hand, it allowed them to claim equal treatment as distinctive peoples:

In an imperial state, which consists of many separate governments each of which hath peculiar privileges and of which kind it is evident the empire of Great Britain is, no simple part, though greater than another part, is by that superiority entitled to make laws for or to tax such lesser part; but all laws and all taxations which bind the whole must be made by the whole.[153]

"How then do we New Englandmen derive our laws?" asked John Adams when arguing with Daniel Leonard: "I say not from parliament, not from common law, but *from the law of nature, and the compact made with the King in our charters.*"[154] Revealing of the common confusion between the two types of contract, using this very quote – a rather clear exemplification of the political contract established via chartering – Michael Zuckert claims instead that "[t]he background theory to which Adams appeals here should be easy to identify: it is the Lockean natural rights/social contract theory."[155] If there is indeed an

---

[150] John Dickinson, *A Speech Delivered in the House of the Assembly* ... (Philadelphia, 1764); Samuel Webster, *The Misery and Duty of an Oppressed and Enslav'd People* ... (Boston 1774), pp. 10 ff (the quotation is at 22). Both quoted in Bailyn, p. 192. See also Lutz, *Colonial Origins*, for a similar argument, as well as Chapter 2.

[151] McConville, *The King's Three Faces*, 51.   [152] Dulany, *Considerations*, 618.

[153] Hopkins, *The Right of the Colonies*, 519.   [154] Novanglus, Essay VIII, 81 (emphasis added).

[155] Michael P. Zuckert (2005), "Natural Rights and Imperial Constitutionalism: The American Revolution and the Development of the American Amalgam" in Ellen Frankel Paul, Fred D. Miller Jr., Jeffrey Paul, eds., *Natural Rights Liberalism from Locke to Nozick* (Cambridge: Cambridge University Press), 41. For a similar confusion, see also Mark Hulliung, *The Social Contract in America*, 2. Despite the evidence, Hulliung claims that, "at the time of the Revolution it was consistently the Loyalists, far more so than the Patriots, who spoke of a contract

"easy to identify" Lockean social theory in *Novanglus*, it is to be found in Essay No. VII, in which Adams made clear, once again, that each colony was a distinct political body, created and maintained in existence by the colonial legislatures, regardless of any common ancestry:

> I agree, that "two supreme and independent authorities cannot exist in the same state," any more than two supreme beings in one universe; and, therefore, I contend, that our provincial legislatures are the only supreme authorities in our colonies. [...] There is no need of being startled at this consequence. It is very harmless. There is no absurdity at all in it. Distinct states may be united under one king. (Novanglus VII, 70, 75)

As such, "[t]he controversy was about the rights of competing legislatures and thus was difficult to resolve."[156] In the words of Cassandra (James Cannon, 1776), the "war of Legislatures [...] between the British Parliament and the Colonial Assemblies" has begun.[157] The colonists refused to be any longer "the subjects of subjects," as Silas Downer put it.[158] Since according to the social contract theory, the legislative was "the soul" of any political body, holding it together, it would have been but a small step from war between different legislatives to war between different peoples, unless the king was accepted as arbitrator, or *compromissarius*, between different peoples.

> [T]he people here still remain under the sacred tie, the subject of the King of Great Britain; but utterly unaccountable to, and uncontroulable by the people of Great Britain, or any body of them whatever; their compact being with the King only, to him alone they submitted, to be governed by him, agreeable to the terms of that compact, contain'd in their charter.[159]

Silas Downer, a Son of Liberty, could not help but agree: "We cheerfully recognize our allegiance to our sovereign Lord, George the third, King of Great-Britain, and supreme Lord of these dominions, but utterly deny another dependence on the inhabitants of that island, than what is mutual and reciprocal between all mankind."[160]

Psychologically speaking, the colonists were already starting to separate from their English brethren and to create their own political identities, despite all the co-sanguinity ties between the two groups. As John Adams observed, "the Revolution was affected before the war commenced. [...] The radical change in the principles, opinions, sentiments, and affections of the people

---

between rulers and ruled ... It was John Locke's social contract, defeated in 1688, that triumphed at the time of the American Revolution, and *Locke explicitly disallowed the notion of a contract between government and the people*" (emphasis added).

[156] Shain, *The Declaration of Independence*, 13.

[157] Quoted in Nelson, *The Royalist Revolution*, 5.

[158] Silas Downer (1768), *A Discourse at the Dedication of the Tree of Liberty*, in Hyneman and Lutz, *American Political Writing*, 102.

[159] Britannus Americanus (1766), *Untitled*, in Hyneman and Lutz, *American Political Writing*, 89.

[160] Downer, *A Discourse at the Dedication of the Tree of Liberty*, 98.

was the real American Revolution."[161] But if the colonists hoped that King George would arbitrate to their advantage, they were soon to discover that they had made a terrible mistake. It has been claimed that "a willingness on the part of King George II and Lord North to compromise and barter ... might have fundamentally transform subsequently word history,"[162] yet "at issue in 1774 was not [the king's] own power, but rather the power of Parliament to legislate for the colonies. On such a fundamental issue he could accept no compromise."[163]

3.4 THE KING "UNKINGS HIMSELF"

The separation of king from the Parliament in the colonial constitutional perception began as early as 1750s, and grew in intensity after the Stamp Act Crisis.[164] By the early 1770s, the king had become the only thread theoretically connecting the colonies to the Empire, as well as the various parts of the empire together. "As the King is the center of union," wrote "American Solon" in 1772, "the various parts of the great body politic will be united in him; he will be the spring and soul of the union, to guide and regulate the grand political machine."[165] As the center of the empire, he was in the position to act as an impartial arbitrator. As late as 1775, Alexander Hamilton argued that the monarch "is under no temptation to purchase the favour of one part of his dominion, at the expense of another; but it is his interest to treat them all, upon the same footing. Very different is the case with regard to the Parliament. The Lords and Commons both, have a private and separate interest to pursue."[166] The idea was not original. The same impartiality had been claimed earlier in Great Britain. In 1734, Attorney General John Willes claimed that only the king could have been objectively impartial, for he had at heart the good of the whole empire, "whereas the people of any county, city, or borough ... may often be induced to give instructions directly contrary to the interest of their country."[167] Yet in the case of the colonists, "conscious of their tendency to quarrel among themselves as well as with the mother country,"[168] the authority of the king to act as a benevolent and paternal arbitrator pacifying turbulent children became essential. Metaphors about "the paternal Care of the

---

[161] John Adams to Hezekiah Niles, February 13, 1818, in Charles Francis Adams, ed. (1850–1856), _The Works of John Adams_, vol. 10 (Boston: Little, Brown), 282.

[162] Sanford Levinson (2013), _Framed: America's 51 Constitutions and the Crisis of Governance_ (Oxford: Oxford University Press), 41.

[163] Marston, _King and Congress_, 41.   [164] McConville, _The King's Three Faces_, 204.

[165] Quoted in Marston, _King and Congress_, 26.

[166] Alexander Hamilton (1775), _The Farmer Refuted: or, A More Impartial and Comprehensive View of the Disputes between Great-Britain and the Colonies_ (New York), 18.

[167] John Willes (1734), _Speech in Common Debates_, quoted in Reid, _The Concept of Representation_, 105.

[168] Marston, _King and Congress_, 26.

Monarch," and "his Paternal Goodness" abounded at the beginning of the 1770s.

For Benjamin Franklin, therefore, the greatest importance of "the King's Supreme Authority over the Colonies," lay in his role as a "dernier resort, for settling all their Disputes, a Means of preserving Peace among them with each other, and a Center in which their Common Force might be united." [The King] was the "sovereign umpire" who resolved all intra-imperial disputes. [...] In short, observed "A Philadelphia," Britain's kings had always served as "the Umpires of our Disputes."[169]

Forced by their own reasoning, some (albeit not all) colonists took the royalist position a step further, arguing something barely imaginable for a Whig, namely that the colonies were governed solely by royal prerogative and that – thanks to the political contract embodied in the royal charters – the king was, properly speaking, the only legitimate representative of the people from each colony. For them, the theory of "actual representation" or "the election theory of authorization" was a nonstarter:

As loyalists and administration spokesmen gleefully pointed out in the late 1760s and early 1770s, if we take the view that an individual cannot be represented by anyone for whom he himself has not voted, we will conclude that every citizen must be given a veto over the election of representatives and that every representative must be given a veto over acts of legislation. But this is simply to embrace anarchy.[170]

The solution was to return to a royalist theory of representation, like the one embraced by the supporters of Charles I. "It is one of the great ironies in this richly ironic story," observes Eric Nelson, "that the raw material of the patriot defense of the Stuarts were initially provided by loyalists."[171] Some of the patriots, such as Edward Bancroft in 1771, took their defense of the king far enough to argue that New England was settled by Puritans fleeing not the king, but the Parliament's tyranny.[172] It was an undoubtedly dangerous path. As William Knox warned these colonists, "they ought to reflect, that whatever might be their condition, they cannot apply to parliament to better it."[173] Lord North, Second Earl of Guilford, was baffled as well. He argued that "if he understood the meaning of the words Whig and Tory ... he conceived that it was characteristic of Whiggism to gain for the people as much as possible, while the aim of Toryism was to increase the [royal] prerogative. That in the present case, the administration contended for the right of parliament, while the Americans talked about their belonging to the crown. Their language therefore was that of Toryism."[174]

---

[169] Marston, *King and Congress*, 26–27.   [170] Nelson, *The Royalist Revolution*, 70.

[171] Eric Nelson (2011), "Patriot Royalism: The Stuart Monarchy in American Political Thought, 1769-75," *The William and Mary Quarterly*, 68:4, 543.

[172] Ibid., 553.   [173] Quoted in Nelson, "Patriot Royalism," 547.

[174] Quoted in Nelson, "Patriot Royalism," 535. For a more developed argument, see Nelson, *The Royalist Revolution*.

It is difficult to pinpoint the precise date when the honeymoon between the Patriots and the king ended, since it occurred at different times in different places for different peoples.[175] Having barely set foot on the shores of New England, Thomas Paine, for example, already considered in 1774 that, "[a]s Britain hath not manifested the least inclination towards a compromise, we may be assured that no terms can be obtained worthy the acceptance of the Continent, or any ways equal to the expence of blood and treasure we have been already put to."[176] He also claimed that the unanimously celebrated Magna Carta was but a compromise, aka a political compact, forced on the king by the people:[177]

The charter which secures this freedom in England, was formed, not in the senate, but in the field; and insisted on by the people, not granted by the crown; the crown in that instance *granted nothing,* but only renounced its former tyrannies, and bound itself over to its future good behaviour. It was the compromise, by which the wearer of it made his peace with the people, and the condition on which he was suffered to reign.[178]

Yet in that same year, after the conclusion of the First Continental Congress in October, "republicanism," understood as anti-monarchical stance, was still a smear word, very much like "democracy." Both stood for the rule of the mob and, ultimately, for anarchy.

How could a multitude of voters, [colonial newspapers and pamphlets] asked, make the decisions that up to then had seemed to require the education and political acumen of an experienced political elite? And how could a state of any extent survive without a monarch as an impartial judge to resolve the conflicts between opposing interest groups? And how could a league of thirteen separate republics endure if it were based on no higher authority than the sovereignty of the people?[179]

As late as July 1775, while rejecting the Parliament's offer of peace and reconciliation (which made moot the taxation issue and made clear to everyone that this was a disagreement of principles), the Congress was still extending an olive brach petition to the king.[180] Although John Adams was in the forefront of the movement for independence, he too used "republicanism" with pejorative connotations as late as November 1775. A major step toward

[175] For a wealth of details, see McConville, *The King's Three Faces,* 286–306.
[176] Thomas Paine (1774), "Thoughts on the Present State of American Affairs," in *The Writings of Thomas Paine, Vol. I (1774–1779)* (Indianapolis: Liberty Fund), 93.
[177] Born and raised Englishman, Paine sometimes uses "compromise" as an equivalent for "compact," like in this letter from 1791, when he talks about "the right of making any such compact, or compromise"; *The Writings of Thomas Paine, Vol. III (1791–1804)* [1791], 90.
[178] Thomas Paine (1774), "To Cato," in *The Writings,* Vol. I (1774–1779), 151.
[179] Willi Paul Adams (1980), *The First American Constitutions: Republican Ideology and the Making of the State Constitutions in the Revolutionary Era,* translated by Rita and Robert Kimber (Chapel Hill: The University of North Carolina Press), 101.
[180] For the full documents, see Shain, *The Declaration of Independence,* 290–292, and 318–322, respectively.

independence – one not really flattering for the patriots – was Lord Dunmore's proclamation offering freedom to slaves in Virginia, a gesture that, in Edward Rutledge's words (December 8, 1775), was "more effectually to work an eternal separation between Great Britain and the Colonies, than any other expedient, which could possibly have been thought of."[181] Yet it took the publication of Thomas Paine's *Common Sense*, in January 1776, for the Americans to start changing their opinion about republicanism in general and monarchy in particular. It happened a day later (January 9) after news that in his speech in Parliament on October 26, 1775, the king had declared the colonies to be in open rebellion and had rejected the olive branch petition. As Levinson put it in grand terms, "a willingness on the part of King George III and Lord North to compromise and barter ... might have fundamentally transformed subsequently world history."[182]

Even so, while beginning to think about "some Method for the Colonies to glide insensibly, from under the old Government, into a peaceable and contended Submission to new ones," John Adams thought that republicanism, while admirable in theory, was no longer a feasible option for an already less virtuous America:

The Form of Government, which you admire, when its Principles are pure is admirable indeed ... But its Principles are easily destroyed, as human Nature is corrupted ... Public Virtue cannot exist in a Nation without private, and public Virtue is the only Foundation of Republics. There must be a positive Passion for the public good, the public Interest, Honour, Power, and Glory, established in the Minds of the People, or there can be no Republican Government, nor any real Liberty. [...] Is there in the World a Nation, which deserves this character. There have been several, but they are no more. Our dear Americans perhaps have as much of it as any Nation now existing, and New England perhaps has more than the rest of America. But I have seen all along my Life, Such Selfishness, and Littleness even in New England ... The Spirit of Commerce is as rampant in New England as in any part of the World ... While this is the Case there is great Danger that a Republican Government would be very factious and turbulent there.[183]

The rationality for breaking with the king, and implicitly with Great Britain, was founded in the same political contract used throughout the Imperial Debate. In *Novanglus*, Essay No. VII, John Adams writes: "It ought to be remembered that there was a revolution here, as well as in England, and that we, as well as the people of England, made an original express contract with King William." It followed, as "Amicus Constitutionis" from New York put it, that if the king fails to fulfill his part of the contract, he "unkings himself."[184] The model to be copied was none other than the Glorious Revolution. William

---

[181] In Shain, *The Declaration of Independence*, 361.   [182] Levinson, *Framed*, 41.
[183] In Shain, *The Declaration of Independence*, 437. See also further Chapter 5 and Gordon Wood's "commercial republic" mentioned above.
[184] Quoted in Adams, *The First American Constitutions*, 103.

Henry Drayton's revolutionary charge from April 1776 employed verbatim the formula used in the Resolution of Lords and Commons in Convention of February 7, 1689: "by breaking the original contract between king and people." Naturally, the main source of inspiration was not Locke and his social contract theory, as Hulliung, among others, claims, but William Blackstone, labeled by Stourzh "Teacher of Revolution,"[185] despite his well-known position against the American colonists.[186]

In the eye of the famous Tory jurist, the Glorious Revolution could be seen as a precedent: If a future prince should "endeavor to subvert the constitution by *breaking the original contract between king and people,* should violate the fundamental laws, and should withdraw himself out of the kingdom, we are now authorized to declare this conjunction of circumstances would amount to an abdication."[187] Although Blackstone agreed that "the supposition of *law . . .* is, that neither the king nor either house of parliament (collectively taken) is capable of doing any wrong," under extraordinary circumstances, "the law feels itself incapable of furnishing any adequate remedy. [. . .] [T]he *prudence* of the times must provide new remedies upon new emergencies."[188] It was precisely the justification that the patriots were looking for, since, as we have seen, prudence and virtue were conspicuously absent from Hobbes's and Locke's contract theories. After showing multiple examples in which Blackstone was used and quoted during the revolutionary era, Stourzh concludes that "the kind of contract referred to most often, whose violation was charged most often, was the governmental contract between ruler and ruled. However, this contract is not part of Locke's system."[189]

Becker's observation, formulated in 1922, still stands:

From this moment the old policy of *compromise* was rapidly abandoned. Those who on this ground would not support the patriot cause had to be ignored or suppressed; and now that independence was the object, it was not only possible but necessary, in formulating the rights of the colonies, to adopt a theory of British-colonial relations in the light of which the act of separation could be regarded as a step that the colonies had always had a moral and legal right to take. Such a theory could only be found in a close union of the natural rights philosophy of government with a conception of the empire as

---

[185] Gerald Stourzh (2010) [1970], "William Blackstone: Teacher of Revolution," in *From Vienna to Chicago and Back: Essays on Intellectual History and Political Thought in Europe and America* (Chicago: University of Chicago Press).

[186] Blackstone was the second most quoted author during the revolutionary era, right after Montesquieu, and significantly ahead of John Locke; see Donald S. Lutz (1988), *The Origins of American Constitutionalism* (Baton Rouge: Louisiana State University Press), 142. Although Zuckert (2003) also discusses Blackstone's impact on the American Revolution, he fails to notice the governmental contract mostly referred to by Blackstone. Other scholars did the same. None of them mentions Stourzh (2010 [1970]), most likely because Stourzh's original text appeared in German.

[187] Quoted in Stourzh, *William Blackstone*, 63 (emphasis added).

[188] Ibid., 21 (emphasis added).   [189] Gerald Stourzh, *William Blackstone*, 70.

a confederation of free peoples submitting themselves to the same king by an original compact voluntarily entered into, and terminable, in the case of any member, at the will of the people concerned.[190]

As Noll observes, the evangelical rhetoric further inflamed the uncompromising spirit.

Patriot Christians moved without hesitation from the observation that some actions of Parliament compromised colonial rights to the conclusion that Parliament was promoting tyranny and that this promotion of tyranny was the Antichrist. Given that leap, it was only appropriate to treat the war with Britain as a climactic struggle between good and evil. [...] They did not feel compelled to look for the ambiguities in the actions of Parliament or in their own reactions, so they fell into black-and-white habits of mind in which the patriots could do no wrong and Britain no right.[191]

By the summer of 1776, the paternal image of the king had been seriously undermined. As early as July 1775, in a Speech to the Six Confederate Nations, the colonists alluded to the king as an unfair father to his American child, but one that was misguided by wicked servants: "They t[old] the father, and advise[d] him to enlarge the child's pack – they prevail[ed] – the pack [wa]s increased – the child [took] it up again – as he thought it might be the father's pleasure ... Those proud and wicked servants ... laughed ... By and by they appl[ied] to the father to double the boy's pack..." Nevertheless, in 1775, "the boy" still "intreat[ed] the father."[192] But a year later, the story was different. In the eyes of the colonists, what he did, in siding with the Parliament, amounted to nothing less than a "paternal betrayal,"[193] and the king became "the perfect scapegoat."[194] As far as George III was concerned, he sided with Parliament in accordance with the principles of the constitutional monarchy. In his understanding, doing anything else would have meant "acting truly tyrannically."[195] However, the Declaration of Independence begged to differ, making King George almost exclusively responsible for all of the colonists' grievances.

With the Declaration's public readings ... the royal father truly came crashing down in a torrent of acts designed to delegitimate royal rule. [...] In Boston, a ceremony "absolving the United Colonies from their allegiance to the British Crown" drew a large crowd which milled in the street until someone decided to destroy all signs of the now-hated king. "On the same evening," it was reported, "the King's arms and every sign with any resemblance of it, whether lion and crown, pestle and mortar and crown, heart and

[190] Carl Lotus Becker (1922), *The Declaration of Independence: A Study on the History of Political Ideas* (New York: Harcourt, Brace and Co., 1922), chapter 3.

[191] Mark A. Noll (1988), *One Nation under God? Christian faith and Political Action in America* (San Francisco: Harper & Row), 48–49.

[192] In Shain, *The Declaration of Independence*, 310.   [193] Marston, *King and Congress*, 24–25.

[194] Stourzh, *From Vienna to Chicago*, 25.   [195] Shain, *The Declaration of Independence*, 15.

crown, etc. together with every sign that belonged to a tory was taken down, and the latter made a general conflagration of in King street."[196]

Still, even with the war in full swing, not everyone lost hope – particularly not the British, who were convinced that a compromise (or a new compact) was possible. After a huge victory against the Americans at the Battle of the Long Island, on August 27, General Howe sent his prisoner, General Sullivan, on parole to meet with Congress. General Sullivan obliged and delivered the message on September 3:

> That he, in Conjunction with General Howe, had full powers to Compromise the Dispute between Great Britain and America, upon terms advantageous to both; the obtaining of which Delayed him near Two months in England, and prevented his arrival at this place before the Declaration of Independence took place. That he wished a Compact might be Settled at this time, when no Decisive Blow was struck, and neither party could say, that they were Compelled to enter into such agreement.

It was an attempt to compromise without being compromised, yet it was, once again, bad timing. After two days of debates, the Congress decided to send Benjamin Franklin and John Adams to meet with Lord Howe (General Howe could not attend). Despite the professed goodwill of all the parties, the meeting could not reach a compromise. Lord Howe suggested the olive branch petition could still be considered a good foundation for a reconciliation but asked the colonists to withdraw their Declaration of Independence. Franklin reminded Howe that the response to the olive branch petition had been Parliament's Prohibitory Act of December 1775, and that the independence of the colonies was a fait accompli, which should be the foundation for any future agreement – a condition deemed unacceptable by Howe.

The effects of the propaganda war from both sides – deplored by King George ("those who have long too successfully labored to inflame my people in America gross misrepresentations") and by Jay ("it has long been the Art of the Enemies of America to sow the seeds of Dissentions among us") – proved too great to be overcome by the goodwill of a few. Both parties, but even more so the Patriots, saw evidence of conspiracy everywhere, which only fueled a paranoid rhetoric.[197] Appeals to reason and moderation fell on deaf ears. David Ramsay, who had a firsthand knowledge of the events, acknowledged as much in 1789 in *The History of the American Revolution*. According to him, "the horrors of the *civil war*" could have been avoided if only the question of where the parliamentary authority ended and the authority of the colonies began should have "never been agitated, but more so, had it been compromised by an amicable compact."[198] But the propaganda wars made such an amicable compact impossible:

---

[196] McConville, *The King's Three Faces*, 307.
[197] Gordon S. Wood (1982), "Conspiracy and the Paranoid Style: Causality and Deceit in the Eighteenth Century," *William and Mary Quarterly*, 3:39, 406–408, 411.
[198] David Ramsay (1798), *The History of the American Revolution*, in Hyneman and Lutz, *American Political Writings*, Vol. 2, 731.

A few honest men properly authorized, might have devised measures of *compromise*, which under the influence of truth, humility and moderation, would have prevented a dismemberment of the empire, but these virtues ceased to influence, and falsehood, haughtiness and blind zeal usurped their places. Had Great-Britain, even after the declaration of independence, adopted the magnanimous resolution of declaring her colonies free and independent states, interest would have prompted them to form such a connexion as would have secured to the Mother Country the advantages of their commerce, without the expense or troubles of their governments.[199]

One cannot fail to notice, however, that the willingness of the British to compromise was not matched by the American revolutionaries. In June 1777, Washington, for example, told Lieutenant-General Howe that, "we appeared to differ so widely, that I could entertain no hopes of a compromise being effected."[200] A year later, from Valley Forge, he wrote dismissively about "the defection of some and temporary inconsistency and irresolution of others, who may desire to compromise the dispute."[201] And yet in London, in 1777, is published the volume *Essays, Commercial and Political, on the real and relative Interests of Imperial and Dependent States, particularly those of Great Britain and her Dependencies: Displaying the probable Causes of, and a Mode of compromising, the present Disputes between this Country and her American Colonies.*[202] Even more touching is the poem entitled *The Compromise*, published the same year by *The Sentimental magazine, or, General Assemblage of science, taste, and entertainment*:

> When mutual passions fire the mind,
> Whate'er the latent cause,
> From nature we are apt to fly,
> And violate her laws.
>
> Friends, brethren, enemies will prove,
> And violate each tie,
> Which ought to link 'em fast in love,
> And strengthen liberty.
>
> Then arts and commerce are no more,
> Religion fails to bind;
> And every sacred bond is lost
> Which holds the human mind.
>
> But e're the fatal hour is come,
> Which ratifies despair,
> Let either seek the other's weal,
> And wish away her care.

---

[199] Ibid., 747.

[200] George Washington (1890), *The Writings of George Washington, Vol. V (1776–1777)*, (New York and London: George Putnam's Sons), 423.

[201] Ibid., Vol. 6, 482.   [202] Newcastle: Printed by T. Saint for the Author and sold by J. Johnson.

Let BRITAIN yield that she is wrong,
America not right;
So may the contest quickly end,
And end this bloody fight.[203]

As we know, it was just wishful thinking. Still, one must ask: What is the possible cause for such obvious discrepancy in the willingness to compromise across the Atlantic? One can, of course, look for pragmatic reasons, although, as we have seen, the Patriots were not willing to compromise even in the face of almost sure defeat. I suspect that the cause is to be found in the two different representations of the people. On the one hand, the idea of individuals being equally represented in Parliament compelled many British to compromise, even with the rebellious Americans. The only issue that they could not compromise on – and for cause, this being the crux of the most admired social contract theory – was that the legislative did not equally represent all individuals. On the other hand, by appealing to the political contract theory, the Patriots embraced, like the Puritans before them, the idea of corporate peoples, whose identities and interests were to be protected against any outside interference, thus becoming hostile to any compromise perceived to be threatening. Yet these peoples from the newly formed states were kept together not by common descent, common traditions, or common religion, but by their own legislatures, elected by their own votes. This, in turn, created a problem. Absent a king, who was supposed to keep these peoples together, and based on which of the competing understanding of the people?

It was a challenge the Patriots had to face even before the Declaration of Independence was signed – and the ways in which it was addressed is the focus of the next chapter.

---

[203] Author unknown (London, August 1777), 182.

4

The Compromising Confederates

"... mounting a body of Mermaids on Alligators"

> [I]t would be a Miracle, if Such heterogeneous ingredients did not at first produce violent Fermentations.
>
> – John Adams

The Founding Era was revolutionary on many levels, and one of the most important revolutions took place in the vocabulary of politics – "a furiously intense struggle over the control of words."[1] Before founding a common people, the American Patriots had to establish a common meaning for the very word "people," which carried, then as now, both political and cultural connotations. As we have seen in the previous chapters, this was no easy task. Most of the foundational documents celebrated today as political statements prove to be, for an attentive reader, less focused on designing a specific form of government than founding distinctive, politically and socially defined peoples. From the Mayflower Compact to the Massachusetts Body of Liberties, and from the Virginia Bill of Rights to the Declaration of Independence, "we have an outline of the major sociocultural norms, not a design for government."[2] As Daniel Shute pointed out in a sermon from 1768, "the line ... between one society, and another, is not drawn by heaven; nor is the particular form of civil government." These are distinctions made by men as "rational and free agents."[3] As I shall try to show in the following pages, the three subcultures described by

---

[1] Daniel T. Rodgers (1987), *Contested Truths: Keywords in American Politics since Independence* (New York: Basic Books), 212.

[2] Donald S. Lutz (1980), *Popular Consent and Popular Control: Whig Political Theory in the Early State Constitutions* (Baton Rouge: Louisiana State University Press), 59.

[3] Daniel Shute (1768), "An Election Sermon" in Charles S. Hyneman and Donald S. Lutz, eds. (1983), *American Political Writing during the Founding Era, 1760–1805* (Indianapolis: Liberty Press), 112.

Daniel J. Elazar – moralistic in New England, individualistic in the Middle Atlantic, and traditionalistic in the South – while important, should not obscure other, even more important differences among and even within each of the colonies.[4]

The challenge of defining "the people" was further complicated by an "unconscious federalism" operating at the intra-colonial level, because each colony was understood as a corporation of distinct corporations.

> Political relationships in colonial America potentially had three levels – intracolonial, intercolonial, and colony-mother country. It is interesting that in the first and third instances, the solution tended to be federalism – although a federalism that was unconscious, was not derived from theory, and had no name to describe it. The colonies were each a collection of towns or counties ... Still, since charters recognize only a single entity, a colony, these various parts had to coordinate policy and control [...] [e]ven when not derived from covenants, colonial governments functioned effectively as federal politics, having been built up from below.[5]

Hence, before even deciding if there was *an* American nation, the Patriots had first to determine if they were three, thirteen, or even more American "peoples," considering the number of potential "peoples" inside the colonies. During the first years of the Revolutionary Era, they could and did muddle the issue, but after the Declaration of Independence they were forced to confront it head on.[6] "It was hard enough to make the representative, say of Hanover County, think in terms of Virginia, let alone of the whole United States." Each town, parish, or county wanted therefore to elect its own representative. "No state adopted a system of indirect election for representatives, because such a system would have betrayed the conception of representation that the colonists had insisted on throughout the quarrel with England."[7] As Formasino observes, "[t]he American Revolution was made more in the name of 'the people' conceptualized in the plural, than for a collective entity or for an American 'nation.' They did not conceive of themselves as a unified people or nation," and the Declaration of Independence clearly reflects this ambiguity.[8]

The period between the Declaration of Independence and the Philadelphia Convention tends to be ignored by contemporary scholars, despite the largely

---

[4] Daniel J. Elazar (1972), *American Federalism: A View from the States* (New York: Thomas Y. Crowell); see alsoCalvin C. Jillson (1988), "Political Culture and the Pattern of Congressional Politics Under the Articles of Confederation," *Publius*, 18:1, 1–26.

[5] Donald S. Lutz (1990), "The Articles of Confederation as the Background to the Federal Republic," *Publius*, 20:1, 56.

[6] Willi Paul Adams (1980), *The First American Constitutions: Republican Ideology and the Making of the State Constitutions in the Revolutionary Era* (Chapel Hill: The University of North Carolina Press), 134.

[7] Morgan, *Inventing the People*, 246–247.

[8] Ronald P. Formisano (2008), *For the People: American Populist Movements from the Revolution to 1850s* (Chapel Hill: University of North Carolina Press), 20.

undisputed role the first state constitutions and the Articles of Confederation played in shaping the future of the United States. As Hoffert noticed, "unfortunately, Americans' obsession with the Constitution of 1787 is matched only by their obliviousness to the Articles of Confederation."[9] The reason might be that "American history is not kind to those who lose, or are perceived to have lost,"[10] and "traditionally ... the Articles of Confederation have played the role of the villain."[11] As a result, "the conventional view of the period ... is that the country came to the very brink of dying in infancy."[12]

At the other end of the spectrum one finds a small but quite enthusiastic minority of scholars, seeing in the first state constitutions and in the Articles of Confederation nothing less than an attempt of popular democracy to oppose either a more elitist form of republicanism, or directly "the anti-democratic forces" that would allegedly take over during the Philadelphia Convention. Undoubtedly, the most "radical" exponent of the latter remains Jensen, who wrote that "the Articles of Confederation were an expression of the democratic philosophy of the eighteenth century and ... the Constitution of 1787 was the culmination of an anti-democratic crusade."[13]

In counterdistinction to both approaches, in the following pages I shall propose a new perspective that goes beyond modern dichotomies that counterpoise "democratic" to "aristocratic republicanism,"[14] "democrats" to "anti-democrats," "radicals" to "conservatives," or "liberals"/"Lockeans" to "republicans." To begin with, most of these labels were not even in use during the period with which I am concerned, or when they were – such as the labels of "democrats" or "republicans" – they had different (and fluid) connotations. In the rhetorical battles of the Revolutionary Era, far from being perceived as

---

[9] Robert W. Hoffert (1992), *A Politics of Tensions: The Articles of Confederation and American Political Ideas* (Boulder: University Press of Colorado), xiii.

[10] Lutz, "The Articles of Confederation as the Background to the Federal Republic," 55. The specification "or are perceived to have lost" is important, considering how often the apparent "losers" of American History have succeeded in implementing their ideas later. See Jeffrey Tullis and Nicole Melllow (2017), *Legacy of Losing in American Politics* (Chicago: University of Chicago Press).

[11] Merrill Jensen (1937), "The Articles of Confederation: A Re-interpretation," *Pacific Historical Review*, 6:2, 120. See also Merrill Jensen (1970), The Articles of Confederation: An Interpretation of the Social-Constitutional History of the American Revolution, 1774-1781 (Madison: University Wisconsin Press).

[12] Eric M. Freedman (1993), "Why Constitutional Lawyers and Historians Should Take a Fresh Look at the Emergence of the Constitution from the Confederation Period: The Case of Drafting of the Articles of Confederation," *Tennessee Law Review*, 60, 785.

[13] Jensen, *The Articles of Confederation*, xv. Besides the authors mentioned above, offering more nuanced interpretations than Jensen, see also Sanford Levinson (2013), *Framed: America's 51 Constitutions and the Crisis of Governance* (Oxford: Oxford University Press), or Gregory E. Maggs (2017), "A Concise Guide to the Articles of Confederation as a Source for Determining the Original Meaning of the Constitution," *George Washington Law Review*, 85:2, 397–450.

[14] Jonathan Israel (2017), *The Expanding Blaze: How the American Revolution Ignited the World, 1775–1848* (Princeton: Princeton University Press).

opposites, both "democracy" and "republicanism" had basically negative connotations, and were used by both sides as disparagement. Later, for more than a decade after 1776, they were often used interchangeably, with both positive and negative connotations.[15]

As a matter of fact, the struggle over a common vocabulary was mainly focused on a different pair of words, namely "sovereignty" and "people." Once again, the distinction between the people's two bodies and the legacy of the Puritan bidimensional covenant shall prove helpful in better understanding this uniquely American "hybrid theory of democracy," this "tacit dimension that is vital in its routine expression, but which is nearly absent or heavily masked in its most familiar, overt explanations of itself." As such, the interpretation advanced here addresses directly "America's intellectual challenge [which] is not to resolve the conflict within the mixed tradition either by denying the reality or by insisting on the purification of the tradition through the domination of one of its two theoretical forms."[16] Each of the two people's bodies will be shown to have played its own crucial role in this revolution of meanings.

Besides its practical advantages, independence from Great Britain in general and from the king in particular posed an entirely new set of theoretical challenges. "The kind of central government that was to replace British rule was as vital an issue as independence itself" – and for good reason.[17] As I showed in Chapter 3, in the years preceding the summer of 1776, the Patriots went to great lengths to emphasize the governmental or political contract that, via chartering, connected the corporate peoples of the colonies solely with the king. The king as such acted as an impartial arbitrator, de facto a *compromissarius*, between competing corporate interests. Thus, as early as 1764, while arguing for the rights of the British colonies and asserting that the "supreme and absolute power is originally and ultimately with the people," James Otis also acknowledged that "the necessity of a common, indifferent, and impartial judge makes all men seek one."[18] Or, as Joseph Galloway argued even more forcefully in the First Continental Congress, in support of his plan of constitutional union with Great Britain, absent "the authority of the Parent State," the colonies would be "in a perfect state of nature" against each other. "[A]nd should that authority be weakened or annulled, many subjects of unsettled disputes ... can only be settled by an appeal to sword, and must involve us all in the horrors of the civil war."[19]

[15] Adams, *The First American Constitutions*, chapter 4.

[16] Hoffert, *A Politics of Tensions*, xiv, xvi.   [17] Jensen, *The Articles of Confederation*, xix.

[18] James Otis (1764), "The Rights of the British Colonies Asserted and Proved" in Bernard Baylin, ed., *Pamphlets of the American Revolution, Vol. I, 1750-1765* (Cambridge, MA: The Bellknapp Press of Harvard University Press), 424–425.

[19] Quoted in Jensen, "The Articles of Confederation," 130.

As I will try to illustrate in the first part of this chapter, previous failed attempts to create an overarching political authority over the colonies, and thus *an* American people, left many wondering whether such a union had even a standing chance of succeeding. Who in this newly created, almost Hobbesian state of nature was to be the new arbitrator between the colonies became an increasingly important question to answer. Even if, in the beginning, the Continental Congress stepped in to fill the shoes of the king, it soon became clear that this was only a provisional solution, and that a permanent one was desperately needed.

To complicate matters even further, the issue of the impartial arbiter was closely related to that of sovereignty. After so many years of arguing in favor of the sovereign's right to charter the creation of a corporate people, where was this sovereignty to reside once there was no longer a king? Apparently, the answer was straightforward: the people were the sovereign. However, such a rhetorical answer was theoretically too vague to offer any practical solutions, thus forcing the colonists, under time constraints, to follow the model they knew best – that of the Puritans. According to this approach, as we have seen, the people were equally entitled to consent, via a majority vote, to the general form of government. They were to elect the wise and virtuous as leaders, after which this natural aristocracy was to be entrusted with the details. This is not to say that there were no exceptions. In Massachusetts, for example, some counties felt free "to take what form of government they please," arguing that, according to the Massachusetts Government Act, they were under no authority, as the contract between the king and the people had been nullified. Nevertheless, such cases were outliers.[20]

As discussed in the second part of the chapter, most of the colonists initially accepted the authority of the provincial legislatives not only to draft but also to ratify the state constitutions. "Within a few years, however," because of the popular pressure exercised from the bottom up, "a second stage was reached, when legislation and constitution making came to be considered two entirely different steps in the political process, each requiring a separate representative body."[21] According to Puritan tradition, popular ratifications were considered the norm, yet such exercises in democracy came with a price, particularly in the colonies further removed from the Puritan practice of town meetings. After "four different constitutions had to be sent to the people [of New Hampshire] between 1779 and 1783, before they found one of their liking, not for another quarter of century, in 1812, did a state outside New England risk sending a constitution to the voters for their approval."[22] "Even after this understanding had taken hold by the mid-nineteenth century, several conventions still opted against submitting their work to the people, whether because delegates were

---

[20] Adams, *The First American Constitutions*, 53.   [21] Ibid., 64.
[22] Rodgers, *Contested Truths*, 87.

not persuaded that popular ratification was essential to ensuring the legitimacy of their work ... or as a result of uncertainty about whether voters would approve of their work."[23]

Despite some notable differences between the constitutions of the eighteenth century and those of the nineteenth, they all shared at least some common features, and all required from their creators a willingness to compromise, usually away from the public eye.[24] This should come as no surprise, since, as Levinson points out, "all constitutions necessarily involve tradeoffs and compromises."[25] The state constitutions and Articles of Confederation were no exception. Once the constitutional conflict with Great Britain was put to rest by the Declaration of Independence, "the problem of large, rival minorities with no majority to control them made compromise a matter of the greatest necessity."[26]

As I shall try to demonstrate in the third part of this chapter, the prominence of the well-known compromises during the Convention of 1787 should not obscure the direct connections between the compromises of the Second Continental Congress and the ones made in Philadelphia, or the role played by the paradigm of the two people's bodies in affecting the willingness to compromise in both cases. As a constitutional lawyer noticed, "the delegates divide initially on the basis of the interest of their states, and then unite, on the basis of shared ideological premises and the practical need for consensus, to reach pragmatically acceptable compromises."[27] Yet Elazar's warning is worth remembering:

The tendency has been to assume either that the philosophic assumptions of the state constitutions are the same as those of the United State Constitution or that state constitutions are worldly patchworks of compromises having little, if any, rhyme or reason. Neither assumption is accurate, and even those constitutions which can be said to be a bundle of compromises reflect the political struggles between representatives of competing conceptions of government within particular states.[28]

4.1 "... A ROPE OF SAND"

As we have seen in Chapter 2, "the colonists were willing to let the legislatures speak for them in matters of self-definition and the creation of governmental institutions but not when it came to forming themselves into a people or

---

[23] John J. Dinan (2009), *The American State Constitutional Tradition* (Lawrence: University Press of Kansas), 17–18.

[24] See, for example, Adams, *The First American Constitutions*, Levinson, *Framed*, or Alan G. Tarr (1998), *Understanding State Constitutions* (Princeton: Princeton University Press).

[25] Levinson, *Framed*, 12.

[26] Peter B. Knupfer (1991), *The Union as It Is: Constitutional Unionism and Sectional Compromise, 1787–1861* (Chapel Hill: The University of North Carolina Press), 16.

[27] Freedman, "Why Constitutional Lawyers ...," 784.

[28] Daniel J. Elazar (1982), "The Principles and Traditions Underlying State Constitutions," *Publius*, 12, 11.

founding a government. *The exception* to the latter is found in those documents founding a federation or confederation of existing towns or colonies."[29] This is precisely what happened in the largely forgotten Articles of the Confederation of the United Colonies, meant initially to better protect the Puritan colonies against the threat of the indigenous tribes helped by the French and the Dutch. The decision was left entirely in the hands of the "elected aristocracy." On the one hand, the practice of Congregationalism made the idea of a Confederation almost natural; on the other, the same practice informed a fiercely protected autonomy, which made compromises between corporate interests more difficult, thus explaining why the union of 1643 was in the making for several years.

In 1638, Winthrop's explanation for the postponing of the confederation was that "another plot the old serpent had against us, by sowing jealousies and differences between us and our friends at Connecticut, and also Plymouth."[30] Yet, in 1640, commissioners appointed by the general courts and invested with "full and absolute power" successfully settled by arbitration a land dispute between Plymouth and Massachusetts Bay, encouraging the idea of a body that could act as a *compromissarius* in solving all intercolonial disputes.[31] Finally, on May 29, 1643, commissioners from Massachusetts Bay, Plymouth, Connecticut, and New Haven met in Boston and drew up the Articles of Confederation. Being "desirous of union and studious of peace, they readily yielded each to other, in such things as tended to the common good."[32] Rhode Island was excluded from the start, its government being considered anarchical and heretical, because "Mrs. Hutchinson and those of Aquiday island broached new heresies every day."[33] Thus, the first intercolonial constitution was born under Puritan auspices – the making of the aristocracy of the virtuous.

Each colony was to be represented by two commissioners, and most decisions were to be made with at least six out of the eight votes, except for the acceptance of new members, which required unanimity. At each meeting, either ordinary or extraordinary, the eight commissioners were to elect a president from amongst themselves, "whose office and works shal be to take care and direct for order and a comely carrying on of all the proceedings,"[34] but who did not have more decisional power than any of the other members. Undeniably, the document introduced features that would be imitated by all future attempts to unite the colonies:

(1) representation by whole states; (2) equal votes for each state; (3) two delegates from each state; (4) a national forum; (5) power to make treatises with foreign states; (6) war

---

[29] Lutz, *Colonial Origins*, xxxvii (emphasis added).
[30] Quoted in Harry M. Ward (1961), *The United Colonies of New England – 1643-90* (New York: Vantage Press), 51.
[31] Ibid., 40.   [32] Quoted in Ward, *The United Colonies*, 42.   [33] Ibid., 42.   [34] Ibid., 389.

powers, such as declaring war and calling into service of the "Country" the militia of the states; (7) regulatory powers, though without enforcement machinery . . .; (8) overseeing of Indian affairs of the colonies; (9) a watchdog for the common welfare; (10) an entrenchment of conservative interests among the majority of its members.[35]

As we have seen, Article Two, for example, would be echoed almost literally, more than a century later, by the first constitution of the United States:

The said United Colonies for themselves and their posterities do joyntly and severally hereby enter into a firme and perpetual league of friendship and amytie for offence and defence, mutual advice and succor upon all just occasions both for preserving and propagateing the truth and liberties of the Gospell and for their owne mutual safety and welfare.[36]

In line with the Puritan tradition, the ratification of the Articles happened in the General Courts of each colony, and the commissioners were also appointed by them, serving as ambassadors of the colony's interests. Thus, it was considered unwise to appoint deputies, understood as representing only particular constituencies inside of the colony, favoring instead general officers. The colonists referred to the board of Commissioners as the "Supreme Court," since its main role throughout its existence was to arbitrate disputes arising among the colonies. However, their decisions were good only so long as they were accepted by the colonies involved.

Without a supreme judicial authority to interpret the "true meaning" of the Articles [as referred to in the first article] and without coercive powers in the Confederation, each colony could interpret the Articles to its liking. Thus, during the course of the Confederation, the Puritan colonies, to their amazement, on occasion found themselves in good faith on opposite sides of the fence.[37]

Despite all these shortcomings, the New England Confederation managed to survive for half a century and enjoyed more than thirty years of peace – no small feat considering all the vagaries it had to endure both internally and externally from the political tumults that reverberated across the ocean from the mother country. In the end, the expansion of the New England settlements "left the individual colonies more cohesive and better able to look out for themselves, thus diminishing the benefits of the union."[38] Reviving the Union would have required a new constitution, and the colonies were in no position to make such an effort. Nevertheless, the experiment demonstrated that, despite their differences, the peoples of the American colonies could eventually combine themselves into one body. It was neither an easy task nor an impossible one, provided that the parties were willing to compromise.

In the following years, several other plans of union were devised, sometimes from Great Britain – such as the Royal Commission to Governor Edmund Andros to unite all of New England, New York, and the Jerseys (1688) – and

---

[35] Ibid., 379–380.   [36] Ibid., 384–385.   [37] Ibid., 52.   [38] Ibid., 366.

sometimes by the colonists themselves, like *A Virginian's Plan* in "An Essay on the Government of the English Plantations on the Continent of America" (1701).[39] The Albany Plan of Union (1754), however, remains the only serious attempt to bring the colonies under one authority before the actual Articles of the Confederation. Devised by Benjamin Franklin with the purpose of uniting the colonies in the face of the impending war with France, the plan had some revolutionary features that, if adopted, would have made the Union even stronger than under the future Articles of Confederation.

The plan was skillfully drafted to promote compromise, both with Great Britain and among the colonies. In Madison's words, it was an attempt "to introduce a compromising substitute, that might at once satisfy the British requisitions, and save [the colonies] own rights from violation."[40] According to the plan, no colony had veto power and, following the colonial pattern, the "president general," assigned by the Crown, was to sign all legislation passed by a common Grand Council endowed with the power to control the purse strings. Yet the strength of Franklin's plan lay in its design for the legislature.

Elected every three years, the representatives were to be apportioned according to the financial contributions of each colony. This would have put the colonies in the position of arguing for a decrease in their respective representation every time they asked for a lower tax levy. [...] It was possible for four out of the eleven colonies to create a majority, but it was also unlikely that this would happen because the three largest colonies were each the centerpiece of a different political subculture. The most likely coalitions were not based on the size of the colonies, but rather on a New England coalition centered around Massachusetts, a southern coalition centered around Virginia, and a center coalition built around Pennsylvania.[41]

Playing on the division between the three American subcultures, as defined by Elazar, was meant to encourage compromise and coalition-building. The division "would later be reproduced almost exactly in the Continental Congress and Articles of Confederation." Furthermore, "when the United States Constitution established the number of seats initially to be allocated to each state in the House of Representatives, the division between regions was very close to Franklin's proposal made in 1754."[42] For the time being, the Albany Plan was rejected both by the Crown, which saw in it an attempt to undermine its authority, and by the colonies, which were unwilling to sacrifice their much cherished autonomy. As a matter of fact, considering the circumstances, what was surprising about it "was not that it was universally rejected, but that it had been proposed and adopted by a conference of leaders in the first place."[43]

---

[39] For a complete list of these plans, see Lutz, "The Articles of Confederation," 58.

[40] James Madison (1985), "Preface" in *Notes of Debates in the Federal Convention of 1797* (Athens: Ohio University Press), 4.

[41] Lutz, "The Articles of Confederation," 60.   [42] Ibid., 61.

[43] Jack P. Greene (1982), "The Background of the Articles of Confederation," *Publius*, 12:4, 33.

Even a decade later, in 1764, the cultural differences between the corporate interests of the peoples from each colony made the prospect of a compromise among them nothing more than a wishful thinking. In his widely read treatise on *The Administration of the Colonies* (London, 1764), former Massachusetts governor Thomas Pownall expressed his strong skepticism of a possible union of the peoples from the colonies, due to

> the different manner in which they are settled, the different modes under which they live, the different forms of charters, grants, and frames of government they possess, the various principles of repulsion ... the different interests which they actuate, the religious interests by which they are actuated, the rivalship and jealousies which arise from hence, and the impracticability, if not impossibility, of reconciling and accommodating these incompatible ideas and claims.

The peoples from the colonies, argued another writer from the era, were all too "peculiarly attached to their respective forms of Government," forms of society, and interests to ever "relish a union with one another." They were but "a rope of sand."[44] Given these marked differences, John Dickinson worried that, without Great Britain's authority, the peoples from the colonies would fall prey to "centuries of mutual Jealousies, Hatreds, Wars, and Devastations."[45]

Under these circumstances, as shown in the previous chapter, the king became, for people like Benjamin Franklin, the overarching Umpire, the *Compromissarius*, a "dernier resort, for settling all their Disputes, a Means of preserving Peace among them with each other, and a Center in which their Common Force might be united."[46] Franklin's compromising attitude toward Great Britain is also apparent in a letter he sent from London to his grand-nephew, Jonathan Williams, on June 6, 1770: "I only know that generally the dispute is thought a dangerous one, and that many wish to see it well compromised in time, lest by a continuance of mutual provocations the breach should become past healing."[47] Yet the inability of the colonists to maintain a united front during the Townsend Acts crisis between 1768 and 1770 was not indicative of any future prospects for Union.

When in May 23, 1774 the New York Committee suggested to the Boston Committee of Correspondence that a congress of deputies from all colonies should be called without delay to pass "some unanimous resolutions formed

---

[44] "Some Thoughts on the Settlements and Government on our Colonies in North America," 10 March 1763, Add. Mss (Liverpool Papers), British Library – quoted in Jack P. Greene (1982), "The Background," 19.

[45] John Dickinson to William Pitt, 21 December 1675, Chatham Papers, PRO 30/8/97, Public Record Office (London).

[46] Quoted in Jerrilyn Greene Marston (1987), *King and Congress: The Transfer of Political Legitimacy, 1774–1776* (Princeton: Princeton University Press), 26–27.

[47] Benjamin Franklin (1904), *The Works of Benjamin Franklin*, Vol. V Letters and Misc. Writings 1768–1772, 186.

in this fatal emergency," they knew the difficulty of the task ahead.[48] "Fundamentally there was no ground for compromise between Great Britain and the radical party in the colonies," yet many were still hoping for a peaceful resolution of the conflict.[49] The prospect of "unanimous resolutions" was further complicated not only by the differences between New England colonies, the Middle colonies, and the Southern colonies but also by the fact that "colonial nationalism," for lack of a better term, was by then so developed as to make unanimity almost impossible.

Each delegate thought of his own colony as his country, as an independent nation in its dealing with England and with its neighbors, with whom relations were often as not unfriendly. It is this simple fact that is too often overlooked. Instead of lamenting the absence of "national feeling," one must recognize that it was there in an intense form, but in the form that is illustrated by the attitude of John Adams when he wrote of Massachusetts Bay as "our country."[50]

As a result, Joseph Galloway maintained his skepticism that, absent a constitutional union with Great Britain, the colonists could ever agree on creating an overarching structure of authority. Remaining instead, in a Hobbesian state of nature against each other.

Their different Forms of Government – Productions of Soil – and Views of Commerce, their different Religions – Tempers and private Interests – their Prejudices against, and Jealousies of, each other – all have, and ever will, from the Nature and Reason of things, conspire to create such a Diversity of Interests, Inclinations, and Decisions, that they can never [long] unite together, even for their own Protection. [...] In this Situation Controversies founded in Interests, Religion or Ambition, will soon embrue their Hands in the blood of each other.[51]

Yet if the colonies were indeed in a state of nature, argued Patrick Henry, on the first day the delegates met, where were the boundaries and landmarks between colony and colony? After previously pleading in favor of large states, such as Virginia, being given more weight in "the general council," he switched sides, famously claiming that "the distinctions between Virginians, Pennsylvanians, New Yorkers, and New Englanders are no more. I am not a Virginian, but an American."[52] Following the supposition that all governments had been eradicated, the logic forced him to conclude that *all* distinctions had been eradicated.[53]

Such a radically populist conception scared many of the moderates in Congress. Gouverneur Morris gave voice to these worries when he bid

---

[48] In *The Correspondence and Public Papers of John Jay* (1890), edited by Henry P. Johnson (4 vols, New York), I: 13.

[49] Jensen, *The Articles of Confederation*, 55.   [50] Ibid., 56.

[51] G Joseph Galloway to [Samuel Verplanck], December 30, 1774, quoted in Greene, "The Background," 20.

[52] Quoted in John Adams, "Notes on the Debates," in *Works*, vol. 2, 367.

[53] See Jensen, *The Articles of Confederation*, 58.

"farewell aristocracy! . . . If the disputes with Great Britain continues, we shall be under the domination of a riotous mob."[54] The people's two bodies were to be reduced to one, and of the worse kind – that of an unruly multitude. For the time being, the issue was put to rest – on the one hand, because there was no data to evaluate the relative weight of each colony in terms of population or property, and on the other, because, as John Rutledge pointed out, the Congress had "no coercive or legislative authority."[55] In the end, each colony received a vote, to the satisfaction of the supporters of a corporatist view of the peoples from the colonies.

For the following years, the main line of division remained the one separating the moderates seeking a protection of Americans' rights inside the empire, through a redefinition of the relations between the colonies and the mother country, and the radicals seeking to sever all connections with Great Britain. This division would persist at least for the First Congress and the early years of the Second.

On one side were congressional radicals – mostly men of New England and Virginia – who moved quickly than others away from the colonies' dutiful adherence to, and even love of, the king and inclusion in the British Empire. On the other side were congressional moderates (and, early on, conservatives, who would in the end remain loyal to the king) – most importantly men of the mid-Atlantic colonies – who were far more cautious about distancing themselves from the Crown and empire and far more hopeful, up to the beginning of 1776, of achieving a just and constitutional reconciliation.[56]

This might not be a coincidence, considering that, as shown in Chapter 3, the colonies of New England and Virginia were vastly more religiously homogenous and thus less prone to compromise their corporate identities. Furthermore, it might not be a coincidence either that the compromisers from the mid-Atlantic colonies "were among those who later pushed more strenuously for the adoption of the Constitution in 1787–1788, as we shall see in more detail in the following chapter.[57]

Because of the balance of power between the two factions, little was accomplished during the first few weeks of the First Continental Congress until, largely thanks to Samuel Adams, the first significant compromise was reached. In Galloway's words, it was Adams "who by his superior application managed at once the faction in Congress at Philadelphia, and the factions in New England."[58] The approval of the Suffolk Resolves gave at least some satisfaction to both sides. To the radicals, it was a big step in the right direction because it declared that the "the commercial intercourse" with Great Britain, Ireland, and the West Indies should be stopped. It also specified how, and what penalties

---

[54] Quoted in Jensen, "The Articles of Confederation," 126.
[55] Quoted in Jensen, *The Articles of Confederation*, 58.
[56] Shain, *The Declaration of Independence*, 10.   [57] Ibid.
[58] *Historical and Political Reflections*, quoted in Jensen, *The Articles of Confederation*, 61.

would occur for disregarding this decision, namely "social ostracism, commercial boycott, and confiscation of property." To the moderates this was acceptable, as it recognized George III as sovereign of the colonies "agreeable to compact." And if the document stipulated, to the satisfaction of the radicals, that the late acts of Parliament closing the port of Boston, etc., were "infractions according to the laws of nature," they were *also* "infractions" according to "the British constitution, and the provincial charter."[59]

This was no small compromise. The matter of the foundation for the granting of colonial rights was heavily disputed. On the one hand, the moderates appealed to the English constitution, the common law, and the charters. On the other, the radicals insisted on natural rights. As John Adams later confessed, he was "very strenuous for retaining and insisting on it [the law of nature], as a resource to which we might be driven by Parliament much sooner than we were aware."[60] Adams's insistence on the inclusion of the appeal to natural rights was revealing for his generally uncompromising stance – a peculiar one even among his fellow Patriots. "From the moment he entered public life, he always seemed to travel the road not taken. Americans have rarely seen a political leader of such fierce independence and unyielding integrity. [...] He would compromise neither with Governor Thomas Hutchinson nor with the Boston mob."[61] As he put it in a letter to Horatio Gates on March 23, 1776, when discussing the hesitancy of some members of Congress to declare independence. "In Politicks the Middle Way is none at all."[62] He was, in Parrington words, "the uncompromising realist" of the Founding Era.[63]

Unsurprisingly, among the Founders, John Adams stood out for consistently using compromise with its negative, French connotations. To give just a few examples from among a long list, he asked Jefferson, "Have I compromised myself or the public in any thing?"; wrote to Secretary Livingston "that the King's dignity and the nation's honor are compromised"; and, speaking of the Duke of Dorcester in a letter to Jay, observed that the Duke "did not incline to compromise himself by hazarding any opinion."[64] Ironically, it was precisely his uncompromising realism that would later make him suspicious of all parties, falling "ideologically between the poles of Jeffersonianism (the advocates of states' rights) and Hamiltonianism (the supporters of a strong activist state)." Revealing of the increased polarization of American politics, his

[59] For more details, see Jensen, *The Articles of Confederation*, 61–64.
[60] John Adams, *Notes on Debates*, quoted in Jensen, *The Articles of Confederation*, 65.
[61] Bradley C. Thompson (2000), *The Revolutionary Writings of John Adams* (Indianapolis: Liberty Fund), ix.
[62] In Shain, *The Declaration of Independence*, 419.
[63] Vernon P. Parrington (1927), *The Colonial Mind*, vol I of *Main Currents in American Thought* (New York: Harcourt, Brace & World), 312, quoted in David S. Brown (2016) *Moderates: The Vital Center of American Politics, from the Founding to Today* (Chapel Hill: University of North Carolina Press), 14.
[64] John Adams (1987), *Complete Works*, Vol. 8 (Indianapolis: Liberty Fund), 315; 9; 249.

uncompromisingly moderate position, placed between "aristocracy" and "democracy," made him suspicious in the eyes of the American public for a long time.

For the time being, a compromise was reached, and the Declaration and Resolves of the First Continental Congress read "That the inhabitants of the English colonies in North-America, by the immutable laws of nature, the principles of the English constitution, and the several charters or compacts, have the following RIGHTS; . . ." The enumeration of rights was largely pleasing for the majority of the delegates, as it emphasized the role of the British constitution, and corporate more than individual rights, while also defending the British monarchy. "These commitments [. . .] stand in sharp contrast with the universal natural rights and popular-consent theorizing associated with Lockean liberalism and the Declaration of Independence."[65] The Declaration also called for a Second Continental Congress the next year.

The First Continental Congress officially ended on October 26, 1774, and the Second opened May 10, 1775. Formally, it stayed in existence until it became the permanent organ of the newly created national government under the Articles of Confederation, although the use of the title "Continental Congress" persisted throughout the Confederation period until the second Constitution went into effect in 1789.[66] It was a period of dramatic shifts in opinions. Even as the evolutions of 1775 and 1776 pushed the delegates closer and closer to accepting the idea of a union, their fears about the impossibility to bridge the divisions among the colonies grew even stronger. As John Adams wrote to Samuel Osgood on November 14, 1775, "In such a Period as this, Sir, when Thirteen Colonies, unacquainted in great Measure, with each other are rushing together into one Mass, it would be a Miracle, if Such heterogeneous ingredients did not at first produce violent Fermentations."[67] Just a few days later, on November 25, he wrote to Joseph Hawley: "I dread the Consequences of this Dissimilitude of Character [among the colonies] and without the Utmost Caution . . . and the most considerate Forbearance with one another and prudent Condenscention . . . they will certainly be fatal."[68]

Such caution was not necessarily foreign to more dismissive attitudes toward other colonies. In the same letter to Hawley, Adams also wrote: "The Characters of Gentlemen in the four New England Colonies differ so much from those in the others . . . as much as [in] several distinct Nations almost. Gentlemen, Men of Sense, or any Kind of Education in the other Colonies are much fewer in

---

[65] Shain, *The Declaration of Independence*, p. 11. See also Greene, "The Background," 25.

[66] Telling for the continuities between the two Continental Congresses, the secretary, Charles Thomson of Philadelphia, was elected at the opening session of 1774 and managed to keep, almost by himself, a journal of every session of Congress, copies of reports of all committees, records of correspondence, etc., until the new government took over in 1787. Sadly, he was given no special recognition during his lifetime.

[67] Quoted in Greene, "The Background," 16.   [68] Ibid., 20.

Proportion than in N. England." Not even the Declaration of Independence managed to improve some of these superior attitudes among the colonists. Speaking of the people of Georgia, on August 27, 1776, Charles Lee, the general from Virginia, commented with disdain in a letter to John Armstrong: "Upon the whole I should not be surpris'd if they were to propose mounting a body of Mermaids on Alligators."[69]

Not discouraged by these intercolonial differences and tensions, and always on the lookout for a feasible compromise, on July 21, 1775, Benjamin Franklin presented to the Congress a draft of the "Articles of Confederation and Perpetual Union [Between] the several Colonies," carefully stipulating that "each colony shall enjoy and retain as much as it may think fit of its own present Laws, Customs, Rights, Privileges ..." But, by the same token, Franklin was also proposing an overall Arbitrator. The "Power and Duty" of the General Congress would extend not only to "Determining on War and Peace" but also to "the Settling [of] all Disputes and Differences between Colony and Colony ..."[70] Unfortunately, the timing was not right. Congress postponed its discussion for almost six months, only to reject it on January 16, 1776.

Not everyone was pleased with the result. At the beginning of 1776, Carter Braxton of Virginia wrote that if independence were to be achieved, "the Continent would be torn in pieces by intestine Wars and Convulsions," unless all intercolonial disputes were settled before independence, and above all "A Grand Continental league must be formed and a superintending Power also."[71] On June 7, 1776, as the logical follow-up to his motion "[t]hat these United Colonies are, and of right ought to be, free and independent States," Richard Henry Lee moved "[t]hat a plan of confederation be prepared and transmitted to the respective Colonies for their consideration and approbation."[72] On July 12, a committee of five members presented the first draft, which the Congress ordered to be printed, requesting that neither the delegates nor the printers disclose its content. The requirement of secrecy became a staple of the era, and almost a prerequisite for reaching any compromise.[73] On August 20, 1776, a revised version was ordered to be printed under the same condition of secrecy.[74] Optimistic, John Witherspoon observed a few days later that "honour, interest, safety and necessity" had concurred in creating "such a degree of union throughout the colonies, as no one would have prophesized, and hardly any would have expected." Only "a well planned confederacy among the states of America" could ensure "their future security

---

[69] Quoted in Freedman, "Why Constitutional Lawyers," 813.
[70] Worthington C. Ford, ed. (1907), *Journal of the Continental Congress*, Vol. 2, 194–199.
[71] Quoted in Jensen, "The Articles of Confederation," 131.
[72] Ford et al., *Journals of the Continental Congress*, Vol. 5, 425.
[73] See further. Also, on the need for secrecy in reaching compromises, see Levinson, *Framed*, 49.
[74] For more details, see Freedman, "Why Constitutionalist Lawyers ...," 798–800.

and improvement."[75] His optimism proved misplaced. The plan for confeder-
ating was dropped from consideration in August 1776, not to be seriously
discussed until April 1777.

Meanwhile, despite the vagaries of war, there was a more pressing matter at
hand – framing the new state constitutions. John Adams once again proved a
realist when, on June 3, 1776, he wrote to Patrick Henry:

It has appeared to me that the natural course and order of things was this: for every
colony to institute a government; for all the colonies to confederate, and define the limits
of the continental Constitution; *then* to declare the colonies a sovereign state, *or a
number of confederate sovereign states*; and last of all, to form treaties with foreign
powers. But I fear we cannot proceed systematically, and that we shall be obliged to
declare ourselves independent States, before we confederate, and indeed before all the
colonies have established their governments.[76]

Some members of Congress entertained for a while the idea of proposing a
common plan for constitutions to all colonies. Concerned that different constitutions would only increase the already extant differences and tensions among
the colonies, Richard Henry Lee asked John Adams in May 1776: "Would not
a uniform plan of government, prepared by America by the Congress, and
approved by the colonies, be a surer foundation of unceasing harmony to the
whole?"[77] Adams replied by insisting that each colony should have the privilege of determining its own constitution – and eventually Congress refused to
impose any particular form of government.[78] Hence, even before the Articles of
Confederation, the framing of the state constitutions became the first ground
for seriously testing all the implications of the people's two bodies' paradigm.

4.2 "WE ARE THE STATE"

When the states were given the opportunity to frame their own constitutions,
they turned to what they knew best, namely the charters on which colonies like
Massachusetts Bay, Rhode Island, Connecticut, Pennsylvania, and Maryland
had been based. There was, however, a theoretical problem: these charters were
made possible by the letters patent of the crown. Absent the royal authority
"to give or grant a constitution," this sovereign power was transferred almost
naturally to "the people."[79] In its resolution of May 10 and 15, 1776, the
Second Continental Congress advised the colonies to reorganize themselves on
the basis of "the authority of the people," without going into specifics, except

[75] John Witherspoon, Speech in Congress [July 30, 1776], in Paul H. Smith et al., eds. (1976),
Letters of Delegates in Congress (Washington, DC), Vol. 4, 584–587.
[76] In Edmund C. Burnett, ed. (1921–1936), *Letters of Members of the Continental Congress*
(Washington, DC), Vol. I, 47 (emphasis added).
[77] In *Works of John Adams*, Vol. IX, 374.
[78] For more details, see Adams, *The First American Constitutions*, chapter 2.
[79] Adams, *The First American Constitutions*, 18.

that "[s]omehow 'the people' had to be originators of the basic law of the land."[80] Yet as late as 1775, this "people" still had a reputation to build, since, as we have seen, both "republicanism" and "democracy" – the two key concepts associated with people's sovereignty – were used predominantly as pejoratives by both Loyalists and Patriots.

It was an established British rhetorical practice to discredit opponents by branding them "republicans." Some Patriots began, rather timidly, to dispel "this dreadful chimera from your imagination,"[81] but not until the publication in 1776 of Paine's *Common Sense* was republicanism presented as a positive good. Even then, the new meaning was far from widely embraced, as evidenced by the fact that none of the eighteen state constitutions adopted between 1776 and 1787 used the term. It is worth noticing that the Declaration of Independence also does not suggest a preference for this form of government. As previously mentioned, John Adams joined Paine in using "republicanism" as a form of government to be sought only in January 1776.[82] For most colonists, being a republican meant being a radical, or even an anarchist.

The same applied to "democracy," used principally as an equivalent of "mob rule." Implying egalitarianism was worrisome for the believers in a natural aristocracy of the wise and the virtuous. A provisional solution to this conundrum came from the Puritan legacy: the specific form of government (i.e., the constitution) was to be determined by the elected few in the legislatures, in the same way the latter had drafted and passed bills. Even before the Declaration of Independence, four legislatures – New Hampshire, South Carolina, New Jersey, and Virginia – adopted "provisional" constitutions, while also expressing their "earnest desire" to reconcile with Great Britain and to put an end to "the present unhappy and unnatural contest with Great Britain."[83] They considered themselves "the full and free representations of the people." Two other legislatives, from Connecticut and Rhode Island, did not even think that a new constitution was necessary, since the nullification of the charters by the king did not affect the desire of the people to live by them.

The practice did not last long. Although, in accordance to the Puritanical legacy of the people's two bodies, most agreed that "the voters should delegate the exercise of the power to a few of the most wise and good,"[84] two questions remained to be addressed: first, if the legislature was still representative of the people in a matter as fundamental as the establishment of a constitution; and second, if the same legislature had the right to approve such a constitution in

[80] Ibid., 63.
[81] "To the People of Pennsylvania," March 1776, signed "Salus Populi," quoted in Adams, *The First American Constitutions*, 104.
[82] Lutz, *Popular Consent*, 3.
[83] South Carolina Constitution of 1776, Preamble; New Hampshire Constitution of 1776, 2.
[84] John Adams to Henry Lee (1775), quoted in Adams, *The First American Constitutions*, 123.

the name of the people. Eventually, the answers in both cases would turn out to be negative.

On the first matter, Thomas Young from Pennsylvania was allegedly the first to distinguish between the "supreme delegate power" of elected representatives and the "supreme constituent power" of the people: "They are the supreme constituent power, and of course their immediate Representatives are the supreme delegate power; and as soon as the delegate power gets too far out of the hands of the constituent power, a tyranny is in some degree established."[85] The fact that Young was a radical from Pennsylvania might not have been a coincidence. When, in the spring of 1776, the uncompromising advocates for independence in the Pennsylvania Assembly came to the realization that they lacked a majority, they demanded that a special convention be called to draft a new constitution. Like their predecessors, they were willing to compromise among themselves but not with the "unbelievers."

Unconsciously adhering to the view of the English Puritans in 1649, [the Provincial Conference of Committee of the Province of Pennsylvania] felt that only those citizens of Pennsylvania who recognized the new regime should have a hand in forming the new government. Thus, only those citizens who rejected the authority of the English crown and wanted a constitution at this time would be allowed to elect representatives to the convention.[86]

The same happened in Delaware, where the loyalist sentiment was even stronger. A petition addressed to the Continental Congress rejecting the idea of a new constitution allegedly had five thousand signatures on it, but it was intercepted and destroyed before it reached the Congress. In the same uncompromising spirit, the assembly restricted the right to vote to the people that swore an oath "to ... support and maintain the independence of this Government."[87]

On the matter of popular ratification, the positions were even stronger. According to the Puritan legacy, the selected natural aristocracy was entitled to draft the constitution, but the power to approve it belonged exclusively "to the inhabitants at large." It was, pointed out "the artisans and the mechanics" from New York, "the right which God has given them, in common with all men, to judge whether it be consistent with their interest to accept or reject a Constitution framed for the State of which they are members." In a similar way, as early as May 1776, a town meeting in Pittsfield, Massachusetts, argued that, once King George had broken his contract, the people *at large* had a duty to approve a new constitution.

The first step to be taken by a people in such a state for the Enjoyment or Restoration of Civil Government amongst them, is the formation of a fundamental Constitution as the Basis and ground work of Legislation.

---

[85] An open letter dated April 11, 1777, *To the Inhabitants of Vermont, a Free and Independent State ...*, quoted in Adams, *The First American Constitutions*, 65.
[86] Ibid., 78.   [87] Quoted in ibid., 75.

That the Approbation of the Majority of the people of this fundamental Constitution is absolutely necessary to give Life and being to it. That then and 'till then is the foundation laid for Legislation ...

That a Representative Body may form, but cannot impose said fundamental Constitution upon a people. They being but servants of the people cannot be greater than their Masters, and must be responsible to them. If this fundamental Constitution is above the whole Legislature, the Legislature cannot certainly make it, it must be the Approbation of the Majority which gives Life and being to it.[88]

The problem with this Puritan legacy, however, was that it required people trained in the art of self-government. While opposing what he saw as the populist constitution of Pennsylvania, Benjamin Rush, writing under the pseudonym of "Sidney," doubted that regular people, while able to judge the principles of a constitution, were equally able to judge the particular form of government:

There is a material difference between the principles and form of government. We judge of the principles of a government by our *feelings* – of its form by our *reason*. The bulk of mankind are judges of the *principles* of a government, whether it be free and happy. Men of education and reflection only are judges of the *form* of a government, whether it be calculated to promote the happiness of society by restraining arbitrary power and licentiousness – by excluding corruption – and by giving the utmost possible *duration* to the enjoyment of liberty or otherwise.[89]

Thus, "it may not be coincidental that popular ratification developed in two New England states, where the institution of town meetings provided a mechanism for asserting the will of the people."[90] In 1778, almost the entire adult male population of Massachusetts had an opportunity not only to vote on the draft of the new constitution but also to propose amendments to it – something unprecedented in the history of modern constitutionalism. Even more impressive was the quality of the debates, "comparable in intensity and sophistication to the debate ten years later over the draft of the new Federal Convention."[91] South Carolina also scheduled a year of public discussion before drafting its 1778 constitution. Naturally, these constitutional exercises were widely followed in Europe, from Prussia to France, where the new state constitutions were republished and publicly discussed.[92]

---

[88] Quoted in ibid., 85, 88.
[89] "Maxims for Republics," *United States Magazine*, I (1779), 18–19. Quoted in Adams, *The First American Constitutions*, 120. Emphases in the original.
[90] Tarr, *Understanding State Constitutions*, 70.
[91] Adams, *The First American Constitutions*, 5.
[92] Robert R. Palmer (1969), *The Age of Democratic Revolution: A Political History of Europe and America, 1760–1800* (Princeton: Princeton University Press). See also Jonathan Israel (2017), *The Expanding Blaze: How the American Revolution Ignited the World, 1775-1848* (Princeton: Princeton University Press).

At the same time, these constitutional exercises were also exercises in the practice of compromise. The task of the convention in Massachusetts was to ratify the constitution "if upon a fair Examination it shall *appear* that it is approved of by at least two thirds of those who are free and twenty one years of age, belonging to this State, and *present to several Meetings*."[93] The problem was that there were more than 174 town meeting resolutions, and most articles were approved only on the condition that they would be amended. It soon became clear that amendments meant to please one town would be rejected by others, and that the process of ratification would have no end. The problem "could be solved only by compromising principles. [...] As article by article of the constitution was read to the convention, the chairman asked, 'Is it your opinion that the people have accepted this article?' The result was 'a very great majority' for every article."[94]

It was certainly a sign of the political maturity of the American founding generation that in the face of such difficulties two obvious dangers were avoided: the theoretically inclined were not allowed to become doctrinaires fighting mainly for the purity of their principles, and those with a taste and talent for the mere exercises of power were not enabled to throw all principles overboard . . .[95]

It also became evident that debates in the conventions were more likely to reach suitable compromises as long as they were kept away from the public eye. The conventions of the eighteenth century were "closet affairs for the most part, meeting at times behind closed doors, rarely printing more than a perfunctory parliamentary account of their proceedings."[96] The advantages of secrecy when drafting a constitution were forgotten neither in the case of the Articles of Confederation nor in Philadelphia in 1787. They were largely ignored in the state conventions of the nineteenth century when the more egalitarian view of society became increasingly popular. Few, like Milton Gregg in the Indiana Convention of 1850–1851, still tried to oppose the trend, if for no other reason than expediency. Public records would only encourage bad rhetoric:

Now here are at least 150 of us, all deeply imbued with the same perhaps laudable, ambition to do something to immortalize our names, and transmit hem to posterity. [...] And how is this desirable end to be attained? Why sir, each of us have got to set out wits to work, to concoct a speech – no matter on what subject, nor how irrelevant it may be to the subject matter under consideration, so it be of sufficient length, and full of sound and fury, signifying nothing.[97]

By that time, however, Gregg was in the minority. For most delegates of the nineteenth-century state conventions, publicity was a must. Sometimes, the

[93] *Resolution of the house of representatives on June 15, 1779*, Taylor, ed., Massachusetts, 117.
[94] Adams, *The First American Constitutions*, 96–97.   [95] Ibid., 97–98.
[96] Rodgers, *Contested Truths*, 94.
[97] Quoted in Dinan, *The American State Constitutional Tradition*, 20–21.

justification was sheer pride, as in the case of Richard Field at the New Jersey Convention of 1844: "I confess I have a little State pride in having these debates correctly reported ... I cannot agree in the belief, that our labors here will be of little value. I see no reason why we may not form a Constitution which will be a model for other States and other Countries."[98] Most often, publicity of the debates was considered a must for a citizenry that would then be called on to pass judgments on the works of the convention:

The constitution that we are to adopt, will be presented to the people for their ratification or rejection, and it is due to them, that the motives and influences that have entered into its adoption by us, should go forth with it, to aid the people in forming an opinion in regard to its merits and value. Let them have the same light and the same means of forming their judgment that we have.[99]

"Though the sovereignty of the people was a common place of the Revolution and the early years of the republic, the phrase rose to full pitch only in the 1830s and 1840s, when more common sorts of men than had ever ruled before seized it to wedge open the machinery of government for the many."[100] In the process, secrecy came to be equated with elitism or, worse, nefarious conspiracies. Publicity and full transparency were the necessary antidotes to such attempts to undermine the sovereignty of the people.

No one recorded the debate over the New York constitution of 1776. The debates in the revisory convention of 1846, in contrast, were scribbled down, more or less verbatim, by two teams of stenographers and set up in close to a thousand pages of double-columned type to be hawked as commercial ventures by rival Albany newspapers.[101]

Indeed, the distinctions between the state constitutions of the eighteenth and nineteenth centuries are hard to ignore, both in terms of length and of content, revealing patterns in the development of American political thinking. "If one excludes the often lengthy preamble to these constitutions, several of the initial documents were even shorter than the federal Constitution."[102] They asserted that "all political power is vested in and derived from the people only," and that the people therefore have "an incontestable, unalienable, and indefeasible right" to "reform, alter, or totally change" their form of government.[103] As a result, there were no constitutional limitations in the constitutional power of "the people."[104] During the eighteenth century, there were no provisions detailing the relationships between state power and local government, or regarding the state's power to manage public finance. Furthermore, "no state imposed detailed constitutional limitation on state legislative power until well

---

[98] Quoted in ibid., 23.
[99] Thomas Campbell in the Illinois Convention of 1847, quoted in Dinan, *The American State Constitutional Tradition*, 22.
[100] Rodgers, *Contested Truths*, 13. See further Chapter 6. [101] Ibid., 94.
[102] Tarr, *Understanding State Constitutions*, 61–62. [103] Ibid., 67.
[104] On the importance of these preambles, see Levinson, Sanford, *Framed*, especially chapter 3.

into the nineteenth century."[105] This applied even to the Bill of Rights. After the Virginia Declaration of Rights, an inclusion of a Bill of Rights became, with some exceptions, the common practice.[106] However, these bills of rights were not regarded as sacrosanct, but rather as subject to change. As Donald Lutz observes, even though "to a certain extent bills of rights were assumed to be anchored in natural law [...] there is no getting around the fact that early state constitutions permitted the legislature to abrogate rights if it was deemed necessary, and legislatures frequently did so."[107] In Shain's interpretation, the states "continued to demonstrate a commitment to preserving their founda-tional Protestant cultures, to shaping the moral character of their residents, and to placing individual rights in an inferior position to those of the majority."[108]

Despite all of these differences between the early and the later state consti-tutions, what is even more important – and surprising – is the degree of uniformity among them. This uniformity does not appear to have been affected by the adoption of any of the three major documents of the Founding era, namely the Declaration of Independence, the Articles of the Confederation, and the 1787 Constitution, respectively. John Adams was proven right when, in replying to Richard Henry Lee's letter expressing concerns that allowing states total liberty in framing their constitutions would destroy the fragile and newly created unity, he expressed confidence that, to the contrary, the result would likely be a greater uniformity than seemed likely only a few months prior.[109]

To interpret these similarities with an eye exclusively on their provisions for greater popular control and for an emphasis on the legislative power is to see only half of the story. At least partially responsible for this theoretical myopia might be the language of these constitutions, which is heavily indebted to the social contract theory. As I have illustrated in the previous chapter, social contract theory obscures the undeniable remnants of the political contract and of the corporatist understanding of the people. The legacy of the bidimen-sional Puritan covenant should help, once again, in disentangling the two, since "the distinction between societal consent and governmental consent is usually overlooked simply because it is difficult to detect."[110] Thanks to the people's two bodies paradigm, one can easily understand why, "unlike the French experiment soon to follow, the American effort was characterized by a great compromise [...] Enlightenment ideas were harnessed to Anglo-American experience and institutions whenever a conflict between the two arose."[111]

---

[105] Alan Tarr (1998), *Understanding State Constitutions*', 63.
[106] New Hampshire, South Carolina, New Jersey, and New York (although there are some rights included in the body of the constitution). As we have seen, Connecticut and Rhode Island still had their colonial charters, and hence no Bill of Rights.
[107] Lutz, *Popular Consent*, 6.
[108] Barry Alan Shain (1994), *The Myth of American Individualism: The Protestant Origins of American Political Thought* (Princeton: Princeton University Press), 144.
[109] See above. *Works of John Adams*, IX, 389.   [110] Lutz, *Popular Consent*, 46.
[111] Adams, *The First American Constitutions*, 121.

Let us start by considering the preamble of the famous first constitution of Massachusetts, which reads: "The body-politic is formed by a voluntary association of individuals: It is a social compact, by which *the whole people* covenants with each citizen, and each citizen with *the whole people*, that all shall be governed by certain laws *for the common good.*" An attentive reader can easily discern that if there is a social contract here, it is in effect the Rousseauian, not the Lockean one, and that its primary *telos* is not the private but the common good. In a similar way, The Declaration of the Rights that followed seemed to descend from clear Lockean principles, as did the Declaration of Independence: "All men are born free and equal, and have certain natural, essential, and unalienable rights; among which may be reckoned the right of enjoying and defending their lives and liberties; that of acquiring, possessing, and protecting property; in fine, that of seeking and obtaining their safety and happiness." Meanwhile, the very next paragraph talked about "the right as well as the duty of all men in society, publicly, and at stated seasons, to worship the SUPREME BEING, the great creator and preserver of the universe," and later about the fact that "no man, nor corporation, or association of men, have any other title to obtain advantages . . . distinct from those of the community," since "government is instituted for the common good."

As Lutz observes, because of this blending of societal and governmental consent, in which the sacred right to trial by jury is followed by appeals to Sunday worship, "Americans have come less and less to understand the distinction between the two."[112] By now, we can clearly understand the differences in assumptions that shape the view of the people as a collection of individuals versus the people as a corporate entity: Groups of individuals form associations for the pursuit of private interests; conversely, people as corporate bodies form hierarchical structures based on merit and pursuit of the common good. The Puritan understanding that constitutions devoid of virtue could not last regardless of how skillfully they were crafted was apparent in the state constitutions. The assumption was that government ought to play a direct and explicit role in the formation of citizens' characters, "and that this commitment should be expressed through constitutional provisions."[113] The 1792 New Hampshire constitution – but one example from at least a half a dozen from the era – stipulated that "a constant adherence to justice, moderation, temperance, industry, frugality, and all the social virtues, are indispensably necessary to preserve the blessings of liberty and good government." Even the constitutions of the nineteenth century "recognized – some explicitly, others implicitly – that there was a good common to the society as a whole, which government was obliged to pursue."[114]

---

[112] Lutz, *Popular Consent*, 71.
[113] Dinan, *The American State Constitutional Tradition*, 4. For a full analysis of such constitutional provisions, see chapter 7 of the same book.
[114] Tarr, *Understanding State Constitutions*, 100.

The corporatist understanding went as far as to compare this corporation with an incorporated trading company, as a Connecticut pamphlet of 1775 explained:

The interest of this common stock is now the property of the whole body, and each individual is benefited in proportion to the good of the whole, and is a good or bad member in proportion as he uniteth to, or counteracteth the interest of the body. [...] As society evidently originates from mutual compact or agreement, so it is equally evident, that the members who compose it, unite in one common interest; each individual gives up all private interest that is not consistent with the general good, the interest of the whole body. And, considered as a member of society, he hath no other interest but that of the whole body, of which he is a member.[115]

Thus, in most cases, the rhetoric of the social contract had nothing to do with the requirement for the individual to sacrifice him/herself for the common good. This was made clear in the ten-point document sent to the delegates to the Massachusetts constitutional convention by a village southwest of Boston. The third point read: "That in the Social Contract every individual is bound to each other to the Supreme Power to Submit to its Control where the good of the whole Requires it."[116]

As a matter of fact, the very popularity of the Bill of Rights reveals the same corporatist understanding of the people and of the political contract between the ruled and the rulers, which developed with a built-in suspicion that the elected officials might abuse their power, like King George III had allegedly done. Hence the "assumption that constitutional violations resulted primarily from officials' deviations from the popular will, rather than from unconstitutional aims among the populace. This in turn was based on the notion that the major political conflict was between governors and governed, rather than among competing groups among the population."[117] In the state constitution, the few, not the many, seemed to pose the greatest threat. The Pennsylvania constitution, for example, explicitly stipulated that "the danger of establishing an inconvenient aristocracy will be effectually prevented."

The breakdown of the people's two bodies' paradigm is manifest in this mistrust. The elected ones were no longer part of the accepted (and respected) natural aristocracy, as in the case of the Puritan bidimensional covenant, but rather a necessary evil to be closely watched and contained. Unlike the future Bill of Rights, the declarations or bills of rights in the state constitutions were focused on protecting both the individual and the community. For example, many state constitutions included limitations on the freedom of the press and on religious practices contrary to the good ordering of society,[118] while others

---

[115] Levi Hart (1775), *Liberty Described and Recommended* (Hartfort, CT), 11.
[116] Quoted in Adams, *The First American Constitutions*, 125.
[117] Tarr, *Understanding State Constitutions*, 73.
[118] See, for example, Pennsylvania constitution from 1790, art. 9, sec. 7; New Hampshire constitution of 1784, art. 1, secs. 4–5.

included provisions recognizing the relationship between religion and civil government and permitting the people to authorize their legislative to support religion, financially or otherwise.[119] Even the rights understood today as individual rights – such as the right to trial by jury – were framed in terms of protecting the community.[120]

Furthermore, while the 1776 Virginia Bill of Rights asserted that "all men are *equally free* and independent, and have certain inherent rights," there was no mention of men being "free *and* equal." John Adams was among the few aware of this distinction. When drafting the Bill of Rights for Massachusetts in 1780, he suggested that the key phrase read "equally free and independent." "But the constitutional convention decided to follow the wording of the Declaration of Independence more closely and declared, 'All men are born free and equal.' No one seemed to feel that there was a significant difference between 'equally free and independent' and 'free and equal.'"[121]

Nevertheless, the first state constitution continued the colonial practice of representing corporate people instead of individuals – towns in New England, counties, or both counties and towns elsewhere. It was, at least in part, the result of the "unconscious federalism" mentioned above, which complicated the search for a common definition of "the people." For years, demands for "equal representation" were framed in the name of the New England "corporate principle," according to which the "principle of corporate equality" prevailed over the "principle of personal equality." "The concept of artificial electoral districts with a comparable number of voters only gradually came to replace the claim of natural, permanent units like towns and counties to equal representation."[122] As the Lincoln town meeting declared, "Corporations are the Immediate Constituant part of the State and the Individuals are only the Remote parts in many respects."[123] As a result, at the beginning of the nineteenth century, all state constitutions guaranteed some representation to counties and towns, regardless of the population, in at least one house. The same even applied to states newly admitted to the Union.

Nonetheless, as the debates over fair apportionment increased, the trend was unmistakably in favor of representation by numbers. "The compromise that presented itself was to divide the legislature in two chambers. The number of inhabitants or voters would determine the composition of one chamber ..., territorial units the makeup of the other. The Essex delegates [in 1776] made just such a proposal. But none of the new state constitutions applied this solution with any consistency."[124] The idea of bicameralism was strongly opposed by the supporters of an egalitarian view of the people – and will

---

[119] See, for example, Massachusetts constitution of 1780, part 1, art. 3.

[120] For a more detailed discussion of these bills of rights, see Tarr, *Understanding State Constitutions*, 76–81, and Dinan, *The American State Constitutional Tradition*, chapter 7.

[121] Adams, *The First American Constitutions*, 175. [122] Ibid., 237.

[123] Quoted in ibid., 237. [124] Adams, *The First American Constitutions*, 239.

continue to be frequently challenged for the next couple of hundred years.[125]
A different compromise between the people's two bodies was in the making.

The idea of the people as collection of equal individuals ruled by a majority got more and more traction. So did the idea of "the people's power" to amend or even radically change a defective constitution, which resulted in the nineteenth-century "orgy of state constitutions."[126] The widespread feeling was that "the people," as represented in the constitutional conventions, could decide … whatever. As George M. Dallas, later vice president of the United States, wrote in anticipation of the Pennsylvanian convention of 1837–1838, "What may [this convention] not do?"

> It may reorganize our entire system of social existence, terminating, and proscribing what is deemed injurious … It might restore the institution of slavery among us; it might make our penal code as bloody as that of Draco; it might withdraw the charters of cities, it might supersede a standing judiciary … it might permanently suspend the writ of habeas Corpus, and take from us … the trial by jury. These are fearful matters, of which *intelligent and virtuous freemen* can never be guilty, but I mention them merely as illustrations of the inherent and almost power of a Convention.[127]

A delegate to the Illinois convention of 1847 was even blunter: "We are the sovereignty of the State … We are what the people of the State would be, if they were congregated here in one mass-meeting. *We are what Louis XIV said he was, 'We are the State.'*"[128]

The shortcomings became clear when Rhode Island's legislature adamantly refused to sanction a new constitutional convention to address the issue of unfair apportionment.[129] In 1848, Thomas Dorr and his followers pushed the doctrine to its logical conclusion: "We contend for [the people's] absolute sovereignty over all Constitutions … Constitutions [are] … but form of expressing, protecting and securing the Rights of the People, intended to remain in use *until the People shall otherwise indicate* and direct."[130] By then, they had already created "a new, people's government in the bowels of the old state." An extralegal (for some) People's Convention met, drafted a new constitution, and submitted it for ratification through another extralegal election. The new proposed constitution extended the vote to adult white males who lived in the state for one year, increased representation ratios for Providence and larger towns, and provided for secret ballots and an independent judiciary. Almost 14,000 voters, including 5,000 freeholders, approved the new constitution.

---

[125] For a detailed discussion of the issue of bicameralism in state constitution, see Dinan, *The American State Constitional Tradition*, chapter 5.

[126] Tarr, *Understanding State Constitutions*, 97.

[127] Quoted in John A. Jameson (1867), *The Constitutional Convention: Its History, Powers, and Modes of Proceeding* (New York: Charles Scribner), 292 (emphasis added).

[128] Ibid., 292 (emphasis added).   [129] Tarr, *Understanding State Constitutions*, 103.

[130] Quoted in William M. Wiecek (1972), *The Guarantee Clause of the United State Constitution* (Ithaca: Cornel University Press), 94–95 (emphasis added).

But since the reformers agreed that the charter government should exercise power until May 1842, in February, "the freeholders reconvened and offered a revised constitution with a compromise on suffrage, opening it to native-born citizens while keeping the property requirements for naturalized citizens."[131]

Eventually, the "revolt" was suppressed, but the problem of the people's sovereignty became even more acute. "The events in Rhode Island forced all that was problematic and troublesome in the term the People to the surface. Which of the two electorates in Rhode Island was – and by what right – the people? What limits bound the people – whoever they were – from taking their sovereignty into their own hands, in whatever way that might choose?"[132]

The solution was a new compromise, and the idea was not entirely new. A comment made most likely by Theophilus Parson on the unsatisfactory 1778 draft of the Massachusetts constitution pointed out that the ideal constitution should incorporate both people's two bodies; thus, including both aristocratic and democratic elements:

Among gentlemen of education, fortune and leisure, we shall find the largest number of men, possessed of wisdom, learning, and a firmness and consistency of character ... Among the bulk of the people, we shall find the greatest share of political honesty, probity, and a regard to the interest of the whole ... The former are called the excellencies that result from an aristocracy; the latter, those that result from a democracy.[133]

Even if they did not fully follow the recommendation from 1776 of the county of Essex, all but three state constitutions created bicameral legislatures, with the declared purpose to (a) offer some satisfaction to the partisans of corporate representation of the people and (b) to create, in Gordon Wood's words "repositories of classical republican honor and wisdom" in the Senate.[134] However, the common way of identifying this natural aristocracy remained, in most cases, wealth; hence many constitutions imposed higher property requirements for their senators. Ironically, it was precisely the equality presupposed by the social contract theory that offered the best argument for creating space for the representation not just of persons but of wealth as well. As Abel Upshur argued in the Virginia Convention of 1829–1830,

If men enter into the social compact upon unequal terms; if one man brings into the partnership, his rights of person alone, and another brings into it, equal rights of person and all the rights of property beside, can they be said to have an equal interest in the common stock? Shall not he who has, not only a *greater* interest, but a *peculiar* interest in society, possess an authority proportioned to that interest, and adequate to its protection?[135]

---

[131] Formisano, *For the People*, 166. [132] Rodgers, *Contested Truths*, 103–104.

[133] In Handlin and Handlin, eds., *Popular Sources*, 335, quoted in Adams, *The First American Constitutions*, 112.

[134] Gordon Wood (1998), *The Creation of the American Republic, 1776–1787* (Chapel Hill: The University of North Carolina Press), 209.

[135] Quoted in Dinan, *The American State Constitutional Tradition*, 147.

In the meantime, amid these state constitutional debates, two federal constitutions were devised, exacerbating the struggle over the proper understanding
of "the people." If the state constitutions were even slightly influenced by them,
they did produce "a political culture considerably evolved from that surrounding the Declaration of Independence."[136]

4.3 "... MUTUAL SACRIFICES SHOULD BE MADE TO EFFECT A COMPROMISE ..."

There is no doubt that "the Articles of Confederation were a compromise."[137]
As Samuel Chase observed in the summer of 1776, "our importance, our
interests, our peace required that we should confederate, and that mutual
sacrifices should be made to effect a compromise of this difficult question."[138]
The war made this union even more urgent. Still, it took more than a year and
three different drafts before the delegates to the Continental Congress agreed to
compromise. The main challenge was not, as expected, the factional divisions
between the large and the small states, nor between the three political subcultures – moralistic in New England, individualistic in the Middle Atlantic states,
and traditionalistic in the South.[139] As attractive as it may sound, the factual
evidence is simply absent: "Over the course of sixteen ballots, the majority
position carried by a resounding 125–30. Only in one case was there a statistically significant split between the northern and southern states, and in no case
was there a statistically significant split between the states with western land
claims and those without."[140]

Rather, what was at stake was the same confrontation that had appeared in
the state constitutions between the principle of corporate representation and the
principle of numerical majorities.[141] "The controversy over representation was
of far more consequence than as evidence of a struggle between large and small
states. It also involved the question of sovereignty: the location of ultimate
political authority."[142] Transferred to the federal level, the issue could be
rephrased as a question of ... orthography. If, in the Declaration of

---

[136] Lutz, *Popular Consent*, xv.
[137] James B. Scott (1920), *The United States of America: A Study in International Organization*
(New York: Oxford University Press), 41.
[138] Thomas Jefferson's *Notes of Proceedings in Congress* (July 12–August 1, 1776), quoted in
Freedman, "Why Constitutional Lawyers ...," 819.
[139] Elazar, *American Federalism*; Calvin C. Jillson (1988), "Political Culture and the Pattern of
Congressional Politics Under the Articles of Confederation," *Publius*, 18:1, 10, 26. For the
persistence of coherent voting blocs originating in sectional conflict, see James H. Henderson
(1974), *Party Politics in the Continental Congress* (New York: McGraw-Hill.)
[140] Freedman, "Why Constitutional Lawyers ...," 815.
[141] Adams, *The First American Constitutions*, 285.
[142] Jensen, "The Articles of Confederation," 135.

Independence, the spelling of "united States" was with a small "u," ought not the first federal constitution redress the balance by using a capitalized Union?

Some of the delegates agreed. James Wilson, of Pennsylvania, was one of them: "It has been said that Congress is a representation of states, not individuals. I say that the objects of its care are all the individuals of the states. [...] We are not so many states, we are one large state. We lay aside our individuality whenever we come here."[143] John Adams also claimed that the aim of the confederation was "to form us, like separate parcels of metal, into one common mass. We shall no longer retain our separate individuality."[144] As a result, he argued in favor of proportional and descriptive representation, "Reason, justice, & equity never had weight enough on the face of earth to govern councils of men. It is interest alone which does it, and it is interest alone which can be trusted. That therefore the interests within doors should be the mathematical representation of the interests without doors."[145] Benjamin Rush pressed a similar position, but from a different angle, arguing that only a proportional representation would pursue the common good of the nation as opposed to the particular interests of the states.

Most of the delegates from the small states begged to differ. John Witherspoon, from New Jersey, for example, considered each state to be a distinct person; thus, he understood the national government as a compact between equal corporations of people, regardless of their respective sizes.

The key point in Witherspoon's position for constitutional design was not that the states should each have one vote, but that the national government should act upon the states rather than directly upon the individuals within a state. Since individuals were seen as part of a community, it made little sense to act upon anything other than the community. *To act upon the individuals was to imply the destruction of the community.*[146]

Merrill Jensen famously labeled the first group "democratic radicals," trying to preserve state rights, and the second "conservatives," looking to preserve their "aristocratic" advantages by creating a strong central government.[147] Attractive as it seems in its simplicity, such a sharp dichotomy, "a really fundamental division of interest and political philosophy between conservatives and radicals," simply does not sustain close scrutiny.[148] Indeed, some delegates saw in the creation of a federal government a way of stopping what they perceived as "democratic" or "populist" excesses. "Only a formal and lasting continental union, as Gouverneur Morris had earlier suggested, could 'restrain the democratic spirit, which the constitutions and the circumstances of the country had so long fostered in the minds of the people'."[149] Yet, as Jensen is

---

[143] Quoted in Jefferson, *Notes on Debates*, I, 46–47, in *The Writings of Thomas Jefferson* (New York: 1982–1989), P. L. Ford, ed.

[144] Ibid., 45.   [145] Ibid.   [146] Lutz, "The Articles of Confederation," 62 (emphasis added).

[147] Jensen, *The Articles of Confederation*. See also Jensen, "The Articles of Confederation."

[148] Jensen, *The Articles of Confederation*, 57.   [149] Greene, "The Background," 36.

the first to acknowledge, the votes in Congress did not follow the conservatives vs. radicals line of division. They were not "consistent" with their economic and political views, there were contradictions in each camp, and arguments were "borrowed" from one camp by another.[150]

Far from being irreconcilably divided, most of the delegates tried hard to find ways of overcoming their differences, not least that between the people understood as corporations and the people conceived as collection of individuals. As a result, a third suggestion was a compromise between the two understandings via some form of bicameralism, much in line with the solution adopted by the state constitutions. As early as May 16, 1776, in a letter to John Adams, Thomas Jefferson recommended a solution of compromise that would be mirrored, almost a century later, by Calhoun's idea of a concurrent majority – the veto power:

[A]ny proposition might be negatived by the representatives of a majority of the people of America, or of a majority of the colonies of America. The former secure the larger the latter the smaller colonies ... The good whigs I think so far will cede their opinions for the sake of the Union ...[151]

Richard Sherman tried to reconcile the two using a different strategy. He began by agreeing that, "We are representatives of States, not individuals," yet he continued: "The vote should be taken two ways; call the Colonies; and call the individuals, and have a majority of both." Samuel Chase also proposed his own version of bicameralism: "[T]he smaller states should be secured in all questions concerning life and liberty, and the greater ones in all respecting property ... in votes related with money, the voice of each colony should be proportioned to the number of his inhabitants."[152] Neither of these proposals got traction in Congress, nor did other "suggestions for compromise, such as giving Rhode island, Delaware, and Georgia one delegate each and the rest of the states one delegate per fifty thousand inhabitants."[153] In the end, the bicameral solution was abandoned, but not the quest for other feasible compromises.

Sharp conflicts based on self-interest indeed arose, but they were followed by compromises designed to appeal to a preexisting political consensus. The paradigm might be called one of constrained consensus; the drafters did have individual interests to represent, but they also faced external pressures (notably the British army) requiring them to craft solutions with broad appeal to get their work through state legislatures.[154]

As it quickly became clear, the problem was not so much in the Continental Congress as in the state legislatures. The first half of the year 1777 was spent in

---

[150] For a detailed criticism of Jensen's position, see Freedman, "Why Constitutional Lawyers ..."
[151] In the *Papers of Thomas Jefferson*, quoted in Freedman, "Why Constitutionalist Lawyers ...," 820.
[152] In Ford et al., *Journals of the Continental Congress*, Vol. 6, 1102.
[153] Adams, *The First American Constitutions*, 285.
[154] Freedman, "Why Constitutionalist Lawyers ...," 791.

essentially futile attempts to create coalitions across and inside state legislatures. In a letter to Robert R. Livingston, dated May 28, 1777, William Duer excused himself saying that "my attention has been so engross'd in defeating the Design of the Mischievous Combination, and in cultivating the Friendship of the Members from the Southern States that I have had … no time to write."[155] Worried about the hidden motives of different states, Thomas Burke wrote to Richard Caswell: "Of the political principles of the respective states I am not yet able to speak very clearly, for they are kept as much as possible out of view […] I am not yet satisfied that there is any combination among them. I rather think that they only combine when they have common interest, which is seldom the case, & I am sure that this is not peculiar to them."[156]

As Freedman observes, "[u]nder these circumstances, no confederation would have been formed at all had it not been for the other delegates' salient characteristic, *their willingness to compromise.*"[157] As Richard Henry Lee advised Roger Sherman on November 1777, "In this great business dear Sir, we must yield a little to each other, and not rigidly insist on having every thing correspondent to the partial views of every State. On such terms we can never confederate."[158] The three successive drafts of the Articles suggest a genuine interest in finding a compromise between the supporters of a strong central government and the ones of decentralization. It would be easy to conclude that the latest camp ended up carrying the day, and that the small "u" in the "united States in Congress assembled" "tells the story" of the winners.[159] Yet this would mean completely disregarding the fact that the first draft was much more in favor of the states than the second, and that "between the second and third versions of the Articles there were similar changes in a centralizing direction."

The third version added to the second a very strong provision granting "the free inhabitants of each of these states … all privileges and immunities of … the several states." The same new article also provided for interstate extradition and required that "[f]ull faith and credit … be given in each of these states to the records, acts and judicial proceedings of the courts and magistrates of every other state."[160]

It was a way of giving Congress power to effectively act upon the individuals directly, thus crafting a revolutionary notion of "dual citizenship." In Lutz's words, "the invention of dual citizenship in the Articles of Confederation structured the way in which national citizenship operated later in the United States Constitution."[161] In effect, a closer reading of the Articles reveals that

---

[155] Quoted in ibid., 813.   [156] Quoted in ibid., 813.   [157] Ibid., 813–814 (emphasis added).
[158] Quoted in ibid., 814.
[159] William F. Swindler (1981), "The Articles of Confederation: Our First Constitution," *American Bar Association Journal*, 67, 168.
[160] Freedman, "Why Constitutionalist Lawyers …," 808.
[161] Lutz, "The Articles of Confederation," 66.

some of the most familiar parts of the future Constitution – such as the Supremacy Clause, the Privileges and Immunities Clause, and the Full Faith and Credit Clause – were directly inspired by the Articles of Confederation.[162] As a result, Freedman argues that the compromises in the Continental Congress paved the way for the future compromises during the Philadelphia convention[163].

As part of the compromise finally achieved, the Congress had pledged to use the land ceded to it for the common good of all the states and in due time to organize it into "distinct republican states." This decision was the first step toward the expansionist federalism that provided the constitutional basis for the settlement of the entire continent in the course of the following century.[164]

Possibly the most revealing example of the willingness of the delegates to compromise once the equality of the parties was accepted were the provisions of Article IX for solving disputes among states. It is worth remembering that the British Parliament accepted compromise as a formalized procedure [*Modi of Parliament*] whenever "the Estates could not agree (or the greater part of the Knights, Proctors, Citizens, &c.). There, by consent of the whole Parliament, *the Matter might be compromised* to 25 chosen out of all Degrees, and to fewer, till at length it might come to 3 who might determine the Case, except that being written it were corrected by Assent of Parliament and not otherwise."[165] As in the classic method of *compromissum*, the number of arbitrators, i.e., *compromissores*, ought to be odd, to prevent further stalemates. The same logic of *compromissum* applied in cases of unsolvable disputes among states. According to Article IX, once all other methods were exhausted,

congress shall name three persons out of each of the united states, and from the list of such persons each party shall alternately strike out one, the petitioners beginning, until the number shall be reduced to thirteen; and from that number not less than seven, nor more than nine as congress shall direct, shall in the presence of congress be drawn by lot, and the persons whose names shall be so drawn or any five of them, shall be commissioners or judges, to hear and finally determine the controversy, so always as a major part of the judges who shall hear the cause shall agree in the determination.

Thus, the beginning of the national court system began with a compromise.[166] A rather timid beginning, granted, but a beginning nevertheless. "Of half a dozen potential cases noted in the journal of Congress, only one was pursued to

[162] Freedman, "Why Constitutionalist Lawyers ...," 784.   [163] Ibid.
[164] Adams, *The First American Constitutions*, 287.
[165] John Sadler (1682), *Rights of the Kingdom, or Customs of Our Ancestors Touching the Duty, Power, Election, or Succession of our Kings and Parliaments* (London: Printed for J. Kidgell), 316; emphasis added. Quoted in Fumurescu, *Compromise*, 88.
[166] Lutz, "The Articles of Confederation," 66.

final judgment, another never reached a point where the congressional commission could take jurisdiction, and the others were either dropped or settled by direct negotiation between the states affected."[167]

Despite its shortcomings, the Articles of Confederation has recently enjoyed a renewed interest, particularly on the part of constitutional scholars. Since the Supreme Court has looked to the Articles in more than 150 cases so far, it appears that the supporters of the continuity thesis are fully vindicated, at least from a judicial perspective. "The Articles of Confederation, indeed, now appear to have almost as much influence in efforts to determine the original meaning of the Constitution as other, key sources, such as the notes from the Constitutional Convention, the Federalist papers, and the records of the state ratifying conventions."[168]

Before the articles went into effect, there was one more important, and more difficult, step to be taken: getting thirteen state legislatures to ratify the final draft. In its appeal to the states for ratification, Congress appeared fully aware of the difficulties of the process, so it pointed to its own delegates' efforts to compromise on behalf of their states as an example to be followed: "To form a permanent union, accommodated to the opinions and wishes of the delegates of so many states, differing in habits, produce, commerce, and internal police, was found to be a work which nothing but time and reflection, conspiring with a disposition to conciliate, could mature and accomplish."[169]

It was a slow-working strategy. If it took Congress more than a year to agree on a draft, it took the last state, Maryland, almost three years to ratify, making the Union finally legitimate. In Madison's words, they "yielded only to the hope that by giving a stable & authoritative character to the Confederation, a successful termination of the Contest [over the western lands] might be accelerated. The dispute was happily compromised by successive surrenders of portions of the territory by the States having exclusive rights."[170] Yet this was but one benefit among many. As James Duane, a delegate from New York, observed, the Union did not only have an important psychological effect on American national consciousness; it also made it easier to raise credit from states such as France, Spain, and Holland, thus increasing the Patriots' military chances. "By the accomplishment of our Federal Union," he declared, "we are become a Nation. In a political view it is of more real importance than a Victory

---

[167] Swindler, "The Articles of Confederation," 168–169.
[168] Gregory E. Maggs (2017) "A Concise Guide to the Articles of Confederation as a Source for Determining the Original Meaning of the Constitution," *George Washington Law Review*, 85:2, 399.
[169] Ford et al., *Journals of the Continental Congress*, Vol. 9, 933; quoted in Freedman, "Why Constituionalist Lawyers . . .," 826.
[170] Madison, *Notes of Debates*, 7.

over all our Enemies." Yet he did not stop there. Since the constitution was subject to amendments, he expressed confidence that further articles, soon to be proposed, would "give vigor and authority to Government."[171]

His predictions were not to be fulfilled, but rather surpassed a mere six years later, when the delegates met in Philadelphia.

[171] January 29, 1781, Burnett, ed., *Letters of the Continental Congress*, V, 551–552; quoted in Adams, *The First American Constitutions*, 287.

5

The Constitution

"... that greatest of all compromises"

... if no compromise should take place, our meeting would not only be in vain but worse than in vain.

– Oliver Ellsworth

When on July 22, 1850, Henry Clay rose in the Senate to claim that the Constitution of the United States was the "greatest of all compromises ... a great, memorable, magnificent compromise, which indicates to us the course of duty when differences arise,"[1] no one denied it, even though some may have disagreed with Clay that on issues such as slavery, compromise represented the unavoidable, let alone the proper, solution. By the time of Clay's speech, the idea that the Constitution was a great compromise had already been well embedded in the minds of Americans.

During the Philadelphia Convention, the framers made constant references to the necessity and benefits of compromise, and they continued to do so, even more forcefully, during the state ratifying conventions. In the eyes of its supporters, compromise was the only way of preventing the disintegration of the newly created United States. When Nicholas Gilman, a delegate from Hew Hampshire, wrote to his brother in the day after the adjournment of the Convention, he endorsed the document in the familiar terms of a choice between compromise and open conflict, between national unity and an unrepairable fragmentation: "It was done by bargain and Compromise, yet notwithstanding its imperfections, on the adoption of it depends (in my

---

[1] Quoted in Peter B. Knupfer (1991), *The Union as It Is: Constitutional Unionism and Sectional Compromise, 1787-1861* (Chapel Hill and London: The University of North Carolina Press), 23.

feeble judgement) whether we shall become a respectable nation, or a people torn to pieces."[2]

Since then, compromise has become "a staple theme of most narrative accounts of the Federal Convention of 1787," even if its benefits, especially when it came to the infamous Three-Fifths Compromise, have at times been vehemently denied.[3] In a display of surprising consensus in an otherwise highly controversial field, hundreds of articles and dozens of books, many impressive in terms of volume of the information displayed, agree on this point: The Constitution of the United States was nothing other than the result of a series of compromises, large and small, that prompted a compromising approach to American politics for centuries to come.[4] This process, then, appears as a fait accompli, about which nothing more could be said.

Nonetheless, it is precisely this overwhelming consensus that is intriguing. After all, as seen in the previous chapters, the idea of constituting a new people upon the com-*promise* of individuals sharing a certain set of beliefs regardless of "consanguinity ties" was nothing new. Not just the Puritans, but the Patriots as well, used consent and compromise to forge new identities, while vehemently refusing to compromise with "outsiders." Since the "British brethren ... have been deaf to the voice of justice and consanguinity," claimed the Declaration of Independence, they were to be held, as the rest of mankind, "Enemies in War, in Peace Friends." If the Articles of Confederation, like the Articles of Confederation of the United Colonies of New England that preceded them by more than a century, were possible at all, it was because these various new, voluntary, and consensual peoples agreed to consider each other equal corporate entities – regardless of each other's actual sizes, thus fulfilling the prerequisite of any compromise.

But here is the puzzle: If, as we have seen, "compromise had been an important means of reconciling differences in the colonial tradition," and if "[t]he framers did not invent compromise," why did "subsequent compromisers (act) as if they had"? Why is "[t]he country's long tradition of devising constitutions, compacts, covenants, and charters to arrange its diverse colonial and state politics ... missing from later discussions of compromise"? And why

[2] Nicholas Gilman to Joseph Gilman, Philadelphia, September 18, 1787, in Max Farrand, ed. (1937), *The Records of the Federal Convention of 1787*, 4 vols. (New Haven: Yale University Press), Vol. 3, 82.

[3] Jack N. Rakove (1996), *Original Meanings: Politics and Ideas in the Making of the Constitution* (New York: Alfred A. Knopf), 57.

[4] The records of the Federal Convention and of the state ratifying conventions aside, among the most impressive monographs on the new Constitution are Michael J. Klarman (2016), *The Framers' Coup: The Making of the United States Constitution* (Oxford: Oxford University Press); Pauline Maier (2011), *Ratification: The People Debate the Constitution, 1787–1788* (New York: Simon & Schuster); Rakove, *Original Meanings*, and David Brian Robertson (2013), *The Original Compromise: What the Constitution's Framers Were Really Thinking* (Oxford: Oxford University Press).

did the same author quoted above also claim that "the distinctive history of compromise ... would *not* be found in the colonial period or even after the Civil War but in the period between the two?"[5] Furthermore, why are scholars even today equating the Constitution with the "*original* compromise,"[6] *the one* that placed compromise "at the heart of American polity"?[7] What makes this Constitution different from other constitutions and compromises during the founding era? It is with these questions that this chapter is concerned.

Thus, the first part of the chapter offers a new theoretical perspective on "the reification of compromise" accomplished by the new Constitution.[8] Previous interpretations have focused on compromises between principles and interests, between national and federal powers, between large and small states, between free and slave states, between economic sectional interests and general ideas about representation, the ideal structure of the executive and the judicial branches, and so forth. While the perspective advanced here does not contradict any of these interpretations, it has the advantage of incorporating them all in a coherent fashion, by once again employing the paradigm of the people's two bodies. I argue that this quasi-unanimous interpretation of the Constitution as "the *original* compromise" is due to the document's status as a *written* compromise between the two understandings of the people, qua corporation of corporations, hierarchically structured, on the one hand and qua collection of equal individuals on the other. By the same token, this compromise managed to combine the different underlying assumptions of the political and of the social contract theories. In some respects, one could claim that the framers managed to recuperate and make permanent the Puritan legacy of the bidimensional covenant at a scale previously difficult to imagine.

Such an emphasis on ideas is not to deny the role played by the sentiment of urgency that mobilized many of the key players, nor to minimize the role of down-to-earth economic interests or even an important degree of serendipity that contributed to the final outcome.[9] The claim advanced here is only that regardless, and oftentimes despite of, its actual causes and motivations, the resulting Constitution did in fact succeeded in "reifying" a reconfiguration of the people's two bodies. While this combination of such contradictory theoretical assumptions was not a new phenomenon of the American founding, it was indeed original insofar as it "formalized," for generations to come, this foundational double helix in the understanding of the people, with all the practical consequences derived from it.

---

[5] Knupfer, *The Union as It Is*, 14, 24, 13 (emphasis added).
[6] Robertson, *The Original Compromise*.   [7] Knupfer, *The Union as It Is*, 1.   [8] Ibid., 15.
[9] Thus, I am not contradicting interpretations that emphasize the role played by interests in crafting the final compromise. See Klarman, *The Framers' Coup*, 6: "While the delegates mostly argued over issues in terms of political principles, often their ostensibly principled arguments simply served as rationalizations for the interests being advanced." I am only claiming that in the long run these interests mattered less than the ideas used to promote them.

The second part of the chapter uses this theoretical framework to interpret some of the well-known compromises that took place during the Federal Convention. Although far from exhaustive, this review aims at providing a better understanding of the discrepancy between the practical considerations *of that time* and their unforeseen long-terms effects. For example, the infamous Three-Fifths Compromise ended up forever binding representation to population, not to property, by driving the southern delegates to insist, for the wrong reasons, on constitutional rules for both census and reapportionment.[10] I shall argue that, paradoxically, by *not* being specifically empowered to craft a radically new constitution, the delegates were able to combine in an original way the two understandings of the people, if for no other reason than to justify their breach of mandate through a higher purpose. As Elbridge Gerry observed on July 5,

> We were ... in a peculiar situation. We were neither the same Nation not different Nations. We ought not therefore to pursue the one or the other of these ideas too closely. If no compromise should take place what will be the consequence. A secession he foresaw will take place; for some gentlemen seem decided on it; two different plans will be proposed; and the result no man could foresee. If we do not come to some agreement among ourselves some foreign sword will probably do the work for us.[11]

This quote captures the sentiment of urgency mentioned above; the choice was a compromise or a doomsday scenario. Most importantly, it proposes a compromise by intentionally avoiding the *rhetorical* trap of one vs. different nations or peoples. It is another proof that most practical problems have rhetorical solutions. There is little doubt that the distinction between one and several nations was in the minds of all delegates, and it laid at the core of many of Philadelphia's disagreements. Yet I shall argue that, in the long run, the real issue was not the obvious tension between the Union and the states, or between the "federal" and the "national" principles, but between the people's two bodies. From Philadelphia on, the American peculiarity could be rephrased: "We are neither a corporate people nor a collection of individuals. We ought not therefore to pursue the one or the other of these ideas too closely." As the history of the United States clearly demonstrates, this is easier said than done.[12]

Finally, the third part focuses on the states' ratifying conventions. Both practically and theoretically, popular ratification was a bold and risky move. Practically speaking, the proviso was meant to bypass the state legislatures entirely, thus avoiding a sure rejection although not ensuring ratification.

---

[10] Rakove, *Original Meanings*, 74.

[11] In James Madison (1985), *Notes of Debates in the Federal Convention of 1797* (Athens: Ohio University Press), 243.

[12] As mentioned in the Introduction, and as demonstrated by many quotes throughout this book, in the American case, the conflation of "people" with "nation," and vice versa, occurred almost naturally, since both were perceived as political creations.

As depicted in the previous chapter, prior experiments with submitting state constitutions to the approval of the people at large had not been very reassuring in terms of producing the desired outcomes. From a theoretical perspective, popular ratification was necessary not only for securing the Constitution by placing it on a level superior to that of any other legislative decision but also for providing it with a legitimacy that would otherwise remain open to contestation.

There was, however, a huge risk. Since these ratifying conventions were supposed to represent the people at large, and thus the ultimate repository of sovereignty, there was no guarantee that the delegates would not take this role so seriously as to propose amendments that eventually could end up destroying the Constitution. "The framers thus left Philadelphia fearful that their new concept of ratification, so useful a device to circumvent the Confederation, could be wielded against the Constitution itself."[13] They were all aware of the fact that "the people" was a powerful, potentially even explosive concept, to be handled with extreme caution.

In order to minimize the potential dangers of the people's sovereignty, the framers offered only a binary choice: either accept or reject the Constitution. Any alterations or amendments were possible only *after* it had been ratified. Thus, a Constitution crafted by an entire series of compromises was to be legitimized by a procedure that precluded any possible compromise. By the same token, they managed to create two seemingly easily recognizable camps in the Federalists and the Antifederalists. As most scholars agree today, both labels were largely misleading. "Moderate or lukewarm adherents to either side were often almost indistinguishable from each other."

There is an impression of a greater unity [among the Federalists] ... because the Federalists were (in general) unified in supporting the Constitution ... That impression has been strengthened by the Federalists' victory and by the massive impact on later generations of the *Federalist Papers* ... There were in fact diverse and contradictory opinions among the Federalists just as they were among their opponents.[14]

Unsurprisingly, some scholars refuse to even employ these labels. "Antifederalist" was a term used by the Federalists to win a fiercely fought PR war for the hearts and minds of the American people.[15] It is a trap some scholars still have a hard time avoiding. "To use the Federalists' language – to tell the story in their terms – tends to give them the game, or at least to tip the story further in their direction."[16] I suggest a more accurate way to describe the two camps during

---

[13] Rakove, *Original Meanings*, 107.

[14] Herbert J. Storing (1985), "Introduction" to *The Anti-Federalist: An Abridgment* by Murray Dry of the Complete Anti-Federalists, Edited, with Commentary and Notes by Herbert J. Storing (Chicago and London: The University of Chicago Press), 3.

[15] The very fact that even today there is no agreement if the word should be spelled as Anti-Federalists or Antifederalists speaks volumes in itself.

[16] Maier, *Ratification*, xiv.

the ratification process would be to employ the terms "compromisers" and "anti-compromisers." After all, some of the more vehement and articulate opponents of the Constitution, such as Samuel Adams, Edmund Randolph, and Melancton Smith, ended up playing a crucial role in the Constitution's ratification in Massachusetts, Virginia, and New York, respectively.[17]

A further proof that these distinctions were largely artificial is the rapidity with which the Antifederalists abandoned their legitimacy challenges once the Constitution was ratified. Even if they lost the battle over ratification, the extent to which they lost the war on its interpretation remains questionable. By forcing the Federalists to compromise over the Bill of Rights, the Antifederalists demonstrated the possible advantages of an uncompromising stance.[18] Two of the main supporters of the Constitution, Thomas Jefferson and James Madison, led the opposition to the Federalists. Some scholars still find the development puzzling: "This is difficult to account for in light of the string and bitter partisan feelings engendered by the ratification debates."[19] Less so, however, once one considers that the paradigm of the people's two bodies can be used to promote not just compromise but an uncompromising attitude as well. Unsurprisingly, in today's polarized politics, the Antifederalists' ideas enjoy a new legitimacy, both on the political left and on the political right, "moving from the fringes to the center of the political debates."[20]

5.1 "THE STATES MUST SEE THE ROD ..."

On September 17, 1787, thirty-nine people signed a document that began with the words "We the People." Yet the proposal they had just authored did not refer only to the signatories, but to all the people of the United States. Regardless of how one chooses to look at this, claiming to speak in the name of not just millions of one's contemporaries but also in that of all generations to come, required a particular mindset. James Wilson of Pennsylvania, for example, had no doubts that he was "acting & responsible for the welfare of millions not represented in this House."[21] His supporters could not help but agree. As the Convention wrapped up its work in Philadelphia, an article in the *Gazette* considered that "[s]uch a body of enlightened and honest men perhaps never before met for political purposes in any country upon the face of the earth."[22] Much later, in the preface to his *Notes*, even Madison expressed his "profound

---

[17] Michael J. Faber (2015), "The Federal Union Paradigm of 1788: Three Anti-Federalists Who Changed Their Minds," *American Political Thought: A Journal of Ideas, Institutions, and Culture*, 4, 526–556.

[18] For the sake of simplicity and of avoiding unnecessary – and likely confusing – turns of phrase, I will keep using these familiar labels.

[19] Faber, "The Federal Union," 554.

[20] Saul Cornell (1999), *The Other Founders: Anti-Federalism and the Dissenting Tradition in America, 1788–1828* (Chapel Hill: University of North Carolina Press), 3.

[21] Madison, *Notes of Debates*, 454.   [22] Quoted in Klarman, *The Framers' Coup*, 2.

and solemn conviction ... that there never was an assembly of men, charged with a great and arduous trust, who were more pure in their motives, or more exclusively or anxiously devoted to the object committed to them."[23]

All these rhetorical exaggerations aside, being able to compromise on so many diverse ideas and interests was nothing short of a miracle, as the same Madison would later confess to Jefferson.[24] Attempts to better the Articles of Confederation began even some weeks before the first constitution went into effect, when Congress asked state legislatures to approve an amendment authorizing it to collect a 5 percent impost on imported goods. None of these attempts were successful. The Annapolis Convention's only accomplishment was that, in a bold move, it gambled on a second convention, in Philadelphia. This last one proved to be a different story. In the words of David Ramsay, "Heaven smiled on their deliberations and inspired their councils with a spirit of conciliations."[25] If so, Madison might as well have acted as its godly instrument.

The Convention was scheduled to begin on Monday, May 14, 1787, but because there were not enough delegates, the official opening was postponed until Friday, May 25. While Washington was vexed and frustrated about the delay, Madison took full advantage of it. He had already prepared well in the preceding months and, unlike most of the delegates, he had a pretty clear idea about what he wanted to achieve. Thus, by the time the Convention begun, the Virginia Plan was penned down and ready to set up the terms of the debates to follow.

There was one more obstacle to overcome before starting the actual negotiations for the new Constitution. While the vast majority of the delegates agreed that the Confederation was defective and needed to be amended, not everyone felt prepared or even authorized to replace it with an entirely new set of principles.[26] The first to "doubt whether the act of Congress recommending the Convention ... could authorize a discussion of a system founded on different principles from the federal Convention" was General Pinckney of South Carolina. Elbridge Gerry of Massachusetts "seemed to entertain the same doubt."[27]

It soon became clear that it was a threefold issue, as William Patterson of New Jersey explained. From a legalistic perspective, he observed "that the articles of Confederation were ... the proper basis of all the proceedings of

[23] Madison, *Notes of Debates*, 19.

[24] Madison to Jefferson, October 24, 1787, *The Papers of James Madison* (Congressional Series), Robert B. Rutland and William M. E. Rachal, eds. (Chicago, 1977), vol. 10, 208.

[25] Quoted in Klarman, *The Framers' Coup*, 2.

[26] For examples of the constitutionalist perspective questioning the legality of the process see, Bruce Ackerman and Neal Katyal (1995), "Our Unconventional Founding," *The University of Chicago Law Review*, 62:2, 475–573.

[27] Quoted in Madison, *Notes of Debates*, 35.

the Convention. We ought to keep within its limits, or we should be charged by our Constituents with usurpation, [for] the people of America were sharp-sighted and not be deceived." From a practical perspective, he argued, the proposal to replace the Articles of Confederation was doomed to fail, because "[t]he idea of a national Government as contradistinguished from a federal one, never entered the mind of any of them, and to the public mind we must accommodate ourselves. We have no power to go beyond the federal scheme, and if we had the people are not ripe for any other." Last, but not least, the issue was a theoretical one as well: Were the representative from the states to *lead*, or to *follow* their constituencies? Patterson was clear on this point: "We must follow the people; the people will not follow us."[28]

A few days later, his arguments were to be echoed by John Lansing of New York. From a legalistic perspective, he observed that "New York would never have concurred in sending deputies to the convention, if she had supposed the deliberations were to turn on a consolidation of the States, and a National Government." From a practical perspective, he too noticed that it was unlikely "that the States would adopt & ratify a scheme, which they never authorized us to propose," and also that "it is vain" to propose a "Scheme ... totally novel." Finally, he believed that the delegates should follow the "present sentiments," which were known, instead of relying "on any change which is hereafter to take place in the sentiments of the people."[29]

Quite a few of their fellow delegates begged to differ. Speaking the same day, right after Lansing and Patterson, James Wilson found an original way to appease the legalistic concerns, arguing that, "[w]ith regard to the *power of the Convention*, he conceived himself authorized to *conclude nothing*, but to be at liberty to *propose anything*." From a practical perspective, "[w]ith regard to the sentiments of the people, he conceived it difficult to know precisely what they are."

He could not persuade himself that the State Government & Sovereignties were so much the idols of the people, nor a National Government so obnoxious to them, as some supposed. Why a National Government be unpopular? Has it less dignity? Will each Citizen enjoy under it less liberty or protection? Will a citizen of *Delaware* be degraded by becoming a Citizen of the *United States*?[30]

Charles Pinckney's doubts were immediately alleviated by Wilson's distinction between "concluding" and "proposing," finding "the Convention authorized to go to any length in *recommending*, which they found necessary to remedy the evils which produced this Convention." Edmund Randolph of Virginia was more radical. Far from breaking the trust of the people, "[w]hen the salvation

---

[28] Quoted in Madison, *Notes of Debates*, 95–96.
[29] Quoted in Madison, *Notes of Debates*, 122.
[30] Quoted in Madison, *Notes of Debates*, 125 (emphases in the original).

of the Republic was at stake, *it would be treason to our trust, not to propose what we found necessary.*"³¹

The next day, Hamilton agreed wholeheartedly. The crisis, he contended in rather Machiavellian terms, "was too serious to *permit any scruples whatever* to prevail over the duty imposed on every man to contribute his efforts for the public safety and happiness. [...] To rely on & propose any plan adequate to these exigencies, merely because it was not clearly within our powers, would be *to sacrifice the mean to the end.*" Instead of following the sentiments of the people, he was convinced that with the help of the delegates, "the people will be shackled from their prejudices."³² In this he agreed with Madison who, a few days earlier, made a similar plea. Instead of focusing on what the people wanted, which was essentially impossible to determine, the delegates' responsibility was to share "the information & lights possessed by the members here."

We ought to consider what was right & necessary *in itself* for the attainment of a proper Government. A plan adjusted to this idea will recommend itself – The respectability of this convention will give weight to their recommendation of it ... and all *the most enlightened & respectable citizens will be its advocate.* Should we fall short of the necessary & proper point, this influential class of Citizens will be turned against the plan, and little support in opposition to them can be gained to it *from the unreflective multitude.*³³

The message lends itself to two possible interpretations. The most obvious one follows in the footsteps of an established tradition. Put it simply, like their Puritan predecessors, the delegates "wanted the new America to be governed by an elite, not by a hereditary elite but by an elite of the virtuous and talented."³⁴ Their distrust in one of the people's two bodies was repeatedly expressed throughout the convention and is well documented in Madison's *Notes*.

[T]he speeches of delegates at the convention attest to their fear of mobs ... Scattered throughout Madison's notes are such phrases and thoughts as "popular intemperance" (Randolph), "popular passions [which] spread like wildfire, and become irresistible" (Hamilton), "the ignorance of the people" (Gerry), "the political depravity of man" (Madison), "the insensitivity to character, produced by a participation of numbers, in dishonorable measures" (Gorham), "the dangerous influence of those multitudes, without property & without principle" (John Dickinson, Delaware), and the need "to protect the people against the transient impressions into which they themselves might be led" (Madison again.)³⁵

---

³¹ Quoted in Madison, *Notes of Debates*, 127 (emphasis added).
³² Quoted in Madison, *Notes of Debates*, 129–130, 137 (emphases added).
³³ Madison, *Notes of Debates*, 107 (emphasis added).
³⁴ Anthony Stephen King (2012), *The Founding Fathers v. the People: Paradoxes of American Democracy* (Cambridge, MA: Harvard University Press), 24.
³⁵ King, *The Founding Fathers v. the People*, 32–33.

The people qua multitude were not to be trusted with all subtleties of devising a particular form of government. This was the role and the duty of the natural aristocracy of the enlightened, who could rise above petty particular interests, crafting a form of government meant to serve common good and public happiness.

By the same token, these "enlightened and respectable citizens" ought to contribute to the progress and enlightenment of the masses. Rather than being led by public opinion, they ought to lead it in the right direction. As Gerry put it bluntly, when the problem of ratification came up, "The rulers will either conform to, or influence the sense of the people."[36] Thanks to the paradigm of the people's two bodies, we are now better equipped to understand "the delegates' profound ambivalence concerning the people" that many scholars are still finding puzzling: "On the one hand, the people were definitely to ordain and establish the new constitution; on the other hand, these same people, as individuals, were by no means to be trusted."[37]

Still a question remained: Were the people to be understood at state level or at national level? For delegates such as Madison or Hamilton, the answer was straightforward: The main problem of the existing Confederation was not as much to be found in the often invoked "imbecility of the Congress" as it was in the incapacity of the states, specifically the state legislatures, to rise up to the task. Therefore, the problem was at the state level. For Hamilton, the state legislatures reproduced, at a larger scale, all of the defects of the people qua multitude: "All the passions then we see, of avarice, ambition, interests, which govern most individuals, and all public bodies, fall into the current of the States, and do not flow in the stream of the General Government."[38]

Likewise, Madison observed that "the evils issuing" from the states "contributed more to that uneasiness which produced the Convention, and prepared the public mind for a general reform, than those which accrued to our national character and interest from the inadequacy of the Confederation to its immediate objects."[39] "The time had come," Madison concluded, "not only to free the Union from its dependence on the states but to free the states from themselves by taking steps that would undo the damage done by the excesses of republicanism," i.e., of democracy.[40] As Jefferson warned a year before in a letter to James Monroe, "The states must see the rod; perhaps it must be felt by some one of them." Thus, only if the Union would have "a negative *in all cases whatsoever* on the legislative acts of the states, as heretofore exercised by the Kingly prerogative," wrote Madison to Washington, could the national government act as an actual arbiter, or

---

[36] Quoted in Madison, *Notes of Debates*, 349.
[37] King, *The Founding Fathers v. the People*, 29.
[38] Quoted in Madison, *Notes of Debates*, 131–132.
[39] Farrand, *The Records of the Federal Convention of 1787*, Vol. 1, 423–424.
[40] Rakove, *Original Meanings*, 34.

compromissarius, a "disinterested & dispassionate umpire in disputes between different passions & interests in the State" – that is, within each of the states.[41]

As we shall see with more concrete examples in the next section, there is little doubt that in the minds of the delegates the dispute was about the final locus of sovereignty – thus, about the proper balance of powers between the states and the federal government. However, the *actual* dispute proved less important in the long run than did the *theoretical* argument against the state legislatures, which amounted to an insidious attack on the much-praised social contract theory.

Attractive as it was, the social contract theory presented two major flaws. First, as shown in previous chapters, according to the Lockean social contract theory, the legislature represented the supreme power of any voluntarily erected polity, for it was the "soul" that kept the political body alive. Yet this central role played by a legislature intended not just to *represent* the people but also to *be* the only legitimate voice of people did not function very well, as the experience of the states had demonstrated. Second, and arguably more important, the cornerstone of the social contract theory was that the majority rules. As such, it was intrinsically inimical to compromises between majority and minority, as it automatically denied the equality of the two. Herein lies the paradox: the social contract *is* fundamentally a compromise (for implying the equality of the parties), but one that prevents any further compromises (by fostering unequal majorities and minorities).

As Madison explained it in a letter to Monroe, prior to the Convention and before he penned *Federalist* No. 10, "[t]here is no maxim in my opinion which is more likely to be misapplied, and which therefore needs elucidation, than the current one that the interest of the majority is the political standard of right and wrong," unless one understands by "interest" the "Ultimate happiness."

But taking it in the popular sense, as referring to immediate augmentation of property and wealth, nothing can be more false. In the latter sense it would be the interest of the majority in every community to despoil & enslave the minority of individuals; and in a federal community to make a sacrifice of the minority of the component states.[42]

Unsurprisingly, "Madison began to fashion a powerful criticism of the majoritarian premise of the republican government – a criticism he could apply to both Congress and the states."[43] This criticism required an appeal to a different body of people – the corporatist one – and thus to a different kind of contract – the political one, without, however, discarding the first one. As he explained years later, in a letter dated February 15, 1830, "[t]he original compact is the one implied or presumed, but nowhere reduced to writing, by which a people agree to form one society. The next is a compact, here for the first time reduced

---

[41] Quoted in Rakove, *Original Meanings*, 51 (emphasis in the original).
[42] Quoted in Rakove, *Original Meanings*, 44–45.   [43] Ibid., 45.

to writing, by which the people in their social state agree to Government over them. These two compacts may be considered as blended in the Constitution of the United States."[44] By conceiving the people as a proper political body for whose health all parts, large and small, ought to be tended to, the political compact theory almost naturally promotes consensus and compromise.[45]

Thus, one can understand why the framers' "tendency to compromise was not accidental," but "was embedded in the very structures of politics in which they carried on their activities."[46] Nelson explains this "original" development by the consistent use of what he labels "instrumental reasoning" conducive to the formation of concurring majorities and thus to compromise, not just in the Convention, but also during the ratification process and the implementation of the federal institutions at the beginning of the 1800s. While correct, the explanation captures only half the story. Far from being just the result of instrumental and cold reasoning, the compromises that took place in the Convention were, to an equal extent, the result of a corporatist and idealist vision of the people requiring punctual sacrifices for the sake of the common, larger good. As a matter of fact, Nelson himself seems to agree with this second leg of interpretation, since he follows in the footsteps of Rousseau, distinguishing between a holistic General Will in counterdistinction to the "will of all," as a simple numerical majority. Furthermore, he acknowledges that the delegates "strove to preserve liberty not by promoting factional divisions, but by arranging compromises that would accommodate all factions and ultimately transform them into a single homogenous community."[47]

The reason for this ambivalence, as we have seen already, is to be found embedded in the structure of compromise itself. As Knupfer astutely observed, mutuality, which stays at the heart of any compromise, "can be understood at two levels, *contractual* and *affective*."

This notion of contractual mutuality suits well the idea that societies comprise aggregations of self-interested individuals whose conflicts require adjustment instead of melioration. The parties to the agreement are acting as independent, rational beings whose creative energy compromise releases instead of restrains. The other level of mutuality is affective: the relationship between the parties reflects a degree of intimacy, of dependence. Compromise in this sense is a communal act ... that ... has an intrinsic value apart from the material gains it produces. The parties seek conciliation, so their arguments for concessions appeal to common symbols of fraternity, honor, affection and duty.[48]

---

[44] Quoted in Gary Rosen (1999), *American Compact: James Madison and the Problem of Founding* (Lawrence: University Press of Kansas), 17.

[45] For a similar observation, but focused on the "constitutional" v. the "radical democratic" vision of the American past, see King, *The Founding Fathers v. the People*, 133–146.

[46] William E. Nelson (1987), "Reason and Compromise in the Establishment of the Federal Constitution, 1787-1801," *The William and Mary Quarterly*, 44:3, 460.

[47] Ibid., 462.   [48] Knupfer, *The Union as It Is*, 9.

It goes almost without saying that, as such, compromise is an intrinsic part of the people's two bodies paradigm, by accommodating both the liberal understanding of the people as a collection of equal and self-interested individuals and the republican language of a corporate, hierarchically ordered people. In the following two sections, I will use this approach to analyze some of the most important compromises during the Federal Convention and the ratifying process.

5.2 "... TO SMOKE THE CALUMET OF UNION AND LOVE"

Even before the dust began to settle on the hard-fought battles over the new Constitution, a Massachusetts newspaper announced with festive optimism that "all appeared willing to bury the hatchet of animosity and to smoke the calumet of Union and love."[49] Such a degree of optimism was nowhere to be found among the delegates when they first gathered in Philadelphia. Considering the diversity of interests and the history of failed attempts to reform the Articles of Confederation, the deck seemed stacked against any perspective of notable success. Even later in the Convention, Pierce Butler saw the interests of Southern and Eastern states "to be as different as the interests of Russia and Turkey."[50] "No sooner were the State Governments formed than their jealousy & ambition began to display themselves. Each endeavored to cut a slice from the common loaf, to add to its own morsel till at length the confederation became frittered down to the impotent condition in which it now stands."[51] Luckily, it was precisely this generalized doomsday feeling that created a sense of urgency among most of the delegates, and the fresh memory of Shay's rebellion played right into it.[52] As Washington described it in a letter to Jefferson, "the situation of the general government, if it can be called government, is shaken to its foundation, and liable to be overturned by every blast. In a word, it is at an end; and, unless a remedy is soon applied, anarchy and confusion will inevitably ensue."[53]

As Rakove observed, "by 1787 Congress had become such an object of scorn that it is a minor puzzle to explain why the framers retained its name for the new legislature." As we saw in the previous chapter, under the Articles of Confederation, "Congress was an essentially executive body – the successor less of the Parliament than of the Crown. In its appearance and deliberation, however, resembled a legislature."[54] What might appear puzzling could also

---

[49] Quoted in Nelson, "Reason and Compromise," 476.
[50] Quoted in Madison, *Notes of Debates,* 549.
[51] Quoted in Madison, *Notes of Debates,* 90–91.
[52] For a detailed review and analysis of the Confederation's flaws, see Klarman, *The Framers' Coup,* chapter 1, and Robertson, *The Original Compromise,* chapter 2.
[53] George Washington to Thomas Jefferson, May 30, 1787, in Farrand, *The Records of the Federal Convention of 1787,* Vol. 3, 31.
[54] Rakove, *Original Meanings,* 206.

be interpreted as another sign of the profound ambivalence shared by the Philadelphia delegates. On the one hand, they wanted a brand-new constitution, based on a different set of principles. On the other, they wanted to reassure the skeptics that the same changes would not affect the features of the old constitution that they had found attractive. Fortunately, by the time of the Federal Convention, the framers benefited from the experience of more than a century and a half of constitutional controversies, resolved – as we have seen – by covenants, compacts, and appeals to charters. Unsurprisingly, "compromise, compact, and contract were clearly interwoven."[55] "Properly conceived and honorable executed, compromise was the expected outcome of republican political action: the reconciliation of principles and interests."[56]

The first sign of the delegates' shared willingness to compromise despite the different interests of their constituencies came in the first days of the Convention, when they adopted rules meant to favor compromise, including the secrecy of the debates. The delegates were to pay undivided attention to every speaker on the floor ("none shall pass between them, or hold discourse with another, pamphlet or paper, printed or manuscript"), and complex issues were to be disentangled: "[a] question which is complicated, shall, at the request of any member, be divided, and put separately on the propositions, of which it is compounded." To ensure time for reflection and to allow the minority voices to be properly heard, "[t]he determination of a question, altho' fully debated, shall be postponed, if the deputies of any State desire it until the next day." Furthermore, since changes of opinion were to be expected and encouraged, the provision to register "the yeas & nays" was struck down, since "such a record of the opinions of members would be an obstacle to a change of them on conviction."[57] Overall, "[t]he rules were designed not to enable a majority to triumph over a recalcitrant minority."[58]

Even when different economic interests – commercial, maritime, agricultural, manufacturing – could be divided along a majority–minority line, compromise required that minorities' voices were not to be ignored. As a matter of fact, "claims of interest were always brought up by minorities that had no hope of triumph. The claims were a device by which defeated minorities insisted that they be accommodated through compromise." But most importantly – and still overlooked by most scholars – some of the most significant issues, from the proper balance between national and state powers to the structure and extent of the executive power, the role of the judiciary, etc., were *impossible* to formulate in terms of group interests, for the simple reason that no one could predict who the future winners and losers would be. Such issues "were not questions about which the delegates could know whether their constituents would benefit from particular outcomes." As a result, "[w]hat was in dispute was not what each

---

[55] Knupfer, *The Union as It Is*, 55.   [56] Ibid., x.   [57] Madison, *Notes of Debates*, 25–26.
[58] Nelson, "Reason and Compromise," 465.

delegate desired for his own group *in the present* but what the delegates expected or fear for *the nation as a whole* in the future."[59] Put differently, they had to identify themselves with the interests of the American people rather than with their respective state interests. Such identification was more than merely rational. It came with a strong affective component as well.

The fact that the framers were divided between "broad nationalists" supporting a strong central government with extensive policy authority (such as Madison, Hamilton, Wilson, or Morris) and "narrow nationalists" supporting the expansion of the powers of the national government in more limited ways (such as Roger Sherman or Oliver Ellsworth) did not prevent all of them from thinking either that their first allegiance should go to the national American identity or at least that the American and state identities were on an equal footing. In turn, this national identification removed the fear of endangering local identities so pernicious to any previous attempts to compromise.[60] As William L. Pierce explained, "[t]ho' from a small State he felt himself a citizen of the U.S." Speaking right after Pierce, Gerry also argued in terms of identities and allegiances. He "urged that we never were independent States, were not such now, & never could be even on the principles of the Confederation. The States & the advocates for them were intoxicated with the idea of their *sovereignty*." By emphasizing their local identities at the expense of the all-comprehensive one, some fellow delegates brought forward the self-interested spirit of bargaining, thus damaging the self-sacrificing spirit of republicanism: "He lamented that instead of coming here like a band of brothers, belonging to the same family, we seemed to have brought with us the spirit of political negotiators."[61] Gouverneur Morris was even more vehement:

He came here as a Representative of America; he flattered himself he came here in some degree as a Representative of the whole human race; for the hole human race will be affected by the proceedings of this Convention. He wished gentlemen to extend their views beyond the present moment of time; beyond the narrows limits of place from which they derived their political origins. If he were to believe some things which he heard, he should suppose that we were assembled to truck and bargain for our particular States.[62]

Only by embracing a wider and timeless vision of the public good did the "republican political skills enable[] them to work through compromise after compromise on Congress, president, the courts, national authority, state powers, economic management, slavery and national defense."[63] Still, in this context, the label "republican" might be misleading. Indeed, George Mason claimed that on two points the mind of the people of America was "well settled. 1. in an attachment to Republican Government. 2. in an attachment

---

[59] Nelson, "Reason and Compromise," 468, 470 (emphases added).
[60] Robertson, *The Original Compromise*, 15.   [61] Quoted in Madison, *Notes of Debates*, 217.
[62] Quoted in Madison, *Notes of Debates*, 240.   [63] Robertson, *The Original Compromise*, 8.

to more than one branch in the Legislature. ... This must either have been a miracle, or have resulted from the genius of the people."[64] However, as shown in the previous chapter, the term "republicanism" carried different meanings for different people – and sometimes for the same ones.

For some, "republicanism" meant simply a non-monarchical form of government. While acknowledging that "we don't propose to establish Kings," Benjamin Franklin was quick to point out, "but there is a natural inclination in mankind to Kingly Government. [...] It gives more of the appearance of equality among Citizens, and that they like. I am apprehensive therefore ... that the Government of these States, may in future times, end in a Monarchy. But this Catastrophe I think may be long delayed."[65] Later in the Convention, Hugh Williamson proved much more of a "contextual republican." "It was pretty certain he thought that we *should* at some time or other have a King; but he wished no precaution to be omitted that might postpone the event as long as possible."[66] It is by now largely forgotten that many founders entertained some degree of monarchical sympathy. If John Adams or Alexander Hamilton's pro-monarchical positions are relatively common knowledge, less known is what George Washington wrote to James Madison on March 31, just before assuming the chairmanship of the Federal Convention: "I am ... clear, that *even admitting the utility, nay, necessity*" of monarchy, "*that period is not arrived* for adopting the change without shaking the peace of this country to its foundation."[67]

For others, such as Mason, "republicanism" equated with a more direct, democratic control of the people on their elected officials. While most of the delegates were willing to accept some degree of "democracy" in the framing of the new Constitution, they also largely agreed that "[t]oo much democracy imperiled the pursuit of national interests."[68] Elbridge Gerry captured well these mixed feelings when declaring on May 31 that "The evils we experience flow from the excess of democracy. The people do not want virtue, but are the dupes of pretended patriots. [...] He had he said been too republican heretofore: he was still however republican, but had been taught by experience the dangers of the levelling spirit."[69] Hamilton observed as well that "[t]he members most tenacious of republicanism ... were as loud as any in declaiming the vices of democracy." The shared emphasis was on striking the proper balance between the two people's bodies.

In every community where industry is encouraged, there will be a division of it into the few & the many. Hence separate interests will arise. There will be debtors & creditors &c. Give all the power to the many, they will oppress the few. Give all the power to the

---

[64] Quoted in Madison, *Notes of Debates*, 158.   [65] Quoted in Madison, *Notes of Debates*, 53.
[66] Quoted in Madison, *Notes of Debates*, 357 (emphasis added).
[67] Quoted in Gerald Stourzh (1970), *Alexander Hamilton and the Idea of Republican Government* (Stanford: Stanford University Press), 39 (emphasis added).
[68] Robertson, *The Original Compromise*, 7.   [69] Quoted in Madison, *Notes of Debates*, 39.

few, they will oppress the many. Both therefore ought to have power, that each may defend itself against the other.[70]

After long debates, the solution came from "the second attachment" of the American mind mentioned by Mason, namely "the attachment to more than one branch in the Legislature." In retrospect, it is easy to wonder why it took so long, since the compromise now seems so "natural" and obvious. As Oliver Ellsworth of Connecticut famously told the Convention on June 29, "The proportional representation in the first branch was conformable to the national principle ... An equality of voices was conformable to the federal principle ... On this middle ground a compromise would take place. He did not see that it could on any other. And if no compromise should take place, our meeting would not only be in vain but worse than in vain."[71]

And yet on the question of representation the delegates were in a stalemate, until General Pinckney "proposed that a Committee consisting of a member of each State should be appointed to devise & report some compromise." Most delegates agreed with Doctor Williamson, who "approved of the Committee, supposing that as the Committee will be a smaller body, a compromise could be pursued with more coolness." The only notable opposition came from Madison, who argued that "[a]ny scheme of compromise that could be proposed in the Committee might as easily be proposed in the House."[72] Luckily, he was for once in the minority.

There is little doubt that no other compromise in American history has received more attention that what has since been labeled the Great Compromise of July 16, also known as the Connecticut Compromise, when the delegates agreed with the principle of proportional representation in the House of Representatives and of equal representation of the states in the Senate. Then as now, people understood different things from the same compromise, some partially overlapping and some not. For most, it was a compromise between the interests of large and small states, or between representing individuals and representing states; for others, as we have seen, it was a compromise between one and several American peoples, or between the federal and the national (or sometimes republican) principles. For others, such as Gouverneur Morris, it was nothing less than a compromise between the aristocratic and the democratic principles, where aristocracy was understood less as one of virtue and of merits than as one of wealth:

[T]he checking branch must have a personal interest in checking the other branch, one interest must be opposed to another interest. Vices as they exist, must be turned against each other. [...] The aristocratic body, should be as independent & as firm as the democratic. If the members of it are to revert to a dependence on the democratic choice,

[70] Quoted in Madison, *Notes of Debates*, 134–135.
[71] Quoted in Madison, *Notes of Debates*, 218.
[72] Quoted in Madison, *Notes of Debates*, 232, 236.

the democratic scale will preponderate. [...] It will then do wrong, it will be said. He believed so: He hoped so. The Rich will strive to establish their dominion & enslave the rest. They always did. They always will. The proper security against them is to form them into a separate interest. The two forces will then control each other. Let the rich mix with the poor and in a Commercial Country, they will establish an oligarchy. Take away commerce, and democracy will triumph. [...] Reason tells us we are but men: and we are not to expect any particular interference of Heaven in our favor. By thus combining & setting apart, the aristocratic interest, the popular interest will be combined against it. There will be a mutual check and mutual security.[73]

Underlying all these different interpretations was a compromise between the people's two bodies: the people qua multitude and the people qua ordered corporation. The visions about the proper ordering of the two bodies differed. For delegates like Morris, they were conceived as equally strong and opposite poles of powers. For people like Madison, it was more of a balanced mixture at various levels of government. For many others, like Wilson or Hamilton, the balance was tilted to the hierarchical side, primarily for "architectural" reasons: "Mr. Wilson contended strenuously for drawing the most numerous branch of the Legislature immediately from the people. He was for raising the federal pyramid to a considerable altitude, and for that reason wished to give it as broad a basis as possible." It was also more of a practical arrangement: "No government could long subsist without the confidence of the people. In a republican Government this confidence was peculiarly essential."[74] For Franklin, the pyramid was reversed: "In free Governments the rulers are the servants, and the people their superiors & sovereigns." Allowing the rulers to return among the people "was not to *degrade* but to *promote* them."[75] And Mason believed that "you should draw the representatives directly from the people. It should be so much so, that *even the Diseases of the people should be represented – if not, how are they to be cured?*"[76]

King's description of this prevailing attitude of the framers captures well the contemporary forgetfulness of the people's two bodies paradigm. For him, like for many contemporaries, there is only one people – the electors:

[The framers] allocated one capacious room – a downstairs room – to the people, in the guise of the electors of each state for the numerous branch of the state's legislature. But for the time being that was the only room the people were allocated. They were given only limited and indirect access, if any access at all, to all of the other rooms in the new

---

[73] Quoted in Madison, *Notes of Debates*, 233–234. For a similar interpretation of John Adams position on aristocracy, see Luke Mayville (2016), *John Adams and the Fear of American Oligarchy* (Princeton and Oxford: Princeton University Press); and Richard Alan Ryerson (2016), *John Adams's Republic: The One, the Few, and the Many* (Baltimore: John Hopkins University Press).

[74] Quoted in Madison, *Notes of Debates*, 40.

[75] Quoted in Madison, *Notes of Debates*, 371 (emphasis in the original).

[76] Quoted in Robertson, *The Original Compromise*, 42 (emphasis added).

house. [...] The people were given a place, to be sure, but they were also to be kept in that place, as securely as could be arranged.[77]

While undoubtedly attractive, such metaphors perpetuate a unidimensional vision of the people that has little to do with how the framers understood it. As in the case of the repeated appeals to social compact theory, words like "people" can be easily misleading. Thus, unless he resigns any hope for intellectual coherence during the founding, the observer must switch focus from *what* words were used to *how* they were used. As we have repeatedly seen, the fact that the founders spoke about "people" and "rulers" (and increasingly about "representatives") did not mean that they conceived the "aristocracy" as distinct from "the people" qua corporate political body. The founders were not versus the people, as King had it in the title of his book. Every single one of them thought about himself as being *part of* and *for* the people.

From a contemporary perspective, it is tempting to play on the built-in ambiguity of the concept of compromise in order to distinguish between the Great Compromise, which "symbolizes compromise in its positive and laudatory aspects," and the Three-Fifths Compromise, "more difficult to endorse, much less celebrate." From this second perspective, the Constitution, "as the abolitionist William Lloyd Garrison later put it, was 'a covenant with death and an agreement with hell.'"[78] The immorality of the Three-Fifths Compromise has been persuasively proven from a multitude of perspectives.[79] Even the participants agreed that there was no basis on which the rule could be justified. On July 11, the delegates argued about this infamous rule in the general context of discussing the principle of representing people versus representing wealth. Wilson "did not see on what principle the admission of blacks in the proportion of three-fifths could be explained. Are they admitted as Citizens? then why they are not admitted on an equality with White Citizens? are they admitted as property? then why is not other property admitted into computation? These were difficulties however which he thought must be overruled by the necessity of compromise."[80]

If there was to be a new Constitution at all and the Union was to be preserved, there was no other solution. "[S]outhern intransigence on slavery led Gouverneur Morris and Roger Sherman to observe that it was 'vain for the Eastern States to insist on what the Southern States will never agree to' and that

---

[77] King, *The Founding Fathers v. the People*, 61–62.   [78] Rakove, *Original Meanings*, 58.

[79] See, for example, Avishai Margalit (2009), *On Compromise and Rotten Compromises* (Princeton: Princeton University Press); Lena Zuckerwise (2016), "'There Can Be No Loser': White Supremacy and the Cruelty of Compromise," *American Political Thought: A Journal of Ideas, Institutions, and Culture*, 5, 467–493; Simon Cabulea May (2018), "No Compromise on Racial Equality" in Christina F. Rostboll and Theresa Scavenius, eds., *Compromise and Disagreement in Contemporary Political Theory* (New York: Routledge), 34–49. For a detailed historical analysis, see Klarman, *The Framers' Coup*, chapter 4.

[80] Quoted in Madison, *Notes of Debates*, 275.

it would be 'better to let the S. States import slaves than to part with them.'"[81]
Even if the southern delegates could have been persuaded, the document
would have never been ratified. Hence, for the abolitionists, there was no
foreseeable gain in terms of weakening the institution of slavery.[82] But unfore-
seeable as well were the long-term benefits. "By limiting the protected categories of property to a single, specified, and exceptional case, it narrowed the
basis on which property in more general could be protected more radically."
By insisting on constitutional rules for both a census and a reapportionment,
the southern delegates unintentionally contributed to the legitimization of
"the principle that representation actually followed population," not wealth.[83]
Michael J. Klarman summarizes well the compromise on slavery:

> In a sense, the delegates were drafting two separate constitutions. As practical politicians
> who understood that slavery would not disappear any time soon, they wrote a
> constitution that protected the interests of slave owners. As idealists who were not
> oblivious to their historical reputations, they wrote a constitution that would require
> little amendment should slavery one day be abolished, as many of them hoped and
> expected it would be.[84]

But when the final version was signed by the thirty-nine, another, longer
political battle was already in the making – the battle for ratification.

5.3 "THE HOUSE ON FIRE MUST BE EXTINGUISHED"

In late August, the delegates grew increasingly impatient and frustrated.
Gouverneur Morris had urged them "to hasten their deliberation to a conclusion." The motivation was eminently practical. The more "the people have time
to hear the variety of objections" against the proposed Constitution, the more
"doubtful" its fate would be.[85] As such, the issue of ratification became an
urgent one – and it was far from generating consensus. There were several
questions that needed to be addressed: Was there supposed to be a National
Ratifying Convention or should the document be sent to the states for ratification? If the latter, was Congressional approval needed before submitting it to
the states? Were the people entitled to bring forward amendments or not?
Ought the ratification be conducted by the state legislatures or by popular
ratifying conventions? If the requirement of unanimity was to be dropped,
how many states were required for the Constitution to be approved?
   The facts are well known by historians. Some of the questions were
answered much quicker than others. Ellsworth's motion to refer the ratification
to state legislatures was struck down, since these legislatures would have had to
approve a Constitution that would reduce their powers. As Randolph noted,

---

[81] Nelson, "Reason and Compromise," 464.   [82] Rakove, *Original Meanings*, 93.
[83] Ibid., 74.   [84] Klarman, *The Framers' Coup*, 265.
[85] Quoted in Rakove, *Original Meanings*, 94.

they "would be adverse to any Change in their Constitutions ... unless expressly called upon to refer the question to the people."[86] Furthermore, it was yet another signal that the framers lost their confidence in the ability of legislatures to properly represent the people. But the other extreme, namely Morris's proposal for a National Ratifying Convention, was also rejected. It would have meant that the "peoples" of the states disappeared, being entirely melded into the all-encompassing people of the United States – a step that few were willing to seriously consider, for either theoretical or practical reasons.[87] Having state ratifying conventions appeared to most delegates the right compromise between these extremes.

The motion for unanimous ratification by the thirteen states, proposed by Daniel Carroll, was immediately struck down. As Wilson argued, "[u]nanimity was of great importance, but [should] not be purchased by the majority's yielding to the minority."[88] The number of states required for ratification was more heavily debated, varying between a simple majority of seven states (Wilson), to ten (Sherman and Dayton), only to be finally agreed at nine (Randolph's initial proposal). Most delegates felt, like Wilson, that there was no time for consideration of minority rights: "The House on fire must be extinguished, without a scrupulous regard to minority rights."[89]

The issue of Congressional approval required more strategic thinking. On the one hand, by sending the new Constitution to the main institutional body under the former constitution and obtaining its approval would have meant a lot in terms of boosting the legitimacy of the proposal and hence its chance for ratification by the states. *Not to ask* for its approval could have been seen as improper and indecorous, treating it as mere messenger. On the other hand, *to ask* for its approval could have been an embarrassment, effectively demanding Congress to approve an act overtly inconsistent with the Articles of Confederation it was supposed to uphold. Finally, a potential refusal by Congress would have delivered a deadly blow to the ratification process. In the end, on August 31, yet another compromise was reached: The document was to be sent to Congress, but the words "for its approval" were to be eliminated.

The problems were far from over. In one way or another, they all had to do with "the people." If successful, agreeing that the people were entitled to ratify the new Constitution by acting as "the fountain of power" for the new government could serve several purposes. As Madison wrote to Washington even before the delegates convened in Philadelphia, on April 16, "[t]o give a new system its proper validity and energy, a ratification must be obtained from the people, and not merely the ordinary authority of the Legislatures."[90] After the beginning of the Convention he reiterated the idea, claiming that "the new

[86] Quoted in Madison, *Notes of Debates*, 349.
[87] For the debates around these two proposals, see Madison, *Notes of Debates*, 347–355.
[88] Quoted in Madison, *Notes of Debates*, 555.   [89] Quoted in Madison, *Notes of Debates*, 562.
[90] Quoted in Rakove, *Original Meanings*, 98.

Constitution should be ratified in the most unexceptionable form, and by the supreme authority of the people themselves."[91] As such, the Constitution would take its place in the respected Puritan legacy according to which the people qua multitude were entitled to approve a particular form of government worked out by an aristocracy of merit. It was also "a viable way of making popular creation and limitation of government viable." "It was fictional, for it ascribed to one set of elected representatives meeting in convention a more popular character than every subsequent set of representatives meeting as a legislature. But it was not too fictional to be believed and not so literal as to endanger the effectiveness of government."[92]

It was more than an attempt to officially place the Constitution on a level of authority above all other legislative acts, thus preventing further attempts to rashly modify or even nullify it by future majorities. It was also a way of providing the new document with a post hoc degree of legitimacy that all delegates, despite their rhetoric, knew it was missing. It was not as much a fear of legal repercussions – after all, "it is difficult to imagine who would have pressed charges against the framers for subverting the Articles of Confederation and circumventing the authority of their own state legislatures, or in what court and under what law they might have been tried."[93] But it was a fear nevertheless. No matter how boldly, for example, Madison would claim in the *Federalist* No. 40 that even if all accusations of illegitimacy were true it does not follow that the Constitution "ought, for that reason alone, be rejected," he also acknowledged that its approbation by the people would "blot out all antecedents errors and irregularities."[94] Absent this undisputable popular blessing, the Constitution would lay on very shaky foundations and thus be open to future contestations.

There were major risks to be considered as well. The radical doctrine of people's sovereignty was a double-edged sword: Once these popularly elected conventions embodied the "true sovereign will" of the people, how could one prevent them from following the resolutions of the Federal Convention? In other words, on what theoretical basis could they have been prevented from making the exact same arguments the delegates of the Convention made when claiming to speak in the name of the "real" will of the people? "If the framers could plead 'revolution principles' to justify abandoning the Articles of Confederation, why should the state conventions not enjoy equal liberty?"[95]

No one seriously denied the possibility of amending the new Constitution, providing that the amendment process would pass a high threshold, enough to discourage momentary populist impulses from affecting rushed changes.

---

[91] Madison, *Notes of Debates*, 70.   [92] Morgan, *Inventing the People*, 91.

[93] Rakove, *Original Meanings*, 129.

[94] *The Federalist* (2001), Edited with an Introduction . . . by George W. Carey and James McClellan (Indianapolis: Liberty Fund).

[95] Rakove, *Original Meanings*, 107.

The question was if the state ratifying conventions should be allowed to *demand* amendments *before* the ratification took place, *conditioning* the latter on the former. Here, the Federalist answer was a resounding "no." By doing so, they could frame the following debates in the binary terms of an "all or nothing" choice – either accepting the Constitution as it was, with the possibility of amending it in an unspecified future, or rejecting it in its entirety. Fortunately for them, their opponents in the state conventions could not move past a theoretical argument to a practical arrangement. Rakove's observation deserves a lengthier quotation, for its ability to capture the intractability of the problem:

> Their difficulty lay not in justifying the right of the state conventions to claim greater authority than federalists would have allowed but in determining how this authority could be exercised. [...] Who would propose a suitable set of amendments? How could consensus be reached among a sufficient number of states – presumably nine – acting separately? If five states ratified the Constitution unamended, would that preclude the adoption of amendments by the other eight? Would a second federal convention be needed to attain consensus on the revisions? If so, who would call and elect it? And would its decisions not have to be referred to the states in their turn? Once begun, how could this cycle of deliberation and revision ever end?[96]

Conciliator, a Federalist from Philadelphia, put it in words that could resonate with many of his compatriots: "The most artful logic in the world *cannot show another line of compromise than the one adopted*, and it would be nothing short of madness to hazard the salvation of our country on a bare chance of its repetition. *Where is the man, who after having drawn a prize, would put his ticket into the wheel again?*"[97] One thing was certain – it was not to be found in the ranks of the Federalists.

After some behind-the-scenes maneuvers, Congress adopted the resolution on September 28 without taking a position for or against; however, they explicitly asked the state legislatures to comply with the procedures recommended for conveying ratifying conventions. For Madison, it was a personal disappointment that Congress had failed to provide open support. In one of the rare reversals when it came to political realism, Washington tried to raise his spirits in a letter dated October 10:

> I am better pleased that the proceedings of the Convention is handed from Congress by a unanimous vote (feeble as it is) than if it had *appeared* under stronger marks of approbation without it. This *apparent unanimity* will have its effect. Not every one has opportunities to peep behind the curtain; *and as the multitude often judge from externals, the appearance of unanimity* in that body, on this occasn, *will be of great importance.*[98]

[96] Ibid., 112.   [97] Quoted in Knupfer, *The Union as It Is*, 49 (emphasis added).
[98] http://founders.archives.gov/documents/Washington/04-05-02-0334 (emphasis added).

Washington proved less able to accurately read public opinion when it came to the recent incident involving the Federalists from Pennsylvania. While people were still waiting to hear back from Congress, the supporters of the new Constitution were eager to replace the radical 1776 state constitution. Their Constitutionalist opponents, however, were in no such rush. Aware of their minority status, nineteen of them refused to show up, leaving the assembly two members short of the quorum required to proceed. The next day, two of them, James M'Calmont and Jacob Miley, were forcibly brought in by the sergeant at arms. Alluding to the incident, Washington expressed his conviction that "some of the seceding members of the legislature of that State" were not representing the overall sentiments of the people. In reality, "the assembly's action evoked sharp criticism throughout the country well into 1788." The "obnoxious" Richard Henry Lee, according to Washington, complained that Pennsylvania's supporters of the Constitution were acting "[as] if the subject of Government were a business of passion, instead of cool, sober, and intense consideration."[99]

There were several lessons to be learned, and the Federalists were good students. First, they learned how important the *appearance* of unity was for the success of their project. From that time on, they tried their best not only to keep the debates inside the "all or nothing" strategy but also to present a unified front in counterdistinction with the obvious fragmentation of their opponents. On some of the most sensitive points, such as the issue of slavery, they tailored the compromises in the Constitution "to suit their needs to local audiences. James Wilson and Tench Coxe claimed that the slave trade clause augured the eventual abolition of slavery, whereas C.C. Pinckney and James Madison claimed that slavery would be perfectly secure under the Constitution."[100] *The Federalist* papers also barely mentioned slavery, while making Madison, Hamilton, and Jay appear like they never disagreed on framing the Constitution and all considered it the fine result of a patriotic compromise.[101]

In this context, Madison's change of heart about compromise is worth noticing. After Oliver Ellsworth told the Convention that "proportional representation in the first branch was conformable to the national principle ... an equality of voices was conformable to the federal principle ... [therefore] on this middle ground a compromise would take place,"[102] James Madison countered him: "'I would always exclude inconstant principles in framing a system of government.' If the delegates were to be consistent, they had to choose one form or another, but not both."[103] It was a considerable difference

[99] Quoted in Rakove, *Original Meanings*, 111–112. For a more detailed description of the incident and its aftermath, see Maier, *Ratification*, 63–65.

[100] Knupfer, *The Union as It Is*, 45.

[101] See also Jay's speeches in New York Convention, and Madison's speeches in Virginia Convention.

[102] Madison, *Notes of Debates*, 218.   [103] Knupfer, *The Union as It Is*, 29.

between *that* Madison and the Madison who, in the *Federalist* No. 39, suggested that the new "mixed constitution" embodied a perfect compromise between the national and the federal principles, not just in the two chambers of Congress it proposed but also in its foundation, sources, and extent of powers, including the ability to introduce amendments.

As a matter of fact, it was during the process of ratification that compromise became so closely associated with the Constitution, the Union, and the idea of self-sacrificing patriotism. Promoting the idea of unity, the Federalists emphasized the spirit of compromise that dominated the Federal Convention, and deserved to be replicated in the state conventions as well. It was the only way of creating unity within diversity, *e pluribus unum*, not just as a mere negotiation of competing interests but as a proof of republican patriotism sacrificing private interests for the sake of the larger common good of all Americans. The implication was that their opponents were unwilling to sacrifice local interests for the common good and would rather see the Union dissolved than agree to compromise. As Washington put it, in a letter to John Armstrong, dated April 25, 1788,

[T]he truth is, men are too apt to be swayed by local prejudices, and those who are so fond of amendments which have the particular interest of their own State in view cannot extend their ideas to the general welfare of the Union – they do not consider that for every sacrifice which they make they receive an ample compensation by the sacrifices which are made by other States for their benefit – and that those very things which they give up will operate to their advantage through the medium of the general interest.[104]

It was the second lesson learned by the Federalists, namely that the appeal to compromise as a foundational idea presented the advantage of versatility. Depending on the circumstances, it could be used to appeal either to interests or to virtues. In contemporary parlance, they could appeal to both liberal and republican arguments. Or, from the perspective proposed here, compromise allowed them to play on the dialectic between the people's two bodies. "The dialectic of the ratification debate" placed the concept of compromise "within the context of history and theory that had been absent from the Convention's discussions of the subject." The mounting opposition by the beginning of 1788, following revelations that their initial positions have not been as unanimous as claimed, "had forced the federalists to supplement their early emphasis on patriotism and concord with specific discussions of the specific conditions under which compromise did and should occur."[105]

Finally, after the incident in Pennsylvania's state legislature, the Federalists learned that rather than trying to force an unconditional approval, they would increase their chances by adopting a more conciliatory, compromising position. They also could afford it. Even if the numbers were not on their side, in most

---

[104] http://founders.archives.gov/documents/Washington/04-06-02-0201.
[105] Knupfer, *The Union as It Is*, 31, 32.

states the press was overwhelmingly sympathetic, and so were the wealthiest, most educated members of the public (i.e., "the enlightened ones") whom Madison had wanted to persuade during the Convention so that they may in turn persuade the masses. From the opposite side, Amos Singletary described them with bitterness as "these lawyers and men of learning, and moneyed men, that talk so finely, and gloss over matters so smoothly, to make us poor little people swallow down the pill."[106]

As Klarman put it with academic restraint, "in some ways," the process of ratification "was not entirely fair."[107] Like the Patriots before them, the Federalists too considered that when the house is on fire, extinguishing it trumped all other considerations of fairness. "They sometimes paid those who took notes on the convention's debates or subsidized the publication of their transcripts. In some places, above all Connecticut, Federalists forcibly blocked the circulation of literature critical of the Constitution. In Pennsylvania ... they even tried to suppress evidence that anyone has anything negative to say about the Constitution."[108] Yet unlike both the Patriots and the Antifederalists, they were more than willing to compromise, both among themselves and with their adversaries, as long as their project moved forward toward completion. Once they had discovered the strategic advantage of compromise, they were not about to let it go. After all, the revolution they proposed was about maintaining the union. Even the fact that during the ratification process the protagonists were forced to adapt their strategies according to the most recent developments in other states played right into the hands of the Federalists, by unconsciously reinforcing a sense of togetherness.

Thus, compromise became both an ideologically and a practically strategic weapon, especially after the first early and easy victories of the Federalists in the conventions of Delaware, New Jersey, Pennsylvania, and even Connecticut. As the battles for ratification became more fiercely and closely contested, the Federalists became more and more willing to compromise. They conceded that amendments could be proposed, but only if they were *recommendations*, not *conditions* for ratification. Once again, the political battles became mainly battles over words. In the New York Convention, for example, after dividing the fifty-five proposed amendments into three categories – explanatory, conditional, and recommendatory – the words "upon condition nevertheless" were replaced with "in full confidence nevertheless." It was yet another proof that compromise was possible amid the direst circumstances as long as its terms were rephrased in such a way as to satisfy the subjective sensibilities of the parties involved.

---

[106] Quoted in Rakove, *Original Meanings*, 119.   [107] Klarman, *The Framers' Coup*, 8.
[108] Maier, *Ratification*, xiv.

5.4 "IT WILL WAIT UPON THE LADIES AT THEIR TOILETT ..."

The entire process of ratification was interwoven with different levels of irony, some more obvious than others. The first and best known was that the Federalists insisted on calling themselves as such, while succeeding in labeling their opponents as Anti-Federalists, to the latter camp's understandable despair. If the new Constitution was framed on *radically* different principles than the Articles of Confederation, it was, paradoxically, because according to its supporters, it was more *moderate* than the constitution it sought to replace. "Federalists argued that unlike the Confederation government, the proposed frame contained institutional restraints that steered the nation toward the political center, encouraged moderate conduct, and therefore avoided the extremes of anarchy and consolidation."[109] In effect, as we have seen, they argued that the *nationalist* principle was needed to counterbalance the excesses of the *federal* principle embodied in the previous constitution.

As such, they should have been called "Nationalists," not "Federalists." According to the accepted meanings of the time, their opponents were the "true Federalists" – and they considered themselves as such. For example, a famous Antifederalist (probably Richard Henry Lee) signed his public writings as "A Federal Farmer," and the New York committee opposing the Constitution was called the "Federal Republican Committee." Nevertheless, thanks to the above-mentioned advantages, the Federalists won this PR war of the words. As Frank Schechter observed as early as 1915, "it would be hard to conceive a more deft and sudden abduction of a valuable verbal party asset, a more skillful appropriation of the enemy's thunder, than that by which ... the metamorphosis of the meaning of the work 'Federal' ... under the pens of Nationalists of America was effected."[110] Regardless of one's personal sympathies, one has to admire Pauline Maier's academic probity when refusing to use the word "Antifederalists" unless absolutely necessary in the context. As we have seen, "[t]o use the Federalists' language ... tends ... at least to tip the story in their direction."[111]

The second level of irony is that the theoretical differences between the two camps, while rhetorically inflated, were sometimes difficult to pinpoint. It was a blurry line that could – and was – crossed both ways. Three of the most vehement opponents of the new Constitution, Samuel Adams, Edmund Randolph (who refused to sign the document in Philadelphia), and Melancton Smith, proved crucial to the Constitution's ratification in Massachusetts, Virginia, and New York, respectively. As Faber persuasively argues, their compromising attitude was, in the end, more principled than pragmatic.

---

[109] Knupfer, *The Union as It Is*, 40–41.
[110] Frank I. Schechter (1915), "The Early History of the Tradition of the Constitution," *The American Political Science Review*, 9, 714.
[111] Maier, *Ratification*, xiv.

"They were consistent in initially opposing the Constitution but ultimately voting for ratification. All three were motivated by a similar set of principles that might be best described as 'Federal Union Paradigm.'" They considered the Union and states' sovereignty to be inseparable. Ensuring the success of the one was securing the chances of the other. "Furthermore, like the Federalists, they saw in outright rejection of the Constitution nothing but disunion and potential anarchy."[112]

When it came to their belief in "a wholly natural aristocracy," there were no clear distinctions between Federalists and their opponents. As Melancton Smith's observed in New York's ratifying convention:

I am convinced that this Government is so constituted, that the representatives will generally be composed of the first class in the community, which I shall distinguish by the name of the natural aristocracy. I do not mean to give offence by using this term … I shall be asked what is meant by natural aristocracy – and told that no such distinction of classes of men exists among us. [. . .] Every society naturally divides itself into classes. The author of nature has bestowed on some greater capacities than on others … In every society, men of this class will command a greater degree of respect.[113]

In the same ratifying convention, Robert R. Livingston opposed the proposal that senators ought to be subject to recall by their state legislatures, with the argument that "the state legislatures being frequently subject to factious and irregular passions, must be unjustly dissatisfied, and discontented with their delegates; and a senator may be appointed one day and recalled the next."[114] Hamilton could not help but agree wholeheartedly, making a similar argument as in the Federal Convention, namely that the state legislatures have all the defects of the people's first body. Pointing out that the state legislatures were "immediate agents of the people," and "so constituted, as to feel all their prejudices and passions," he asked rhetorically: "Is not the state of Rhode Island, at this moment, struggling under difficulties and distresses, for having been led blindly the spirit of the multitude? What is her legislature but the picture of a mob?"[115]

Nor did the Antifederalists differ from their adversaries when it came to distrust of human nature. Both Federalists and Antifederalists fit Cecelia's Kenyon famous label, *Men of Little Faith*, as she was the first to acknowledge, after providing plenty of examples from their speeches and writings:

The attitude of the Anti-Federalists toward the people as distinguished from their representatives, and toward the general problem of majority rule, was not radically different from that of their opponents. It is a curious and remarkable fact that during the

---

[112] Faber, "The Federal Union Paradigm," 529.
[113] Quoted in Bernard Bailyn, ed. (1993), The Debate on the Constitution: Federalist and Anti-federalist Speeches, Articles, and Letters during the Struggle over Ratification (New York: The Library of America), 760.
[114] Quoted in Bailyn, *The Debate*, 792.   [115] Quoted in Bailyn, *The Debate*, 810–811.

course of this great debate in which the most popular national constitution ever framed was submitted to the public for the most popular mode of ratification yet attempted, there was very little tendency on either side to enthrone "the people" or to defer automatically to their judgment. [...] Rather was the contrary true, and some of the Anti-Federalists expressions of this attitude could easily have fitted into the dark picture of human nature presented in The Federalist.[116]

"The important point to note" about the rhetorical battles between the Federalists and the Antifederalists, observes King in a similar vein, "is that to a remarkable degree they were fought on the same philosophical ground." "Nowhere in the anti-federalists' numerous essays, letters, and speeches are the people either glorified in moral terms or credited with preternatural sagacity. There is scarcely any mention in any of the anti-federalists papers of the desirability of empowering the people *beyond according them the right to elect*," very much in line with their Puritan predecessors.[117] Even more, in many instances, famous Antifederalists such as Patrick Henry, Richard Henry Lee, George Mason, or Melancton Smith expressed their serious doubts about the wisdom of the electors. As the leading expert in Antifederalist thought, Herbert J. Storing, observed, the Federalists and the Antifederalists "were, at a deeper level, united with one another. Their disagreements were not based on different premises about the nature of man or the ends of political life."[118]

Still, some questions persist: If the Federalists and the Antifederalists "fought on the same philosophical ground," shared the same distrust in both "multitudes" *and* oftentimes in their elected representatives, and if both camps argued in favor of checks and balances precisely for this reason (the Antifederalists even more so than the Federalists), then *what* was the main source of disagreement between the two camps? If nothing else, what made one camp more willing to compromise than the other? And why did the losing camp accept its defeat so fast and so graciously once the rhetorical battles were over?

The answers are to be found, seemingly paradoxically, in the sovereignty of the people implied in the opening of the Constitution – "We the People" – yet conspicuously absent from this foundational text. The paradox is only apparent for "the people" the delegates were referring to there were not the same people as the "changeable multitudes" they were worried so much about. As we have seen, the fact that this phrase was left undefined allowed significant room to maneuver between different understandings of the people during the ensuing debates.[119] And this is the third level of irony: In this theoretical no-man's-land, political combatants often ended up unknowingly changing places. To stick

---

[116] Cecelia M. Kenyon (1955), "Men of Little Faith: The Anti-Federalists on the Nature of Representative Government," *The William and Mary Quarterly*, 12:1, 33.

[117] King, *The Founding Fathers v. the People*, 80, 72 (emphasis added).

[118] Storing, "Introduction" to *The Anti-Federalist*, 3.

[119] King, *The Founding Fathers v. the People*, 25.

with the war metaphor, in the confusion of the battle they sometimes ended up in their opponents' trenches.

Prima facie, the difference between the two camps can be summarized as follows: While the Antifederalists were first and foremost concerned with the *concentration of power*, the Federalists' main concern was, in Hamilton's blunt words, the *concentration of democracy*. Differently put, while the former camp was concerned with the dangers of elitism, the latter was worried about the excesses of populism. In other words, they were each concerned mostly with one of the people's two bodies. The Federalist Farmer framed it this way:

> To be for or against the constitution, as it stands, is not much evidence of a federal disposition; if any names are applicable to the parties, on account of their general politics, they are those of republicans and anti-republicans. The opposers are generally men who support the rights of the body of the people, and are properly republicans. The advocates are generally men not very friendly to those rights, and properly anti republicans.[120]

The Antifederalists were rather satisfied with the basic principle of representation as embodied in the Articles of the Confederation, for it assumed the representation of people not *qua* individuals, but collectively, as corporations, much as the Congregationalists had understood them a century before. A compromise between different corporate entities on the principle of equality of the parties was to be welcomed. As Brutus emphasized, "[t]he idea of a confederated government is that of a number of independent states entering a compact for the conducting certain general concerns, in which they have a common interest, leaving the management of their internal and local affairs to their separate governments."[121]

From here the famous rhetorical question raised by Patrick Henry: "Who authorized them to speak the language of, *We, the People*, instead of *We, the States*?"[122] From here, also, the Antifederalists' belief, of Puritan pedigree, that "the people" ought to be apprehended as a society of orders, and thus that a republican government can operate only on small areas. According to them, that was the only way of ensuring a descriptive representation of various corporate interests – of farmers, merchants, artisans, and the like. Although somewhat concerning, populism was not their primary worry. In the Federal Farmer's words, "[b]ecause we have sometimes *abused democracy*, I am not among those men who think a democratic branch a nuisance; which branch shall be sufficiently numerous, to admit some of *the best informed men of each order in the community* into the administration of government." Having the best of each "order" elected to represent a specific group's interests represented the last (and the most beneficial) of the three kinds of aristocracy he identified: "constitutional" (encompassing all electors and the elected), "a junto of

---

[120] Quoted in Storing, *The Anti-Federalist*, 67–68.
[121] Quoted in Storing, *The Anti-Federalist*, 133.   [122] Quoted in Bailyn, *The Debate*, 596.

unprincipled men, often distinguished by wealth and abilities," and, finally, "a natural aristocracy." Yet he was quick to add "this term we use to designate a respectable order of men, *the line between whom and the natural democracy is in some degree arbitrary.*"[123] Not surprisingly, in the opinion of many Antifederalists, since a society is composed of many orders, the number of representatives ought to reflect this multiplicity. "To make representation real and actual," argued George Mason as well in the Virginia Convention, echoing many of the arguments of the Patriots (of whom he was one), "the number of Representatives ought to be adequate; they ought to mix with the people, think as they think, feel as they feel, ought to be perfectly amenable to them."[124]

There was an irony hidden in the argument's logic. As we have seen, if the Antifederalists adopted an uncompromising position, it was to protect their various corporate identities, which they considered to be threatened by the new Constitution.

It is to be observed that when the people shall adopt the proposed constitution it will be their last and supreme act; it will be adopted *not by the people of New Hampshire, Massachusetts, etc., but by the people of the United States,* and wherever this constitution, or any part of it, shall be incompatible with the ancient customs, rights, the laws of the constitutions heretofore established in the United States, it will entirely abolish them and do them away.[125]

Since they were familiar with constitutions as political compacts between the corporate people and their rulers, they could not think otherwise about the new one. In Brutus's words, "this constitution considers the people of the several states as one body corporate, and its intended as original compact; it will therefore dissolve all contracts which may be inconsistent with it."[126] From here springs the Antifederalists' distrust of any concentration of power removed from the people, the demands for short periods in office, and the repeated appeals for a Bill of Rights. The political contract that they embraced with the same enthusiasm as during the revolutionary era came with a built-in suspicion of any men in power.

The state legislatures are obliged to take notice of the bill of rights of their respective states. The bill of rights, and the state constitutions, are fundamental compacts only between those who govern and the people of the same state. In the year 1788 the people of the United States make a *federal constitution, which is a fundamental compact between them and their federal rulers*; these rulers, in the nature of things, cannot be bound to take notice of any other compact. [. . .] It is part of the compact between the people of each state and their rulers, that no *expost facto* laws shall be made. But the

---

[123] Quoted in Storing, *The Anti-Federalist*, 61, 76 (emphases added).
[124] Quoted in Bailyn, *The Debate*, 607. See also, for example, Kenyon, *Men of Little Faith*.
[125] The Federal Farmer (1788), quoted in Storing, *The Anti-Federalist*, 55 (emphasis added).
[126] Quoted in Storing, *The Anti-Federalist*, 133.

convention, by Art. 1 Sect. 10 have put a sanction upon this part even on state compacts.[127]

Such a tutelary, far-reaching power frightened many. In some respects, it anticipated a much later fear – that of the Big Brother:

> This power, exercised without limitation, will introduce itself into every corner of the city, and country—It will wait upon the ladies at their toilett, and will not leave them in any of their domestic concerns; it will ... sit beside them in the carriages, not it will desert them even at church; it will enter the house of every gentleman, watch over his cellar, wait upon the cook in the kitchen ... and watch him while he sleeps; ... it will watch the merchant in the counting-house or in his store; it follow the mechanic to his shop, and in his work, and will haunt him in his family, and in his bed.[128]

Ironically, it was this very fear that compelled the uncompromising Antifederalists to press for a more egalitarian view of the people and thus to "unwittingly play into the federalist hands."[129] "The growing strength of [the Federalist] doctrine of individualism could only undercut the town and county as the unit of representation."[130] The emphasis on local communities and virtues that they were trying so desperately to protect was in danger of being replaced by the doctrine of individual interests, and the corporate vision of the people by populism.

The Federalists, on the other hand, dusted off the British appeal to the virtual representation of "every single Englishmen" and adapted to the new reality. As a result, they started off with the declared attempt of replacing the representation of local corporations with the representation of the American individuals. Unsurprisingly, they were willing to compromise for the sake of what they essentially perceived to be a new social compact. In the *Federalist* No. 15, Hamilton harshly attacked his opponents on the "the principle of LEGISLATION for STATES or GOVERNMENTS, in their CORPORATE or COLLECTIVE CAPACITIES and as contradistinguished from the INDIVIDUALS of whom they consist," defining it as "the great and radical vice in the construction of the existing Confederation."[131] Consequently, Hamilton also deplored the idea of electing representatives in the likeness of their electors and argued in favor of representatives that would refine the views of their electors and be able to transcend interest group politics. According to him, lawyers were best equipped to fulfill these requirements, as they were not attached to any single interest group. Furthermore, he argued that increasing the ratio of constituents to representatives would ensure the election of the "best" men.[132] While the

---

[127] The Federal Farmer (1788), quoted in Storing, *The Anti-Federalist*, 57 (emphasis added).
[128] Brutus (1788), quoted in Storing, *The Anti-Federalist*, 141.
[129] Lutz, *Popular Consent*, 167.   [130] Ibid.
[131] *The Federalist* (2001), 71 (emphasis in the original); see also, for example, Robert R. Livingston in Bailyn, *The Debate*, 776.
[132] Jean Yarbrough (1979), "*Thoughts on the Federalist's View on Representation*," Polity, 12:1, 65–82. See again Robert R. Livingston in Bailyn, *The Debate*, 777–778.

Federalists had initially opposed the Bill of Rights, for according to the tenets of the social compact theory it would be absurd to "protect against oneself," once they embraced their opponents' accusation of trying to create a corporate *American* people, and agreed with the first ten amendments, they left the other camp without its main ammunition.

That the concentration of power might bring about corruption did not worry Hamilton, who accused the other side of exaggerated cynicism: "They [the Antifederalists] seem to suppose that the moment you put men into the national council, they become corrupt and tyrannical, and lose their affection for the fellow-citizens."[133] On the contrary, it was the "concentration of democracy" that he perceived as the greatest danger. In a letter written the day before he met Aaron Burr in his mortal duel, he confessed his belief that "diluting" democracy by spreading it over a large territory was the only "relief to our real disease, which is *democracy*, the poison of which, by a subdivision, will only be the more concentrated in each part, and consequently the more virulent."[134]

In the end, the difference between the two camps boiled down to different expectations about the possibility of human nature to excel once men were placed in a position of power. The radical Whig assumption was that all men would be "good" if they were deprived of power and "bad" if they wielded it.[135] They would have wholeheartedly agreed with Lord Acton, who would famously claim a century later that "power tends to corrupt and absolute power corrupts absolutely. Great men are almost always bad men."[136] On the contrary, despite their present-day reputation as hard-core "realists," the Federalists were in effect the ones who had to defend themselves against accusations of excessive optimism and even idealism. There is no doubt the claim was exaggerated. After all, Madison, for example, repeatedly warned that "enlightened statesmen will not always be at the helm" (*Federalist 10*), and that neither men nor their governors are angels, hence the necessity "to enable the government to control the governed; and in the next place oblige it to control itself" (*Federalist 51*).[137] Yet the Federalists had much more faith than their adversaries in the ability of (at least some) representatives to serve the common good rather than factional interests. Discussing Smith's concern that only the natural aristocrats, mentioned above, would be at the helm of the new government, Livingston argued with sarcasm:

I hope, Sir, we are all aristocrats. [...] But who, in the name of common sense, will he have to represent us? [...] Why, those who are not virtuous, those who are not wise; those who are not learned: These are the men, to whom alone we can trust our liberties.

[133] Quoted in Bailyn, *The Debate*, 798.
[134] Quoted in Stourzh, *Alexander Hamilton*, 40 (emphasis in text).
[135] Stourzh, *Alexander Hamilton*, 186.
[136] John E. Acton (1887) [2011], *Acton-Creighton Correspondence* (Indianapolis: Liberty Fund), 9.
[137] *The Federalist*, 45, 269.

[...] Where will he find them? Why, he must go out into the highways, and pick up the rogue and the robber: He must go the hedges and ditches and bring in the poor, the blind and the lame.[138]

Obviously, Livingston exaggerated for dramatic effect, and Smith went on to reply vigorously, but the fact of the matter remains: The Federalists tended to have more faith in the ability of great statesmen to resist corruption and work for the common good.

As the Puritans before them, the Federalists believed that no government, no matter how well devised, could survive absent the existence of virtuous men, able to apply general laws to particular circumstances. Nevertheless, they were hardly idealists, as their adversaries often implied. As Hamilton argued, "men will pursue their interests. It is as easy to change human nature as to oppose the string current of selfish passions." However, "*a wise legislator will gently divert the channel, and direct it, if possible, to the public good.*"[139] In direct opposition to "men of little faith," Hamilton claimed that "the supposition of universal venality in human nature, is little less an error in political reasoning, than that of universal rectitude. [...] [T]here is a portion of virtue and honor among mankind, which may be a reasonable foundation of confidence: and experience justify the theory" (*Federalist 76*).[140] Realism told them that virtue and corruption do not differentiate among rulers and the ruled. According to this view, if the charge of lack of realism ought to have been placed anywhere, it should have been in the camp of those under the illusion that well-devised institutional arrangements would make "the aristocracy of merit" unnecessary.[141]

As a matter of fact, the final factor that made the Federalists more willing to compromise than their opponents was precisely the propensity of the latter for grand ideas and abstract theory.[142] As Madison reminded his opponents in *Federalist 37*, as men of good faith, they "will keep in mind that they themselves also are but men, and ought not to assume an infallibility in rejudging the fallible opinions of others." Some topics "complicated in their nature ... have never been distinguished and defined, with satisfactory precision, by all the efforts of the most acute and metaphysical philosophers."

Besides, the obscurity arising from the complexity of objects, and the imperfection of human faculties, the medium through which the conceptions of men are conveyed to each other, adds a fresh embarrassment. The use of words is to express ideas. [...] But no language is so copious as to supply words and phrases for every complex idea, or so correct as not to include many, equivocally denoting different ideas.

---

[138] Quoted in Bailyn, *The Debate*, 779.
[139] Quoted in Bailyn, *The Debate*, 814 (emphasis added).   [140] *The Federalist*, 395.
[141] Stourzh, *Alexander Hamilton*, 181. For a similar interpretation of Hamilton's position, see Michael P. Federici (2012), *The Political Philosophy of Alexander Hamilton* (Baltimore: Johns Hopkins University Press).
[142] It is an interesting aside in this context that a similar accusation had been brought by Edmund Burke against the French revolutionaries.

Madison's observation came in the context in which he was trying to defend the new Constitution's attempt to combine "the genius of republican liberty" – demanding "not only that all power should be derived from the people, but that those entrusted with it should be kept in dependence on the people" – with the principle of stability, which required the opposite. In other words, he was indicating that the word "people" included many "equivocally denoting different ideas." This became even more obvious when he defended the great compromise between the large and small states. "We may well suppose, that neither side would entirely yield to the other, and consequently that the struggle could have been terminated only by compromise." As some compromises are more beneficial than others, the framers had to depart from abstract thinking and take into consideration the existing realities. "Would it be wonderful if, under the pressure of all these difficulties, the convention should have been forced into some *deviations from that artificial structure and regular symmetry*, which an abstract view of the subject might lead an ingenious theorist to bestow on a constitution planned in his closet or in his imagination?"[143]

The Federalists' efforts paid off once New Hampshire became the ninth state to ratify the Constitution, with Virginia a close tenth.[144] Yet the fact that the new document was adopted did not mean an agreement about its three key words, "*We, the People.*" Revealing of the persistent confusion, only a couple of years later, in 1790, John Adams explained himself to his cousin, Samuel Adams: "Whenever I use the word republic with approbation, I mean a government in which the people have collectively, or by representation, an essential share in sovereignty." To which his cousin replies: "Is not the whole sovereignty, my friend, essentially with the people?"[145] In the decades to follow, the battles over the proper interpretation of the Constitution would be further complicated by the Federalists' appropriation of the people *qua* corporation at a national level, and by the Antifederalists' increased support of egalitarianism and populism. From then on, the differences between the two camps' understandings of "the people" would become increasingly blurred, making the battles of interpretation increasingly hard to fight – sadly, not only in the political arena but also on the actual battlefields.

---

[143] *The Federalist*, 180–184. See also *Federalist 62* for similar observations.

[144] The "detail" is disturbing for some constitutional scholars, by raising questions about the eligibility of George Washington. As a citizen of Virginia he was *not* a citizen of the United States at the time of the adoption of the Constitution under Article VII, and hence was ineligible under Article II: "No Person except a natural born Citizen, or a Citizen of the United States, *at the time of the Adoption of this Constitution*, shall be eligible to the Office of President." See Vasan Kesavan (2002), "When Did the Articles of Confederation Cease to Be Law," *Notre Dame Law Review*, 78:1, 35.

[145] Quoted in Lutz, *Popular Consent*, 16.

6

"This Is Essentially a People's Contest"

"Shall We Compromise?"

A compromise, a middle place between freedom and slavery, is as easily tenable a position as one between heaven and hell.

– *The Liberator*, March 21, 1845

We will compromise any measures tending to prevent the extending of slavery. We will compromise as to the particulars of its death, laying out, and burial.

– *The Independent*, March 21, 1850

As easy as it is to dispassionately discuss the compromises of the eighteenth-century American founding, it is as hard to do the same with the compromises of the nineteenth century, because most of the famous ones have the institution of slavery looming in the background. How could one objectively interpret the series of compromises that, through a variety of strategies, made possible the embarrassing survival of slavery well into the second half of the nineteenth century?[1] Yet to properly understand the era extending from the ratification of the Constitution to the Civil War, we must shed our contemporary moralizing lenses. For instance, one must acknowledge that in the first decades following the ratification the issue of slavery was far from being in the forefront of the political debates. "Like most of the nation's founders, for many northerners slavery constituted a 'distraction,' not a moral issue."[2] Even when it became a

---

[1] See, for example, Avishai Margalit (2009), *On Compromise and Rotten Compromises* (Princeton: Princeton University Press); Lena Zuckerwise (2016), "'There Can Be No Loser': White Supremacy and the Cruelty of Compromise," *American Political Thought: A Journal of Ideas, Institutions, and Culture*, 5, 467–493; Simon Cabulea May (2018), "No Compromise on Racial Equality" in Christina F. Rostboll and Theresa Scavenius, eds., *Compromise and Disagreement in Contemporary Political Theory* (New York: Routledge), 34–49.

[2] Ronald P. Formisano (2008), *For the People: American Populist Movements from the Revolution to the 1850s* (Chapel Hill: University of North Carolina Press), 213.

central issue of division, the main focus of the political debates remained on the preservation of the Union, not on the institution of slavery. As late as August 1862, during the war, Abraham Lincoln himself displayed a "tragic pragmatism" when claiming in a famous letter to Horace Greely, the editor of the influential New York *Tribune:*[3]

My paramount object in this struggle is to save the Union, and is not either to save or to destroy slavery. If I could save the Union without freeing any slave I would do it, and if I could save it by freeing all the slaves I would do it; and if I could save it by freeing some and leaving others alone I would also do that. What I do about slavery, and the colored race, I do because I believe it helps to save the Union; and what I forbear, I forbear because I do not believe it would help to save the Union.[4]

But if slavery was *not* the cornerstone of American politics during the first part of the nineteenth century, what was? Since by then the idea of people's sovereignty had become the widely accepted doctrine, the answer is rather straightforward – the proper definition of "the people." The ground of the Gettysburg Address was laid down decades earlier when, in 1830, Daniel Webster told Robert Hayne: "It is, Sir, the people's Constitution, the people's government, made for the people, made by the people, and answerable to the people."[5] Twenty years later, furious at Webster's position during the Compromise of 1850, Theodor Parker accused Webster himself of betraying "a government of all the people, by all the people, for all the people."[6] In Lincoln's own words, even the war was nothing other than "essentially a people's contest."[7]

The distinction between the people's two bodies became further blurred once the Federalists moved away from their initial emphasis on individuals and adopted the corporatist and hierarchical understanding of the people, transferring it from the state to the national level. At the same time, the Antifederalists began embracing a more egalitarian, sometimes even populist understanding of the people at state level, while switching the emphasis from corporate to individual rights. The simple fact that the Constitution was ratified and its opponents acknowledged the authority and legality of the new document did not make these ambiguities disappear overnight. While everyone agreed that the Constitution was both a compact and a compromise, there was no

---

[3] John Burt (2013), *Lincoln's Tragic Pragmatism: Lincoln, Douglas, and Moral Conflict* (Cambridge, MA: The Belknap Press of Harvard University Press).

[4] Roy P. Basler et al. (1953), *The Collected Works of Abraham Lincoln* (New Brunswick: Rutgers University Press), Vol. 5, 389.

[5] *The Writings and Speeches of Daniel Webster* (1906), National ed., 18 vols. (Boston: Little, Brown), 6:54, quoted in Rodgers, *Contested Truths*, 91.

[6] Theodor Parker (1916)[1969], The Slave Power (New York: Arno), 250, quoted in Rodgers, *Contested Truths*, 92.

[7] Abraham Lincoln (1861), *Message to Congress in Special Session*, in *The Collected Works of Abraham Lincoln* (1953), Vol. 4, 439.

consensus on a definition of "the people," nor on the type of compact and compromise. The cards of people's sovereignty were shuffled once again at both national and state levels.

Some, like John Marshall or Daniel Webster, saw the Constitution as a compact agreed on by the American people to form a nation. Others, like Andrew Jackson, were sure that it was a compact among the states, so that during the Nullification Crisis of 1832, both Webster and Jackson attacked Calhoun's theory, only from opposite sides.[8] Even Thomas Jefferson, who thought that Jackson was "one of the most unfit men I know [for the presidency]," because "he has had very little respect for laws and constitutions," agreed with him when it came to interpreting the Constitution.[9] Many years after he famously claimed in his First Inaugural Address, "We are all Republicans, we are all Federalists," the same Jefferson praised John Taylor's book, *Construction Construed*, as "the most effectual retraction of our government to its original principles which has ever yet been sent by heaven to our aid."[10] Yet in this "heavenly" book, Taylor asserted that "the federal is not a national government; it is a league between nations." According to him, each state was a nation and "the natural rights of nations ... are more universally recognized than the rights of individual men."[11] No future secessionist could have interpreted the Constitution in terms more radical than these.

The few who refused to embrace either one of these two interpretations, trying to maintain instead the dialectic between the two poles, were unable to stir the popular enthusiasm. John Adams is a case in point. Faithful to the Puritan heritage, he was not prepared to give up the paradigm of the people's two bodies to favor one at the expense of the other. As previously shown, he was an "uncompromising realist," refusing to side with any simplified vision, no matter how politically profitable it was.[12] But if "in 1776, John Adams did not merely appear to be at the center of America's new political culture, he appeared to be that center" by the 1780s and even more so by the 1790s; he became an outlier, refusing to choose between the "democrats" and the "aristocrats," finding both sides unsatisfactory.[13] Not surprising, Adams, soon to be followed by his son, John Quincy, inaugurated the unflattering list of the one-term presidents, remaining up until recently a marginalized figure in the Founders' Pantheon. Telling for the turn toward polarization that American

---

[8] Knupfer, *The Union as It Is*, 108.

[9] Quoted in Davis S. Brown (2016), *Moderates: The Vital Center of American Politics, from the Founding to Today* (Chapel Hill: University of North Carolina Press), 94.

[10] Thomas Jefferson to Archibald Thweat, January 19, 1821, in Paul Leicester Ford, ed., (1899), *The Writings of Thomas Jefferson* (New York: G.P. Putnam), Vol. 10, 184.

[11] John Taylor (1820), *Construction Construed and Constitutions Vindicated* (Richmond: Shepherd and Pollard), 234, 171.

[12] Vernon P. Parrington (1927), *The Colonial Mind*, Vol. 1 of *Main Currents in American Thought* (New York: Harcourt, Brace & World), 312.

[13] Ibid., 3, 423. See also Brown, *Moderates*, 14.

politics was about to take, "Hamilton and Jefferson, by contrast, conveniently ascended from men to myths. They came quickly to personify the poles of American politics."[14]

This is not to say that extreme polarization conquered the spirit of compromise overnight. As we saw in the previous chapter, the debates in Philadelphia, and even more so the ones surrounding the ratification process, firmly planted in the American psyche the idea that the Constitution was a praiseworthy compromise. For the decades to follow, politicians and civic educators alike worked diligently to reinforce the idea that the Union would not have been possible – and could not be maintained – absent this spirt of compromise. When, for example, Jefferson wanted to convince the reluctant Alexander Hamilton to establish the federal capital on the Potomac River (Washington, DC), he invited him "and another friend or two, bring[ing] them into conference together," thinking "it impossible that *reasonable men, consulting together coolly, could fail, by some mutual sacrifices of opinion, to form a compromise which was to save the union.*"[15] The compromise that followed resulted in what came to be known as the Resident Act.

Half a century later, President John Tyler, too, argued that the Union was "the great interest, equally precious to all," and "should be fostered and sustained by mutual concessions and the cultivation of that spirit of compromise from which the Constitution itself proceeded."[16] His sentiments were echoed by James K. Polk who, at his inauguration in 1845, also declared that in order to preserve the Union, "the compromises which alone enabled our fathers to form a common constitution ... must be sacredly and religiously observed. *Any attempt to disturb or destroy these compromises, being terms of the compact of union, can lead to none other than the most ruinous and disastrous consequences.*"[17] These are only a few examples from literally hundreds of appeals to the Union as compact and commendable compromise. They were made indiscriminately by supporters and opponents of slavery alike.

A survey of the usages of the term "compromise" during this period reveals that the *only* instances in which "compromise" was used with negative connotations were those in which religion constituted the main subject. For example, in a "Tale for Young People" by Jane Taylor, published in the *Christian Register and Moral Theological Review*, we learn how a young and rather pious Emily "found herself unwilling to make that entire surrender of the heart to God which he requires, and without which religion is ... a fruitless effort to

---

[14] Brown, *Moderates*, 13.
[15] Thomas Jefferson [1905], *Autobiography* (1760–1770), in *The Works of Thomas Jefferson*, Vol. 1, 176 (emphasis added).
[16] Third Annual Message, December 1843, quoted in Knupfer, *The Union as It Is*, 115.
[17] Quoted in Knupfer, *The Union as It Is*, 117 (emphasis added).

compromise between God and the world."[18] From *The Christian Disciple and Theological Review* one was reminded how "[i]t is delightful to remember that there have been men, who, in the cause of truth and virtue, have made no compromises for their own advantages and safety."[19] In a similar vein, *The Methodist Quarterly* observed that "[w]e may compromise with conscience for a low rate of obedience; but we will discover at last that God has not endorsed the compromise, and therefore it is worthless."[20] This refusal to compromise, reminiscent of the Puritan and evangelical approaches, coincided with the rise of "religious populism," which in turn "occurred as conflicts percolated in various states over disestablishment and the role of the church in society."[21] It was a foretelling sign for the future of political compromise in a society in which the paradigm of the people's two bodies increasingly gave way to populism.

In order to detail this change, the first part of this chapter analyzes the ways in which the rise of American populism eroded little by little the aura of virtue surrounding political compromises. This should come as little surprise, considering the doctrine of majority rule associated with populism, when left unchecked, was intrinsically inimical to compromise. Although forgotten by many, the first threats to the spirit of compromise for the sake of the union, and – the Kentucky and Virginia Resolutions aside – the first more or less transparent calls to secession were made not because of slavery but due to the perceived peril of populism, and were heard not from the South but from the North, as early as the start of the nineteenth century.

Nevertheless, one must be careful not to adopt a one-sided and unidirectional perspective on a period that for decades has been labeled the Age of the Common Man or the Age of Egalitarianism, allegedly increasingly inclusive, increasingly liberal, and increasingly democratic.[22] "The oft-repeated narrative of the 'rise' of democracy between the American revolution and the Civil War can obscure as much as it reveals. Historians have found it hard to resist imposing a teleological account of political development onto an era that imagined politics very differently from our own."[23] There are several reasons to be cautious. The first one is methodological:

---

[18] "Display, Maternal Solicitude, & C..." (no author) in *Christian Register and Moral Theological Review*, 1:2 (January 1, 1817) (New York: T. & J. Swords), 387.

[19] "Thoughts on True and False Religion" (no author) in *The Christian Disciple and Theological Review*, 2:11 (September 1, 1820) (Boston: Cummings and Hilliard), 337.

[20] *The Methodist Quarterly Review*, 7 (1855) (New York), 9.

[21] Formisano, *For the People*, 45.

[22] See, for example, Sean Wilentz (2005), *The Rise of American Democracy: Jefferson to Lincoln* (New York: Norton); Daniel Walker Howe (2007), *What Hath God Wrought: The Transformation of America, 1815–1848* (Oxford: Oxford University Press).

[23] Daniel Peart and Adam I. P. Smith (2015), "Introduction" in Daniel Peart and Adam I. P. Smith, eds., *Practicing Democracy: Popular Politics in the United States from the Constitution to the Civil War* (Charlottesville and London: University of Virginia Press), 2.

If history must be moving progressively toward better government or more civil rights – more inclusion, more liberty, more social justice – then anyone who blocks the march of progress must be attacked. There are only two sides; people are either right or wrong. These tendencies have not disappeared in either popular or academic scholarship, nor in contemporary American politics. Balance is rare.[24]

There are also historical reasons for refusing such an approach. As we shall see, the egalitarian thrust was followed by a "counter-attack" led mostly, yet not exclusively, under the flag of the Scottish Enlightenment and its Common-Sense Philosophy. Discourses about the state of nature and natural rights began to be replaced by arguments about duties to the community, and about order as the guarantor of liberty. But there is yet another historical reason for being cautious about labels such as the Age of the Common Man: Despite the unstoppable extension of the electoral franchise, not all people were as lucky as white, native-born men in seeing their rights expand throughout the period. Women and free blacks, who, contrary to popular beliefs, were *not* formally prevented from voting in many states at the beginning of the 1790s, saw their rights restricted in the decades to follow.[25] Furthermore, as mass political parties consolidated, political rhetoric began increasingly to favor blatant appeals to racial, ethnic, and religious discrimination. Identity politics grew hand in hand with the first mass political parties, and none of these developments were favorable to political compromise.

Therefore, the second part of the chapter uses this period in order to question the orthodoxy that connects the rise of mass parties with increased democratization, while arguing that partisanship is conducive to political compromises. From Clinton Rossiter's claim – "No America without democracy, no democracy without politics, no parties without compromise and moderation" – to the most recent statement made by Russel Muirhead that "[a]lmost all partisanship is a compromise – not always with rival partisans, but always with our fellow partisans," there is an entire tradition of equating the best form of partisanship with a compromising spirit.[26] Since America was the first country to witness the emergence of mass political parties, it goes almost without saying that it was also the frontrunner of democratization. According to this narrative, the major compromises that marked the first half of the nineteenth century are but historical proofs of this argument. Unfortunately, even a brief survey of the era tells a different story.

[24] Douglas Bradburn (2015), "'Parties Are Unavoidable': Path Dependence and the Origins of party Politics in the United States" in Peart and Smith, *Practicing Democracy*, 26.

[25] Andrew W. Robertson (2015), "Jefferson Parties, Politics, and Participation: The Tortuous Trajectory of American Democracy" in Peart and Smith, *Practicing Democracy*.

[26] Clinton Rossiter (1960), *Parties and Politics in America* (Ithaca: Cornell University Press); Russell Muirhead (2014), *The Promise of Party in a Polarized Age* (Cambridge, MA: Harvard University Press), 18.

Far from being conducive to compromises, the emergence of mass political parties increased the polarization of public life and made political rhetoric increasingly vicious. Even if most politicians still refrained from launching blatant ad hominem accusations against their opponents, an increasingly well-oiled party apparatus and obedient newspapers were happily doing such dirty jobs on their behalf. The major compromises of the era, from the Missouri Compromise to the Compromise of 1850, were made in spite, not because, of the increased partisanship, and most of them took advantage of major realignments inside party systems while trying to prevent party alignment along sectional lines. Appeals were made not to party ideologies or partisan interests, but to the Union, "the people," and the need to overcome narrow partisanship as the founders had done decades earlier.

However, considering the long-established tradition of antiparty rhetoric, a puzzle persists: How is it that the antiparty Americans invented the first mass political parties? The answer, I suggest, is to be found in a radical, albeit incremental, change in the understanding of compromise. As previously discussed, compromise has two components: a contractarian one, with an emphasis on bargaining interests; and an affective one, with an emphasis on amity and mutual self-sacrifices for the common good. As long as the "chords of affection" binding together one people were, more or less consciously, cultivated through a wide variety of strategies, the second component managed to balance the first one.[27] But in the decades after 1800, economic, social, technological, and demographic changes created the "Market Revolution," and consequently a change in mindsets.[28] The rise of individualism and the myth of the self-made man eroded these "chords of affection," producing a marketization of politics.[29] Thus, the Compromise of 1850 was unlike the ones from 1820 to 1821. It marked the transition from this binary understanding of compromise to a one-sided, strictly contractual understanding, thanks largely to the works of the maverick of mass party politics, Stephen Douglas. Ironically for Douglas at least, 1850 also marked the beginning of the end for the compromises meant to preserve both the Union and the institution of slavery. William Freehling refers to the Compromise of 1850 as the *Armistice* of 1850, precisely because, far from solving the tensions between North and South, it exploded into full-fledged war a mere decade later.[30]

---

[27] Emily Pears (2017), "Chords of Affection: A Theory of National Political Attachments in the American Founding," *American Political Thought: A Journal of Ideas, Institutions, and Culture*, 1–29, 6.

[28] Formisano, *For the People*, 68.

[29] The *Oxford English Dictionary* credited Henry Clay with coining the phrase "self-made men" in an 1832 speech: "In Kentucky, almost every manufactory known to me, is in the hands of enterprising and self-made men, who have acquired whatever wealth they possess by patient and diligent labor"; quoted in Brown, *Moderates*, 104.

[30] William Freehling (1990), *The Road to Disunion: Secessionists at Bay, 1776–1854* (New York: Oxford University Press), 487.

The last part of this chapter is dedicated to analyzing these disturbing connections between compromise and slavery. As expected considering the importance of the topic, there is a vast amount of literature from both historical-practical and ethical-philosophical perspectives on the topic. Despite the time and energy put into this debate, the jury is still out in determining if the compromises of the nineteenth century were justifiable or not. Persuasive arguments have been made that, had secession occurred in 1850 or earlier, the Confederacy might have been successful. Yet equally persuasive arguments claim the opposite. As Sanford Levinson observes, after reviewing some of this literature, "[a]t the very least, this illustrates the inevitable admixture of abstract principle and empirical consequences in making basic decisions about the legitimacy of compromise – and about the selection of one's heroes."[31]

While I will be employing the work of some of the scholars involved in this debate, my aim is not to take sides. Instead of trying to decide if these compromises were defensible or not, either from a theoretical or from a practical perspective, I shall direct the focus to what made these compromises possible and what factors eventually made them obsolete. The hope is that this approach will at least illuminate some rather disturbing puzzles that otherwise tend, rather conveniently, to be overlooked. For example, why did nativist Know-Nothings, openly anti-Catholic and anti-immigration, end up in the new Republican, anti-slavery party, while pro-slavery Democrats were very successfully courting the votes of new immigrants? Why did war erupt because of the Southern rather than of the Northern refusal to compromise? I shall argue that the willingness, or lack thereof, to compromise may be explained by a combination of two factors: one largely objective – namely the establishment of long-lasting majorities and minorities; the other largely subjective – namely a perceived group identity. Both, however, were related to fluctuating understandings of "the people" at state and national levels. "We the people of the Confederate States," as the first words of the Constitution of the Confederate States read, clashed on the battlefields with "We the people of these United States," in the name of the same revolutionary principle of popular sovereignty earlier employed by the Patriots. It was, indeed, as Lincoln put it, "a people's contest."

6.1 "... FRESH FROM THE LOINS OF THE PEOPLE ..."

> This day (Feb. 8, 1788) ... the news arrived in this town (Newsburyport) that the federal Constitution was yesterday adopted and ratified ... I have not been pleased with this system, and many acquaintances have long since branded me

---

[31] Sanford Levinson (2012), *Framed: America's Fifty-one Constitutions and the Crisis of Governance* (New York: Oxford University Press), 46. For arguments that far from "buying time for the North" to develop industrially, the Compromise of 1850 actually "bought time for the South" to strengthen its position, see Paul Finkelman (2011), "The Cost of Compromise and the Covenant with Death," *Compromise and Constitutionalism, Pepperdine Law Review*, 38, 845–888.

with the name of an anti-Federalist. But I am now converted though not convinced. I think it is my duty to submit without murmuring against what is not to
be helped.[32]

This fragment from young John Quincy Adams's diary captures the so-branded
Antifederalists' almost-overnight change of heart regarding the Constitution. Yet
if, like John Quincy, most were converted, fewer were convinced about the
"official" interpretation promoted by the Federalists. On the contrary, many
were arguing that, properly interpreted, the Constitution did not – and could
not – create an "American people." After all, it was ratified by popular consent at
state and not at national level. As Jefferson's favorite interpreter of the Constitution, John Taylor, argued, "Common consent is necessary to constitute a
people, and no such consent, expressly or implied, can be shewn, by which all
the inhabitants of the United States have ever constituted themselves into *one*
people. *This could not have been effected without destroying every people constituted within each state*, as one political being called a people cannot exist within
another."[33] And yet, went the argument, the undisputed state constitutions
proved the contrary. The constitution of New Hampshire, for example, stated
that, "The people of this state have *the sole and exclusive* right of governing
themselves as free, *sovereign* and independent state."[34] The state constitutions of
Massachusetts, New York, Pennsylvania, Delaware, Maryland, and so forth
proved beyond any doubt the existence of "the people" of those states and their
right to self-government – a claim never contested by the federal Constitution.[35]

The Federalists knew from the beginning that they had an uphill battle ahead
of them to impose their national interpretation. Once overlooked, the commonalities between the peoples of different states could have become a huge liability
in the eventuality of an open conflict similar to those between the colonists and
Great Britain during the Revolutionary War. As Joseph Story warned with
uncanny premonition, "Our very animosities will, like those of other kindred
nations, become more deadly, because our lineage, our laws, and our language
are the same."[36] Unfortunately, the attachments that existed in America at the
time of the founding were "wholly on the side of the state governments."

[32] C. F. Adams, ed. (1903), *Diary of John Quincy Adams* (Boston), 94, quoted in Frank
I. Schechter (1915), "The Early History of the Tradition of the Constitution," *The American
Political Science Review*, 9, 710.

[33] John Taylor (1820), *Construction Construed and Constitutions Vindicated* (Richmond: Shepherd and Pollard), 234, 46–47 (emphasis added).

[34] Quoted in Taylor, *Construction Construed*, 40 (emphasis in the original).

[35] Telling for the persuasiveness of the argument is Judge Clarence Thomas's similar one, made in
1995: "The ultimate source of the Constitution's authority is the consent of the people of each
individual State, not the consent of the undifferentiated people of the Nation as a whole" (*U.S.
Term Limits, Inc. v. Thornton*, 514 US. 846).

[36] Joseph Story (1840), A Familiar Exposition of the Constitution of the United States: containing a
brief commentary on Every Clause ... (N.p.), 270, quoted in Knupfer, *The Union as It Is*, 57.

"While the American Union might well have possessed the potential and basis for strong nationalism, it did not possess the political attachments between citizen and federal government that the new republican system would require."[37]

But what was required was more than merely rational, political attachments. Since the Union was a compromise, and a compromise requires both a contractarian, rational component, *and* an affective one, having one at the expense of the other would not have been enough. Therefore, Gordon Wood is only partially right when he argues that "tying people together, creating social cohesiveness, making a single nation out of disparate sections and communities *without relying on idealistic republican adhesions*, this was the preoccupation of the federalists and explains much of what they did."[38] Even Tocqueville's "rational patriotism," while forged through the active participation of citizenry in the government of society, ended up forging a national pride "stooping to every puerile expression of individual vanity."[39] Ideals, like foundational myths, are necessary for the maintaining of the cohesion of *any* people, newly created or not – and at least some of the Federalists were consciously trying to establish such bonds of affection at a national level.[40]

This was not a single-man job, nor a single-pronged approach.[41] "'It may be an easy thing to make a republic, but it is a very laborious thing to make republicans," the common-school reformer Horace Mann remarked. In America, good citizens had to be made; they were not born to the role.[42] These citizens needed ideals, myths, and even idols. One of the most important steps, if not the first step, was raising the Constitution on a pedestal of respect in American political culture paralleled probably only by the Declaration of Independence. As Judge Addison put it in 1791, "[m]an must have an idol. And our political idol ought to be our Constitution and laws. They, like the ark of the covenant among the Jews, ought to be sacred from all prophane touch."[43]

Politicians and civic educators alike complied willingly with this duty. According to William Duer, the Constitution was to be praised as the result

---

[37] Pears, "Chords of Affection," 3.

[38] Gordon Wood (2011), *The Idea of America: Reflections on the Birth of the United States* (New York: Penguin), 256 (emphasis added).

[39] Alexis de Tocqueville [2004], *Democracy in America*, translated by Arthur Goldhammer (New York: The Library of America), Vol. II, 271.

[40] See Edmund S. Morgan (1988), *Inventing the People: The Rise of Popular Sovereignty in England and America* (New York and London: W. W. Norton & Co.), 13.

[41] Emily Pears in "Chords of Affection" identifies three strategies: the utilitarian, the participatory, and the cultural one. Although she differentiates between nationalism and political attachments, according to her interpretation, Tocqueville's "rational patriotism" would fall in the participatory category.

[42] Knupfer, *The Union as It Is*, 60.

[43] Quoted in Frank I. Schechter (1915), "The Early History of the Tradition of the Constitution," *The American Political Science Review*, 9, 733.

"of the benignant influence of peaceful deliberation and calm decision, combined with a spirit of moderation and conciliation."[44] Mordecai McKinhey's
Constitutional Manual asked, "Is the federal constitution to be regarded as the
result of concession and compromise?" It also answered unequivocally: "Yes."
Afterwards, the answer became more ambiguous: "It was the act of the people
of the original States, voluntarily uniting, through mutual concession and
compromise in relation to various local interests and other matters, in establishing a government for the Union."[45] To his merit, Washington McCartney
was not only less equivocal than many civic educators and politicians of the
time but also more faithful to the dual understanding of people's sovereignty,
arguing that "viewed in the light of the compromise which gave it existence, the
Constitution is neither a compact of States, nor a directly popular government,
but it is the *Constitution of the United States.*"[46]

All these concerted efforts payed off. From then on, the Constitution would
serve as the background and the common denominator for all political confrontations to follow, cutting across all sectional interests, including slavery.
Regardless of the camp in which one was situated, as a responsible politician,
one could not fail to make appeals to the Constitution as compact and/or
compromise. For example, in the "unanimously approved Address to the
People of the Slaveholding States," the Democratic Republican Members of
Congress from These States stated:

> You cannot fail to have perceived the striking fact, that wherever in the North the Whigs have
> the ascendancy, there Abolition goes stronger; but wherever the Democrats govern, there the
> rights of the South, and the Compromises of the Constitution, are sacredly regarded. [...]
> [Our constitution] is called "a compact," "a compromise." It is a written compact? Then we
> are not to vary or control it by parol. [...] It is a compromise? Then you may be sure it was
> carefully penned. A compromise imports a mutual surrender of rights interests and preju-
> dices. [...] The extent of the surrender is limited by the terms of the contract.[47]

As we shall see later, this was not the only instance in which the
Constitution, presented as *the* original compromise, was used by pro-slavery
advocates as a conservative tool. But the conservative dimension of the Constitution – and implicitly of political compromise – was not confined to this
single issue. "Compromise, no longer a justification for launching a risky
experiment in republican government, became a conservative tool for

---

[44] William Duer (1843), A Course of Lectures on the Constitutional Jurisprudence of the United
States ... (New York), 41, quoted in Knupfer, *The Union as It Is*, 78.

[45] Mordecai McKinney (1845), The United States Constitutional Manual; being a Comprehensive
Compendium of the System of Government of the Country ..." (Harrisburg), 30, quoted in
Knupfer, *The Union as It Is*, 78.

[46] Washington McCartney (1847), *The Origin and Progress of the United States* (Philadelphia),
239, quoted in Knupfer, *The Union as It Is*, 79.

[47] C. C. Clay, R. C. Nicholas, W. S. Fulton, Thomas Francis, et al. (1840), *The Crisis. Devoted to
the Support of the Democratic Principles*, Vol. 1, Issue 28, (Richmond, VA), 217.

preserving the new system."[48] We have seen how, for the Federalists, it was an indisputable truth that any political society is one of orders and that those elected to national office should constitute a natural aristocracy acting for the common good.[49] As we know by now, what Formisano labels "democratic elitism" was none other than the manifestation of the people's two bodies' paradigm, of Puritan descent. Not just the Federalists but even their rising rivals, the Jeffersonians, embraced the same deferential approach.

> As much as the Federalists, the republicans also regarded themselves as mentors of the people. Even Jefferson "heard little authority in the faint dissonant voice of the people." Indeed, like some ardent republicans of 1790s, Jefferson was not comfortable with the word 'democrat'. [...] The early republic (1789–1828) ... was a mixed period, deferential and democratic, elitist and participatory at the same time.[50]

Therefore, there is nothing "ironic," as Formisano claims, in the fact that "the Revolutionary generation of presidents (through James Monroe), though having a more constricted view [of the people], used the term somewhat more often than their [populist] successors." Since the first presidents still took for granted the paradigm of the people's two bodies, there is nothing surprising in that *none* of these multiple references "sounded what might be called a populist note in reference to the people."[51]

James Monroe's First Inaugural Address captures well the distinction between the two understandings of the people: "It is only when the *people* become ignorant and corrupt, *when they degenerate into a populace*, that they are incapable of exercising the sovereignty." Even John Quincy Adams, after losing the popular vote and being elected president via vote in the House of Representatives, made warm appeals in the First Inaugural to "the will of the people." He also became the first president to use "democracy" in a public discourse, but changed his tune just a few months later, in the first annual message: "[W]ere we to slumber in indolence or fold up our arms and proclaim to the world that we are palsied by the will of our constituents, would it not be to cast away the bounties of Providence and *doom ourselves to perpetual inferiority?*"[52]

---

[48] Knupfer, *The Union as It Is*, 56. Recently, Michael J. Klarman (2016), *The Framer's Coup: The Making of the United States Constitution* (Oxford: Oxford University Press) also argues that the Constitution was a conservative tool, but uses the term with an economic meaning – meant to preserve and enhance the wealth of the few.

[49] Kenneth Owen (2015), "Legitimacy, Localism, and the First Party System" in Daniel Peart and Adam I. P. Smith, eds., *Practicing Democracy: Popular Politics in the United States from the Constitution to the Civil War* (Charlottesville and London: University of Virginia Press), 173.

[50] Formisano, *For the People*, 46. For a wealth of examples about the survival of "deferential politics" well into the nineteenth century, see the contributions in Peart and Smith, *Practicing Democracy*.

[51] Ibid., 65.   [52] Quoted in Formisano, *For the People*, 66–67.

Furthermore, from this conservative perspective, the adoption of the Constitution "of the people, by the people, and for the people" meant that popular acts of resistance, let alone of rebellion, were no longer justified. For no matter what the discontent was, one could never exhaust the "peaceful means of redress." As the former revolutionary Samuel Adams told the Massachusetts legislature in 1795, "What excuses then can there be for forcible opposition to the laws? If any law shall prove oppressive in its operation, the future deliberations of a freely elected Representatives, will prove a constitutional remedy."[53] The fact that even the otherwise radical Samuel Adams was concerned about popular rebellions is telling for a phenomenon that in the 1780s and 1790s spread beyond the well-known Shay's rebellion. "Throughout the country, crowds attacked tax collectors and court officers and released debtors and taxpayers from prison. Courthouses were burned in Virginia and assaulted by crowds in South Carolina, Maryland, and Massachusetts."[54] The so-called Whiskey Rebellion, prompted by the 1791 federal excise tax on distilled spirits, was concerning enough for President George Washington to personally lead an army of 13,000 to quell the unrest. Meanwhile the Fries's Rebellion of 1798 mobilized some four hundred militiamen to demand the release of seventeen men imprisoned in Northampton County for resisting a new tax on houses, land, and ... slaves.

None of these popular revolts posed a real threat to the stability of the new republic. They were, however, revealing for the persistence of the revolutionary spirit well past 1776 or even 1787. The right of popular resistance was an intrinsic part of the revolutionary tradition, and the appeals to "peaceful means of redress" at times fell on deaf ears. Like many of the elites, populist leaders learned firsthand that majorities in the state or federal legislatures were not always protective of minorities' interests. "Experience with the powerful democratic legislatures of the late 1770s and the early 1780s suggested that danger to liberty lay not only in kings and magistrates, but that the people themselves – the majority – was also prove to abuse its power at the cost of minorities."[55]

If all these populist movements evoked the revolutionary tradition and people's sovereignty, they failed to notice that the Patriots drew on *both* populist *and* anti-populist arguments. No matter how "backward" rather than "forward-looking" were the populisms of the late eighteenth and early nineteenth centuries, they still favored one of the people's two bodies, namely the horizontal, egalitarian one. This was the main reason why, unlike Jefferson, the well-balanced John Adams looked with reserve, to say the least, at both all these popular insurrections *and* at the coming of commercial capitalism. In his view, both extremes were dangerously wrong. In his late correspondence with Jefferson, he made clear his dislike of both Thomas Paine and Alexander

---

[53] Quoted in Pauline Maier (1981), "The Road Not Taken: Nullification, John C. Calhoun, and the Revolutionary Tradition in South Carolina," *The South Carolina Historical Magazine*, 82:1, 8.

[54] Formisano, *For the People*, 27.   [55] Maier, "The Road Not Taken," 4.

Hamilton, considering the two equally dangerous, for embracing one of the people's two bodies at the expense of the other.

Considering his rather bleak view of human nature – of declared Puritan descent as well – Adams felt naturally vindicated when his Burke-like prophecies about the outcome of the French Revolution came true, and did not miss the opportunity to remind Jefferson how wrong he had been to place his optimistic support behind it: "You was well persuaded in your own mind that the Nation would succeed in establishing a free republican Government, over five and twenty millions people, when four and twenty millions and five hundred thousands of them could neither write nor read ... [Such a self-government] was as unnatural and impracticable ... as it would be over the Elephants Lions Tigers Panthers Wolves and Bears in the Royal Menagerie, at Versailles."[56]

As a matter of fact, the French Revolution served as a catalyst for speeding up the differentiation between two camps, yet not between the "aristocrats" and the "democrats," but between the ones who chose to tilt the balance one way or another, and those of the likes of Adams, who tried – without necessarily succeeding – to keep it more or less even-keeled. The fact that the paradigm of the people's two bodies was applicable at both national and state levels complicated this task even further.

Since the first populist movements were local and of grassroots origins, modeled after the Antifederalists' fear of centralizing power and praise of local communities, it went almost without saying that the natural aristocracy would be differentiated by its larger, nonlocal perspective. Unfortunately, went the argument, most of the members of state legislatures "were too narrow in outlook, too attached to local interests, too subject to corrupt or partisan influences. They were, it might be said, *too representatives.*"

People, argued [William Pitt Bears in *An Address to the Legislature and People of the State of Connecticut* in 1791] were of two kinds, those with large views and sound judgment (natural aristocrats) and those biased by local interests and prejudice. The first kind, always a small minority, were scattered thinly through any state. [...] Local candidates would gain only local votes, while men of larger views would be more widely-known, even though their local following might be small.[57]

Yet the practice proved more disappointing than the theory – and for good reason. Those divisions among elites that would eventually be conducive to the creation of the Federalist and Republican parties ended up fostering, rather unintentionally, "a populist spirit, particularly as competing elites appealed to hitherto only sporadically mobilized sectors of the population. [...] Eventually, a more active electorate was one unintended consequence of gentry exertions, as well as middling and ordinary people's acquiring an enhanced sense of their own virtue and thus their capacity as citizens."[58]

---

[56] Quoted in Brown, *Moderates*, 27.   [57] Morgan, *Inventing the People*, 251–252.
[58] Formisano, *For the People*, 44.

As the electoral rolls increased and expanded, so did the necessity for reality to catch up with the myth of people's sovereignty. On the positive side, property qualifications were rapidly abandoned. Delaware was the first state to abandon them altogether in 1792; by the mid-1850s, the requirement (for white male citizens) were practically abandoned everywhere. Perhaps even more revealing is that none of the new states admitted to the Union after 1790 included property qualifications.[59] Yet even if before the end of the eighteenth century elections were not contested under party labels, newspapers did openly assume partisanship. Appeals continued to be made to the common good instead of sectional interests, but the rhetoric grew increasingly vicious in this period. Each side accused the other one of being "a party," driven by particular interests, while denying themselves that same label.

Paralleling in many respects the Great Awakening's democratization of religion, deferential politics were rapidly losing ground, and any association with aristocracy – of merit or otherwise – became a political liability. In the eyes of a Kansas populist, they were "the aristocrats, plutocrats, and all the other rats."[60] "The people were now portrayed as constituting not merely 'the demos' or 'the plebs,' but rather the brilliant sun, located, or deserving to be located, at the heart of a strictly Ptolemaic political universe."[61] Intellectual references were no longer received with admiration, but with contempt. When during the Virginia Convention of 1850–1851 the authority of John Locke was invoked in favor of a mixed government, John M. Boots wondered if someone would dare to go out and make the same haughty philosophical reference in front of his constituency.

I did not come here to study the science of government. [...] I believe we are a different people from any other that ever did live, or ever live on the face of the earth. I believe that this Anglo Saxon race of people in the United States of America are the only people ever formed by the hand of God, that are capable of self-government. And believing this, I shall endeavor to make a constitution for the people of the present day, and not for the people of the days of John Locke.[62]

The quote captures yet another development of the era worth noticing: As the populist rhetoric increased and became more vitriolic, it began making appeals to racial, ethnic, and religious discriminations, giving preference to "the Anglo Saxon race." Thus, identity politics was born as populism's twin. By 1800, the presidential race was already framed not in terms of political differences, but in terms of piety. As the *Gazette of the United States* put it on its October 14 issue, "At the present solemn moment the only question to be asked by every American, laying his hand on his heart, is 'Shall I continue in

---

[59] For more details, see King, *The Founders v. the People*, 100–104.
[60] Quoted in Formisano, *For the People*, 11.   [61] King, *The Founders v. the People*, 82.
[62] *Register of the Debates and Proceedings of the Virginia Reform Convention* (1851) (Richmond: Ro. H. Gallaher), 221, quoted in Rodgers, *Contested Truths*, 91.

allegiance TO GOD – AND A RELIGIOUS PRESIDENT; or impiously declare for JEFFERSON – AND NO GOD!"[63]

Real policies were not far behind this identity rhetoric. If in 1790 only Virginia, South Carolina, and Georgia explicitly reserved the right to vote for white males, by 1855 only five states – and all in New England – allowed free blacks to vote on the same basis as whites. This was not a matter of "aristocrats," i.e., Federalists, versus "democrats," i.e., Republicans. Since in the early 1800s women and free blacks tended to vote Federalists, the Republicans worked successfully to deny both categories this right.[64] And while the anti-immigrant wave would have to wait until 1850 to start materializing in the Know-Nothing party, other populist movements realized rather quickly that the only way to become effective was to use the formal political channels, become political parties, and throw their hats into the election ring, with various degrees of success.

Under different labels, the Working Men's parties of 1829–1835, for example, had only modest electoral scores, not because of their populist ideology, but because of their radicalism. And in yet another strange mixture of political sympathies and values, "many lower- and middle-class wage earners and independent artisans engaged in mob actions against abolitionists and African Americans."[65] At the other end of the spectrum, one finds the Anti-Masonry movement, which enjoyed considerable success, paralleling the Second Great Awakening of the 1820s and 1830s. Freemasons were seen as a threat not only to Christianity and traditional morals but also to egalitarianism, and the proof of their obvious elitism was the exclusive entrance into the fraternity, combined with the veil of secrecy that characterized most of their activities.

For the Anti-Masons, Freemasons came to embody all of what they perceived as powers beyond people's control. An Anti-Mason complained that the government was "treating the people like children that do not know what is good for themselves." This was unacceptable. It was a declaration of war between the people's two bodies. As a Young Men's Anti-Mason state convention put it in 1830, "The people, the democracy of the country, have passed sentence of extermination against the Free Masonry. *From their judgment there is no appeal*, and against their will it is folly to contend." "Antimasonry," charged Masons in return, "like the cholera ... dwells among the lower classes."[66] The result of this war between the people's two bodies was a growing distrust in both elites and populist movements that threatened to rip the foundational double helix apart.

---

[63] Quoted in Robertson, "Jefferson Parties, Politics, and Participation," 107.

[64] Robertson, "Jefferson Parties, Politics, and Participation," 114–118.

[65] Formisano, *For the People*, 87.

[66] Quoted in Formisano, *For the People*, 115, 114, 128 (emphasis added).

Such controversies underscore the importance of these mechanisms. *There was no one ideal of a "representative body" that could supplant other competing claims in and of itself.* Governmental representation was suspect because of representatives' seeking to aggrandize power; extra-governmental mobilization was suspect because it was impossible to prove the deliberative or representative character of these mechanisms. What lay at the core of the use of these means, though, was the idea that action in the name of an individual or a self-interested group was illegitimate, whereas *action in the name of a community was the expected goal of a republican society.*[67]

The solution found by mainstream politicians was to co-opt the populist rhetoric. Already by the end of the 1820s, "when electoral politics became permeated with an egalitarian ethos, even candidates for office born on plantations ... preferred to present themselves to the electorate as born in rude log cabins."[68] Thus, rather than being the artisan of the populist style in American politics, Andrew Jackson was more its by-product. After attending Jackson's swearing-in ceremony and the reception that followed, Supreme Court Justice Joseph Story was in despair: "The reign of KING MOB seemed triumphant."[69] From then on, electioneering would no longer be possible unless one dressed and acted as "one of the people." The candidates, as numerous newspapers and campaign documents advertise them, were allegedly all "fresh from the loins of the people."[70]

Justice Story was neither the first nor the last to be worried by what he and others perceived not as a fulfillment, but rather as a betrayal, of the republican revolutionary principles. In effect, so huge was the rift between the two understandings of the people that the rise of Jeffersonian-Republicans by the beginning of the nineteenth century brought to the foreground the first thoughts of secession. For the "Old Puritans," populism was nothing but a weapon used by an "artificial aristocracy" to better control the easily manipulated masses. In yet another display of historical irony, their arguments paralleled in more ways than one those proposed by the Loyalists less than a half-century before. The "deluded Vulgar were charmed ... like the poor harmless Squirrel that runs into the Mouth of the Rattlesnake, the Fascination in the Word Liberty threw the People into the harpy Claws of their Destroyers; & for what?"[71]

Deeply concerned by the huge losses of the Federalists between the Sixth Congress (1799–1801) and the Seventh (1801–1803), as well as by the rise to

---

[67] Owen, "Legitimacy, Localism, and the First Party System," 175 (emphasis added).

[68] Formisano, *For the People*, 3.

[69] Quoted in King, *The Founders v. the People*, 96–97 (capitalization in the original).

[70] Daniel Peart and Adam I. P. Smith (2015), "Introduction" in Daniel Peart and Adam I. P. Smith, eds., *Practicing Democracy: Popular Politics in the United States from the Constitution to the Civil War* (Charlottesville and London: University of Virginia Press), 14.

[71] Peter Oliver [1961], *Origin & Progress of the American Rebellion: A Tory View*, edited by Douglass Adair and John A. Schutz (Stanford: Stanford University Press), 65.

power of the Republican-Democrats, the Massachusetts statesman Timothy Pickering wrote to a Philadelphia judge in 1803:

Although the end of all our Revolutionary labors and expectations is disappointment, and our fond hopes of republican happiness are vanity, and the real patriots of '76 are overwhelmed by the modern pretenders to that character, I will not yet despair: I will rather anticipate a new confederacy, exempt from the corrupt and corrupting influence and oppression of the aristocratic Democrats of the South. There will be – and our children at the farthest will see it – a separation.[72]

After Federalists' hopes were once again crushed as the Jeffersonians retained control of the government in 1812, the New Englanders felt that they had become an oppressed minority, and called for a convention of New England states to discuss their common grievances. Ironically, this time around, the "Old Puritans" were the ones concerned, on the one hand, by the increase rise of the federal government powers and, on the other, by its perceived inability to manage the war with Great Britain. They thus turned toward their state governments for relief. Although this was not properly speaking a secession movement, "it did have the potential to move in that direction," and Madison entertained enough concerns to send a special emissary to the Hartford Convention to report on the debates. Fortunately, a series of military victories, culminating with Jackson's triumph at New Orleans, were enough to make the New Englanders thoughts of secession obsolete, and they were quick to drop their arguments. Yet interestingly enough, as Brown observes, "history has dealt more kindly with the 'lost cause' of southern nationhood than with the 'lost cause' of New England nationhood. [...] Matched against the moonlight-and-magnolias mythology, the Hartford conventioneers long ago lost any chance to claim historiographical high ground."[73]

Nevertheless, the largely forgotten Northern secessionist movement is significant in more than one respect. First, it shows that the threat of secession, i.e., of the unwillingness to compromise even for the sake of the Union, appeared first when a minority felt permanently discriminated against by a hostile populist majority. Second, it points toward the fact that, far from inimical to an aristocracy of wealth, populism can, as a matter of fact, encourage it. The Age of Egalitarianism came, rhetorically, at a time of growing economic inequalities.[74] John Adams's warnings about the risks of a plutocracy enabled by and profiteering from "the Many" left unprotected proved largely correct. Last but not least, if the New Englanders were concerned by the betrayal of the Patriots' ideals by the new populist trend, it was also because, as we have seen, it came to be associated with an inflation of identity politics that ran contrary to a long-established tradition.

---

[72] In Henry Adams, ed. (1877), Documents Relating to New England Federalism, 1800–15 (Boston: Little, Brown, and Company), 338, quoted in Brown, *Moderates*, 43.
[73] Brown, *Moderates*, 67, 69.   [74] Formisano, *For the People*, 160.

As shown in Chapter 2, the American Puritans created new peoples on the shores of New England, *despite* their acknowledged commonalities of blood, traditions, and even religion with their brethren from across the Atlantic. According to their understanding, what created and maintained a people into existence was their consent and, even more importantly, the government erected by the bidimensional covenant. More than a century later, their legacy was revived by the Patriots when the latter decided "to dissolve the Political Bands" that connected them with their "British Brethren," for "[t]hey too have been deaf to the Voice of Justice and of consanguinity" (Chapter 3). And it was the same understanding of the people as primarily *political* communities that made both difficult *and* possible the adoption of the Articles of Confederation (Chapter 4) and, eventually, of the Constitution (Chapter 5). Not surprising, the feverish adoption of identity politics, based on consanguinity, religion, ethnicity, and so forth, was perceived, especially in New England, as a direct threat to this enduring legacy and implicitly to the possibility of future political compromises.

Such a serious threat was to be met with the expected counterreaction.

6.2 "PARTY SPIRIT ... ONLY ASK TO LICK THE SORES OF THE BODY POLITIC"

Louis Hartz's claim that, with very few exceptions,[75] liberalism has dominated the intellectual background of the founding unchallenged has proven, in the past few decades, to be largely false.[76] Yet, as proof of its long-lasting legacy, more than a half-century after Hartz, Mark Hulliung still argued that "[i]n antebellum politics the trump cards were always held by the theorists of the social contract."[77] As many scholars have noticed, beginning with the 1830s and the 1840s, an intellectual countermovement became prominent – one that attacked the basic tenets of liberalism regarding the state of nature, the foundation of government, and the will of fleeting majorities.[78] However, to label this movement a conservative or a Burkean "counter-revolution" is to ignore that its existence, although at times less evident, has never been interrupted.[79] As we have seen repeatedly throughout the previous chapters, the paradigm of the people's two bodies consistently prevented the embracement of the basic tenets of liberalism from the very beginning of the founding.

[75] Notably Fisher Aimes and George Fitzhugh.
[76] Louis Hartz (1955), *The Liberal Tradition in America: An Interpretation of American Political Thought since the Revolution* (New York: Harcourt, Brace & World).
[77] Mark Hulliung (2007), *Social Contract in America: From the Revolution to the Present Age* (Lawrence: University Press of Kansas), 43.
[78] See, for example, Rodgers, *Contested Truths*; Knupfer, *The Union as It Is*; King, *The Founders v. the People*.
[79] Rodgers, *Contested Truths*, pp. 114–115.

True, the idea of a people being formed through a voluntary compact or a compromise has never been seriously contested at the state level. Thus, as an article on government explained in the *Nassau Literary Magazine*, by the mid-nineteenth century, there were only two possible theories about "the nature of the government" "interwoven in the texture of almost any political creed." One was the outdated theory of its divine institution, the other the theory of the social compact that "*suppose[d] men to form themselves into a body politic by a compromise of their several rights*, each individual yielding up a portion of his natural liberty, in order to establish an independent power which shall protect him in the enjoyment of the reminder."[80] From this perspective, nothing much has changed since Gilbert Burnett claimed the same about the social compact in seventeenth-century Great Britain.[81] What did remain highly disputable was *how* and *if* the same theory could apply to the national level, as well as all of the other basic tenets of a Lockean liberalism. "It is telling that Locke was published in America in 1773 but never again for the next 164 years. By contrast, Burlamaqui, who offered a nonrevolutionary, Whiggish revision of Pufendorf, was reprinted six times before the Civil War," while the conservative Edmund Burke enjoyed sixteen editions during the same period of time.[82]

What represented a new development, indeed, was the switch of emphasis from "the people" to "the State," preferably with a capital S. The Whig Rufus Choate shuddered at the potentially destructive idea of a State founded on contract and the will of the majority. Since "[b]y the middle of the century his likes (if not his wit and exaggeration) were legion," he deserves a lengthier quotation:[83]

Having learned from Rousseau and Locke, and our revolutionary age, its theories and its acts, that the State is nothing but a contract, rests in contract, springs from contract; that government is a contrivance of human wisdom from human wants; [...] and that the State itself were held to be no more than an encampments of tents on the great prairies, pitched at sun-down, and struck to the sharp crack of the rifle next morning, instead of a structure, stately and eternal, in which the generations may come, one after another, to the great gift of social life. On such sentiments as these, how can a towering and durable fabric be set up? [...] It is a tendency to regard the actual will of that majority as the law of the State. It is a tendency to regard the shortest and simplest way of collecting that will, and the promptest and most irresistible execution of it, as the true polity of liberty.[84]

[80] "Government" (no author), *The Nassau Literary Magazine*, 15:2 (October 1854) (Princeton), 41 (emphasis added).

[81] Fumurescu, *Compromise*, 265.

[82] Hulliung, *Social Contract in America*, 44, 129. Interesting, despite this evidence that he himself notices, Hulliung continues to claim a towering Lockean influence throughout most of the nineteenth century.

[83] Rodgers, *Contested Truths*, 114.

[84] Rufus Choate (1862), *The Works of Rufus Choate, with a Memoir of His Life*, by Samuel Gilman Brown, 2 vols. (Boston: Little, Brown, and Company), 423–424; 425. Mentioning in the

The move from invoking "the people" to invoking "the still higher, person eclipsing abstractions – Nation, State, and Society – on which political science was to lay its foundations for the rest of the century" was seen a necessary one, yet in the long run it created at least as many problems as it sought to address.[85]

As a signer of the Declaration of Independence and of the Articles of Confederation, as well as a supporter of the ratification of the Constitution, John Witherspoon is proof that liberalism was never left unattended by either a Christian republicanism or the Scottish Common Sense philosophy.[86] As the president of the College of New Jersey (now Princeton University) for many years (1769–1794), he influenced generations of students, including James Madison, and thus helped shape the intellectual background of the first half of the nineteenth century. The emphasis on virtue, both Christian and Roman, and the need to sacrifice one's personal interest for the sake of the common good, found fertile ground in the piety-saturated colleges across the early republic, and was further inflated by the series of revivals that came to be known as the Second Great Awakening.

Sometimes, the enthusiasts went so far as not only to deny the basic assumptions of the social compact theory but also to openly reclaim the divine origin of government:

> The whole theory [of the social compact] is wrong ... It came from the infidel philosophy of Hobbes and his successors. It assumes that man is an *independent being*, at liberty to choose his own course of life, the law by which he will be governed; or that he may deny to be governed by any law at all. ... No, sir, Government is founded on no such weak and miserable device as *social compact*. It is of divine origin; not the invention of man – but the appointment of God.[87]

Yet such extreme claims were outliers. There was, however, a quite widespread consensus that "God created man subject to law, and that is his natural state,"[88] "that the idea of right cannot be philosophically stated without the idea of obligation,"[89] and that "[a] man has rights in order that he may do right."[90] Government was not only natural but moral as well. It was not a

---

same breath of both Rousseau and Locke, without mentioning any significant differences between the two, is yet another proof of how carelessly these names were thrown around.

[85] Rodgers, *Contested Truths*, 115.

[86] See, for example, Mark A. Noll (2002), *America's God: From Jonathan Edwards to Abraham Lincoln* (Oxford: Oxford University Press); Jeffry H. Morrison (2005), *John Witherspoon and the Founding of the American Republic* (South Bend: University of Notre Dame Press).

[87] Quoted in Benjamin F. Wright (1931), *American Interpretation of Natural Law* (Cambridge, MA: Harvard University Press), 192 (emphasis in the original).

[88] Joseph B. Burleigh (1848), *The American Manual*, 2nd ed. (Philadelphia: Grigg and Elliot), 49.

[89] "Inaugural Address of Francis Lieber" (1858), in *Addresses of the Newly-Appointed Professors of Columbia College, February 1858* (New York: Columbia College), 97.

[90] Mark Hopkins (1862), *Lectures on Moral Science* (Boston: Gould and Lincoln), 256, quoted in Rodgers, *Contested Truths*, 120.

necessary evil, as the social compact theory had it, not "the badge of lost innocence," as Thomas Paine claimed in *Common Sense*, but a positive good.

Excessive cynicism could destroy it, as Daniel Webster pointed out: "Can there be nothing in government except for the exercise of mere control? Can nothing be done without corruption, but the imposition of penalty and restraint? Whatever is positively beneficent, whatever is actively good [...] – must all this be rejected and reprobated as an obnoxious policy ...?"[91] Obviously then, the vision promoted by influential civic educators such as Francis Lieber was Aristotelian, not Lockean, as the orthodoxy still has it:

> The state is aboriginal to man; – it is no voluntary association, no contrivance of art, or invention of suffering, no company of shareholders; no machine, no work of contract by individuals who lived previously out of it; no necessary evil, no ill of humanity which will be cured in time and by civilization; no accidental thing, no institution above and separate from society, no instrument for one or few – the state is a form and faculty of mankind to lead the species toward perfection – it is the glory of man.[92]

During the first decades of the early republic, such critics of the main tenets of Lockean liberalism were at the same time both the beneficiaries and the promoters of the anti-party spirit that permeated the American founding. Faithful to the spirit of the Philadelphia convention, they emphasized the Union over the states, which in turn required overcoming the doctrine of majoritarianism, triumphantly stated by Andrew Jackson in 1828: "The first principle of our system ... [is] that the majority is to govern."[93] It was a doctrine already vehemently opposed by Madison in *Federalist 10*, worried "that measures are too often decided, not according to the rules of justice, and the rights of the minor party, but by the superior force of an interested and overbearing majority."[94] Their guiding principle, at least at a declarative level, was the Aristotelian one, according to which the interests of a faction – majoritarian or not – ought to be secondary to the interest of the whole; from here, too, the requirement of making mutual sacrifices and compromises for the sake of the common good.

Even as the first party system emerged, the rhetoric took a long time to adjust to reality. As we have seen, the label of "party" was always reserved for the opposite camp, precisely due to the stigma associated with it well into the nineteenth century. It is beyond the scope of this chapter to analyze the

[91] Daniel Webster (1830), "First Speech on Foot's Resolution," in *The Works of Daniel Webster* (1851) (Boston: Charles C. Little and James Brown), Vol. III, 260.
[92] Francis Lieber (1838–1839), *Manual of Political Ethics*, 2 vols. (Boston: Little and Brown), Vol. I, 171.
[93] Andrew Jackson (1835), *Annual Messages, Veto Messages, Protests, Etc. of Andrew Jackson, President of the United States* (Baltimore), 10 quoted in Daniel Peart and Smith, "Introduction," 3.
[94] James Madison [2001], "Federalist 10," in Alexander Hamilton, John Jay, and James Madison, *The Federalist* (The Gideon Edition) (Indianapolis: Liberty Fund), 42.

evolution of parties in antebellum America. There is an impressive body of literature that has already done this, with classifications varying from Burnham's "five party systems"[95] to three or two, or even twenty-four state party systems "based on long standing local political rivalries and, equally importantly, on durable Atlantic affinities with either Britain or France."[96] In recent years, many of the generally accepted interpretations, from parties' role in increasing political participation and democratization to the distinction between the Federalist-Republican and Whig-Democrat party systems, have been questioned.[97] What is of interest, from the perspective proposed here, is the extent to which the development and entrenchment of party spirit promoted political compromise – as the orthodoxy has it – or rather the contrary.

What the history of the era can teach us in this respect is to avoid the confusion between *parties* and *partisanship*. As overlooked as it is today, the distinction between the two was in the forefront of political thought in the era with which this chapter is concerned.[98] Few, if any, of the founders denied the existence – and, to a certain degree, the necessity – of parties, oftentimes understood as factions, or simply as divisions between a majority and a minority. But most, if not all, of them were just as quick to condemn the spirit of partisanship. Ideally, even the most loyal party members ought to have crafted their actions with an eye to the common good and to the building of bridges between majorities and minorities. As Madison wrote in the National Gazette on 23 January 1792, "In very political society, parties are unavoidable." To "*combat this evil,*" he continued, it was necessary for "one party [to be] a check on the other, so far as the existence of parties cannot be prevented, nor their views accommodated." He concluded: "If this is not the language of reason, it is that of republicanism," for which taking into consideration the views of *both* the majority and of the minority is a fundamental tenet.[99] Later the same year, Madison argued that it was the duty of every "contemplative statesman to trace the history of parties in a free country," coming to the conclusion that his contemporaries were already witnessing the emergence of ... the third party system! According to his interpretation, the first parties were the Loyalists and the Patriots, between 1774 and 1783, the "friends of order" and the "friends of liberty," respectively. Between 1784 and 1787 "there were parties in abundance" within the states, lacking any national coherence.[100] Finally, by the end

---

[95] Walter Dean Burnham (1967), "Party Systems and the Political Process" in William Nisbet Chambers and Walter Dean Burnham, eds., The American Party Systems: Stages in Political Development (New York: Oxford University Press).

[96] Robertson, "Jefferson Parties," 100.

[97] For a recent review of the literature on this topic, see Peart and Smith, "Introduction."

[98] For the contemporary scholarship on this issue, see further Chapter 7.

[99] Quoted in Bradburn, "'Parties Are Unavoidable'," 34 (emphasis added).   [100] Ibid., 35.

of the 1790s, "the 'national' party coalitions of Federalists and Republicans were a heterogeneous mash-up of local practices and personalities."[101]

Civic educators did their best to further embed the distinction between parties and partisanship (or party spirit as it was called) into American political culture. Andrew Young, for example, agreed that, "where freedom of opinion and of speech is tolerated, *parties* must necessarily exist to some extent. [...] But *party spirit*, when unrestrained, becomes intemperate and revengeful." According to him, "it must be evident to all who have observed the effects of party spirit among us, that the evils flowing from it overbalance all the good which can produce."[102] Washington McCarthy, too, wrote in his civic manual that the "bloodless warfare" of parties in fact "demonstrated that democracy on an extended scale is practicable in these United States," but only as long as the parties "stand on the common platform of republicanism, and fire a common artillery upon the diminishing ranks of legitimacy." Yet he quickly specified, "We do not wish to be understood as defending or encouraging the spirit of partyism." And Benson Lossing, in his *Pictorial History of the United States*, advised against the use of vitriolic rhetoric in party politics: "Mutual recriminations, ungenerous expressions, and flippant censures, only tend to alienate the affections of those who ought to live as brothers, conceding to each other sincerity of feeling and honesty of motives."[103]

Journals and magazines were filled with condemnations of party spirit as the greatest danger that threatened the Union. For example, in an 1828 issue of *Western Luminary*, a Presbyterian newspaper, one could read a full column on the dangers of party spirit, which began rather abruptly with: "Party Spirit Prostrates every thing which is venerable and sacred within the sphere of its commotion. It directs the attention of the people from their own common interest to the means of gaining ends to which prejudice and passion may direct them; and the attention of the government from public good to the means of its own political existence."[104] Unlike contemporary authors, mid-nineteenth-century writers were convinced that, far from promoting compromise, party spirit promoted "universal anarchy and universal hate. And to what other result do such sweeping and absurd charges in both parties tend? How little to these leaders, on either side, care to what extent they inflame these already too morbid passions of the multitude beneath them, provided that they can secure votes, VOTES, VOTES."[105]

The amount of the game now, is, the whigs want a bank of some sort, the democrats don't. The whigs want a tariff in one way, the democrats want it a shade different, and

[101] Bradburn, "'Parties Are Unavoidable'," 38.
[102] Andrew Young (1836), Introduction to the Science of government and Compend of the Constitution and Civil Jurisprudence of the United States ... (Warsaw, NY), 300–301, quoted in Knupfer, *The Union as It Is*, 81.
[103] Quoted in Knupfer, *The Union as It Is*, 82.   [104] April 16, 1828, 4, 42.
[105] *Niles' National Register*, July 29, 1843, 14, 22.

but a shade. On both these questions, the great mass of the people of these United States, if left alone, would at this moment substantially agree, except in the mere questions of modes and forms, and the public mind would be calm, rational, tranquil, open to reason, and open to truth. But no – they cannot be let alone – they must be harangued, inflamed, literally dragged up to the ring by party demagogues and party office seekers.

The anonymous writer from 1843 was worried that party spirit, "instead of appealing to the reason of the people, and placing before them their principles that they may judge between the two parties ... appeal[ed] to their passions, conceal their principles, and endeavor to entrap the mass by diverting them from the true issue." At times, the description became truly poetic. Party spirit "crawls and creeps, and fawns, and leers, and whines around the multitude, and only asks to lick the sores of the body politic, and feed upon the crumbs that fall from its table."[106] With a comparable literary talent, A. A. Forbes wrote in *The Rural Repository Devoted to Polite Literature* about party spirit:

There is a spirit of giant form, and demoniac aspect, marching in terror over our beautiful land from the North, to the South, and from the shores of the Atlantic, to the Western wilderness. Ruin marks his progress, and moral desolation like a pestilence follows him. He has placed his withering hand on the bonds of union which unite us together as a Nation. He has laid his axe at the root of the glorious "tree of Liberty," which has so long overshadowed us.[107]

Yet even more surprising is that some of the most seasoned politicians and party members agreed with the dangers that party spirit was thought to present for the Union. Jacob Collamer, a prominent Whig senator, nominated Postmaster General by President Taylor, wrote in *The American Review: A Whig Journal*, that the first among the elements "which are supposed to tend to disunion" was "the predominance of an excess of party spirit. [...] Leave it as it is, and the abuses of power which would threaten and overawe the freedom from which it springs, will always find a master in it."[108] A shrewd party player such as Henry Clay acknowledged the existence of parties as a necessary evil. In a response to Reverend William Ellery Channing, who was advocating the extinction of parties, he replied with an argument that resonated with Madison's *Federalist 10*: "I am afraid that the desire to put down parties, which you express, has more of humanity than practicability in it. They can only, I apprehend, be extinguished, by extinguishing their cause, free Government, a free press, and freedom of opinion." The only option left was to tame the spirit of partyism. "The effort of the wise and the good should be rather directed to moderate their asperity."[109]

---

[106] Ibid., 22.   [107] August 31, 1844, 21, 1.
[108] Jacob Collamer (1849), "Dangers and Safeguards of the Union," in *The American Review: A Whig Journal*, III:II, February, 115.
[109] Quoted in Knupfer, *The Union as It Is*, 135.

Nevertheless, the towering figure of this movement against the spirit of "partyism" was – and to a certain extent remains – George Washington, whose Farewell Address is as frequently invoked now as it was two centuries ago.[110] In it, Washington claimed that it is "the *unity* of government which constitutes you *one* people … The name of American, which belongs to you in your national capacity, must always exalt the just pride of patriotism more than any appellation derived from local discriminations." The danger of sectional parties was in the forefront of his concern – "I have already intimated to you the danger of parties in the state, with particular reference to the founding of them on geographical discriminations." But on a more general level, and in the long run, even more concerning was the *spirit* of party:

Let me now take a more comprehensive view and warn you in the most solemn manner against the baneful effects of the *spirit of party, generally*. This spirit, unfortunately, is *inseparable from our nature*, having its root in the strongest passions of the human mind. It exists under different shapes in all governments, more or less stifled, controlled, or repressed; but in those of the popular form it is seen in its greatest rankness and is truly their worst enemy.

The reason for "the common and continual mischiefs of the spirit of party" is that it destroys the bonds of affection and mutuality necessary for the maintenance of *one* people. "It agitates the community with ill founded jealousies and false alarms, kindles the animosity of one part against another, foments occasionally riot and insurrection." Far from encouraging the spirit of compromise, party spirit is inimical to it.

"There is an opinion that *parties* in free countries are useful checks upon the administration of the government and serve to keep alive the spirit of liberty. This *within certain limits is probably true*," concedes Washington. "But … in governments purely elective, it is a *spirit* not to be encouraged. From their natural tendency, it is certain there will always be enough of that spirit for every salutary purpose." Thus, the spirit of partisanship is "[a] fire not to be quenched, it demands a uniform vigilance to prevent its bursting into a flame, lest instead of warming it should consume."[111]

Like the Puritans, Washington and his fellow Federalists did not believe that a people could be held together as one people solely on a contractual basis, absent the "chords of affections" and the virtuous sacrifice of particular interests, including state interest, to the interests of the whole. Their opponents, from Jeffersonians and Republicans to Democrats, were fervent supporters of states' rights and critics of the federal government. For this brand of Lockeans,

---

[110] The Farewell Address was regularly read in the Senate from 1888 until today (since 1893 on Washington's birthday,) and in the House from 1899 until 1984.

[111] George Washington (1796) [2000], *The Farewell Address* – 106th Congress, 2nd Session, Senate Document No. 106–201 (Washington, DC: US Government Printing Office) (emphasis added).

as for the Patriots before them, and for the Antifederalists, whose name they quickly abandoned after the ratification because of the stigma of "political atheism,"[112] the social compact applied only to the creation of the people of Virginia, Rhode Island, and so forth. If the Constitution was a compact, it was not one among the American people, nor even one among the American people and their federal government, but one among states retaining a large degree of autonomy.

Unsurprisingly, when the Alien and Sedition Act sought to extend the powers of the federal government, then Vice President Thomas Jefferson penned the Kentucky Resolutions of 1798 and 1799, arguing that

to this compact each state acceded as a state, and is an integral party, its co-States forming, as to itself, the other party; that this government, created by this compact, was not made the exclusive or final judge of the extent of the powers delegated to itself, since that would have made its discretion, and not the Constitution, the measure of its powers; but that, as in all other cases of compact among powers having no common judge, each party has an equal right to judge for itself, as well of infractions as of the mode and measure of redress.[113]

The resolution warned that such Acts, "unless arrested at the threshold, necessarily drive these States into revolution and blood," and claimed that "it would be a dangerous delusion were a confidence in the men of our choice to silence our fears for the safety of our rights."[114] As even the sympathetic Jean Yarbrough acknowledges, the "appeal to natural rights was a dangerous game. Had Kentucky actually moved to nullify the Alien and Sedition Acts, and not just assert its natural right to do so, it might very well led to the destruction of the Union."[115] And although during his presidency Jefferson expanded the executive power and strengthened the federal government during the war of 1812, he never abandoned the idea of states' rights to nullification.

After John Quincy Adams was elected in 1824, he prepared a "Draft Declaration and Protest of the Commonwealth of Virginia" in 1825, in which he replayed the argument that the Constitution was a confederation and a compact among states; yet he went a step further, dangling the threat of secession. The Virginians, claimed the Draft, had no intention of seceding from the Union. They "would, indeed, consider such a rupture as among the greatest calamities which could befall them; *but not the greatest. There is yet one greater, submission to a government of unlimited powers.*" Thanks mainly to Madison's opposition, the Draft was never publicized, but it remains nevertheless revealing of the major differences separating the compromisers for the sake

---

[112] Schechter, "The Early History," 715.
[113] http://avalon.law.yale.edu/18th_century/jeffken.asp   [114] Ibid.
[115] Jean M. Yarbrough (2003), "Thomas Jefferson and the Social Compact" in Ronald J. Pestritto and Thomas G. West, eds., *The American Founding and the Social Compact* (Lanham: Lexington Books), 155.

of the Union from those less willing to do so, in order to safeguard states' interests and people's sovereignty at state level.

One of the main grievances of the Draft was that the Federalists "claim[ed], for example, and . . . commenced the exercise of a right to construct roads, open canals, and effect other internal improvements within the territories and jurisdictions exclusively belonging to the several States."[116] The federal development of a system of roads and canals was part of a plan labeled by Henry Clay as the American System, aiming at using economic development in order to strengthen and unify the nation, and also including higher tariffs to protect American industry and the preservation of a Bank of the United States able to stabilize the currency and rein in state and local banks. Inspired by Alexander Hamilton's ideas, the plan was supported by politicians as different as John Quincy Adams and John C. Calhoun, and was meant to back up the national bonds of affection with more reliable trans-sectional economic interdependencies. For their opponents, however, such attempts were nothing but further proof that a handful of oligarchs were trying to override the people's sovereignty at state level.

In the aftermath of the War of 1812, the election of James Monroe as president bracketed for a short while the growing spirit of partisanship, and both Republicans and Federalists praised him for pursuing political harmony above petty partisanship. On this wave on anti-partyism, he was reelected in 1820 practically without opposition. In 1817, Benjamin Russell, a Boston newspaper editor, went as far as to declare it the beginning of the "Era of Good Feelings." The formula was so catchy that many historians still use it today. However, the accuracy of the label has been recently questioned, and for good reason. Underneath the appearance of political harmony, plenty of political tensions were boiling up. If it ever was one, the Era of Good Feelings did not last.

As hinted at before, this shuffling of theoretical cards resulted in some peculiar – and sometimes quite toxic – alliances. Faced with the growing wave of state populism, the Federalists kept losing electoral ground throughout the first decades of the nineteenth century. Their two bases remained the northern largely anti-slavery organizations and a much smaller southern aristocracy, still attracted by their refusal to give up the idea of a natural aristocracy. This was not enough to prevent the Republicans from maintaining their supremacy thanks to an equally strange combination of appeals to egalitarian tropes, to identity (and exclusionary) politics, and to pro-slavery Southerners, eager to protect their states' interests. Faced with this reality, the Federalists changed strategies, trying to defeat their opponents on their own turf – that of states' interests.

The Missouri compromises of 1820–1821 were the first to exemplify this new strategy. As a general rule, parties were – and still are – vulnerable not in

---

[116] http://avalon.law.yale.edu/19th_century/jeffdec1.asp (emphasis added).

the face of complex issues, beyond the general public's grasp, but before simple, binary choices, from banning alcohol or not, to religious qualifications for office, and so forth. "Single-issue pressure groups could mobilize voters on these issues without having to worry, as mainstream parties did, about the difficulties of building and maintaining diverse coalitions to win elections."[117] When Missouri requested in 1819 to join the Union as a slave state, the issue of slavery became such a binary choice almost overnight, presenting party leaders with a dilemma: either ignore the popular pressure coming from their constituencies or run the risk of transforming slavery into a sectional party issue. For the Federalists it was a chance to revive the party by dividing southern from northern Republicans over the issue of slavery.

None of the parties contested the constitutional Three-fifths Compromise, but disagreements emerged rapidly over its proper interpretation. For the supporters of the restriction on slavery, the compromise was meant to apply exclusively to the thirteen states existing at the time of ratification but not to the new ones, and surely not to those above the informal line marked by the Ohio River. In their view, the ban of the slave trade was a sure sign that the intention of the founders was to let slavery die of "natural causes." "In sum, the three-fifths rule was a temporary concession to slavery, while the slave trade ban was a permanent restriction on the institution; together, they signaled the Constitution's antislavery intent, forming a 'silent compact,' as Pennsylvania's John Sergeant put it, 'with an afflicting necessity.'"[118] For their opponents, however, the three-fifths rule was *the* compromise that made possible both the Constitution and the Union. In the words of John Holmes of Maine district, "It was a compact and we are bound by it; and if it was a bad or a good bargain, I will never complain of it on the one hand, nor boast of it on the other."[119] To make things even worse, the pro-slavery camp tied the Three-Fifths Compromise to the Great Compromise. If the former did not apply to the newly created states, neither should the latter, which ensured each state two senators.

Faced once again with the South's stubbornness on this matter, many considered that the issue was not worth the threat to the Union, and sought a compromise acceptable to both parties. The details of the 1820 Missouri Compromise are well known, but what is worth emphasizing is its ambivalence. On the one hand, it formally accepted an expansion of slavery in the newly created states – a major and embarrassing step back for the abolitionist camp. Yet on the other hand, it also confirmed Congress's power to legislate on slavery in a territory – something that created a worrisome precedent in the eyes of the pro-slavery camp. The result of these dissatisfactions on both sides required a second compromise, after Missouri pushed things further, by

---

[117] Peart and Smith, "Introduction," 13.   [118] Knupfer, *The Union as It Is*, 95.
[119] Quoted in Knupfer, *The Union as It Is*, 96.

mandating the exclusion of free blacks and persons of mixed ancestry from the state. Tempers were lost again, on both sides, and it was the opportunity of Henry Clay to step in and forge the compromise of 1821. If nothing else, the compromise earned Clay the title of "great compromiser" – a title he never shied from wearing as a badge of honor.[120] After all, this was still, allegedly, the Era of Good Feelings.

The Republicans' willingness to compromise made possible the survival of their party across sectional lines, and meant the final dismissal of the Federalists. Their success, however, was not long lasting. The election in Congress of John Quincy pushed a disgruntled Andrew Jackson to split off the party, thus marking the beginning of the Second Party System, even though its full-blown mass character and new party organization would manifest only a decade later. Meanwhile, the nullification crisis of 1828–1833 brought forward, once again, the rhetoric of compromise. Like the crisis of 1820–1821, the nullification also threatened to disrupt the Union, but now the question of the tariff was placed, primarily thanks to Calhoun, within a larger context of majority rule and minority rights. It also revealed "much of the process by which revolutionary principles were at once developed and rejected in the early nineteenth century," and by doing so emphasized one more time the deep connections between political compromises and the paradigm of the people's two bodies.[121]

Two visons of compromise and of the people clashed during the nullification crisis, one mainly orchestrated by Calhoun, the other by Clay. Under the banner of the former, South Carolinians appealed to their revolutionary ancestors in order to defend the right of the people to resist encroachments on their liberties. At the Jefferson Day dinner on April 1830, George McDuffe toasted "the memory of Patrick Henry: the first American statesman who had the soul to feel, and the courage to declare, that there is no treason in resisting oppression."[122] The key word here was "resistance," more in line with the Stamp Act resistance of 1765 and 1766, than with the revolution of 1776. Since, as Calhoun argued, even the Constitution, "this celebrated work admit – most explicitly, and in the fullest manner – that the constitution derives all its powers and authority from the people of the several States, acting, each for itself, in their independent and sovereign character as States," it followed that the peoples within the states constituted the ultimate constitutional tribunal.[123]

According to Calhoun, the Supreme Court could not act as the final arbiter in case of conflicts between the states and the federal government because it was itself part of the federal government, and therefore part of the conflict. And "if each party has a right to judge, then, under our system of government, the

---

[120] For a detailed exposition of all the intricacies of the compromises of 1820–1821, see Knupfer, *The Union as It Is*, 90–102.

[121] Maier, "The Road Not Taken," 2.   [122] Quoted in Maier, "The Road Not Taken," 6.

[123] John C. Calhoun (1992), *Union and Liberty: The Political Philosophy of John C. Calhoun*, Ed. Ross M. Lence (Indianapolis: Liberty Fund), 110.

final cognizance of a question of contested power would be in the States, and not in the General Government."[124] After all, "[t]he relation ... in which the States stand to the system, is that of the creator to the creature," and only under a despotic federal government, "a thorough revolution has been effected, the creature taking the place of the creator."[125] Thus, nullification, or "state interposition," as he called it, was not, at least in his eyes, meant to destroy the Union and the Constitution, but on the contrary to ensure the survival of both. "The South Carolina Convention of 1832 followed Calhoun's lead when it called 'to restore the Constitution to its original principles, and thereby to perpetuate the Union.'"[126]

Even though Madison denied that the Virginia and Kentucky resolutions provided a precedent for state interposition, Calhoun did not hesitate to claim that Madison had served as his inspiration, and professed his unconditional admiration for his predecessor. Like Madison, he, too, believed that great statesmen, willing to compromise between majorities and minorities for the sake of the common good, would "not always be at the helm." Therefore, he wanted to embed the imperative to compromise into the nation's institutions, mostly via an imposition of the concurrent majority principle at the national level. It was, in his view, the only way of forcing a majority to compromise with a minority, and the constitution of South Carolina proved in practice how well such a system could work. The adoption of the concurrent majority "made, emphatically, the government ... of the whole people of South Carolina, and not of one portion of its people over another portion. The consequence was, the almost instantaneous restoration of harmony and concord [...] Kind feelings, and mutual attachments between the two sections took their place."[127]

For many others, however, it was simply Calhoun's and his fellow Southern Carolinians' way of holding of the Union hostage by a disgruntled minority. A rather strange coalition opposing the doctrine of nullification formed, including John Quincy Adams, Joseph Story, Daniel Webster, Andrew Jackson, and Henry Clay (recently defeated in his presidential bid by Jackson). Some, like Daniel Webster, argued against nullification, claiming that a union of American citizens preceded and ratified the Constitution, while the states served as mere vehicles for this national popular sovereignty. Secession was an alternative that he simply refused to consider. As he replied to Robert Hayne in a fine piece of rhetoric, "I have not allowed myself, Sir, to look beyond the Union, to see what might lie in the dark recess behind. [...] I have not accustomed myself to hang over the precipice of disunion, to see whether with my short sight I can fathom the depth of the abyss below."[128]

---

[124] Ibid., 383.   [125] Ibid., 268.   [126] Maier, "The Road Not Taken," 8.

[127] Calhoun, *Union and Liberty*, 284.

[128] Quoted in Scott M. Reznick (2017), "On Liberty and Union: Moral Imagination and Its Limits in Daniel Webster's Seventh of March Speech," American Political Thought: A Journal of Ideas, Institutions, and Culture, 6, 382.

Others, like Jackson, agreed that the states preceded the Union, but the true Jeffersonian states' right doctrine implied the rule by a constitutional majority. Precisely because the Union was a compact among states, no single state could decide, against the will of the majority, to nullify federal laws or to secede. Jackson's stance soon became more aggressive. He requested that Congress gave him the power to crush nullifiers if they resisted enforcement of the tariff laws, and issued a harsh Proclamation in December 1832, which was followed by a Force Bill sponsored by his supporters in January 1833.

In the eyes of the moderates, such a stance was as militant as South Carolina's, and instead of defusing the situation only made it worse. "With the Democrats facing an internal sectional revolt, with Jackson in an uncompromising temper and drawing closer to Webster, and with Calhoun waiting in anticipation of forcing the government to yield, Henry Clay stepped in to renew a compromise proposal that he had been formulated since 1832."[129] He successfully put together a package of mutual concessions, by making appeals to moderates in both North and South.

Clay's compromise differed from Calhoun's in that it did not involve a constitutional amendment to formalize the concurrent majority principle. Instead, Clay's concurring majorities acted through Congress, in a similar way as they had during the Missouri compromises of 1820–1821. Yet the fact that such compromises passed by Congress were not strictly immune to repeal did not mean that in the eyes of many, especially Clay, they did not share in some of the aura of permanency with which the Constitution was endowed. Clay asked:

What man, who is entitled to deserve the character of an American statesman, would stand up in his place, in either House of Congress, and disturb this treaty of peace and amity? ... [That] great principle of compromise and concession which lies at the bottom of our institutions [will] remove that alienation of feeling which has so long existed between certain parts of this widely spread confederacy, so as to enable us to transmit to after-times the substantial blessings, as well as the name, of the glorious fabric of wisdom which our father bequeathed to us.[130]

The following decades proved that such men did exist, and that their hopes were misplaced.

6.3 "THE DAY OF COMPROMISE HAS PASSED"

When John C. Calhoun insisted on embedding the concurrent majority principle into the Constitution, Henry Clay insisted on building concurrent majorities in Congress. Both politicians understood very well the reasons behind their respective strategies. At stake was the institution of slavery. If Clay, an opponent of slavery in theory, otherwise a slave owner himself, was willing

---

[129] Knupfer, *The Union as It Is*, 111.   [130] Quoted in Knupfer, *The Union as It Is*, 113.

to compromise on this issue to preserve the Union, it was because he was convinced that history was on his side: "Public opinion alone can bring about the abolition of slavery, and public opinion is on the march," he told Thomas Speed in 1833. "We should wait in patience for its operation without attempting measures that might throw it back."[131] His professed disciple, Abraham Lincoln, would make a similar remark during the first debate with Stephen Douglas: "Public sentiment is everything. With it, nothing can fail; against it, nothing can succeed. Whoever, molds public sentiment goes deeper than he who acts statutes, or pronounce judicial decisions."[132]

Both Clay and Lincoln would be proven right. Slowly but steadily, public sentiment marched in the right direction – a major concern for Southerners such as Calhoun who, by the end of 1837, claimed with evident exasperation: "Expediency, concession, compromise! Away with such weaknesses and folly. Right, justice, plighted fight, and the Constitution: These, and these only, can be relied on to avert the conflict!"[133] Calhoun's exasperation came in the context of his attempt to pass six resolutions to bind the Senate against anti-slavery agitation and to acknowledge that the Constitution was meant to respect and protect each state's domestic institutions, notably slavery, "and that *no change of opinion or feeling* on the part of other States of the Union in relation to it can justify them or their citizens in open and systematic attacks thereon with the view of its overthrow," as the fourth resolution read.[134]

Henry Clay voted for the first four resolutions but not the fifth and sixth ones. The fifth opposed any attempt to abolish slavery "in any of the Territories on the ground, or under the pretext, that *it is immoral or sinful.*"[135] Fearing a partisan maneuver to destroy his potential next bid to presidency, Clay offered his own set of resolutions, basically no less pro-slavery than Calhoun's but omitting the impossibility to attack slavery on grounds of immorality. This was sufficient to launch Calhoun into yet another diatribe: "This agitation has produced one happy effect at least; it has compelled us to [sic] the South to look into the nature and character of this great institution, and to correct many false impressions that even we have entertained in relation with it. *Many in the South once believed that it was a moral and political evil; that folly and delusion are gone.*"[136] Indeed, gone were the days in which the slave owners were largely apathetic and apologetic on this painful topic.

---

[131] Henry Clay (1904), *The Works of Henry Clay, Comprising his Life, Correspondence and Speeches* (New York and London: G.P. Putnam's Sons), Vol. 8, 652.

[132] Abraham Lincoln (2008), *The Lincoln–Douglas Debates*, Eds. Rodney E. Davis and Douglas L. Wilson (Urbana and Chicago: The Knox College Lincoln Center and the University of Illinois Press), 32.

[133] Quoted in Archibald Dixon (1903), *History of Missouri Compromise and Slavery in American Politics: A True History of the Missouri Compromise and Its Repeal, and of African Slavery as a Factor in American Politics*, 2nd ed. (Cincinnati: The Robert Clark Company), 151–152.

[134] Ibid., 140 (emphasis added).   [135] Ibid., 140 (emphasis added).

[136] Ibid., 148 (emphasis added).

Initially, the Southerners felt safe to discuss slavery as a political but not as a moral evil. After all, as William Harper put in his *Memoir on Slavery*, "To say that there is evil in any institution, is only to say that it is human."[137] William Smith of South Carolina claimed in Congress, not without some irritation: "When we entered into this confederation, we did it from political, not from moral motives, and I do not think my constituents want to learn morals from the petitioners; I do not believe they want improvement in their moral system, if they do, they can get it at home."[138] Only "at home," in the South, the chances of changing "their moral system" were rather slim, as Bishop Asbury observed: "I am brought to conclude that slavery will exist in Virginia perhaps for ages; there is not a sufficient sense of religion nor of liberty to destroy it; Methodists, Baptists, Presbyterians, in the highest flights of rapturous piety, still maintain and defend it."

George Thatcher from Massachusetts jumped on the opportunity, in 1800, during the Sixth Congress. If slavery was a political evil, then it is the right and the duty of Congress to legislate about it. The institution, he argued, was "a cancer of immense magnitude that would some time destroy the body politic, except a proper legislation should prevent the evil." James Jones replied immediately: "I ask him how he would remedy this evil as he calls it? but I do not think it is an evil ... I believe it might have been happy for the United States if these people had never been introduced among us, but I do believe that they have immensely benefitted by coming amongst us."[139]

For quite a while, the Southerners were convinced that, regardless of whether morally right or wrong, they held the higher ground politically speaking, since the institution of slavery was acknowledged as such by the Constitution; therefore, it was an intrinsic part of the original compact and compromise founding the Union. After all, three clauses mention it specifically: Art. I, sec. 9, cl. 1, for keeping the slave trade open until 1808; Art. I, sec. 2. Cl. 3, also known as the Three-fifths Compromise; and Art. V, sec. 2, cl. 3, requiring the return of persons "held to service of labor" escaping into other states. The only concern of the pro-slavery camp were the "political speculatists, who deriving their ideas of government from abstract theorems, and estimating man more by he ought to be, than what he is, [wish] to erect an Utopian Constitution on a sandy basis."[140] These were the "philosophical abolitionists" who, like the French revolutionaries, were foolishly trying to

---

[137] William Harper (1838), *Memoir on Slavery: Read before the Society for the Advancement of Learning, of South Carolina, at Its Annual Meeting at Columbia* (Charleston: James S. Burges), 8.

[138] Quoted in William Sumner Jenkins (1935), *Pro-Slavery Thought in the Old South* (Chapel Hill: The University of North Carolina Press), 51.

[139] Quoted in ibid., 54–55.

[140] William Smith in an Independence Day oration at Charleston in 1796, quoted in Jenkins, *Pro-Slavery Thought in the Old South*, 61.

impose some abstract, if not entirely wrong, ideals on an existing reality for which they, like James Jones, did not feel responsible. Such idealists were making "eccentric excursions into the fields of Natural Law and Natural Rights, collecting brilliant but poisonous wild flowers with which to dazzle the eyes and drug the senses of the multitude."[141]

As to be expected, the most frequent reference made by their opponents was to the Declaration of Independence and the idea of natural, inalienable rights, and it was on these arguments that the counterattack initially concentrated. According the Joseph Clay of Pennsylvania, "The Declaration of Independence is to be taken with a great qualification. It declares men have an inalienable right to life; yet we hang criminals – to liberty, yet we imprison – to the pursuit of happiness, yet we must not infringe upon the rights of others. If the Declaration of Independence is taken in its fullest extent, it will warrant robbery."[142] During the Missouri debates, when the issue became heavily disputed, William Pinkney argued even more vehemently: "The self-evident truths announced in the Declaration are not truths at all, if taken literally, and the practical conclusions contained in the same passage of that declaration prove that they were never designed to be so received."[143] For William Harper too, the invocation of natural rights was "well sounding, but unmeaning verbiage of natural equality and inalienable rights." How could anyone claim that "all men are born free and equals. Is it not palpably nearer the truth to say that no man was ever born free, and that no two men were ever born equal?"[144]

As we have seen with Calhoun, by the time Harper read these statements in front of the Society for the Advancement of Learning (!) of South Carolina, in 1838, the pro-slavery camp was no longer apologetic and on the defensive. It was the same year in which Calhoun would acknowledge that, "[m]any in the South once believed that it was a moral and political evil; that folly and delusion are gone." Politically, the Missouri Compromise established the precedent – from then on it was accepted that Congress could legislate on issues pertaining to slavery. And morally, the abolitionist movement had become increasingly radicalized. As Harper was the first to admit, "the inhabitants of the slave holding States of America" were "insulated." "If any voice is raised among ourselves to extenuate or to vindicate [slavery], it is unheard. The judgment is made up. We can have no hearing before the tribunal of the civilized world."[145] A different, more offensive strategy was needed.

Far from being defended as a necessary evil for whose existence the Southerners were not to be held responsible, but rather regarded merely as

---

[141] James Henry Hammond, quoted in Jenkins, *Pro-Slavery Thought in the Old South*, 130.

[142] Joseph Clay (1806), *Annals of the Congress of the United States* (9th Congress, 2nd Session, December 29), 227.

[143] William Pinkney (1820), *Annals of the Congress of the United States* (16th Congress, 1st Sess., February 15), 405.

[144] Harper, *Memoir on Slavery*, 9, 6.   [145] Ibid., 3.

cautious administrators, slavery was now promoted as the best possible way of life, the only able to resolve the contradictions and the shortcomings of both capitalism and socialism. According to Hammond, it was as close to a Paradise on earth as one could get. Unfortunately, "into ... Eden is coming Satan in the guise of an Abolitionist!"[146] In his message to the legislature of South Carolina, in 1829, Governor Stephen D. Miller had already claimed that "slavery is not a national evil; on the contrary, it is national benefit," and by 1835, Governor McDuffie argued that slavery was a blessing to both white and black races. Instead of being an evil, it as "the cornerstone of our republican edifice."[147] All that was needed was a more philosophically articulated, ideally even "scientific" case for slavery. Two of the most influential pro-slavery books claimed to be books of "sociology." George Fitzhugh's *Sociology for the South* was the first book published in the English language to use the word "sociology" in its title, and the same year (1854) Henry Hughes published *Treatise on Sociology: Theoretical and Practical*, in which he aimed to replace the label of "slavery" with "warranteism," in order to escape the stigma associated with the word. Also, Hammond's "mudsill theory," according to which in any society there must be a lower class on which civilization can be raised, was presented as a "sociological theory."

One way of doing this was to accept the basic premises of the "philosophical abolitionists" about the social contract and the natural rights, while turning them against their opponents. Hammond, for example, claimed that "[i]f we travel back with the philosophers who refer all human institutions to an original contract, I will still engage to find a place for slavery there. Let it be regarded as a compact between the master and the slave."[148] To make the contract of slavery more palatable, other Southerners, such as Albert Taylor Bledsoe, James Henry Thornwell, or Edmund B. Bryan, suggested that the master owned the slave's labor but not the man.[149] "The property of man in man is only the property of man in human toil. The laborer becomes capital, not because he is a thing, but because he is the exponent of a presumed amount of labor ... In its last analysis, slavery is nothing but an organization of labor, and an organization by virtue of which labor and capital are made to coincide."[150]

Professor of mathematics at the University of Virginia, Bledsoe acknowledged that "no man has a right to alienate his rights. All natural rights are, indeed, in so far as they are real and existing, inalienable." But the most frequently invoked rights did not fall into this category, for "both life and

---

[146] James Henry Hammond (1844), *Letter to an English Abolitionist*, quoted in Drew Gilpin Faust, ed. (1981), *The Ideology of Slavery: Proslavery Thought in the Antebellum South, 1830–1860* (Baton Rouge: Louisiana State University), 168.
[147] Quoted in Jenkins, *Pro-Slavery Thought in the Old South*, 76, 78.   [148] Quoted in ibid., 112.
[149] See Hulliung, *Social Contract in America*, 57.
[150] Quoted in Jenkins, *Pro-Slavery Thought in the Old South*, 109–110.

liberty may be taken away by society for its own highest good. It is on this ground that I justify the institution of slavery. Not on the ground that society may divest the slave all his natural right to personal freedom, but on the ground that he possesses no such natural right." He pushed the argument even further: "In the true sense of the term *liberty*, slavery is not its opposite. Its opposite, its *antagonistic* principle, is *license*. By the institution of slavery for the blacks, license is shut out, and liberty is introduced. It is introduced for the slaves themselves. [...] Let this institution be abolished, and they will no longer enjoy their natural rights."[151]

For most Southerners, however, the social compact theory was a nonstarter. For Calhoun, "nothing c[ould] be more absurd and false" than "the prevalent opinion that all men are born free and equal."

It is, indeed, difficult to explain how an opinion so destitute of all sound reason, ever could have been so extensively entertained, unless we regard it as being confounded with another, which has some resemblance of truth; – but which, when properly understood, is not less false and dangerous. I refer to the assertion, that all men are equal in the state of nature; meaning, by a state of nature, a state of individuality, supposed to have existed prior to the social and political state. [...] But such a state is purely hypothetical. It never did, nor can exist; [...] It is, therefore, a great misnomer to call it the *state of nature*. Instead of being the natural state of man, it is, of all conceivable states, the most opposed to his nature – most repugnant to his feelings, and most incompatible with his wants.[152]

Yet the most flamboyant promoter of slavery remains, indisputably, George Fitzhugh. He vituperated against the "unobservant, abstract thinkers and closet scholars, who deal with little of the world and see less of it."[153] According to him, the idea that men were free and equal was part of the laissez-faire philosophy, meant to promote the interests of the strong at the expense of the weakest, including women, the poor, and the ignorant. "In free society none but selfish virtues are in repute ... In such society virtue loses all her loveliness, because of her selfish aims. Good men and bad man have the same end in view: self-promotion, self-elevation."[154] Shocking phrases such as "liberty is an evil which government is intended to correct," "all government is slavery," or "some were born with saddles on their backs, and others booted and spurred to ride them" abound in his writings and were far from accidental.[155] Like a Salvador Dali of pro-slavery thought, he self-consciously made his work "odd, eccentric, extravagant, and disorderly," as he confessed to George Frederick Holmes in 1855, in order to increase his visibility and sales.[156] But when he

---

[151] Albert Taylor Bledsoe (1856), "Review of His Reviewer," *Southern Literary Messenger*, XXIII, 22–25.
[152] John C. Calhoun (1851), *A Disquisition of Government and a Discourse on the Constitution and Government of the United States*, Ed. Richard K. Crale (Columbia: A.S. Johnston), 57–58.
[153] George Fitzhugh (1854), *Sociology for the South or the Failure of Free Society* (Richmond: A. Morris), 7–8.
[154] Ibid., 24.   [155] Ibid., 170, 179.   [156] Faust, *The Ideology of Slavery*, 18.

proposed to extend slavery to white men, his fellow Southerners began to dissociate themselves from what they perceived as more of a crackpot.

In effect, what Fitzhugh did was nothing other than push to its logical extreme the pro-slavery argument, in an uncompromising way that mirrored William Lloyd Garrison's own radical position. During a Fourth of July rally sponsored by the Massachusetts Anti-Slavery Society in 1854, Garrison famously burned the Constitution, shouting that it was "a covenant with death, and an agreement with Hell." As the document was burning to ashes, he cried out: "So perish all compromises with tyranny!"[157] By then, there was no room left for compromise. After the passing of Kansas-Nebraska Act on May of the same year, William Herndon, Lincoln's law partner, recalled that Lincoln declared: "The day of compromise has passed. These two great ideas [freedom and slavery] have been kept apart only by the most artful means. They are like two beasts in sight of each other, but chained and held apart. Some day these deadly antagonists will open or the other break their bonds, and then the question will be settled."[158] It turned out to be a prophetic observation.

The last serious attempt to compromise on slavery for the sake of the Union had taken place four years earlier, but the Compromise of 1850 differed from both the Missouri Compromise and the Compromise on Tariffs. The crisis was ignited after the war with Mexico, when the United States acquired a vast tract of land – all of present-day California, Utah, and Nevada, most of Arizona and New Mexico, and parts of Colorado, Wyoming, and Texas. Almost overnight, the issue of slavery in the territories became one with huge implications. Initially, the doctrine of popular sovereignty's "seductive ambiguity about the timing of the territory's decision about slavery" appeared capable of calming down the most inflamed spirits.[159] Yet the stakes were simply too high, and tensions exploded once California demanded access into the Union as a free state. Threats of secession became, once again, frequent.

Demoralized but not yet broken after losing all his bids to the presidency, Henry Clay seized the opportunity and stepped into the fray to confirm, once again, his reputation of Great Compromiser – and some historians are still impressed by his tour de force to save the Union "from the edge of the precipice." In this view, the Compromise of 1850 was the "happy result of satisfying both northerners and southerners at the same time while forcing each to make a concession."[160] Others are far less enthusiastic, considering the compromise heavily skewed in favor of the Southerners, conceding to the

---

[157] Massachusetts Historical Society (July 2005), www.masshist.org/object-of-the-month/objects/a-covenant-with-death-and-an-agreement-with-hell-2005-07-01

[158] Quoted in Lewis E. Lehrman (2008), *Lincoln at Peoria – The Turning Point: Getting Right with the Declaration of Independence* (Mechanicsburg: Stackpole Books), 12.

[159] Knupfer, *The Union as It Is*, 174.

[160] Robert V. Remini (2010), *At the Edge of the Precipice: Henry Clay and the Compromise That Saved the Union* (New York: Basic Books), 6.

Northerners only what they would have gained anyway, namely a free California and the largely symbolic interdiction of the public slave trade in the District
of Columbia.[161] What is missing from both interpretations, however, is a detail
of crucial importance: Initiated by Clay and supported by Webster, after the
two worked out the details behind the scenes, the compromise eventually
passed thanks to Stephen Douglas and President Fillmore. It was the proof that
the appeal to mutual sacrifices was no longer working. The "chords of affection" were already broken, and the only way to pass the compromise was to
appeal to cold interests.

True, after Clay introduced his compromise at the end of January 1850,
through a series of resolutions, many thought that they would assist to a similar
pattern as in 1820s or 1830s. On February, *Baltimore's Sun's* Washington
correspondent assured his readers: "After a few more speeches, we shall begin
to feel comfortable, and then we shall compromise; first back to back, then
shoulder to shoulder, and at least face to face, with a cordial shake of hand, as
becomes two great sections of a country guided by the prestige of future world-
domination."[162] His optimism took a serious hit on March 4, when Calhoun,
too weak to speak, asked Senator James Murray Mason of Virginia to deliver a
speech on his behalf. If scholars such as Finkelman are correct in their claims
that the compromise blatantly favored the South and the institution of slavery,
the dying Calhoun surely did not see it. In forty-two pages of manuscript, he
argued that the North wanted nothing less than to control the entire government and would not stop until slavery would be abolished in all states. The
intended permanent sectional equilibrium ratified by the Constitution being
destroyed by broad constructionists and fanatic abolitionists, the only solution
left for the South was a peaceful separation, for at stake was more than a
principle; it was a way of life.

On March 7, Webster took the floor to support Clay's compromise in a
controversial speech known as "The Constitution and the Union." Like Clay
and Calhoun's speeches, Webster's, too, drew an impressive audience. After all,
it was the last rhetorical battle of a dying generation – both literally and
figuratively. Webster attacked all of Calhoun's arguments and enthusiastically
supported Clay's compromise. For the hard-core abolitionists, Webster's
endorsement of the amendment of the Fugitive Slave Act was anathema. And
yet, as John Burt notices, Lincoln's own support of the Fugitive Slave law was
"on exact the ground Webster had taken in the Seventh of March Speech, as the
price of a bargain that came out on balance for freedom."[163] A *Liberator*
headline read, "On the Late Satanic Speech of Daniel Webster," and "Ralph
Waldo Emerson proclaimed that it put Webster on 'the side of abuse and
oppression and chaos' rather that the 'side of humanity and justice.'"[164]

[161] See, for example, Finkelman, "The Cost of Compromise."
[162] Quoted in Knupfer, *The Union as It Is*, 159.   [163] Burt, *Lincoln's Tragic Pragmatism*, 51.
[164] Reznick, "On Liberty and Union," 372.

The same *Liberator* was worried by the effectiveness of Webster's appeal to compromise: "[I]t is to be feared he has so 'sugared o'er the devil' of compromise, that multitude will swallow the gilded pill."[165]

The *Liberator* journalist was right as far as the moderates from both parties were concerned. Between February and April 1850, appeals to compromise, peace, and union, made in the spirit of Clay and Webster, gathered huge crowds on both sides. In New York, Joseph L. White promised, "We will compromise – we will continue to compromise, for the principle of Union is far above all other principles." In Baltimore, William Fell Giles told the crowd that the Union "originated in the sanctities of compromise and sacrifice, and no one party has the right to dissolve it without the consent of the whole."[166] "As a conservative journalist put it back in mid-March: 'The very object of any compromise is, to put an end to the agitation, and to 'save the ship,' not as Mr. Webster eloquently remarked, to select a 'fragment on which to float from the wreck'."[167]

Yet for all this heartfelt rhetoric, Clay's compromise would not have passed through Congress if not for the more practical approach of politicians like Stephen Douglas. The rise of mass politics and the explosion of newspapers inflamed popular passions on both sides, and by 1850 made obsolete the old-style disinterested statesman's approach, grand strategy, and design. What was required now for any politician's survival was a rapid and accurate reading of his constituency's mood, followed by an even more rapid accommodation. Appeals to mutuality and moderation were by now doomed to fall mostly on deaf ears. "The politics of pragmatic interest-group compromise, characteristic of the new generation of Stephen Douglas and Millard Fillmore was the crucial element in the tactical maneuvering and eventual passage of the Compromise."[168] The Compromise of 1850 was not intended to last. It was a compromise "without heart."

In the end, Southerners' initial impulse to engage abolitionism solely on political grounds while avoiding moral confrontations proved to be the right one for their purposes. The end of slavery was determined neither by political nor by philosophical considerations. The slaveholders' main enemies were not, as they had thought for decades, the "speculatists," the "abstract thinkers and closet scholars," and not even the seasoned politicians. Their main enemy was "a new social imaginary" crafted mainly by Harriet Beecher Stowe's *Uncle Tom's Cabin*, with 310,000 copies sold in 1852, and by the popular songs of the likes of Stephen Foster. Under popular pressure, the second party system

---

[165] N, H. W. (1850, March 29). MR. WEBSTER'S COMPROMISE SPEECH. *Liberator (1831-1865)*, 20, 51. Retrieved from http://search.proquest.com.ezproxy.lib.uh.edu/docview/91106634?accountid=7107

[166] New York *Herald*, February 26, 1850; *New York Herald*, March 3, 1850. For more examples, editorials, and letters, see Knupfer, *The Union as It Is*, 187–188.

[167] Knupfer, *The Union as It Is*, 187.   [168] Knupfer, *The Union as It Is*, 161.

crumbled. The Whig Party disintegrated, and the Know-Nothing Party, nativist and resentful, enjoyed only an ephemeral success. "In the end, anti-slavery, not nativism, framed the agenda of the northern public." The cultural performances of the like of Stowe and Foster "drove metaphoric action in a liminal moment, raising the political stakes of the slavery debate to new heights."[169]

Disregarding the change in public mood, an overconfident Stephen Douglas pushed the Kansas–Nebraska bill, which effectively repealed the Missouri Compromise. Added to the new Fugitive Slave Act, which nationalized slavery, it proved to be the straw that broke the back of the Democratic Party, preparing the ground for the future success of the new Republican Party. Douglas found himself caught between the two definitions of "the people." During the famous Lincoln–Douglas debates, he made appeal to the sovereignty of the people both at state and territory levels, on deciding if they accept slavery or not, and to the people at a national level, when supporting the Fugitive Act. The contradiction did not escape unnoticed, and on a banner during the Galesburg, Illinois debate he was depicted unsuccessfully trying to ride two donkeys at the same time, one labeled "Popular Sovereignty," the other "Dred Scott." The people's contest had already begun, and an astute observer such as Lincoln could not fail to notice that "a universal feeling, whether well or ill informed, can not be safely disregarded."[170] As previously mentioned, Lincoln's diagnosis proved correct in the long run: "Public sentiment is everything. With it, nothing can fail; against it, nothing can succeed."[171] He was right. Harriett Beecher Stowe was on his side.

In 1852, the Free Soil Party's presidential candidate, John P. Hale, gathered less than 5 percent of the popular vote. Yet two years later the new Republican Party was born, and by 1856 its national platform concluded that "the main-tenance of the principles promulgated in the Declaration of Independence ... are essential to the preservation of our Republican institutions," while inviting "the affiliation and cooperation of the men of all parties, however differing from us in other respects, in support of the principles herein declared."[172] The remnants of the nativist Know-Nothings and of the Free Soil Party answered the invitation. The promise to restore the principles of the Declaration appealed simultaneously to the supporters of state rights and to the "philosophical abolitionists." Shuffling the cards of "the people" allowed the new Republicans to claim to be the true Democrats. As Lincoln explained in a letter to group of prominent New Englanders,

---

[169] John L. Brooke (2015), "Party, Nation, and Cultural Rupture: The Crisis of the American Civil War," in Peart and Smith, *Practicing Democracy*, 78, 87.

[170] Rodney O. Davis and Douglas L. Wilson, Eds. (2008), The Lincoln–Douglas Debates (Urbana and Chicago: The Knox College Lincoln Study Center and the University of Illinois Press), 20.

[171] Ibid., 32.   [172] Quoted in Brown, *Moderates*, 106.

I remember once being much amused at seeing two partially intoxicated men engage in a fight with their great-coats on, which fight, after a long, and rather harmless contest, ended in each having fought himself *out* of his own coat, and *into* that of the other. If the two leading parties of the day are really identical with the two in the days of Jefferson and Adams, they have performed the same feat as the two drunken men.[173]

In 1858, Lincoln's brilliant rhetoric was not yet enough to prevent the victory of his opponent, Stephen Douglas, but was enough to raise his national profile, making him a viable candidate for the presidency. Two years later, he defeated Douglas as the North Democratic candidate, among others, and won the White House amid public threats of secession.

Lincoln's desperate attempts to find a compromise between radical abolitionists and radical supporters of states' rights were not enough to prevent secession. His conciliatory First Inaugural Address fell on deaf ears. The Southerners were too obsessed with what they perceived to be a direct threat to their particular identities to be willing to compromise once again. So the Civil War began. The days of compromise were, indeed, gone. In a Special Session Message, Lincoln told Congress: "No compromise by public servants could in this case be a cure; not that compromises are not often proper, but that no popular government can long survive a marked precedent that those who carry an election can only save the government from immediate destruction by giving up the main point upon which the people gave the election."[174] What was at stake was more than the issue of slavery. It was the definition of "the people."

As Lincoln put it in his Gettysburg Address, it was a war to guarantee that "government of the people, by the people, for the people, shall not perish from the earth." In Garry Wills's brilliant phrases,

He would cleanse the Constitution – not as William Lloyd Garrison had, by burning an instrument that countenanced slavery. He altered the document from within, by appeal from its letter to the spirit, subtly changing the recalcitrant stuff of that legal compromise, bringing it to its own indictment. By implicitly doing this, he performed one of the most daring acts of open-air sleight of hand ever witnessed by the unsuspecting. Everyone in that vast throng of thousands was having his or her intellectual pocket picked. The crowd departed with a new thing in its ideological luggage, the new Constitution Lincoln had substituted for the one they had brought there with them. They walked off from those curving graves on the hillside, under a changed sky, into a different America.[175]

---

[173] Quoted in ibid., 107–108.

[174] Abraham Lincoln (1861), "Special Session Message" in Life and Public Services of Abraham Lincoln, Sixteenth President of the United States; and Commander-in-Chief of the Army and Navy of the United States *1864* (Philadelphia: T.B. Paterson & Brothers), 116.

[175] Gary Wills (2012), "The Words That Remade America: The Significance of the Gettysburg Address," *The Atlantic*, www.theatlantic.com/magazine/archive/2012/02/the-words-that-remade-america/308801/

More than 600,000 deaths later, the institution of slavery was formally eradicated and a new world had begun: The United States *are* became the United States *is*. As an article from the April 24, 1887, of the *Washington Post* read,

There was a time a few years ago when the United States was spoken of in the plural number. Men said "the United States are" – "the United States have" – "the United States were." But the war changed all that. Along the line of fire from the Chesapeake to Sabine Pass was settled forever the question of grammar. Not Wells, or Green, or Lindley Murray decided it, but the sabers of Sheridan, the muskets of Sherman, the artillery of Grant. . . . The surrender of Mr. Davis and Gen. Lee meant a transition from the plural to the singular.

The change from "are" to "is" put forever to rest the question of whether or not there is an American people. Less so if this *one* people has but one or two bodies.

7

Conclusions

Resuscitating the People's Two Bodies

"Who in the world am I? Ah, that's the great puzzle."
— *Lewis Caroll, Alice in Wonderland*

The story of the American people began with a firm conviction of exemplarity for the rest of the world: "For wee must consider that we shall be ... as a city upon a hill. *The eies of all people are upon us*" (John Winthrop, Chapter 2).[1] "The cause of America is in a great measure *the cause of all mankind*," wrote Thomas Paine, in *Common Sense*, even before the Revolutionary War was in full bloom (Chapter 3).[2] Such claims appeared to be confirmed when the first state constitutions were widely republished and discussed in Europe, as the first written constitutions made under the authority of sovereign peoples, no matter how ambiguous the concept of "the people" remained (Chapter 4). In his Preface of the *Notes of Debates in the Federal Convention of 1787*, James Madison wrote about the struggles to frame "a Constitution on which would be staked the happiness of *a people great even in its infancy*, and possibly *the cause of Liberty throughout the world*," while during the Philadelphia convention Gouverneur Morris "flattered himself he came here in some degree as a Representative of the whole human race; for the hole human race will be affected by the proceedings of this Convention" (Chapter 5).[3] And in his Special Session Message, on July 4, 1861, Abraham Lincoln told Congress that

---

[1] John Winthrop (1630), *A Model of Christian Charity*, in Miller and Johnson, *The Puritans*, 199 (emphasis added).

[2] Thomas Paine (1776), *Common Sense*, in Gordon S. Wood, ed. (2015), *The American Revolution: Writings from the Pamphlet Debate, II: 1773-1776* (The Library of America), 651 (emphasis added).

[3] James Madison (1985), *Notes of Debates in the Federal Convention of 1797* (Athens: Ohio University Press), 17 (emphasis added); quoted in Madison, *Notes of Debates*, 240.

the Civil War "presents *to the whole family of man* the question whether a constitutional republic, or democracy – a government of the people by the same people – can or cannot maintain its territorial integrity against its own domestic foes" (Chapter 6).[4] The examples could go on and on.

As I have tried to demonstrate throughout this book, it was an exemplary birth indeed, yet one more fortuitous than the actors and the promoters of American exceptionalism had (and oftentimes still have) in mind. All well-known considerations – geographical, sociological, and historical – aside, what set the birth of the American people apart was the unique *practical* combination of the people's two bodies. As shown in Chapter 2, this is not to say that the Puritans who came to the shores of the New World did so driven by a programmatic political philosophy or even that politics was in the forefront of their preoccupations. Forced by circumstance and by their religious beliefs, they actually managed to combine de facto two understandings of the people.

The first one was akin to the social compact theory that would be later proposed by Hobbes and Locke. It conceived of the people as a collection of free and equal individuals, unanimously covenanting to create new theologico-political communities. But once this new people was created, it was understood as an organic and hierarchically structured corporation, in which the responsibility for establishing the details of the government and for running its operations was entrusted in the hands of an elected aristocracy of visible saints. This was the second covenant, between the electors and their rulers, modeled after the medieval political compacts, establishing a fragile balance between "the authority of the magistrates and the liberty of the people."[5]

Fortuitous as it was, this foundational double helix proved crucial for the nurturing of an intellectual versatility for centuries to come – a versatility with which scholars still struggle when trying to find some coherence in the ideological origins of the American founding. By now we should be better equipped to understand why so many of the founders, like the Puritans before them, appeared riddled with "striking incongruities and contradictions," "with no coherent intellectual pattern."[6] Hence the contemporary struggle to determine if the ideology of liberalism or the one of republicanism constituted the main component of the founding. Hence the insistence upon virtue, that colored even the most Lockean of arguments, yet was conspicuously absent from Locke's theory, for undermining its egalitarian premises. As previously mentioned, the contrast between the *active* liberty in civic humanism or in the classical republican paradigm (to participate in the political decision-making process) and the *passive* liberty in the natural rights tradition (a liberty that may be possessed

---

[4] Abraham Lincoln (1861), "Special Session Message" in Life and Public Services of Abraham Lincoln, Sixteenth President of the United States; and Commander-in-Chief of the Army and Navy of the United States *1864* (Philadelphia: T.B. Paterson & Brothers), 102 (emphasis added).

[5] John Winthrop (1645), *Little Speech on Liberty*, quoted in Frohnen, *The American Republic*, 34.

[6] Bailyn, *The Ideological Origins*, 33.

without political activity) is easily understood once one accepts the paradigm of the people's two bodies from the Puritan tradition.

This unique implementation in practice of the bidimensional covenant shaped the Puritans' attitude toward compromise as well. While they were willing to compromise among themselves in most matters, for being "knit together by this bond of loue," the Puritans vehemently refused to compromise in matters of faith, not just with outsiders but also among themselves.[7] The fact that this attitude was responsible for the rapid fragmentation of the movement and its subsequent demise, despite later attempts to compromise, can teach us a valuable lesson: While "the chords of affection" that keep a people together are conducive to compromise, the moralized attitudes toward others are not.[8] The fact that in the case of the Puritans these moralized attitudes were the result of a particular set of religious beliefs is only of secondary relevance. As recent "evolutionary, neuroscientific, and cognitive perspectives in psychology" have confirmed, "moralized attitudes reorient behavior from maximizing gains to adherence to rules," and thus "lead citizens to oppose compromises, punish compromising politicians, and forsake material gain."[9]

Let us remember that the Puritans effectively created not just new societies, but new peoples – and that these were, first and foremost, *political* peoples. True, their declared purpose when crossing the Atlantic was to create purified churches, but what held them together was not their religious beliefs, which they shared both with the English Puritans and with other New Englanders, nor their common language, traditions, or even the king. What held them together as *one* people were the elected magistrates and later the elected legislatives. Compromising inside these communities was desirable. Only when their religious beliefs led them to adopt moralizing attitudes toward anyone perceived as different did compromise become unacceptable. In many respects, it was the beginning of identity politics on American soil.

The distinction between the chords of affection holding a people together beyond common interests and the passionate protection of a people's identity from any perceived "otherness" is worth emphasizing, for it would leave its mark throughout the entire American founding period and beyond. As we saw in Chapter 3, by making salvation a personal matter, the Great Awakening ended up effectively destroying the former theologico-political communities. Absent the willingness of the New Lights to compromise with the Old, or even among themselves, the Great Awakening did not prove so great after all, and ended as fast as it had begun, largely cannibalizing itself. In its aftermath,

---

[7] John Winthrop (1630), *A Model of Christian Charity*, in Miller and Johnson , *The Puritans*, 197.

[8] Emily Pears (2017), "Chords of Affection: A Theory of National Political Attachments in the American Founding," *American Political Thought: A Journal of Ideas, Institutions, and Culture*, 6:1, 1–29.

[9] Timothy J. Ryan (2016), "No Compromise: Political Consequences of Moralized Attitudes," *American Journal of Political Science*, 61:2, 409.

religious denominations became a subjective choice, old authorities began to be questioned, and new political identities were needed. In the process, thirteen new *political* peoples were forged, one for each colony, once again regardless of an otherwise common ancestry, language, or tradition. The elected colonial assemblies became the primary bond holding together these peoples.

It is easy to understand why so many scholars see in these new developments the beginning of American democratization and the success of Lockean contractarianism. However, as I have tried to demonstrate, none of these interpretations sustain historical scrutiny. While an emphasis on the horizontal, Lockean understanding of the people is undeniable, this is only half of the story. The colonists started off by being more British than even their mainland British brethren. Their enthusiasm for British monarchy surpassed that of the metropole,[10] and they began to see their colonial assemblies as British Parliaments in miniature, "and consequently deeply resent[ed] an intervention in their affairs from either Whitehall or Westminster."[11] But the idea that their elected representatives constituted a natural aristocracy of the wise and virtuous was never abandoned by the colonial *Weltanschauung*.

Indeed, Locke was cited quite frequently, although not as frequently as Montesquieu or even Blackstone, but rather carelessly, "as he could be relied on to support anything the writers happened to be arguing."[12] Furthermore, as we have seen, Locke's work was first published in America in 1773, without any subsequent reprints for the next 164 years, while Edmund Burke's work, for example, enjoyed sixteen editions before the Civil War.[13] As I suggested, responsible for this widespread misinterpretation are the overlooked differences between the social and the political compacts, and thus between the people's two bodies. From this perspective, the Patriots proved quite versatile, making appeals alternatively to both the social and the political compacts, pending on the circumstances. Once they realized that even an actual representation in the British parliament would have done them no service, since their representatives would have always amounted to an insignificant minority, they abandoned entirely any pretense that the British legislative could possibly represent them, and claimed that the only connection with Great Britain was through the political compact of each colonial people with the king.

From the moment these corporate colonial identities were openly embraced, compromise with the Parliament became impossible. When King George refused to side with the colonies, the political compacts with him were declared void, and he became, in the Declaration of Independence, the perfect scapegoat. The legacy of "political peoples" encouraged the Patriots' lack of hesitation when they declared their "British brethren ... deaf to the Voice of Justice and

---

[10] Bernard McConville (2006), *The King's Three Faces: The Rise and Fall of Royal America, 1688-1776* (Chapel Hill: University of North Carolina Press), 40, 43.

[11] Rhoden, "The American Revolution," 263.   [12] Bailyn, *The Ideological Origins*, 28–29.

[13] Hulliung, *Social Contract in America*, 44, 129.

consanguinity ... and hold them, as we hold the rest of Mankind, Enemies in War, in Peace, Friends." Nonetheless independence made the question of defining people's sovereignty much more pressing. For a while, Congress took on "the executive and administrative responsibilities that had been exercised by or under the aegis of the king's authority [...] Those powers that were exercised or claimed by Parliament, however ... were just as firmly allocated to the states."[14]

Prompted by Congress to adopt their own constitutions, even before the Revolutionary War ended, the peoples from the states took the idea of popular sovereignty seriously. Nevertheless, as shown in Chapter 4, the legacy of the vertical apprehension of a corporate people, ruled by an elected aristocracy of merit, proved initially powerful enough to trust the state legislatures with both the drafting and – Massachusetts aside – the approval of the new constitutions. However, it did not last long. Under mounting popular pressure, constitutional conventions were set up and popular ratifications became a must. When the secrecy of the debates in the convention gave way to demands for transparency, populist rhetoric began to creep in, and some of the delegates came to believe that there were no limits to what they could decide. As a delegate to the Illinois convention of 1847 put it, "We are the sovereignty of the State ... We are what the people of the State would be, if they were congregated here in one mass-meeting. *We are what Louis XIV said he was, 'We are the State.'*"[15] This is not to say that the Puritan legacy was entirely forgotten, as demonstrated by the commitment of these constitutions to preserve and enhance the moral character of the citizens for the sake of the corporate whole.[16]

It was precisely this assumed corporate identity of the people that made possible the first constitutional compromise, the Articles of Confederation. Like in the case of the United Colonies of New England more than a century before, these corporate people were able to compromise, since the equality of corporations, regardless of their respective sizes, was assumed. As I have tried to demonstrate, despite its bad reputation, the Articles of Confederation did more than simply create a loose confederation – they began to forge an American people out of an eclectic collection of identities. According to Donald Lutz, the Articles de facto created the dual citizenship, and inspired many of the future features of the second Constitution, from the Supremacy Clause to the Full Faith and Credit Clause. Furthermore, these first constitutional compromises paved the way for the compromises to come during the Philadelphia Convention.[17]

---

[14] Jerrilyn Greene Marston (1987), *King and Congress: The Transfer of Political Legitimacy, 1774-1776* (Princeton: Princeton University Press), 303–304.

[15] Quoted in John A. Jameson (1867), *The Constitutional Convention: Its History, Powers, and Modes of Proceeding* (New York: Charles Scribner), 292 (emphasis added).

[16] Barry Alan Shain (1994), *The Myth of American Individualism: The Protestant Origins of American Political Thought* (Princeton: Princeton University Press).

[17] Freedman, "Why Constitutionalist Lawyers ...," 784.

If the majority of scholars of the American founding could agree on one thing, it is that the Constitution was the result of a series of compromises – between large and small states, free and slave states, national and state power, the powers of the three branches, etc. As a matter of fact, as shown in Chapter 5, beginning with the participants in the Convention and ending in the Civil War, the Constitution was not only presented as a compromise but was *praised* precisely for this reason. Back then, compromise was not yet a dirty word; rather the opposite: politicians willing to compromise were hailed by public opinion for putting the common good above petty and selfish interests. I suggested that the main reason for this quasi-unanimous interpretation of the Constitution as "the *original* compromise" is to be found in the crafting of a *written* compromise between the two understanding of the people, *qua* corporation of corporations, hierarchically structured, on the one hand, and *qua* collection of equal individuals, on the other. One might argue that it formalized for centuries to come the paradigm of the people's two bodies, precisely because it never spelled out who the famous "We the People" in fact were.

This ambiguity made room for both understandings of the people, not only at the state level but also at the national level. Nevertheless, the social compact theory suffered a serious blow. Thanks to the separation of powers and the system of checks and balances put into place, the legislative was no longer "the soul" that kept the people together, but only one of several necessary ingredients. By making the principle of majority its cornerstone, the social compact theory prevented compromises between majority and minority by automatically denying the equality of the parties – a major concern for many of the delegates in Philadelphia. As previously mentioned, from this perspective, the social compact theory is something of a paradox: it *was* fundamentally a compromise (for implying the equality of the parties), but one that prevented any further long-lasting compromises (for creating inequality between majorities and minorities).

Both the supporters of the new Constitution and their opponents were worried about the potential excesses of populism, but while the first were mostly concerned with the dangers of the Many left unchecked, the latter were more anxious about the Few abusing their power, at the expense of the Many; hence their insistence on supplementing the Constitution with a Bill of Rights. Both fears were motivated, as history has repeatedly demonstrated, since emphasizing one of the people's two bodies at the expense of the other could come with serious potential dangers. Luckily, the resulting compromise between the two fears proved in the long run to be an astounding success, mainly because of its built-in versatility.

However, the Constitution also incorporated a compromise that, although perceived as justifiable at the time, was not meant to last, and threatened the very definition of the American people. This was the compromise over slavery. Notwithstanding, as seen in Chapter 6, the institution of slavery was not initially at the forefront of preoccupations in the newly created United States of America. Embarrassing as it is to acknowledge, the issue was initially largely perceived as an economic rather than a moral one. The main cause of division was the proper interpretation of the Constitution and, implicitly, of what people's sovereignty actually entailed. While practically everyone agreed that the Constitution was both a compact and a compromise, disagreements appeared over who were the parties of the compact and of the compromise: individuals or states. To simply claim, as did Daniel Webster in 1830, that, "It is, Sir, the people's Constitution, the people's government, made for the people, made by the people, and answerable to the people," did not help much in clarifying the confusion.[18] The question still remained: Who were the much-invoked "people"? For most Federalists, the answer was "the American people," now understood as a corporate entity, ruled by an aristocracy of merit. For the Republicans, it was mostly the peoples of each state, whose interests were oftentimes ignored by an almost monarchical central government.

Neither of the two camps was yet prepared to accept the existence of a permanent party system; each side blamed the other for falling prey to a selfish factionalism at the expense of the public good. It took decades for the practice of deferential politics to disappear and for politicians to abandon the rhetoric of an aristocracy of merit in favor of a more egalitarian one. The rapid disappearance of property requirements and the ensuing expansion of electoral franchise to all white males marked the beginning of mass politics and the emergence of the first mass party system. Yet these democratic developments came with a price; women and free blacks who in many states were not initially prevented from voting lost this right, and populist movements began to lash out against various categories, such as immigrants, Catholics, Masons, and the moneyed aristocracy. As new forms of identity politics began to develop and the number of newspapers exploded, the public rhetoric became increasingly vicious, and the idea of a *political* people, encompassing all other identities, came under attack. Threats of secession ensued. For a while, removing this threat was made possible by repeated appeals to the compromising spirit of the Constitution, trying to appease both the concerns of the majority and those of the minority, by building concurring majorities. Such appeals were made by skillful politicians, who proved able to not only to bring together congressmen of various interests but also, and most importantly, to rally public opinion behind their proposals to compromise.

By now, it should be evident that, as meaningful compromises have both a rational and an affective component, binding a people together requires an appeal both to rational interests and to more elusive "chords of affection." If the paradigm of the people's two bodies appears so versatile, it is precisely because it appeals to the former via the horizontal understanding of the people

---

[18] *The Writings and Speeches of Daniel Webster* (1906), National Ed., 18 vols. (Boston: Little, Brown), 6:54, quoted in Rodgers, *Contested Truths*, 91.

as self-interested individuals, in a liberal-Lockean sense, and to the latter via the corporatist, republican understanding, emphasizing the virtue of sacrificing private or sectional interests for the sake of the common good. When either one of the two components is absent, compromise or the cohesiveness of a people become vulnerable.

This is precisely what happened in the United States after the fragile compromise of 1850, a compromise "without a heart," passed thanks to the new pragmatic, interest-group-oriented politicians such as Stephen Douglas and Millard Fillmore. Followed by the Kansas–Nebraska Act, which effectively repealed the Missouri Compromise, and by the Fugitive Slave Act, which nationalized slavery, it proved to be the beginning of the end for the slave states. As Lincoln prophetically told his law partner, "The day of compromise has passed. [...] Some day these deadly antagonists will open or the other break their bonds, and then the question will be settled."[19] One must remember, however, that what finally brought down slavery was a change in public opinion. Lincoln proved right once again when arguing that "a universal feeling, whether well or ill informed, can not be safely disregarded."[20] Once the war was over, no one questioned any longer if there was *one* American people. Nevertheless, the quest for the elusive American people's two bodies was – and still is – far from over.

For this reason, the remaining sections of this chapter will tackle some of the possible lessons from the founding of the United States that may serve us well today. I will begin from where the previous chapter ended, by discussing the contemporary dangers of confounding party membership with partisanship and explaining why such theoretical *and* rhetorical confusion is inimical to the spirit of compromise. Since I claim that the change in understandings of the self, nurtured by the digital revolution, is at least partially responsible for the worrisome loss of trust in parties and in the formalized channels of political representation, I shall return to the Puritan purged individualism in order to see what we may, politically speaking, expect from this change. I shall conclude with some considerations about the importance of rhetoric in shaping public opinion and, hopefully, in resuscitating the people's two bodies.

7.1 PARTIES WITHOUT PARTISANSHIP?

"It is chic to be anti-partisan today."[21] This observation rings even truer now than it did over a dozen years ago, and could have rung equally true some two

---

[19] Quoted in Lewis E. Lehrman (2008), *Lincoln at Peoria – The Turning Point: Getting Right with the Declaration of Independence* (Mechanicsburg: Stackpole Books), 12.

[20] Rodney O. Davis and Douglas L. Wilson, Eds. (2008), The Lincoln–Douglas Debates (Urbana and Chicago: The Knox College Lincoln Study Center and the University of Illinois Press), 20.

[21] Russell J. Dalton and Steven Waldon (2005), "Public Images of Political Parties: A Necessary Evil?" *West European Politics*, 28:5, 937.

centuries earlier. Not just declared Independents and civic activists but even quintessential party members claim to be anti-establishment. If there could possibly be any doubt about it, the overall negative apprehension of parties is well documented not only by dwindling numbers of party members but by other measures as well, all over the world.[22] We are living in what Nancy Rosenblum called the "post-party depression" era, a time when self-organized identity groups on both Left and Right seek new and allegedly more meaningful ways of political involvement.[23]

The stakes are high, since for decades the common knowledge has been that political parties are the backbone of liberal democracies. James Bryce's statement that "No one has shown how representative government could work without (parties)" remained largely undisputed for nearly a century.[24] Among other merits, parties are supposed to mediate between society and the state, distribute political information via shortcuts, mobilize and motivate citizens, nurture inclusiveness and responsibility, develop and implement policies, serve as watchdogs when in opposition, and foster meaningful political compromises, unlike other "anti-party parties" and populist movements. Given these purported benefits, the crisis of parties signals an urgent need to reconsider their role in contemporary liberal democracies as mounting empirical evidence points toward their decline in the electorate. By and large, "scholars have associated such seemingly contradictory trends as the disengagement of citizens from mass politics and the radicalization of citizens' political passions to the shortcomings of political parties."[25]

It is encouraging that in the last decade there has taken place a rapid development of the literature intended to address the preexisting gap between democratic theory and party studies, in a declared effort to find new theoretical bases for the appreciation of parties *and* of partisanship, two concepts that until recently were the "indisputably orphans of political philosophy."[26] Indeed, there is an entire philosophical tradition of ignoring (in the best case) or of deploring (most common) the existence of parties. Against this long-established tradition, the recent body of theoretical literature claims that parties *and*

---

[22] See, for example, Ingrid van Biezen, Peter Mair, and Thomas Poguntke (2012), "Going, going … gone? The Decline of Party Membership in Contemporary Europe," *European Journal of Political Research*, 51:1, 24–56; Lise Esther Herman (2017), "Democratic Partisanship: From Theoretical Ideal to Empirical Standard," *American Political Science Review*, 111:4, 738–754; Carlo Invernizzi-Accetti and Fabio Wolkenstein (2017), "The Crisis of Party Democracy: Cognitive Mobilization, and the Care for Making Parties More Deliberative," *American Political Science Review*, 111:1, 97–109; Peter Mair (2103), *Ruling the Void: The Hollowing of Western Democracy* (London: Verso); Susan Scarrow (2015), *Beyond Party Members: Changing Approaches to Partisan Mobilization* (Oxford: Oxford University Press).

[23] Nancy L. Rosenblum (2008), *On the Side of Angels: An Appreciation of Parties and Partisanship* (Princeton and Oxford: Princeton University Press), 13.

[24] James Bryce (1921), *Modern Democracies* (New York: Macmillan), 119.

[25] Herman, "Democratic Partisanship," 738. [26] Rosenblum, *On the Side of Angels*, 6.

partisanship are to be seen not just as necessary evils, but rather as positive goods, able to develop an "ethical partisanship," "inclusiveness, comprehensiveness, and disposition to compromise."[27]

Recently, these normative approaches have been sympathetically criticized for not being conceptualized "in such a way as to allow for political scientists to evaluate the democratic merits of real-world partisans."[28] Other criticisms of normative approaches range from providing "little empirical traction," being "formulated at a very high level of abstraction ('party at their best')," or disregarding that "all the empirical literature on political parties points in the direction of partisan *de*-alignment and *de*-mobilization."[29] Various remedies to this alleged disconnect of the normative from the empirical have been proposed, including making parties more deliberative and more democratic, as well as making them more ideologically cohesive.[30]

As I have alluded to in Chapter 6, the history of the first party systems in the United States teaches us that there is an alternative to these approaches, which is equally sympathetic to the effort to stimulate an appreciation of parties without disregarding empirical evidence. This alternative attacks one contemporary fundamental assumption that has so far gone largely unchallenged, namely that parties and partisanship are inseparable. Even when scholars observe that "a key to grasping party as an accusatory term, is revulsion to partisanship," and agree that "[t]he two are separable," they still believe that this decoupling is artificial. The separation is thought to be the result of "*contemporary* political thought where parties may be grudgingly accepted for instrumental reasons, but partisans ... are judged inferior to superior 'Independents.'"[31] The "basic fact" that "a pragmatic defense of parties does not necessarily entail an appreciation of party spirit" is seen as motivation for defending the latter.[32] In such accounts, the assimilation of *party membership* with *partisanship* is taken for granted, and the only alternative left is a more-or-less illusory "independence."

[27] Russell Muirhead (2006), "A Defense of Party Spirit," *Perspectives on Politics*, 4:4, 713–727; Russell Muirhead (2014), *The Promise of Party in a Polarized Age* (Cambridge, MA: Harvard University Press); David Ragazzoni (2018), "Political Compromise in Party Democracy: An Overlooked Puzzle in Kelsen's Democratic Theory" in Christian F. Rostball and Theresa Scavenius, eds., *Compromise and Disagreement in Contemporary Political Theory* (New York and London: Routledge); Rosenblum, *On the Side of Angels*; Jonathan White and Lea Ypi (2016), *The Meaning of Partisanship* (Oxford: Oxford University Press). For a somehow different approach to compromise by White and Ypi, see further.

[28] Herman, "Democratic Partisanship," 740.

[29] Invernizzi-Accetti and Wolkenstein, "The Crisis of Party Democracy," 98 (emphasis in the original).

[30] See, for example, Herman, "Democratic Partisanship," and Hans Noel (2014), *Political Ideologies and Political Parties in America* (New York: Cambridge University Press).

[31] Rosenblum, *On the Side of Angels*, 53 (emphasis added).

[32] Ragazzoni, "Political Compromise in Party Democracy," 99.

Yet, as we have seen in the previous chapter, far from being a *contemporary* approach, the appreciation of parties but *not* of partisanship – or of *party spirit*, as it used to be, more appropriately, called – enjoys a long and respectable tradition. Furthermore, I argue that the distinction between the two has had, and continues to have, both theoretical and practical importance. First, according to the classic understanding, it is precisely party spirit that threatens to metamorphose parties into dangerous factions, "against" not "of" the whole.[33] Thus, despite many recent claims to the contrary, partisanship, far from being conducive to compromise, is adverse to it, as the history of the American founding demonstrates with plenty of examples. It is a conclusion reached by contemporary empirical studies as well.[34] Second, the same history teaches us that the development of the first mass parties, despite increasing electoral franchise, came hand in hand with the explosion of identity and exclusionary politics fomented by populist rhetoric. As such, the shrinking party membership that is so concerning to many a contemporary scholar might prove to be a blessing in disguise. Last but not least, it is extremely unlikely that partisan de-alignment can be stopped by persuasive theoretical argumentation, or that the revulsion to partisanship can be reversed by well-intentioned academic fiat.

From this perspective, parties seem to be ahead of academia, by encouraging "multi-speed membership" and by redefining what it means to be an active and engaged partisan. They are "more interested in what their active supporters do than in whether or not they hold party membership."[35] After all, just as one may be a party member without being a partisan, one may also be a partisan without being a party member. For once, it appears that theory must catch up to the practical (and historical) distinction between party members and partisans. Considering all of the above, if one wants to make parties "chic again," one must sacrifice party spirit. One cannot save them both.

Beginning with Clinton Rossiter's claim – "No America without democracy, no democracy without politics, no parties without compromise and moderation" – there has been an entire tradition of equating parties with democracy and with a compromising spirit.[36] This might very well be true, but only, as history teaches us, if one restores the forgotten distinction between parties and partisanship. By 2013, the unwillingness to compromise in politics and the increased polarization of political life all around the world, and particularly in the United States, appeared worrisome enough for the American Political Science Association to create an impressive Task Force for analyzing and

---

[33] Rosenblum, *On the Side of Angels*; Ragazzoni, "Political Compromise in Party Democracy."

[34] See, for example, Jane Mansbridge and Cathie Jo Martin, eds. (2013), *Negotiating Agreement in Politics: APSA Task Force Report* (Washington, DC: American Political Science Association).

[35] Scarrow, *Beyond Party Members*, 206.

[36] Clinton Rossiter (1964), *Parties and Politics in America* (Ithaca and London: Cornell University Press), 1.

interpreting the phenomenon.[37] The results were rather unanimous, pointing to the rise of excessive partisanship, deep ideological divisions, and electoral and partisan politics that would "lead members to reject compromise that would be acceptable if public policy were the only consideration."[38] To summarize, the overall conclusion was not that parties in themselves are responsible for these worrisome developments, but that the rise of partisanship is.

Equally aware of these dangers, and trying to remove the stigma that has come to be associated with parties, theorists largely concede that "the high point of antipartyism today is aversion to partisanship specifically," and even acknowledge that "antipartisanship is a distinct theme in the tradition of antipartyism."[39] Some go so far as to accept that partisanship not only increases polarization but is actually capable of creating new poles of passionate disagreements. "Party spirit," observes Muirhead, "does not merely reflect divisions already there; it can create divisions."[40] At the same time, theorists are so persuaded by the assumption that parties and partisanship are inherently tied together that they try various ways of circumventing the host of problems brought forward by partisanship.

The main strategy is to differentiate between two forms of partisanship: "high" (or even "light") and "low,"[41] "ethical" and "extremist,"[42] or "normal" and "pathological."[43] The first types would be beneficial and conducive to meaningful compromises, while the latter would be rightfully condemned as detrimental to the political fabric of any society. In other words, "partisans *should* express allegiance to a supra-partisan idea of the political community, which includes all social groups and political identities, yet transcend them."[44] Put simply, what theorists paradoxically require from "ideal partisans" is that they overcome their much-praised partisanship, or even that they "give up admirably qualities of thought and character, [as long as] ordinary citizens and knowledgeable elites benefit." This amounts to saying that partisans "are worthy in themselves" insofar as they unconsciously sacrifice their personal independence of mind and even morality.[45]

As acknowledged by even the most sympathetic critics, the main problem with these approaches is that they largely ignore how partisanship *really is*, focusing almost exclusively on how it *should be*. Russell Muirhead is right to prefer "the eighteenth-century phrase 'party spirit' to the social-scientific 'partisanship.' Partisanship is not a dispassionate 'identification' [. . .]; it is

---

[37] Mansbridge and Martin, *Negotiating Agreement*.

[38] Sarah Binder and Frances Lee (2013), "Making Deals in Congress," in Mansbridge and Martin, *Negotiating Agreement*, 67. See also Michael Barber and Nolan McCarthy (2013), "Causes and Consequences of Polarization," in Mansbridge and Martin, *Negotiating Agreement*, 19–53.

[39] Rosenblum, *On the Side of Angels*, 15, 55.   [40] Muirhead, *The Promise of Party*, 3.

[41] Muirhead, *The Promise of Party*.   [42] Rosenblum, *On the Side of Angels*.

[43] White and Ypi, *The Meaning of Partisanship*.

[44] Herman, "Democratic Partisanship," 744 (emphasis added).

[45] Rosenblum, *On the Side of Angels*, 101.

spirited or prideful"; yet he too fails to acknowledge that this affective component is precisely what made it suspicious in the eyes of the first defenders of parties.[46] For them, this was an affection misplaced. Although some of the criticized scholars acknowledge this shortcoming to a certain extent, others embrace it unconditionally. "Rather than adapt the ideal to better fit the practice, our aim should be to improve our understanding of the ideal ... so that can it better act as a critical yardstick."[47] Such an unwavering commitment to partisanship as a "civic ideal," when all the empirical evidence points to the contrary, is also manifest in the constant tendency to read through contemporary lenses the classic assessments of the distinction between parties and party spirit made long ago.

As we know by now, few if any of the founders, from Washington and Madison to Collamer and Clay, denied the existence – or the necessity – of parties. But most, if not all, of them were just as quick to condemn the spirit of partisanship. These founding figures argued, each in their own way, that even the most loyal party members ought to tune their actions and requests with an eye on the common good and on the building of bridges between majorities and minorities via long-lasting political compromises. Luckily for them, the debates in the Constitutional Convention, and even more so those surrounding the ratification process, firmly planted in the American psyche the idea that the Constitution was a praiseworthy compromise. For decades to follow, politicians and civic educators alike worked diligently to reinforce the idea that the Union would not have been possible – and could not be maintained – absent this spirt of compromise inimical to party spirit. Sometimes, as previously mentioned, the attacks on party spirit amounted to brilliant rhetoric: party spirit "crawls and creeps, and fawns, and leers, and whines around the multitude, and only asks to lick the sores of the body politic, and feed upon the crumbs that fall from its table."[48]

It seems that today's defenders of party spirit forgot what during the eighteenth century most actors displayed an awareness of – that a partisan identity, by definition, cannot be conducive to the reinforcement of "the chords of affection" that values the community of citizens above any other identifications. White and Ypi's request that *partisans* address the political community *as a whole* remains a theoretical impossibility, consistently refuted by practice. As long as partisanship is understood as "the array of practices *and discourses* attached to *party identification,* membership, or leadership in support of a shared conception of the public good,"[49] little advance can be made in reviving much-needed political compromises, both for parties "in government" and for parties "in the electorate." Rhetoric matters. One has to accept the obvious –

---

[46] Muirhead, *The Promise of Party,* x.   [47] White and Ypi, *The Meaning of Partisanship,* 25.

[48] Anonymous, *Niles' National Register,* July 29, 1843.

[49] Herman, "Democratic Partisanship," 741 (emphasis added).

"pluralist partisans" are not, properly speaking, partisans, and "bipartisan-ship" is not partisanship.[50]

Even if *mass political parties* are about to become a thing of the past, *mass politics* is not. Old identities are replaced by new ones, more fluctuating and yet, precisely because of that, more aggressively defended – much like during the American founding, when populist movements started to coalesce around a variety of scapegoats, from immigrants to Masons, from Catholics to abolition-ists. Of course, one could argue that the lessons from nineteenth-century America do not apply to America of the twenty-first. After all, the risks of disunion that were frequently associated with the dangers of the party spirit were put to rest after the Civil War. One may also argue that political science has evolved since then, or simply that all of the people mentioned above were merely employing empty rhetoric when distinguishing between parties and party spirit – a rhetoric tinted with a touch of hypocrisy.

Still, to the first observation, one could reply that if the Union is no longer in any present danger, the extreme polarization of American society remains a real threat. "The most common diagnoses of Washington's ailments center on the emergence of excessive partisanship and deep ideological divisions among political elites and office holders."[51] Not only that, but "the polarization of political parties in the United States Congress has been associated on the one hand with the growing citizen disengagement and on the other with a similar polarization of the American electorate along partisan lines."[52] Movements of political mobilization outside of party politics, from Occupy to self-organized identity groups of all flavors, tend to radicalize their discourses rapidly, com-peting with the polarization of political parties. Such extreme polarization might threaten the very fabric of society, and ought to be seriously considered.

To the second observation, one might simply reply that if the lessons of the past are inherently outdated, there is no point in wasting time discussing either the first political party systems or the pioneers of party theory. Yet the most recent attempts to make "existing theories of partisanship ... comprehensive for political scientists to empirically evaluate the democratic merits of partisan discourses and practices on their basis" insist on taking into account "both philosophical principles and historical insight."[53] If so, then understanding what this history has to teach us, with as little contemporary bias as possible, is crucial for the success of the enterprise.

Finally, even if one accepts the possibility that the declared anti-partisanship of so many seasoned politicians and civic educators throughout the latter part of the eighteenth and the bulk of the nineteenth centuries was more or less hypocritical rhetoric, one cannot discard the real impact that such rhetoric had

---

[50] Barber and McCarthy, "Causes and Consequences of Polarization"; Herman, "Democratic Partisanship."

[51] Barber and McCarthy, "Causes and Consequences of Polarization," 19.

[52] Herman, "Democratic Partisanship," 738.   [53] Ibid., 738, 740.

on the general public. One cannot ignore how this rhetoric, then as now, could change both electoral dynamics and parties' behavior in the legislative. Considering the entire history of political philosophy, political theorists should be at the forefront of this battle over words, since they acknowledge that, "The site of political conflict is ... the discursive field as a whole, including its vocabulary, its sedimented meanings, and indeed its silences, as much as consciously articulated views."[54] Ironically, as the state of the discipline now stands, theorists either refuse to grant normative merits to parties or try to praise both parties and partisanship, misreading the lessons of the past.

In itself, however, the distinction between parties and partisanship is not enough to explain why the attempt to normatively salvage both parties *and* partisanship is not only prone to failure but also dangerous for the very practical goal of reviving the practice of meaningful political compromises. If the normative is not to be too far removed from reality, as discussed in the Introduction, one has to take into consideration the empirical evidence. The fact that secrecy in negotiations plays a crucial role in the ability of political actors to reach compromise was largely accepted – and became a requirement – from negotiating the Articles of Confederation to the Philadelphia Convention and all of the first state constitutions (Chapters 4 and 5). Once this requirement was dropped, under populist demands for transparency, the debates became not just public but also publicized, oftentimes at the expense of the interested actors. As a result, the rhetoric inflamed, party spirit crept in, and compromises became highly unlikely.

The same applies today, when both politicians and political scientists (yet not the majority of political theorists) agree that "allowing negotiations to take place in private settings encourages pondering rather than posturing," thus facilitating the "search for fair compromise."[55] It is an indirect indictment of partisanship, yet not of parties, nor of politicians. When removed from the sight of their electorates, politicians are less affected by party spirit. Following in the footsteps of Anthony Downs and Joseph A. Schlesinger, John H. Aldrich claims that politicians, in effect, are nothing but rational actors, willing to compromise as long as it serves their interests.[56] Nevertheless, this is precisely what makes them untrustworthy in the eyes of the general public, furthering the negative image of parties and politicians.

As repeatedly illustrated, meaningful compromises presuppose, besides a contractarian, rational-bargaining side, an affective component of mutuality and self-sacrifice. It was this latter component that was consciously and carefully cultivated during the founding era by responsible politicians and civic educators. It fostered praise among the general public for the virtue of

---

[54] White and Ypi, *The Meaning of Partisanship*, 66.
[55] Cathie Jo Martin (2013), "Negotiating Political Agreements," in Mansbridge and Martin, *Negotiating Agreement in Politics*, 2.
[56] John H. Aldrich (2011), *Why Parties? A Second Look* (Chicago: Chicago University Press).

political compromises transcending party spirit and promoting a vision of political unity and public good, going beyond the majority vs. minority dichotomy. The case is entirely different today. Many scholars have noticed that the increased erosion of trust in parties is accompanied by a rise of identity politics or what is called "the politics of difference." This development is far from being conducive to political compromises precisely because it involves nonnegotiable identities.[57] It is a fertile ground for the concerning growth of the new partisanship without parties. "The new information technology makes it easier than ever to conjure up an *esprit de parti* out of almost nothing, simply by allowing immediate responses to present events to cascade through the system."[58]

Realistically speaking, the problem of electoral identity remains the main challenge that parties have to face nowadays. As Richard S. Katz noticed a few years ago, the principal-agents models that so far have dominated the empirical studies of political parties are no longer relevant, since there is no longer a unified "principal," i.e., electorate. "Parties in office" are supposed to be the "agents" of the electorate; however, this electorate is characterized by deep identity fragmentation, both at the collective and individual levels.[59] What the first generations of American statesmen knew instinctively is also confirmed by recent studies in political psychology:

All social identity theories share the recognition that individuals can – and usually do – derive their identities from more than one social group ... [and] managing multiple identities is something like an intellectual juggling act. [...] In a large, pluralistic society ... multiple crisscrossing social identities can become a source of increasing fractionalism or enhanced social stability, *depending on how competing identities are managed.*[60]

Thus, the problem is one of properly managing various identities, including political ones. Party identity, or the ideologically distinctive identity of a party, is one thing. Partisanship, understood as personal and passionate identification with a party, is another. On the one hand, parties are necessary and beneficial for a representative democracy, for they propose competing grand visions of the common good. Qua individuals, on the other hand, we are not defined by any single identity, and the all-encompassing one, from a political perspective, should be the political community of citizens. Inside this community, multiple identities are not only possible but also unavoidable. One can be, for example,

---

[57] Invernizzi-Accetti and Wolkenstein, "The Crisis of Party Democracy"; Mark Lilla (2017), *The Once and Future Liberal: After Identity Politics* (New York: HarperCollins); Rosenblum, *On the Side of Angels.*

[58] David Runciman (2010), "The Paradox of Immediacy," *Political Theory* 38:1, 154.

[59] Richard S. Katz (2014), "No Man Can Serve Two Masters: Party Politicians, Party Members, Citizens, and Principal-Agents Models of Democracy," *Party Politics*, 20:2, 183.

[60] Marilynn B. Brewer (2001), "The Many Faces of Social Identity: Implications for Political Psychology," *Political Psychology*, 22:1, 121, 123 (emphasis added).

an American and a member of a religious community, an American and gay, an American and Latino, or a combination thereof; one may favor the Republican Party on some issues and the Democratic Party on others, voting a Republican for sheriff and a Democrat for the board of education, etc. Since each of us has more than one identity, no single party or politician can properly represent all of them.

So far, "parties as organizations" have only *re*acted to these new developments, addressing the crisis of "parties in the electorate" by encouraging "multi-speed membership," and by redefining what it means to be an active and engaged partisan. Unfortunately, by doing so, parties and ambitious politicians are succumbing to the lead of their fragmented electorates, falling prey to the *new partisanships*, thus nurturing more radical divisions inside of the political community. "The predicted consequences of polarization in this environment [of divided government with cohesive partisanship] are not benign. Increased policy differences shrink the set of compromises that both parties are willing to entertain."[61]

I advance as a working hypothesis the possibility that the reason for increased polarization, and the resulting unwillingness to compromise, might be found in the rapid *identity fragmentation* brought forward primarily (although not exclusively) by the digital revolution. These developments have changed not only "the technology of politics" but also the understanding of political and self-representation.[62] Only apparently paradoxical, it is precisely on this point that the Puritan experience might provide some valuable clues.

7.2 PURGED INDIVIDUALISM AND FACEBOOK[63]

As we have seen, two main features set the American Puritans' experience apart: their purged individualism and their bidimensional covenant. Although both stem from the same source, namely their peculiar theology, and both informed each other, the survival of one did not depend on the survival of the other. Their purged individualism all but disappeared long before the First Great Awakening, yet the bidimensional covenant and the paradigm of the people's two bodies associated with it became an enduring staple of the American founding. It is a lesson worth remembering whenever one attempts to gauge the impact of the digital revolution on political and self-representation.

---

[61] Barber and McCarthy, "Causes and Consequences of Polarization," 37.
[62] See, for example, Aldrich, *Why Parties?*, 6; Dalton and Waldon, "Public Images of Political Parties," 11–12.
[63] In the pages to follow I use "Facebook" as a shortcut for all the new social media, from Instagram to Twitter to Snapchat and beyond. This section is partially informed by Alin Fumurescu (2018), "The Role of Political and Self Representation in Compromise," in Christian Rostboll and Theresa Scavenius, eds., *Compromise and Disagreement in Contemporary Political Theory* (New York: Routledge), 179–194.

As previously discussed, modernity began in Europe by splitting the medieval dialectic of the self between *forum internum* and *forum externum*, in a centripetal and a centrifugal form of individualism, the former focusing on *forum internum*, the latter on *forum externum*.[64] Thus, the bidimensional individual was forgotten, being replaced by the one-dimensional, either liberal or communitarian, man. By and large, the liberal individual came to define modernity, at least in the Western world. Thus, the idea of a "Western self" has had a long-established tradition and, according to some neurophysiological experiments, even has a neural basis. Neuroimaging the medial prefrontal cortex (MFPC) shows distinct types of self-representation between the Western *independent* self and the Asian *interdependent* self, "providing evidence that culture shapes the functional anatomy of self-representation."[65] The so-called liberal self is described as self-centered, self-constructed, autonomous, and one-dimensional. It has been presented as a modern evolution from the classical, embedded self of medieval times, in which – or so the argument goes – the person was defined solely in terms of the community/communities to which s/he belonged, as in other, more traditional cultures.

The much-praised liberal self was rather quickly found lacking, first from a philosophical perspective and later from a political one as well.[66] The idea that one cannot have a "healthy" political life based solely on a liberal, self-centered self has been argued from a wide variety of perspectives.[67] The generally accepted argument is that an active and informed citizen is one with a strong sense of belonging to a certain political community, involved in an open and honest dialogue with others, regardless of how one defines "otherness."

Unfortunately for some, the digital revolution appears to only exacerbate the popularity of the (neo)liberal self – the "one that uses market rationality to manage its self as though the self was a business that attempts to balance risks and responsibility appropriately in its alliances with other selves/business."[68] The new social media, according to this view, encourage quantity over quality – hits, posts, followers, "friends," or "connections" (usually, these numbers are

---

[64] See Fumurescu, *Compromise*, especially chapters 4–6; Fumurescu, "The Role of Political"; Chapters 1 and 2 of this volume.

[65] Yiing Zhu, Li Zhang, Jin Fan, and Shihui Han (2007), "Neural Basis of Cultural Influence on Self-Representation," *Neuroimage*, 34, 1310.

[66] It is worth noticing that both totalitarian and uncompromising movements that plagued the twentieth century, namely Fascism and Nazism on the one hand and Communism on the other, emphasized the community over the individual. The "communitarian" self replaced for a while the "liberal" self, yet preserved intact the one-dimensional perspective.

[67] See, for example, Hans-Georg Gadamer (1989), *Truth and Method*, tr. and rev. J. Weinsheimer and D.G. Marshall (New York: Continuum); Jürgen Habermas (1984), *The Theory of Communicative Action*, tr. Thomas McCarthy (Boston: Beacon Press); Charles Taylor (1989), *Sources of the Self: The Making of Modern Identity* (Cambridge, MA: Harvard University Press).

[68] Ilana Gershon (2011), "Unfriend My Heart: Facebook, Promiscuity, and Heartbreak in a Neoliberal Age," *Anthropological Quarterly* 84:4, 866.

public and extremely visible). "[T]he number of friends one has on Facebook-
. . ., the number of page-hits one gets on one's blog, and the number of videos
featured on one's YouTube channel are the key markers of success . . . and
details such as duration, depth of commitment . . . become the boring preoccupations of baby-boomers stuck in the past."[69]

In an effort to preserve the uniqueness of the self in such an atomized society,
selective self-presentation in digital media is meant to enhance self-esteem,
supporting the Hyperpersonal Model from computer mediating communication (CMC).[70] As a result, some authors argue that the younger generation is
more selfish and less collectively minded than previous generations are, but
also that it prefers compromise to confrontation – most as the early-modern
Englishmen had.[71] Not surprising for these exhibitionist selves, the photog-
rapher has taken center stage. The former family album has now become more
of an individual album of selfies.[72] This thirst for a unique self also helps
explain why people are more willing than ever to disclose their personal lives
to other Little Brothers, in search of self-confirmation, as long as they do not
feel their privacy encroached on by a nefarious Big Brother.[73]

By now, one should realize that, despite many claims to contrary, this mass
phenomenon of voluntary disclosure of one's most private moments and
thoughts is not unprecedented. It was what the Puritans did during their
conversion narratives, relations, or "admission tests," as they were more frequently called. As one recalls from Chapter 2, a detailed description of what
went through the soul of the aspirant in the preconversion preparation for grace
needed to be authenticated by "the saints." Furthermore, absent a superior
authority to serve as judge, the selection of the "pillars of the church" had to
rely on reciprocal scrutiny and detailed interrogations. Big Brother was
replaced by many smaller ones.

Nothing might seem more different than the Puritans' mindset and the
mindset of millennials or of Generation X. The former wanted their infested
souls – these "varnisht pot[s] of putrid excrements" – to be purged by rooting

[69] Jodi Dean (2009), *Democracy and Other Neoliberal Fantasies: Communicative Capitalism and Left Politics* (Durham: Duke University Press), 17.

[70] Amy L. Gonzales and Jeffrey T. Hancock (2011), "Mirror, Mirror on My Facebook Wall: Effects of Exposure to Facebook on Self-Esteem," *Cyberpsychology, Behavior and Social Networking*, 14:1–2, 79–83.

[71] Elizabeth J. Westlake (2008) "Friend Me If You Facebook: Generation Y and Performative Surveillance," *TDR, The Drama Review*, 52:4, 23 published by The MIT Press, 37.

[72] See, for example, Ori Schwarz (2010), "On Friendship, Boobs and the Logic of the Catalogue: Online Self-Portraits as a Means for the Exchange of Capital," *Convergence*, 16:2, 163–183; Zizi Papacharissi (2002), "The Self Online: The Utility of Personal Home Pages," *Journal of Broadcasting and Electronic Media*, 46:3, 346–368.

[73] Catalina L. Toma and Jeffrey T. Hancock (2013), "Self-Affirmation Underlies Facebook Use," *Personality and Social Psychology Bulletin*, 39:3, 322.

out "the Devils poison and venome or infection of Self."[74] Only by effectively transforming one's *forum internum* into one's *forum externum* could one hope to be saved by grace. The latter want only to affirm their uniqueness in an atomized world, and to be confirmed as "authentic" by as many people as possible, regardless of whether this authenticity is contrived or not. Despite these differences in outlook, the same rationale pushes them to externalize the inner self (or the pretense of it) for everyone to see and judge – the need of group confirmation.

As seen in Chapter 2, for the Puritans, the turning of the inside self out meant that both the characteristics of *forum externum* (i.e., sameness and conformity) and the ones of *forum internum* (i.e., uniqueness and authenticity) had to be revealed in the process. Unsurprisingly, then, the relatively few confessions whose documentation has survived reveal that these narratives had to meet a double standard. On the one hand, they had to respect a certain structure, touch on certain points, and were oftentimes rehearsed before being actually delivered, "coached by the ministers and vetted by senior saints."[75] On the other hand, they had to come across as "unique" and "authentic," and the best way to do so was by being emotionally persuasive. Nowadays too, the selves seem also to be swinging between conformity ("if you are not on Instagram, Twitter, Snapchat, and the like, you do not exist") and a cry for authenticity via intimate disclosures.

However, more cynical analysts consider that, far for "improving the self," this type of approach is nothing but a desperate call for attention to one's uniqueness that will end up falling on deaf ears, since everybody is calling but no one is actually listening. Because of this new form of purged individualism, Samuelson, for example, called the internet the ExhibitioNet. "Everything about these [social network] sites is a scream for attention. Look at me. Listen to me. Laugh with me – or at me ... People can now lead lives of noisy and ostentatious desperation."[76]

Such studies notwithstanding, there are scholars who interpret both the symptomatology and the diagnosis in radically different ways. For them, the digital revolution was able to directly address the problems of the neoliberal self, by increasing open communication and by renewing the sense of belonging. For some, this revolution has been a quick fix for citizens' disenchantment, by mobilizing previously passive segments of the citizenry and by helping them "bloom into both active and capable citizens."[77] Wright, for

---

[74] Quoted in Bercovitch, *The Puritan Origins*, 16, 18.

[75] Michael McGiffert, ed. [1972] (1994), *God's Plot: Puritan Spirituality in Thomas Shepard's Cambridge* (Amherst: University of Massachusetts Press), 137.

[76] Robert J. Samuelson (2006), "A Web of Exhibitionists," *The Washington Post*, September 20, A 25.

[77] Henrik S. Christensen and Asa Bengtsson (2011), "The Political Competence of Internet Participants," *Information, Communication & Society*, 14:6, 897.

example, is convinced that we are witnessing nothing short of a genuine revolution in the democratic process and in the civil sphere, and that "politics as usual" died the moment the classical hegemonic media of from-one-to-many was replaced by the fundamentally democratic new media of from-many-to-many.[78]

There is still a lot of enthusiasm left about the new venues opened by the digital revolution, especially when it comes to the youngest demographics, the so-called millennials. It is claimed that, "contrary to the prevailing attitudes of Baby Boomers and Generation X-ers that Generation Y is somehow socially and politically disengaged because of technology, the opposite is true."[79] There is "an unmistakable expansion of youth interest in politics and public affairs."[80] For these scholars, the increased use of social media such as Facebook and Twitter has strategic and political implications and has led to new patterns of protest for the youth, in which virtual and actual movements intersect.[81] When one chooses to belong to (or to withdraw from) a certain online community, one reveals something about where one considers oneself to belong as peer, as equal. From this perspective, an online community fills the social role played at other times by pubs and coffeeshops – a "third place," situated between the privacy of the home (first place) and of the workplace (second place) in which hierarchy and discipline dominate relationships: here, on the contrary, are regulars who know each other, feel that they are accepted as equals, and can freely speak their mind.[82]

Notwithstanding, numerous findings show that social media in itself appears unable to sustain long-term commitments, for communities organized online lack long-term identities.[83] They are dissatisfied with political representation as it stands but don't know what to replace it with, and "smart mobs" can organize only ephemeral movements of protest.[84] Despite some indisputable and palpable successes of "hashtag activism," "the thorny question ... remains

[78] Scott Wright (2012), "Politics as Usual? Revolution, Normalization and a New Agenda for Online Deliberation," *New Media and Society*, 14:2, 245.

[79] Westlake, "Friend Me If You Facebook," 23.

[80] Thomas H. Sander and Robert D. Putnam (2010), "Still Bowling Alone? The Post-9/11 Split," *Journal of Democracy*, 21: 9–16, 11.

[81] Jeffrey S. Jurris (2012), "Reflections on #Occupy Everywhere: Social Media, Public Space, and Emerging Logics of Aggregation," *American Ethnologist*, 39:2, 260.

[82] Constance Steinkuehler and Dmitri Williams (2006), "Where Everybody Knows Your (Screen) Name: Online Games as 'Third Places'," *Journal of Computer-Mediated Communications*, 11:4, 885–909.

[83] Lance W. Bennett, Christian Breunig, and Terri Givens (2008), "Communication and Political Mobilization: Digital Media and the Organization of Anti-Iraq War Demonstrations in the US," *Political Communication*, 25, 269–289.

[84] Howard Rheingold (2003), *Smart Mobs: The Next Social Revolution* (New York: Basic Books).

of whether social networking can result in long-term meaningful engagement."[85] Furthermore, a closer look reveals some important differences between the classical *universitates* and these online communities. First, by emphasizing the sameness of its members, the contemporary neo-communitarian self tends to overlook or minimize the uniqueness of each individual, still manifest in the medieval and the Puritan self, thanks to the idea of a unique "calling." Second, the assumption of equality inside of the group is nowhere to be found either in the medieval or in the Puritan understanding, once the community is actually formed. According to the latter, each member is a distinct and unique (even irreplaceable) member, precisely because each fulfills a unique role in an organic hierarchy.

As in the case of the Puritans, this emphasis on group identity tends to come at the expense of other, larger and more encompassing identities. From this perspective, this attitude shares with centripetal individualism the same fear of compromise, perceived in this case as a threat to the identity of individual *qua* member of a group. In many cases, such identitarian communities tend to shrink and radicalize instead of expanding and becoming more tolerant. Thus, when it comes to political compromise, social media appears to be, like Puritanism, a double-edged sword. On the one hand, it helps individuals engage in acts of identity disclosure and voluntary construction, encouraging in-group compromises. On the other hand, it promotes group conformity and ideological "Balkanization" as it pushes individuals toward more extreme positions in online rather than face-to-face interactions.[86]

It appears that the cyberworld simultaneously creates conditions for praising "otherness" and provides means to hate "the other" as the enemy with which no compromise is possible. Perhaps unsurprisingly, "post-truth" was nominated as "the word of the year 2016" by *Oxford English Dictionary*. The term describes "circumstances in which objective facts are less influential in shaping public opinion than appeals to emotion and personal belief," and is being often associated with politics and the new media.[87] As recent psychological studies have revealed, "although individuals lack introspective access to reasons for their opinion, they do reliable have a visceral perception (a metacognition) that certain opinions are a matter of right and wrong," and thus not subject to compromises.[88]

---

[85] Johanna Herman (2014), "Hashtags and Human Rights – Activism in the Age of Twitter." *Carnegie Council for Ethics in International Affairs*, www.carnegiecouncil.org/publications/ethics_online/0099

[86] Kathleen H. Jamieson and Joseph N. Capella (2008), *Echo Chamber: Rush Limbaugh and the Conservative Media Establishment* (New York: Oxford University Press).

[87] *Oxford Dictionaries* traced its first use to a 1992 essay by late Serbian-American playwright Steve Tesich in *The Nation* magazine about the Iran-Contra scandal and the Gulf War. "We, as a free people, have freely decided that we want to live in some post-truth world," Tesich wrote.

[88] Ryan, "No Compromise," 4.

Employing the Puritan purged individualism, one may understand why scholars looking at the same evidence when trying to assess the impact of the digital revolution come to conclusions as radically opposed as the neoliberal and the neo-communitarian selves, either self-constructed or prey to manipulation. One has to remember that, like contemporary individualism, the Puritans, too, have come to be interpreted either as "proto-liberals" or as "medieval communitarians" – and for cause: both features were present in the Puritan *Weltanschauung*, thanks to their bidimensional covenant and the associated paradigm of the people's two bodies. But one also has to remember that if the bidimensional covenant proved an enduring legacy, it was precisely for its ability to practically combine the two understandings of the people and of political representation – *qua* collection of equal individuals, and *qua* corporation structured by a hierarchy of merit. Having one without the other comes with a price.

One may say that the Puritans were able to politically put in practice the medieval dialectic of the individual to such an extent as medieval men could hardly have imagined. However, what they, like all their early modern contemporaries, were not able to do was to preserve the subtle balance between *forum internum* and *forum externum*. Although the purged individualism was different from both the centripetal and the centrifugal one, it remained one-sided and thus victim to all the shortcomings of the one-dimensional man.[89] In effect, as we have seen, far from being an advantage, purged individualism proved to be a liability, for by making the Puritans unwilling to compromise their religious identity it contributed decisively to the rapid fragmentation of the movement and its eventual demise.

It is a lesson to be remembered when trying to understand the political consequences of contemporary representations of the self. Once the paradigm of the people's two bodies begins to be forgotten, as it was during the Great Awakening, certain developments are bound to take place – and they have. First, as in the case of the enthusiasts denying the authority of the Old Lights, accusing them of hypocrisy for caring more about the "dead bark" than about the living soul,[90] people nowadays have begun to lose trust in parties and in "the establishment," feeling that they are not properly represented. Thus, they have begun to "shop" for alternatives that will acknowledge and encourage their subjectivity. Second, the horizontal understanding of the people at the expense of the vertical, corporatist one is accompanied, then as now, by a refusal of "elitism" and by calls to direct democracy. Last but not least, this "shopping for authenticity" is prone to encourage the explosion of various forms of identity politics, unwilling to compromise with "the others." If history

---

[89] See Fumurescu, *Compromise*, chapter 9 – "Compromising the Art of Compromise: The One-Dimensional Man."

[90] Uriam Oakes (1673), *New England Pleaded with ...*, quoted in Miler and Johnson, *The Puritans*, 71.

can teach us anything is that at some point this fragmentation becomes unbearable, and compromises between camps become unavoidable, like the ones between the Old and the New Lights, which in turn will fuel new frustrations and accusations of hypocrisy.

The appeal of the dialogical self theory (DST) in recent years can be understood in this context, despite – or precisely because of – not being a unified, grand theory, but rather a collection of quite different strains. Its main claim broadly construed can be formulated as follows: the self is the result of an ongoing dialogue taking place both inside and outside the individual, between the individual and others. "In this process of positioning, repositioning and counterpositioning, the I fluctuates among different and even opposed positions (both within the self and between self and perceived or imagined others)."[91] Not surprising, DST is considered by many to be the most suitable theory to address contemporary challenges, since "the processes of globalization and localization are not just realities outside the individual but are rather incorporated as a constituent of a dialogical self in action."[92]

However, not everyone is so optimistic. Hevern, for example, argues that while the internet alters the personal and social experience of Cartesian space and time, and hence the self, it may either foster or undermine dialogical exchange and even facilitate the expression of extreme forms of monologicality.[93] "These phenomena can be represented by a hybridizied form of the strategies used by the postmodern self in confronting uncertainty; namely, a multiplication of positions functioning in relative autonomy and the simultaneous sharpening of position boundaries *within the self* rather than between the self and others."[94] Put differently, our selves are presented with the alternative of either opening to otherness or relishing in the echo chambers of their choice. Unfortunately, it appears that the latter path is easier than the former.

In this postmodern understanding of the self, like in the case of purged individualism, the boundaries between *forum externum* and *forum internum* vanish. "[O]ur external identity and internal sense of self are imaginary constructs or working hypotheses subject to constant reform."[95] Then, the self-construction online is also a co-construction and reverberates into the self-construction offline, just as virtual, online communities can become actual communities. Still, one could wonder to what extent this ever-changing, rootless self is able to perform in real life as well as it does on paper, let alone

---

[91] Hubert J. M. Hermans and Thorsten Giersen (2012), "Introduction" in Hubert J. M. Hermans and Thorsten Giersen, eds., *Handbook of Dialogical Self Theory* (Cambridge: Cambridge University Press), 2.

[92] Ibid., 5.

[93] Vincent H. Hevern (2012), "Dialogicality and the Internet" in Hermans and Giersen, *Handbook of Dialogical Self Theory*, 188.

[94] Ibid., 195 (emphasis in the original).

[95] Russell W. Belk (2013), "Extended Self in a Digital World," *Journal of Consumer Research*, 40:3, 479.

how a strategy to address the contemporary challenges that political representation is facing nowadays can be devised starting from such premises. Despite his depiction in broad strokes, Mark Lilla's diagnosis deserves a somewhat lengthy quotation:

If [a young student] accepts the all-American idea that her unique identity is something she gets to construct and change as the fancy strikes her, she can hardly be expected to have an enduring political attachment to others, and certainly cannot be expected to hear the call of duty toward them. Instead she will find herself in the hold of what might be called the Facebook model of identity: the self as a homepage I construct like a personal brand, linked to other through associations I can "like" and "unlike" at will. [...] I can even self-identify with a group I don't objectively seem to belong to. [...] If all identification is legitimately self-identification, there is no reason why this woman could not claim to be anything she imagined herself to be. And to drop that identification the moment it became too burdensome, or just a bore. Whatever.[96]

The stakes are high, for – as we have seen in the case of the Puritans – being insecure about one's identity, *qua* individual or *qua* community, has the paradoxical effect of fostering an overly protective attitude toward one's perceived identity and refusing all compromise with "the other," regardless of how one choses to define otherness. "As soon as you cast an issue exclusively in terms of identity you invite your adversary to do the same."[97] In the words of Mark Lilla, this quest for "authenticity" is the appanage of "political romanticism."

Its names are legion: authenticity, transparency, spontaneity, wholeness, liberation. That the world be as one. And when the world politely declines this request, the romantic is left torn between opposed impulses. There is the impulse to flee so as to remain an authentic, autonomous self; and there is the impulse to transform society so that it seems like an extension of the self. The romantic wants to create a world where he or she will possess a fully integrated, unconflicted integrity—where the answers to the questions *Who am I? What are we?* are exactly the same.[98]

So, what can be done under these circumstances? I suggest that in order to restore the health of our liberal democracies, the battles to come will be, once again, battles over political and self-representation. Implicitly, there will be battles over shaping what Abraham Lincoln labeled "public sentiment." Let us remember: "Public sentiment is everything. With it, nothing can fail; against it, nothing can succeed. Whoever, molds public sentiment goes deeper than he who acts statutes, or pronounce judicial decisions."[99] Thus, there will be battles over meanings. Thus, there will be battles over words – rhetorical battles.

---

[96] Mark Lilla (2017), *The Once and Future Liberal: After Identity Politics* (New York: Harper Collins), 87–88.

[97] Ibid., 129.   [98] Ibid., 71–72.

[99] Abraham Lincoln (2008), *The Lincoln–Douglas Debates*, Eds. Rodney E. Davis and Douglas L. Wilson (Urbana and Chicago: The Knox College Lincoln Center and the University of Illinois Press), 32.

7.3 "WE, THE PEOPLE ..."

> [John] Adams ... complained that the scientific language of politics was being
> "employed like paper money, to cheat the Widow and the fatherless and every
> honest man."[100] [...] But just as paper was destined to become the currency of the
> United States, so words like "democracy" and "republic" could not be preserved
> from the inevitable human tendency to inflate the value of anything that has a
> surface appeal.[101]

Even more so for the word "people," one might add, in a democracy in which
the people are supposed to be sovereign. As we have seen throughout the book,
words do change meanings over time, and the process can go both ways – from
negative to positive or the other way around. Sometimes it takes centuries, as in
the case of "compromise," which was used as a neutral method of arbitration
or election throughout the entire Middle Ages, only to split its meaning into a
positive and a negative one at the beginning of modernity. Other times, the
change took only a few decades, as in the case of Puritans, who were able to
embrace and transform in their favor a pejorative label; or even mere months,
as in the case of "republicanism," which from a negative term in 1775 became a
positive one in 1776, all the while acquiring anti-monarchical undertones.
In the decades following the Declaration of Independence, it was the turn of
"democracy" and "natural aristocracy" to slowly but surely switch places in
the public sentiment.

The case of "the people" is more complicated. As I have tried to demonstrate
throughout this intellectual journey, thanks to the legacy of people's two
bodies, the meaning kept changing between "the people" understood as
corporation and "the people" understood as a collection of individuals, at
either colonial or state level, and at the national one, depending on the actors
and circumstances. As long as this pendulum kept swinging, without getting
stuck to one extreme or the other, political rhetoric was able to use both
meanings in order to justify compromises for the sake of preserving the unity
of *one* political people, by making appeal to both interests and affections. Even
when compromises were no longer possible, the Civil War was doubled by a
war over words like "secession" or "rebellion." Nothing surprising here. It has
long been acknowledged that "political words do more than mystify; they
inspire, persuade, enrage, mobilize. With words minds are changed, votes
acquired, alliances secured, unpopular programs made palatable."[102]

---

[100] Quoted in Bradley C. Thompson (1998), *John Adams and Spirit of Liberty* (Lawrence: University of Kansas Press), 186.

[101] David Runciman (2008), *Political Hypocrisy: The Mask of Power from Hobbes to Orwell and Beyond* (Princeton and Oxford: Princeton University Press), 102.

[102] Daniel T. Rodgers (1987), *Contested Truths: Keywords in American Politics since Independence* (New York: Basic Books, Inc.), 4.

Thus, as we have seen over and over again, if the breaking down of the dialectic of the self has affected the modern individual's understanding of representation, the emphasis of one of the people's two bodies at the expense of the other always comes with a high political price. As discussed in the Introduction to this volume, Achen and Bartels's main claim in *Democracy for Realists* is that that the credibility of "folk theory" of democracy, according to which people rule either directly or indirectly, through their representatives, "has been severely undercut by a growing body of scientific evidence."[103] According to their argument, "voters, even the most informed voters, typically make choices not on the basis of policy preferences or ideology, but on the basis of *who they are* – their social identities. In turn, those social identities shape how they think, what they think, and where they belong in the party system."[104] However, as these scholars would readily acknowledge, despite the fact that "an enormous body of experimental, quantitative and qualitative evidence has accumulated ... precise causal mechanisms remain in dispute. Are group attachments dark irrationalities or simply an often misguided attempt to pursue rational self-interest? Do people's group-related ideas and attachments derive primarily from their own needs or from elite cues and messages?"[105]

The paradigm of the people's two bodies offers some clues about how to solve this conundrum, both theoretically and practically. On the theoretical side, it helps us understand how people in their horizontal dimension do indeed pursue what they perceive to be rational self-interests and needs. In their vertical, corporatist dimension, they also derive their "group-related ideas and attachments ... from elite cues and messages." Yet by refusing to take seriously into consideration the idea of the people's two bodies, Achen and Bartels placed themselves in the impossible position of theoretically coping with what otherwise appear to be two contradictory explanations. Ironically, they also acknowledge that while "the concept of identity was widely adopted within political science ... even now [it] is too often imperfectly integrated in the study of political behavior."[106] On the practical side, the paradigm of the people's two bodies offers an alternative mode of not only *thinking* but also *talking* about the rule *by* the people (with populism as its extreme) and *for* the people (with elitism or technocracy as its other extreme), thus overcoming the either-or approach to responsiveness (*to* the people) and responsibility (*for* the people).

One main problem pointed out in *Democracy for Realists* is that "identities are not primarily about adherence to a group ideology or creed. They are *emotional* attachments that transcend thinking" – and we have just seen how important the new social media is in forging and re-forging these group

---

[103] Christopher H. Achen and Larry M. Bartels (2016), *Democracy for Realists: Why Elections Do Not Produce Responsive Government* (Princeton: Princeton University Press), 11.
[104] Ibid., 4 (emphasis added).   [105] Ibid., 221.   [106] Ibid., 229.

identities.[107] As the history of the Founding teaches us, the issue is not the affectionate embracing of several identities – most if not all of today's identities existed back then as well – but their rapid politicization. However, one may also claim that the very term "identity politics" is something of an oxymoron, since identity "is actually a depoliticizing force."[108] Lilla calls it anti-politics or pseudo-politics. In this respect, the story of the American people may also offer some valuable lessons.

Precisely because such group identifications are primarily emotional attachments, they remain subject to manipulation. The very word "manipulation" might raise some eyebrows, for it suggests infringing upon individuals' autonomy and freedom of choice. Yet in recent years scholars have become infatuated with the concept of "nudging," which practically amounts to the same thing, exploiting the fact that choices and decisions are more often than not based on emotions rather than on a rational cost–benefit analysis. It is, in the language of psychology, an "affective and nonconscious thought process."[109] Developed initially in the field of behavioral economics, the concept was made popular by Rachard H. Thaler and Cass R. Sunstein book, *Nudge*, and its application extended rapidly from health to environmental issues, retirement savings, organ donations, and beyond.[110]

Defined broadly as the rearrangement of a choice context with the intention of gently suggesting a specific option, nudging was labeled by Thaler and Sunstein as "libertarian paternalism." As they explained it, the "libertarian aspect of our strategies lies in the straightforward insistence that, in general, people should be free to do what they like – and to opt out of undesirable arrangements if they want to do so." In turn, the paternalist aspect comes from the claim that it is "legitimate for choice architects to try to influence people's behavior in order to make their lives longer, healthier, and better." Although the jury is still out in terms of the ethical implications,[111] it did not take long until researchers (including Sunstein, appointed head of White House Office of

---

[107] Achen and Bartels, *Democracy for Realists*, 228 (emphasis added).

[108] Lilla, *The Once and Future Liberal*, 137. As a declared liberal himself, Lilla focuses almost exclusively on liberal identity politics. Nevertheless, his diagnosis applies as well to other identities groups, from evangelical to Alt-Right. This is not to say that I endorse all of the claims he makes.

[109] David R. Marchiori, Marieke A. Adriaanse, and Denis T. D. De Ridder (2017), "Unresolved Questions in Nudging Research: Putting the Psychology Back in Nudging," *Social and Personality Psychology Compass*, 11, 2.

[110] Richard H. Thaler and Cass R. Sunstein (2009), *Nudge: Improving Decisions about Health, Wealth, and Happiness* (New York: Penguin Books); see also the most recent Cass R. Sunstein (2014), *Why Nudge? The Politics of Libertarian Paternalism* (New Haven and London: Yale University Press).

[111] See, for example, James J. Chriss (2015), "Nudging and Social Marketing," *Social Science and Public Policy*, 52, 54–61; Luke Gelinas (2016), "Rights, Nudging, and the Good of Others," *The American Journal of Bioethics*, 16:11, 17–19; Brent Pickett (2018), "The New Paternalists," *Polity*, 50:2, 300–329.

Information and Regulation Affairs by the Obama administration) have been co-opted to advise politicians about the use of nudges, from the United States and Canada to the Netherlands and Denmark. This ought to come as no surprise, since the concept has elements that appeal to both Left and Right. It allows for elite intervention all the while respecting individuals' freedom of choice.

In effect, nudging is what politicians have always done – it was called political rhetoric or sometimes "principled rhetoric." "Principled rhetoric provides competing partisans with a shared rationale to support a given public policy, even if their specific policy preferences diverge."[112] What I propose is both less and more ambitious than nudging or principled rhetoric. Less ambitious because it does not aim directly at making individuals live healthier and better lives, nor at implementing particular public policies beneficial to the environment, life expectancy, and the like. But, in a way, more ambitious because it aims at nothing less than restoring the health of the people's two bodies.

Throughout this long quest for the elusive American "people" we have come across many useful lessons, two standing out from the rest. First, that there is no inherent public rejection of elitism built into the American psyche, as long as this status remains one of merit, and is not associated with unfair (usually inherited) advantages, such as "being born with a silver spoon in the mouth" (although contemporary politics offers plenty of counterexamples). True, Americans tend to root for the underdog, but they do not do so simply because s/he is an underdog. They do so because s/he is an underdog who, like them, has *the right* to dream big and *a chance* to achieve this dream of becoming part of the *elite*. The explosion of populism and the frantic rejection of elitism (including "the establishment" associated with it) was, at the time of the Founding as now, the result of a demagogical rhetoric promoted even – or even more so – by the wealthiest actors, in a desperate attempt to appear in the eyes of the Many "fresh from the loins of people." One should be worried about the dangers of (fake) elitism only when public acknowledgment and praise of true elitism disappears from the general conversation and from political speeches. But here is the good news: What is rhetorically done can be rhetorically undone.

The second lesson of this quest is that, despite many scholarly claims to the contrary, the emphasis on the horizontal, fragmented and egalitarian body of the people, far from promoting a hegemonic and homogenous vision of the people, does, in effect, the opposite: it starts a process of splitting and re-splitting the body politic into smaller and smaller identity groups until this disintegration becomes unbearable. As discussed in the Introduction, Daniele Caramani is a case in point. Fairly recently, she argued that the representation

---

[112] Mark A. Scully (2018), "Principled Rhetoric as Coalition Management: Speech in Reconstruction Presidencies of Franklin Roosevelt and Ronald Reagan," *Polity*, 50:1, 129.

model of party democracy is under attack from two sides: the populist and the elitist/technocratic. "For populism, the general interest can be identified through the *will* of the people. For technocracy, the general interest can be identified through *rational* speculation and scientific procedures."[113] The "confrontation," therefore, would be one of "will vs. reason," both applied to an alleged homogenous people.

Nevertheless, the history of the founding teaches us a completely different lesson, one in which both will and reason can be taken into consideration, while acknowledging they perform differently in each of the two bodies. The people have to consent to the general form of government; they select their leaders and can remove them "at will." But, by the same token, the same people agree that the details and the operations of government ought to be entrusted in the hands of an aristocracy of merit, "the best and the brightest," to employ another formula used today predominantly with disparaging connotations.[114] Furthermore, the same history teaches us that, far from being homogenous, "the people" are better understood and represented as a *political* corporation of lesser corporate identities – and this is where, once again, rhetorical persuasion may come into play. Thus, if one wants to reverse the increased polarization both among politicians and among the electorate, one has to resuscitate the idea that the American people was from its very foundation and still is to this day a *political* people. More specifically, *one political people with two bodies*.

In order to do so, one has to make an appeal, as in the case of any meaningful compromise, to both rational interests and to "the chords of affection," much like the founders of various political colors did, consciously and programmatically, when trying to implement the so-called American System, meant to nurture the conscience of one American people.

Citizens are made, not born. Sometimes historical forces do the work. [...] The best one can hope for is that democratic citizens will be formed through an education in the principles of self-government. But that's only a start. For those principles to then motivate action they must be rooted in a feeling we are not born with. And feelings can't be taught; they have to be conjured up. It's the closest thing to a miracle that exists in politics.[115]

---

[113] Daniele Caramani (2017), "Will vs. Reason: The Populist and Technocratic Forms of Political Representation and Their Critique to Party Government," *American Political Science Review*, 111, 1, 62 (emphases added). For a more detailed discussion of Caramani, see Fumurescu, "The People's Two Bodies."

[114] Made popular by David Halberstam's *The Best and the Brightest* (Random House 1972), about the origins of the Vietnam War, the expression is attributed to "Junius," an anonymous author who published several articles in the *Public Advertiser* from 1769 to 1772. In a letter from February 1769 he mocks King George III's ministers with this appellative.

[115] Lilla, *The Once and Future Liberal*, 131.

And so it is. The digital revolution is a double-edged sword. It can be used to fuel the fragmentation of the body politic and nurture hatred and rejection of otherness. But it can equally be used to "nudge" or "rhetorically persuade" the people that they are first and foremost Americans because they are citizens.[116] In other words, there are plenty of digital venues to remind them that they are *politically* alike, all other identifications aside. Thus, there is nothing preventing them and their representatives from being willing to compromise with the others, regardless of how one defines "otherness." This is not to say that racial, ethnic, religious, sexual, or other identities are to be discarded, ignored, or fully depoliticized. After all, the paradigm of the people's two bodies serves as a reminder that not just individual but also group interests ought to be equally represented. Yet above all of these groups, there still is *one* American people whose two bodies are to be equally acknowledged and cherished.

After all, there might be a reason for why the thirteen-letter traditional motto inscribed on the Great Seal, *E pluribus unum*, remains so popular even today among the Americans, some two and half centuries later.

---

[116] On this point, I fully subscribe to Lilla's specification that "nothing I say here about citizenship should be taken to imply anything about who should be granted it or how noncitizens should be treated. I am interested here only in what citizenship *is*"; Lilla, *The Once and Future Liberal*, 121. The very fact that such specifications are deemed necessary speaks volumes about the general level of distrust in public discourse.

Index